T0329878

LONDON RECORD SOCIETY
PUBLICATIONS

VOLUME XXVII
FOR THE YEAR 1990

THE OVERSEAS TRADE
OF LONDON
EXCHEQUER CUSTOMS
ACCOUNTS
1480–1

EDITED BY
H. S. COBB

LONDON RECORD SOCIETY
1990

Phototypeset by
Wyvern Typesetting Ltd., Bristol
Printed and bound in Great Britain
by 4edge Limited

CONTENTS

ACKNOWLEDGEMENTS

In editing this volume, I have received help from many quarters. My wife, Eileen, painstakingly typed the text from a difficult script. Dr. Elspeth Veale gave generous assistance with the compilation of the index. Invaluable help has been given by the staffs of the Public Record Office and the Department of Manuscripts of the British Library. The London Record Society is indebted to the Keeper of the Public Records for permission to publish the documents contained in this volume.

I am most grateful to Dr. DeLloyd J. Guth for allowing me to make extensive use of his unpublished thesis on 'Exchequer Penal Law Enforcement, 1485–1509'. Those who have generously advised on specific points include Professor Sydney Anglo, Mr. J. L. Bolton, Miss Heather Creaton, Dr. Brian Dietz, Mr. Geoffrey Harris, Dr. Derek Keene, Mr. Rhys Robinson and the late Mr. John Nevinson.

My special thanks are due to Mr. William Kellaway, the general editor of the London Record Society from 1964 to 1983, who not only suggested this project, but also offered steady encouragement throughout its very slow progress towards completion.

ABBREVIATIONS

A	Alien
Acts of Court	*Acts of Court of the Mercers' Company 1453–1527*, ed. Laetitia Lyell and Frank D. Watney (Cambridge, 1936)
Beaven	A. B. Beaven, *The Aldermen of the City of London, Temp. Henry III–1912*, 2 vols. (1908–13)
B.L.	British Library, Department of Manuscripts
brl(s).	barrel(s)
C. (centum, centena, centenarium)	A hundredweight or a hundred by tale, varying according to commodity, *see* Glossary
C.67	P.R.O., Chancery, Pardon Rolls
C.C.R.	*Calendar of Close Rolls*
C.F.R.	*Calendar of Fine Rolls*
C.P.R.	*Calendar of Patent Rolls*
cont.	containing
D	Denizen
del.	deleted
Dietz	*The Port and Trade of Early Elizabethan London, Documents*, ed. Brian Dietz (London Record Society, 8, 1972)
doz.	dozen
E.122	P.R.O., Exchequer King's Remembrancer, Customs Accounts
E.159	P.R.O., Exchequer King's Remembrancer, Memoranda Rolls
E.356	P.R.O., Exchequer Lord Treasurer's Remembrancer, Enrolled Customs Accounts
E.H.R.	*English Historical Review*
England's Export Trade	E. M. Carus-Wilson and Olive Coleman, *England's Export Trade 1275–1547* (Oxford, 1963)
fo(s).	folio(s)
Gras	N. S. B. Gras, *The Early English Customs System* (Cambridge, Mass., 1918)
grs.	gross
Guth	DeLloyd J. Guth, *Exchequer Penal Law Enforcement, 1485–1509* (Unpublished Ph.D. Thesis, University of Pittsburg, 1967)
H	Hanse
hhd(s).	hogshead(s)
K.R.	King's Remembrancer of the Exchequer

L. and P.	*Letters and Papers, Foreign and Domestic, Henry VIII*, ed. J. S. Brewer and others, 21 vols. (1864–1920)
lb(s).	pound(s)
L.T.R.	Lord Treasurer's Remembrancer of the Exchequer
m.	membrane
M. (mille, millena, millenarium)	Ten hundreds or hundredweights, *see* Glossary *sub* C.
marg.	margin
Middle English Dictionary	*Middle English Dictionary* (Ann Arbor, University of Michigan Press, 1954 onwards, in progress)
Mills, 'Collectors'	Mabel H. Mills, 'The Collectors of Customs' in *The English Government at Work, 1327–1336*, ed. William A. Morris and Joseph R. Strayer, vol. 2 (Cambridge, Mass., 1947)
MS(S)	manuscript(s)
O.E.D.	*Oxford English Dictionary*
Overseas Trade of Bristol	*The Overseas Trade of Bristol in the later Middle Ages*, ed. E. M. Carus-Wilson (Bristol Record Society, VII, 1937)
pc(s).	piece(s)
Power and Postan	*Studies in English Trade in the Fifteenth Century*, ed. Eileen Power and M. M. Postan (1933)
P.R.O.	Public Record Office
qr(s).	quarter(s)
Rot. Parl.	*Rotuli Parliamentorum; ut et petitiones et placita in parliamento* (1278–1503), 6 vols. (1767–77)
Royal Commission of 1552	*The Report of the Royal Commission of 1552*, ed. W. C. Richardson (Morgantown, 1974)
S	The Surveyor's Account of London Petty Custom, 1480–1 (E. 122/194/24)
Smit, 1150–1485	H. J. Smit, *Bronnen tot de geschiedenis van den Handel met Engeland, Schotland en Ireland, 1150–1485*, 2 vols. (Rijks Geschiedkundige Publicatien, nos. 65–6, 's-Gravenhage, 1928)
Smit, 1485–1585	Ibid. *1485–1585*, 2 vols. (nos. 86 and 91, 1942, 1950)
Sp	Spanish
Stat. Realm.	*Statutes of the Realm* (1101–1713), ed. A. Luders *et al.*, 11 vols. (Record Commission, 1810–28)
val.	value
vol(s).	volume(s)
w.g.	without grain, *see* Glossary *sub* Grain
Willan, *Rates*	*A Tudor Book of Rates*, ed. T. S. Willan (Manchester, 1962)
yd(s).	yard(s)

INTRODUCTION

London Customs Records: 1461–1509

The documents which are calendared in this volume consist of a controller's account of petty custom recording particulars of general imports and exports (other than wine, wool and hides) by alien merchants, and of cloth exports by alien and denizen merchants, in the port of London[1] from Michaelmas 1480 to Michaelmas 1481; together with certain less detailed accounts for wool, wine and other commodities, which supplement the incomplete record of the trade of the port contained in the petty custom account. Particular Accounts (such as the 1480–81 Petty Custom account) were kept by royal officials in each customs port, who recorded in them each ship entering or leaving the port with customable goods,[2] frequently with its name and home-port, the name of the master, the date of arrival or departure,[3] the merchant in whose name goods were shipped (usually with the designation denizen, alien or Hanse), each item of customable cargo (with a valuation if it was subject to an *ad valorem* duty) and, in the case of collectors' accounts only, the amount of duty payable. The Particular Accounts were brought to the Upper Exchequer at the end of each financial year (or of a particular official's period of office) to be audited and entered, in summary form, on the Enrolled Customs Accounts.

The Enrolled Accounts (which were intended to be a permanent record) detail for each customs port the total quantities imported or exported annually of wool, cloth, wine, hides and wax, on which specific duties were paid, and the total value of miscellaneous goods on which *ad valorem* duties were paid, together with the amount of custom due in each case. Details of individual merchants and their goods only appear on the Enrolled Accounts in cases where the merchants enjoyed partial or complete exemption from the payment of particular duties. Economic historians have for long appreciated the value of the Enrolled Accounts of customs (which survive almost complete from 1279 to 1547) for the study of trends in English overseas trade in the later Middle

---

[1] In the fifteenth century the customs port of London extended as far as Gravesend on the Kent shore and Tilbury on the Essex shore (*England's Export Trade*, 182, 190).

[2] Like the later Port Books, the Particular Accounts only recorded laden ships and not those in ballast. Duty-free goods, such as ships' stores and small quantities imported for the owner's personal use, were not recorded (Willan, *Rates*, x; Dietz, xviii–xix).

[3] The destination or provenance of ships is not recorded in the late fifteenth century London Accounts, although it is in some of the outport accounts, e.g. Bristol (*Overseas Trade of Bristol*, 203–289).

Ages.[4] A large proportion of the annual totals of trade contained in the Enrolled Accounts has now been published.[5]

A considerable number of Particular Accounts, brought to the Exchequer for auditing (but of little official use thereafter), have survived for each port, although these are only a small proportion of the total originally compiled.[6] More than fifty years ago, N. S. B. Gras described the various types of Particular Accounts and printed examples of them in his study of the medieval English customs system. Since that time, however, few of the medieval Particular Accounts (and none of the longer London accounts) have been published.[7]

The customs duties which were levied in the fifteenth century comprised, firstly, the customs and subsidies on wool, woolfells and hides which combined (from 1353) the Ancient Custom, New Custom and Subsidies on these commodities. The Ancient Custom had been imposed in 1275, at specific rates, on all wool, woolfells and hides exported by denizen and alien merchants. This permanent duty was levied without interruption for the next three centuries.[8] The New Custom on alien exports of wool and hides was levied at specific rates from 1303 onwards. The Subsidies on denizen and alien exports of wool were levied at irregular intervals and varying specific rates from the late thirteenth century and from 1340 onwards they were granted to the sovereign by parliament.[9] The rates of the wool subsidies continued to fluctuate until they were finally fixed in 1471.[10] Secondly, there was the New (or Petty) Custom imposed in 1303 on all goods imported or exported by alien merchants, with specific duties on wool, hides,[11] cloth, wine,[12] and wax and an *ad valorem* duty of 3d in the £1 on all other wares.[13] An additional cloth custom was imposed in 1347 on denizen and alien merchants (other than the Hanse). Petty custom and cloth

---

[4] They are also a source of information concerning customs officials, their allowances, accommodation and equipment and the use to which the customs revenue was put by the Crown.

[5] For a survey of work on the Enrolled Accounts from their first systematic use by Schanz, in 1881, in his study of English trade under Henry VII and Henry VIII, to the publication in 1963 by Professor Carus-Wilson and Miss Coleman of the figures of wool and cloth exports from all the customs ports between 1279 and 1547, see *England's Export Trade*, 4–7.

[6] They are listed in *Public Record Office, List of Exchequer K.R. Accounts* (List and Index Society, vols. 43 and 60, 1969–70).

[7] The main exceptions to this are the Bristol accounts printed in *The Overseas Trade of Bristol*, 167–289, the Lynn accounts in D. M. Owen (ed.), *The Making of King's Lynn. A Documentary Survey* (British Academy, Records of Social and Economic History, IX (1984), 337–78) and Wendy R. Childs (ed.), *The Customs Accounts of Hull 1453–1490* (Yorkshire Archaeological Society, CXLIV (1986)).

[8] *England's Export Trade*, 1–2.

[9] It was not until 1398 that they were granted to a sovereign for life (Gras, 78–80, 84).

[10] *England's Export Trade*, 194.

[11] The duties on wool and hides were later, as stated above, collected with the Ancient Custom.

[12] From the beginning of the reign of Edward III, this was collected and accounted for separately by the King's butler (who also collected the prise on wine) and later called 'butlerage' (Gras, 66–7, 87 and see below, **605–622**).

[13] Gras, 257.

custom were levied without interruption, and at unchanged rates, from their original imposition until 1558 and they came to be recorded on the same, petty custom, accounts.[14] Thirdly, and lastly, there were the subsidies of Tunnage and Poundage. Poundage was a temporary *ad valorem* duty first imposed in the 1340s on all goods (except wool, hides and wine) exported or imported by denizen and alien (but not Hanse) merchants.[15] Tunnage was a temporary specific duty imposed from the 1340s on all denizen and alien wine imports. Both tunnage and poundage were granted intermittently by parliament in the fourteenth century and the first grant for life to a sovereign was not made until 1415.[16]

At first, separate accounts for each type of duty were rendered at the Exchequer by various port officials but in the mid-fourteenth century a process of consolidating the customs and subsidies began. As a result, by the early fifteenth century the customs administration had been simplified and, in most ports, one body of officials (usually two collectors and a controller) rendered one account (with a controlment) for all the duties (except butlerage) collected in that port.[17] The chief exception, however, to this trend towards consolidation was the port of London where separate accounts continued to be rendered by separate bodies of officials for each of the three main types of customs, presumably because London's trade was so much greater in volume than that of other ports.[18] Consequently, three series of London Particular Accounts (for wool custom and subsidy; for petty custom and cloth custom; and for tunnage and poundage) are to be found throughout the fifteenth century. Since each type of duty varied in its incidence, both as regards merchants and goods, it would obviously be necessary for all three accounts to have survived for anything approaching a completely detailed picture of London overseas trade in any one year to be obtained. Needless to say, the accidents of survival have seen to it that

---

[14] *Ibid.*, 72, 435; *England's Export Trade*, 194.

[15] It was, however, occasionally levied on the Hanse at times of conflict between the Hanseatic League and England. Grants of poundage usually exempted imports of fresh fish, meat and grain. Until Henry VI's reign denizen merchants were occasionally charged poundage on their cloth exports but were usually specifically exempted after that time (Gras, 81–3; *England's Export Trade*, 194–5).

[16] Edward IV received a life grant of all three subsidies in 1465 but not until Richard III was such a life grant made in the first year of the reign (Gras, 83–4). At the beginning of the reigns of Richard III and Henry VII, the Merchant Adventurers successfully petitioned against the levying of tunnage and poundage until these subsidies had been granted by parliament (*Acts of Court*, 149–54; *Materials for a history of the Reign of Henry VII*, ed. W. Campbell (Rolls Series no. 60, 1873) I, 273).

[17] Gras, 85–9, 110, 634; D. Burwash, *English Merchant Shipping 1460–1540* (University of Toronto, 1947), 204.

[18] The demands of patronage may also have been a factor in the appointment of three sets of customs officials in London, *see* O. Coleman, 'Collectors of Customs in London under Richard II' in *Studies in London History*, eds. A. E. Hollaender and W. Kellaway (1969), 183. In times of crisis some offices were combined and joint accounts rendered. Thus, in 1469–70, first Richard Passemere and then Ralph Hastyngs were controllers of both petty custom and tunnage and poundage (*C.P.R. 1467–77*, 168, 175). William Brette and Thomas Litley rendered a combined account for petty custom and tunnage and poundage 22 August – 17 October 1485 (E.122/78/3).

although some fifty London Particular Accounts (covering periods of
from ten days to fourteen months) are extant for 1461–1509, there is not
one year in this period for which all three accounts have survived.[19] A
further complication is that separate accounts were rendered for each
type of duty by the collectors, the controller and (from 1478) the
surveyor, and in a number of cases parallel accounts for one type of
custom have survived in a particular year.[20] Whilst such duplication may
be regretted when there are so many gaps in the accounts, collation of
the duplicates can provide additional information since it appears that
the controllers' and surveyors' accounts were not simply copies of the
collectors' accounts.[21]

The Particular Accounts thus constitute the main source for details of
the ships, merchants and cargoes involved in English medieval overseas
trade.[22] They may also, sometimes, as in the case of the surviving
London petty custom and tunnage and poundage accounts between
1473 and 1495, substantially modify the picture of London trade which is
presented by the Enrolled Accounts for those years.[23]

The Customs Officials

The normal establishment of officials in the London customs during the
later fifteenth century was two collectors and a controller each for wool
custom, petty custom, and tunnage and poundage, (from 1478) a
surveyor of the other officials and of their accounts, a searcher, a tronager, the deputy of the chief butler and a number of clerks and other
servants of these officials.[24] By 1490 there were some 42 officials in all.[25]
The very frequent changes in the personnel of the London customs
between 1461 and 1485 make generalisation for the period difficult but
when compared with the personnel between 1485 and 1509 some
general differences between the two periods emerge. Some one hundred
and ten appointments of London collectors, controllers, surveyors,
searchers and tronagers are recorded on the Patent and Fine Rolls

[19] See the list of accounts in Appendix below. But, for example, even fewer London Port
Books survive for overseas trade in the reign of Elizabeth I (*Descriptive List of
Exchequer, Queen's Remembrancer, Port Books, Part I, 1565 to 1700*, P.R.O.).

[20] Such duplication occurs for nine years between 1461 and 1509.

[21] See below, pp. xxvi, xliv, and the collation of the surveyor's with the controller's
account of petty custom 1480–1 in this edition.

[22] Merchants' account books are almost completely lacking for the fifteenth century.

[23] See H. S. Cobb, 'Cloth Exports from London and Southampton in the Later Fifteenth
and Early Sixteenth Centuries: A Revision', *Economic History Review*, 2nd ser., vol.
xxxi (1978), 601–9.

[24] These were all royal officials. Other offices closely connected with the port – the cloth
packer, gauger of wines and garbeller of spices – were from 1461 onwards in the hands
of the City (*C.P.R. 1461–7*, 70). Between 1432 and 1461 these offices had been granted
out by patent to royal servants, a cause of great friction between the Crown and the
City (Caroline M. Barron, 'London and the Crown 1451–61' in *The Crown and Local
Communities in England and France in the Fifteenth Century*, eds. J. R. L. Highfield
and Robin Jeffs (Gloucester, 1981, 90–1, 99–100, 105–9).

[25] Only two less than in 1552, see below n. 71. The largest establishment in an outport
appears to have been at Bristol which in 1506 had 2 collectors, 1 controller, 1 searcher,
4 waiters and 'clerks in diverse creeks' (E.122/163/7).

between 1461 and 1485. Only about forty such appointments are recorded between 1485 and 1509.[26] It would appear that frequent changes in personnel were the general rule until the mid-1470s when a trend towards greater stability emerges.[27] In the earlier part of Edward IV's reign, however, some individuals occupied a succession of offices in the London customs and may thereby have acquired considerable experience in their duties.[28] Others had had previous experience of customs office in the outports, chiefly Sandwich.[29] After the political upheavals of Richard III's reign and in the early years of Henry VII, long tenure of office (20 years or more) became a regular feature throughout the London customs system and a number of Henry VII's officials had careers which extended well into Henry VIII's reign.[30]

The collectors and controllers appointed between 1461 and 1485 included a fairly large proportion of prominent merchants, most of whom rose to high civic office. These appointments were probably in part connected with loans to the Crown.[31] Important merchants are noticeably lacking amongst those appointed to customs posts between 1485 and 1509 but, instead, there would appear to have been a larger proportion of royal servants appointed in the later period. The increase in the proportion of royal servants, the longer periods of office and

---

[26] These figures include the movement of an individual from one office to another but not his re-appointment in the same office. The appointments ('during pleasure') of collectors and searchers usually appear on the Fine Rolls and those of controllers, surveyors and tronagers on the Patent Rolls.

[27] The political crises of the earlier period must have been responsible for many of the changes. The changes may also have been partly a device to invalidate tallies levied on named collectors of customs and thus to delay payment to the Crown's creditors, as had been done in the 1440s (G. L. Harriss, 'Fictitious Loans', *Economic History Review*, 2nd ser. vol. viii (1955–6), 195). Longer terms of office may be one aspect of the reform of royal finances and the customs which has been observed in the 1470s (C. Ross, *Edward IV* (1974), 375–380). Examples are Thomas Fowler, controller of petty custom 1472–85 and Robert Fitzherbert, collector of petty custom 1478–96 (see below pp. xxix, xliv–xlv).

[28] E.g. John Brampton, collector of wool custom 1464, petty custom 1466, re-appointed 1469 and 1470 (when he was also collector of tunnage and poundage), collector of wool custom 1473; William Hampton, collector of petty custom 1464, re-appointed 1469 (when he was also collector of tunnage and poundage); William Martyn, controller of tunnage and poundage 1470, re-appointed 1471, collector of tunnage and poundage 1475, collector of petty custom 1483 (see below, nn. 38, 44).

[29] E.g. Robert Cosyn, mercer, controller of the search in London 1461, collector of tunnage and poundage 1464, 1465 and 1470, had previously been a collector of custom and subsidy in Sandwich (*C.P.R. 1461–7*, 17, 20; *C.F.R. 1461–71*, 5–7, 131, 149, 263; Pardon Rolls, C.67/49, m.26). William Chattok, fishmonger, collector of petty custom 1461, re-appointed 1464, collector of wool custom and subsidy 1466, had been a collector of custom and subsidy in Sandwich and Ipswich during the reign of Henry VI (*C.F.R. 1461–71*, 6, 96, 178, 181; C.67/49, m.24).

[30] E.g. William Treffry, surveyor 1485–1504; John Myllys, controller of tunnage and poundage 1486–97, surveyor 1506–9; John Heron, controller of tunnage and poundage 1497–1509, surveyor 1509–16; John Shurley, controller of wool custom 1489–1524 (H. S. Cobb, 'Books of Rates and the London Customs, 1507–1558', *The Guildhall Miscellany*, iv, No. 1 (1971), 6–8); William Bulstrode, collector of wool custom 1496–1524 or later (*C.F.R. 1485–1509*, 245; *L. and P.* I, 65; E.122/204/5).

[31] See below pp. xvii–xviii.

greater financial rewards[32] which are to be found in the London customs administration in the later years of Edward IV and under Henry VII suggest that the customs service was becoming more professional and less a part-time duty and source of additional profit, as it appears to have been in, at least, the early years of Edward IV.

In the reign of Richard II those responsible for the collection of the wool custom both in London and in the outports had been of a different calibre from the collectors of the other customs. During this time seven of the 15 collectors of wool custom became mayor whilst only one of the 12 collectors of petty custom and of the 14 collectors of tunnage and poundage did so. This difference between the collectors of wool custom and the other collectors does not, however, appear to have been maintained in the later fifteenth century.[33] Due to the pre-eminence of the wool customs and subsidies as a source of revenue the collectors of wool custom in the later fourteenth century handled much larger sums of money than their counterparts in other branches of the customs and, in London, were often responsible for arranging loans to the crown which were secured on the wool customs.[34]

Wool custom and subsidy were still by far the largest source of customs revenue in the later fifteenth century although their yield had declined considerably, both absolutely and in relation to that of the other customs duties, since the end of the fourteenth century. The potential annual revenue from London wool custom and subsidy (i.e. what was theoretically due on recorded exports before allowing for assignments from the customs and for special exemptions) averaged about £10,000 in the last full ten years of Edward IV's reign (1472–82). Over the same period the potential annual revenue from cloth custom was about £2,600, from poundage £4,000, from tunnage £500 and from petty custom nearly £400.[35] This did not mean, however, that the collectors of wool custom continued to handle much larger sums of money than did the other collectors. From the early fifteenth century groups of the wealthiest members of the Staplers' Company were making loans to the Crown and in return were allowed to retain a part or the whole of the custom and subsidy on wool shipped from certain ports. More particularly, under the terms of the 'Act of Retainer' of 1466 the Company was to collect all the custom and subsidy on wool shipped from England, with the exception of that going to Italy by the 'Straits of Marrock'. Out of this and other revenues, the Staplers were to recover the money which they had loaned to Edward IV, and to pay the wages of the

---

[32] See below pp. xxi–xxii.

[33] Between 1461 and 1485 only one of the 19 collectors of wool custom became mayor, whilst three of the 21 collectors of tunnage and poundage, and two of the 16 collectors of petty custom (also collectors of tunnage and poundage) did so (Coleman, *op. cit.*, 184 and see below, nn. 38, 44).

[34] Coleman, *op. cit.*, 183–7; A. Steel, 'The Collectors of the Customs in the Reign of Richard II' in *British Government and Administration*, eds. H. Hearder and H. R. Loyn (Cardiff, University of Wales Press, 1974), 29.

[35] For the reign of Richard II wool custom and subsidy averaged about £18,000 p.a., cloth custom nearly £1,000 p.a., poundage about £3,000 p.a. and tunnage and petty custom a few hundred pounds each (Coleman, *op. cit.*, 183–4).

garrison at Calais and the fees of the collectors and controller of wool custom in the port of London and of certain other officials.[36] The custom and subsidy on wool shipped to Calais were therefore collected at London or Calais by officers of the Staple (and not by the customs collectors) and the Company rendered account for them at the Exchequer.[37]

From 1466, the London Particular Accounts of wool custom, apart from recording custom collected on wool shipped through the Straits of Marrock, were chiefly a check on the accounts rendered by the Staplers. Prominent merchants were, under this system, less likely to be attracted to the office of collector of wool customs, but the presence of a number of royal servants amongst the collectors and controllers appointed after 1466 suggests some official concern to oversee the Staplers' activities. Of the nineteen collectors of wool custom appointed between 1461 and 1485, three attained civic office[38] and one was an important royal servant.[39] Five collectors of wool custom were appointed between 1485 and 1509, one of whom was a royal servant.[40] One of the eleven controllers of wool custom appointed during the reign of Edward IV may have been a royal servant.[41] The controller appointed at the beginning of Richard III's reign was a royal servant as were two of the three controllers who served under Henry VII.[42]

---

[36] The arrangement was to last for eight years and was renewed for another sixteen in 1473 (E. E. Power, 'The Wool Trade in the Fifteenth Century' in Power and Postan, 74–5). It was continued under Henry VII and Henry VIII (*The Ordinance Book of the Merchants of the Staple*, ed. E. E. Rich (Cambridge, 1937), 9–10). Cf. a Warrant of 1468 for the collectors and controller to obtain their annual fees from the Company. (P.R.O. Exchequer of Receipt, Warrants for Issues, E.404/74/1/10).

[37] The accounts are to be found amongst the Exchequer, Various Accounts, France. For an example, see below, **598–602**.

[38] John Brampton, stockfishmonger, alderman, collector in 1464 and 1473, represented the City in parliament 1472–5 (*C.F.R. 1461–71*, 129, 131; *ibid.* 1471–85, 64–5; Beaven, I, 273). Brampton was also a collector of tunnage and poundage 1469–70 and of petty custom 1466, 1469–70 (*C.F.R. 1461–71*, 179, 249, 251, 271, 274). William Heryot, draper, collector in 1469, sheriff 1468–9, mayor 1481–2, knighted 1482, M.P. for the City 1483–4 (*C.F.R. 1461–71*, 248, 250; Beaven, II, 14). Humphrey Starkey, collector 1464, recorder of the City (*C.F.R. 1461–71*, 129, 131; C.67/49, m.16).

[39] John Fitzherbert, collector 1478–85 and at the same time one of the Tellers of the Exchequer and, from 1480, King's Remembrancer (*C.F.R. 1471–85*, 159, 256, 263, 283; *C.P.R. 1476–85*, 202, 534; C.67/51, m.16). Amongst Exchequer officials, Fitzherbert made the largest individual loan to the Crown (£827) in the decade 1475–85, but this may have been more as King's Remembrancer than as a collector of customs (A. Steel, *The Receipt of the Exchequer 1377–1485* (Cambridge, 1954), 332).

[40] Richard Cholmeley kt. collector from 1506, knight for the body, re-appointed 1509 (*C.F.R. 1485–1509*, 378; *L. and P.* I, 63).

[41] William Grymmysby, controller from 1477–83, was probably also one of the two surveyors of all customs in London appointed in 1478. He may also have been the William Grimsby who was a former royal servant (of Henry VI) and a member of parliament for Grimsby in 1472 (*C.P.R. 1476–85*, 38, 101; J. C. Wedgwood, *History of Parliament, House of Commons 1439–1509, Biographies*, 400–1).

[42] Nicholas Southworth, King's servant, controller 1483, 1485 and 1487–8 (*C.P.R. 1476–85*, 404, 536; E.122/78/6); John Shurley, controller 1489–1524, chief clerk of the kitchen and, from 1509, Cofferer of the Household (Cobb, 'Books of Rates', *op. cit.* 7–8; *L. and P.* I, 205).

For tunnage and poundage, the duties whose collectors (after 1466) handled the largest receipts from the customs, twenty-one collectors were appointed between 1461 and 1485, making it the customs office which most frequently changed hands at this period.[43] Of the twenty-one, five attained civic office,[44] and two, early in Edward IV's reign, were the nominees of magnates.[45] It is noticeable that four of the London collectors of tunnage and poundage were amongst the largest individual lenders to the Crown in the period 1462 to 1485.[46] These men may well have undertaken office partly as security for the repayment of their loans out of the customs receipts, and probably received an allowance for interest as well.[47] One of the seven collectors of tunnage and poundage appointed between 1485 and 1509 became a royal servant.[48] Of the seven controllers of tunnage and poundage appointed between 1461 and 1485 one attained civic office[49] and two were royal servants.[50] Both the controllers of tunnage and poundage in the reign of Henry VII were London mercers.[51]

For petty custom and cloth custom, the duties with the lowest yield at this time, sixteen collectors were appointed between 1461 and 1485, four of whom attained civic office.[52] There were ten collectors of petty

---

[43] The number is increased to thirty-seven if re-appointments are included.

[44] John Middleton, collector 1463, sheriff 1450–1, member of parliament for the City 1453, master of the Mercers' Company at various times, 1452–75 (*C.F.R. 1461–71*, 197; Beaven, II, 10; C.67/49, m.28); John Brampton (see above, n. 38); William Hampton, fishmonger, collector 1469, knighted 1471, mayor 1472–3, member of parliament for the City 1478 (*C.F.R. 1461–71*, 249; Beaven, II, 12). Hampton was also collector of petty customs 1464–70 (*C.F.R. 1461–71*, 130, 251). Hugh Bryce, goldsmith, collector 1471–4, sheriff 1475–6, mayor 1485–6, knighted 1485, Master of the Mint 1480–96 (*C.F.R. 1471–85*, 10; Beaven, II, 15). William Martyn, skinner, collector 1475–81, sheriff 1483–4, mayor 1492–3, knighted 1494, master of the Skinners' Company at various times 1485–1502 (*C.F.R. 1471–85*, 103; Beaven, II, 17; C.67/50, m. 4). Martyn was also a controller of tunnage and poundage 1470–1 and a collector of petty custom 1483 (*C.P.R. 1467–77*, 216; *C.F.R. 1471–85*, 255).

[45] Henry Auger, appointed collector 31 December 1462, nominated by the Earl of Warwick; Ralph Wolsley, appointed collector 5 August 1463, nominated by the Earl of Worcester and Robert Styllyngton (*C.F.R. 1461–71*, 73, 98).

[46] Between 1462 and 1475, John Brampton lent £933 6s.8d. on his own and £133 6s.8d. with a colleague; Sir William Hampton lent £1,143 on his own and £1,026 with friends; and Hugh Brice lent £2,850 himself and £800 with a syndicate. Between 1475 and 1485 one of the very few large lenders was Thomas Cotton (collector 1481–5) who lent £1,160 (Steel, *op. cit.*, 334–5, 345).

[47] This had certainly been one motive for wealthy London merchants to take up customs offices in the earlier fifteenth century (G. L. Harriss, 'Preference at the Medieval Exchequer', *Bulletin of the Institute of Historical Research*, XXX (1957), 26).

[48] Ralph Bukberd, collector 1506–9, probably the gentleman usher appointed in 1509 (*C.F.R. 1485–1509*, 376 (where he is misnamed John); *L. and P.* I, 14, 163).

[49] William Martyn (see above, n. 44).

[50] Ralph Hastyngs, controller 1470, esquire of the body (*C.P.R. 1461–67*, 21, 47; *ibid. 1467–77*, 75); he was also a controller of petty custom 1462–3, 1470 (E.122/194/12). Peter Curteys, controller 1478–84, acting keeper of the great wardrobe 1478 onwards, keeper 1480–4 (A. F. Sutton and P. W. Hammond (eds.), *The Coronation of Richard III* (1984), 327–8).

[51] John Myllys, controller 1486–97, John Heron, controller 1497–1509, both became surveyors of the London customs (Cobb, 'Books of Rates', *op. cit.*, 6–7).

[52] Henry Waver, draper and shipowner, collector 1462, 1464, sheriff 1465–6, knighted

custom between 1485 and 1509, one of whom was a royal servant.[53] Of the nine controllers of petty custom between 1461 and 1485, two were royal servants.[54] Two controllers of petty custom were appointed between 1485 and 1509, one of whom was a royal servant.[55]

Three surveyors were appointed between 1478 and 1485, one of whom had previously been a sheriff.[56] The two surveyors appointed under Henry VII were respectively a royal servant and a mercer.[57]

Seven searchers were appointed for the port of London between 1461 and 1485, the longest serving of whom was a merchant, and another was a royal servant.[58] Of the three searchers during Henry VII's reign, two held civic office (one of whom was a royal servant).[59] Two 'controllers of the search' were appointed in 1461 and 1462[60] respectively and two 'surveyors of the search', successively, in 1461[61] but both offices appear to have died out by the late 1460s. The searchers had one or more deputies at Gravesend and the occupants of the office appear to have been relatively humble in status.[62]

1465 (*C.F.R. 1461–71*, 71, 96; Beaven, II, 13; P.R.O. Early Chancery Proceedings, C.1/44/220); William Hampton (see above. n. 44); John Brampton (see above. n. 38); William Martyn (see above, n. 44).

[53] William Treffry, esquire, collector 1497–1504, an usher of the king's chamber (*C.F.R. 1485–1509*, 247; *C.P.R. 1485–94*, 264; *ibid. 1494–1509*, 388); he was also a surveyor of London customs 1485–1504 (Cobb, 'Books of Rates', *op. cit.*, 6).

[54] Ralph Hastyngs (see above, n. 50); Thomas Fowler, controller 1472–4, 1476–85, an usher of the king's chamber (*C.P.R. 1467–77*, 550, 592; *ibid. 1476–85*, 252), and see below, p. xlv and his account for 1480–1 edited in this volume.

[55] Symon Dygby, esquire, controller 1489–1514, king's servant (*C.P.R. 1485–94*, 222, 269); *L. and P.* I, 125, 1177).

[56] William Weston, surveyor 1480–4, sheriff of Surrey and Sussex 1477–8 (*C.P.R. 1476–85*, 225; C.67/51, m.20); for his Survey of Petty Custom 1480–1, collated with the controller's account, see below, p. xliv. The two surveyors appointed jointly in 1478 were William Grymmesby who was probably the man previously appointed controller of wool custom (see above, n. 41) and Robert Fitzherbert, who may have been the Robert Fitzherbert, draper, appointed collector of petty custom late in 1478 (*C.P.R. 1476–85*, 101; *C.F.R. 1471–85*, 159).

[57] William Treffry (see above, n. 53), John Myllys, surveyor 1506 (previously controller of tunnage and poundage), dismissed in 1509 for 'manyfold mysdemeanours' (Cobb, 'Books of Rates', *op. cit.*, 6–7). Both these appointments were for life in contrast to appointment during pleasure for other customs officials.

[58] William Baldry, searcher for most of the period between 1462 and 1479, a London draper and formerly an Ipswich merchant (*C.F.R. 1461–71*, 79, 112–13, 251, 278; *ibid. 1471–85*, 11; C.67/51, m.24). His surviving accounts run from 1462–7, 1469–74 (E.122/186/1, 3, 4, 7, 8). William Dawbeney, searcher 1480, 1483, Clerk of the Jewels of Edward IV and Richard III (*C.P.R. 1476–85*, 223; *C.P.R. 1471–85*, 256; C.67/53, m.7).

[59] John Shaa or Shaw, searcher 1492–1504, goldsmith, sheriff 1496–7, knighted 1497, mayor 1501–2, member of parliament 1495, 1503, Joint Master of the Mint 1493, 1495–8 (*C.P.R. 1485–94*, 372; Beaven, II, 19). Nicholas Pakenham, searcher 1504, town clerk (*C.P.R. 1494–1509*, 352; P.R.O. Early Chancery Proceedings, C.1/260/25).

[60] For Robert Cosyn, mercer, appointed in 1461, see above. n. 29.

[61] John Skelton was appointed surveyor of the search in 1461 'for his good service to the king and his brothers the duke of Clarence and Richard'. An account survives for his survey 1465–7 (*C.P.R. 1461–7*, 52; E.122/186/4).

[62] E.g. 1466, Robert Brooke of Melton by Gravesend 'yoman' alias late of Gravesend 'osteler', deputy at Gravesend of William Baldry, searcher in the port of London

Seven tronagers were appointed between 1461 and 1485, one of whom was a royal servant.[63] Of the five tronagers appointed between 1485 and 1509, two were royal servants.[64]

Apart from royal servants, the large majority of collectors, controllers, surveyors, searchers and tronagers were London merchants.[65] Each of the officials had a clerk and these, when they can be identified (since they were not appointed by the Crown but by the officials), appear to have been mostly lesser merchants.[66] References to 'waiters'[67] in the port of London appear in the late 1470s. In 1478 allowances were made by the collectors and controller of tunnage and poundage for payments to their three clerks and 'to diverse other persons waiting ('vigilant') and searching both by day and by night, by land and by water'.[68] The number and permanence of the waiters in the London customs system prior to 1490 are uncertain but from that time onwards there is evidence that there was a large and regular establishment of such officials both for tunnage and poundage and petty customs. From 1490 the collectors of tunnage and poundage were regularly allowed a sum for 'rewards' which as later accounts show, included payments to ten waiters.[69] Similarly, the collectors of petty custom were, from 1491,

---

(*C.P.R. 1461–7*, 536) and William Floure alias Aston of Gravesend 'chapman' alias 'yoman', late deputy at Gravesend of Baldry (*ibid.* 545).

[63] John Scot, esquire, granted the office of tronage and pesage for life in 1461 (*C.P.R. 1461–7*, 11, 15).

[64] Roger Cotton, tronager 1487, knight of the king's body, and John Roye, 'tronator' of wool 1502, king's servant (*C.P.R. 1485–94*, 159, 172; *ibid. 1494–1509*, 264).

[65] Mercers and drapers predominated but there were also fishmongers, skinners, haberdashers, tailors, goldsmiths, ironmongers and salters. A number of others were described as 'gentlemen'.

[66] E.g. pardons to: 1480, John Thomas of London, mercer, late one of the clerks of the petty custom in London and clerk of John Middleton (1463), John Rogers (1465) and Hugh Brice (1471), collectors of tunnage and poundage (*C.P.R. 1476–85*, 175); 1471, Richard Wyscard of London, draper, formerly one of the clerks of the collector of wool custom in London (C.67/48, m.24); 1468, William Brette, draper of London, late deputy or servant of William Bertram, searcher (*C.P.R. 1467–77*, 122); 1484–5, Edward Froddesham of London, goldsmith, formerly clerk and deputy of William Daubeney, searcher (1483) (C.67/52, m.4; 53, m.15); 1500, William Sever, alias Sevier, of London, salter, late deputy of John Shaa, searcher (*C.P.R. 1494–1509*, 202).

[67] Customs inspectors who boarded vessels before they docked to investigate their cargoes (tide-waiters) and special searchers who inspected the cargoes of ships after landing (land-waiters), with powers to seize uncustomed goods (*Royal Commission of 1552*, 176, 180).

[68] P.R.O. Tellers' Roll, E.405/66, m.4r. Hugh Lawton 'oon of the keepers of the waterside in the office of oure custume and subsidie' was paid at the rate of £4 per annum for his services in 1482–3 (P.R.O. Warrants for Issues, E.404/78/3/27). The same rate was paid to waiters in the sixteenth century (E.122/163/7, 8). They must have relied on augmenting their income with rewards for seizures.

[69] The collectors were allowed a total of £253 6s.8d. for themselves, the controller and their clerks (E.356/23, ms. 37–40). A breakdown of the total is to be found in Views of Account from 1496 onwards which show that four 'waiters' acted for the collector on exports, three for the controller and three for the collector on imports (E.122/163/6, 7, 8). This is one less than the establishment of 1552 (A. P. Newton, 'The Establishment of the Great Farm of the English Customs', *Transactions of the Royal Historical Society*, 4th ser., I (1918), 131).

allowed a sum for 'rewards' which included payments to seven waiters.[70] The customs establishment in the port of London in the 1490s was closely similar to that to be found in 1552.[71]

The financial rewards for those serving in the London customs during the fifteenth century are a matter of some uncertainty but there is evidence that the Crown's direct payments to certain of the officials greatly increased in the latter part of the century, even if their opportunities to profit from the customs in other ways were diminishing. The commissions of appointment in Edward IV's reign of controllers, tronagers and deputy butlers state that they were to receive 'the accustomed fees' (amount not specified), but mention of fees is omitted from the collectors' commissions. It would appear, however, that the collectors were receiving fees and/or 'rewards' at this time.

At the beginning of the reign the two collectors of wool custom received a joint 'fee' of £40 per annum and the controller 'wages' of £10.[72] There was also an allowance of £4 per annum for rent of a house for tronage of wools, with other rooms and a solar to accommodate the collectors and controller and their clerks.[73] The rent of £4 continued as a regular allowance into the sixteenth century but the fees and wages of the collectors and controller ceased to be recorded on the Enrolled Customs Accounts as, under the terms of the 'Act of Retainer' of 1466, the Staplers' Company was made responsible for paying £100 a year for the fees of the London collectors and controller of wool custom.[74] A breakdown of this total shows that by 1466 each collector of wool custom was receiving a total of £40 per annum and each controller £20.[75]

At the beginning of Edward IV's reign the two collectors of petty custom were being allowed a joint fee of twenty-three marks (£15 6s.8d.) per annum, with a further £5 'pro misis et expensis' in collecting cloth

---

[70] The collectors were allowed a total of £170 for 1491–2 for themselves and their clerks. From 1498 this became set at £167 6s.8d. (E.356/23, ms.44–7). Views of Account from 1507 onwards show that there were three waiters for the petty custom outwards and four for the petty custom inwards, the same establishment as in 1552 (E.122/163/7, 8; Newton, *loc. cit.*).

[71] Apart from one extra waiter for the subsidy inwards, the only official mentioned in 1552 but not in the 1490s was the holder of the joint office of 'solicitor, surveyor and receiver of 12d. for every three kerseys in London and Southampton' (Newton, *loc. cit.*; *Royal Commission of 1552*, 13).

[72] E.356/21, ms.1–4. From 1316 onwards the collectors of ancient and petty customs had received a lump sum of £40 a year 'pro misis et expensis'. The controller had received an annual wage of £10 since 1307 (R. L. Baker, 'The English Customs Service, 1307–1343: A Study of Medieval Administration', *Transactions of the American Philosophical Society*, new series, vol. 51, pt. 6 (Philadelphia, 1961), 7n, 16, 25n; Mills, 'Collectors', 175, 177).

[73] The same rent had been paid since the building of the tronage house in 1383 (M. H. Mills, 'The London Customs House in the Middle Ages', *Archaeologia*, lxxxiii (1933), 323).

[74] Power and Postan, 75.

[75] Receipts for these payments by the Staplers' Company show that each collector received annually a fee of £20 and a 'reward' of £20 and the controller a fee of £10 and a 'reward' of £10 (E.122/225/74–5, 78–80, 82–3). Similar fees and 'rewards' had been paid in the 1370s (*Chaucer Life-Records*, ed. M. M. Crow and C. C. Olson (Oxford, Clarendon Press, 1966), 151, 220–46).

custom.[76] They were also allowed 33s.4d. for the rent of the house used for collecting petty custom.[77] In some years, at least, of the 1460s the collectors and controllers of petty custom were receving a joint 'reward' of £50 per annum and in 1478 each collector received a 'reward' at an annual rate of some £40 and the controller £20.[78] By at least 1491 these rewards of £40 and £20 had become regular payments. Each of the three petty custom clerks was receiving £10 a year, whilst the seven waiters received £4 a year each. There was also an allowance of £9 6s.8d. per annum for boat-hire, which was divided between the two collectors.[79]

No fees for the collectors and controller of tunnage and poundage are recorded on the Enrolled Customs Account. However, as with the petty custom, there is evidence of large 'rewards' allowed to the collectors and controller of tunnage and poundage from at least the 1460s onwards. In 1467 the two collectors and controller received a joint 'reward' of £82, and in 1478 the two collectors £133 6s.8d. between them, and the controller £40.[80] By 1490 these latter had become regular payments, namely one hundred marks to each collector and £40 to the controller. Each of the three tunnage and poundage clerks was paid £10 a year and the ten waiters £4 each. There was an allowance of £10 for boat-hire and £1 for rent of a customs house for the subsidy.[81]

The surveyor of London customs, William Weston, was granted in 1480 a fee of 100 marks a year with £10 for his clerk.[82] The size of this fee (an indication of the importance originally attaching to this office) has been the subject of much comment,[83] but, as we have seen, two years earlier an equal sum was paid to each of the collectors of tunnage and poundage. Also, it appears that the surveyor's fee was reduced early in the sixteenth century, a sign, probably, of a decline in the status of the office at that time.[84]

[76] E.356/21, ms.6–11. There is no reference here to a controller's fee. The same fees and expenses had been paid in the 1380s (*Chaucer Life-Records, op. cit.*, 248–53).

[77] This amount had been allowed for rent from the 1380s onwards (Mills, 'The London Customs House', *op. cit.*, 314–15; *Chaucer Life-Records, op. cit.*, 248, 253).

[78] P.R.O. Issue Rolls, E.403/827 A, m.5; 839, m.7; 848, m.12.

[79] These details are to be found in a View of Account of 1507 (E.122/163/8) but a total amount was allowed to the collectors from 1491 onwards which was the sum of all these payments (see above, n. 70). The clerks had received £10 each in 1478 when there had also been a payment of £28 'for waiters ... about the shore of the Thames' and £8 13s.4d. for boats hired for the waiters (P.R.O. Issue Roll, E.403/848, m.12).

[80] The payment to the collectors in 1478 was said to consist of £100 accustomed reward with a further 50 marks special reward (P.R.O. Issue Rolls, E.403/839, m.5; 848, ms.6–7).

[81] These details are to be found in Views of Account from 1496 onwards but from 1490 a total amount was allowed to the collectors which was the sum of all these payments (see above, n. 69). The collectors and controller had been allowed £10 for each of their clerks in 1477–8 (P.R.O. Tellers' Roll, E.405/66, m.4r.).

[82] No fee is specified for the first two surveyors who were appointed in 1478. The fee of 100 marks was granted to Weston's successor, William Treffry, in 1485 (*C.P.R. 1476–85*, 225; *ibid. 1485–94*, 15).

[83] It has been pointed out that the London surveyor's fee was equivalent to the income of one of the richer gentry and that even the king's proctor in the papal court at Rome was paid only £130 (J. R. Lander, *Conflict and Stability in Fifteenth-Century England* (1969), 105; C. Ross, *Edward IV* (1974), 384).

[84] Cobb, 'Books of Rates', *op. cit.* 6–7.

'Patents for the appointment of London searchers usually specified that they were to receive not fees but a 'moiety of the forfeitures' of uncustomed goods and prohibited exports which they had seized.[85] The searchers and their deputies also took certain fees from individual ship-masters and merchants. The London searcher levied a fee of from 20d. to 6s. for making out a bill of discharge for each ship leaving the port, which was delivered to the purser when the searcher was satisfied that all the goods for export had been customed. Each alien passenger on the ship paid 'headmoney' of 4d. to the searcher.[86] The searcher's deputies at Gravesend also levied charges of from 8d. to 2s.8d. on ships and 4d. on outgoing alien passengers.[87]

The tronager would appear to have been another official who was remunerated by fees levied on individual merchants and not by a fixed salary.[88]

The collectors and controllers also levied fees from individual merchants. Thus the collectors of wool custom accounted at the Exchequer for a fee of 2d. per cocket from each merchant exporting wool, hides or woolfells.[89] It appears that cocket money was paid on the export and import of other goods but this was not accounted for at the Exchequer.[90] A further source of revenue for the collectors of petty custom and tunnage and poundage was an allowance of £4 for each £100 collected in custom and subsidy on alien cloth, which was given from at least 1509 onwards.[91]

Although the fees paid to customs officials (particularly from the 1470s onwards) were thus quite considerable, it seems probable that customs posts in the later fifteenth century still also had their attractions

---

[85] E.g. *C.F.R. 1461–71*, 79, 112–13, 251, 277–8. It has been pointed out, however, that the gift of the moiety was at the discretion of the Crown and was not usually paid unless the smuggler had been caught with the goods (Guth, 181).

[86] These amounts were said to have been levied since at least the beginning of the sixteenth century (G. Schanz, *Englische Handelspolitik Gegen Ende des Mittelalters* (Leipzig, 1881), II, 360–1).

[87] Again these rates were said to date back at least to the beginning of the sixteenth century (Schanz, *op. cit.* II, 362–3). In 1486 a fee of 3s.4d. was paid to the searcher at Gravesend on the departure of the 'Margaret Cely' to Bordeaux (*The Cely Papers*, ed. H. E. Malden (Camden Soc. 3rd ser. I, 1900), 185).

[88] In the fourteenth century merchants paid the London tronager a fee of ½d. per sack for the weighing of wool and this was accounted for at the Exchequer but this accounting does not appear to have happened in the later fifteenth century (Baker, *op. cit.*, 8). The Celys paid the weigher's clerk 1d. per sack (Alison Hanham, *The Celys and their World* (Cambridge, 1985), 123).

[89] E.g. E.356/22, m.33; E.122/73/40. The cocket fee of 2d. for each receipt showing the payment of ancient custom was fixed by the end of Edward II's reign (Baker, *op. cit.*, 9n.).

[90] According to the collectors of tunnage and poundage in 1545, the merchant paid 5d. to the collector for a cocket for each ship in which he had goods for export which were liable for petty custom or for tunnage and poundage. The shipmaster also paid 1d. for entering in the customs books the particulars of each ship which was outward bound. Similarly for imports, the shipmaster paid 1d. (divided equally between the collectors and controllers) for entering his ship and its merchandise in the customs books. For receipts for payment of custom, 2d. was paid to the collector and 1d. each to the controller and the surveyor (Schanz, *op. cit.* II, 356–9).

[91] E.122/163/7, 8.

from a commercial point of view as they had had in the fourteenth century. Thus it appears that collectors continued to make temporary use of customs money for their own profit.[92] Customs officials were favourably placed to engage in trade, to gather information concerning their fellow merchants and to pay their custom at their own convenience.[93] Between 1461 and 1509 several London customs officials, including collectors, controllers, searchers and even clerks, were pardoned for having engaged in trade contrary to the Statute of 1442, or were licensed so to trade in the future, but there was apparently a decline in the number so licensed later in the period.[94] The importance of the London collectors of tunnage and poundage as lenders in the Crown between 1462 and 1485 has already been noticed but this role vanished with the cessation of short-term loans to the Crown after 1490.[95] The financial attractions of London collectors' posts are shown by the large sums which certain men were prepared to pay to obtain them in the latter part of Henry VII's reign.[96]

The Compilation and Audit of the Particular Accounts

In 1428 it had been laid down in an ordinance of the Council that a sealed book should be sent out annually from the Exchequer to the customs collectors of each port, each book containing a specific number of folios of which a record was to be kept in the Exchequer. In this book, and no other, were to be entered the names of merchants entering and leaving the port, the quantity of their merchandise and its value. No erasures were to be made of any details entered, under pain of imprisonment and fine.[97] Judging from the surviving accounts, it would appear that this ordinance was largely observed in the port of London until the end of Henry VI's reign. Between 1461 and 1509, however, the only surviving London particular accounts in book form are those of the collectors of wool custom.[98] For this period the surviving accounts of the collectors of petty custom and of tunnage and poundage, as well as of all controllers and surveyors, are in roll form, consisting of long, narrow parchment membranes (some 20 cm. wide by 76 to 90 cm. long) tied at the head in Exchequer style.[99]

---

[92] Baker, *op. cit.*, 9; Coleman, *op. cit.*, 184–5. The 1552 Commissioners complained that the London customers paid in their receipts of customs money only twice a year and recommended that they should make monthly payments into the Treasury (*Royal Commission of 1552*, 174).

[93] Baker, *op. cit.*, 9.

[94] *C.P.R. 1461–71*, 536, 545; *ibid. 1467–77*, 415, 546; *ibid. 1476–85*, 175, 228, 230, 246, 252; *ibid. 1485–94*, 46, 58; *ibid. 1494–1509*, 514.

[95] See above, p. xviii; S. B. Chrimes, *Henry VII* (1972), 217.

[96] In 1506 Ralph Bukberd paid 250 marks to be a collector of tunnage and poundage in London and Nicholas Waryn 200 marks for the same office. John Warnett paid 200 marks to be a collector of petty custom and he also paid £20 'to have liberty to make his clerk in the custom house' (Edmund Dudley's Book of Debts, B. L. Lansdowne MS. 127, fos. 16, 16v, 30). [97] *C.C.R. 1422–9*, 429.

[98] E.122/73/4, 32, 35, 37, 40; 78/5, 10; 79/3, 9, 17; 162/1; 203/5, 6. It was not until the issue of the Book of Orders of 1564 that all the customs accounts kept in the ports were again entered in special parchment books (Dietz, xi).

[99] The heading of the account states the names of the officials, type of custom, port and

In these accounts each ship's cargo is (usually) consolidated under one heading and one date, although the loading or unloading of a ship might be spread over a period of days or even weeks.[100] It appears, therefore, that the collector or, more probably, his clerk[101] accumulated bundles of merchants' bills and cockets and entered them in the accounts from time to time.

The stages in the process of making entries in the particular accounts were, officially, that first, the master of any ship entering or leaving the port paid for the entering in the accounts of his name and the ship's name and homeport. For imports the master or the purser also made a declaration in writing of the goods on board. Then each merchant presented the clerk with a bill of content in which he gave details of the ship or ships in which his cargo had been or was to be carried, the type and number of containers and the amount and nature of the goods.[102] Wool, cloth and other goods for export were examined and packed by the official packers who were to see that the goods were entered in the custom books.[103] Then, goods were valued for the *ad valorem* duties of petty custom and poundage. Parliamentary grants of tunnage and poundage between 1439 and 1510 specified that the goods of denizen merchants were to be valued at the price which the merchant or his factor had paid for their purchase, the amount being certified on oath by the merchant or factor or by letter from a factor overseas.[104] There is evidence, however, that by the later fifteenth century the valuations of many commodities were becoming fixed for customs purposes.[105] The

---

period of the account. The collectors' accounts (particularly for wool custom) frequently specify the dates of the patents under which the collectors had been appointed.

[100] In this the Particular Accounts contrast with the London Port Books of 1565 onwards in which goods were entered as they were declared by individual merchants, so that one ship's cargo might be mixed with others and spread over many pages (Dietz, xxi; N. J. Williams, 'The London Port Books', *Transactions of the London and Middlesex Archaeological Society*, xviii (1955), 16).

[101] Each collector, controller and surveyor had his own clerk in the later fifteenth century (see above, p. xx). It would seem almost certain that the clerks wrote up the accounts. Only the controllers' patents continued to specify that they were to execute their office in person, but this did not necessarily mean that they wrote their own accounts, cf. the surviving controlments of Thomas Fowler (see below, n. 207).

[102] Schanz, *op. cit.* II, 356–9; *Royal Commission of 1552*, 175. In 1479, in the course of their dispute with Edward IV over the payment of poundage, the Mercers agreed on the form which the bill of content should take (*Acts of Court*, 118).

[103] Schanz, *op. cit.* II, 358. There is a reference to a 'packer's book' in 1404 in which the packer entered the number of cloths which he had packed for export and which had been checked by the controller (E.159/181, Recorda, Mich. 6 H.IV, rot.20). No packers' books survive until the later sixteenth century, e.g. P.R.O. Exchequer Port Books E.190/4/5, packer's book 1570–1.

[104] Alien merchants' goods had been valued on the same basis since 1303 (Gras, 263–4; Cobb, 'Books of Rates', *op. cit.*, 2–3).

[105] In the 1480–1 Petty Custom account the valuations of most staple commodities remain stable throughout the account (it is difficult to determine the valuation of particular manufactured goods as these are usually valued together in one consignment). Also the valuations of a number of commodities in 1480–1 correspond with those given in the 1507 Book of Rates. Only in the case of a few staple commodities is a clear increase

merchant then paid the custom which was due, or gave adequate assurance that it would be paid,[106] and the clerks made out cockets or sealed indentures in two parts, one sent to the searcher and the other retained by the collectors who delivered it up at the Exchequer when accounting. The cocket specified the name of the merchant and the nature, quantity and value of the goods which had been customed.

The collector's clerk, after making his entries, passed the bundles of bills of content and cockets to the controller's clerk who entered the details (with the exception of the amount of custom paid) on to his counter-roll. In like fashion, after 1478, the surveyor's clerk entered the details on his roll. That the controllers' and surveyors' rolls were not straight-forward copies of each other and of the collectors' accounts, but separate copies made from the bills of content, is shown by the fact that, where parallel accounts survive, the order of the entries varies although the details usually agree apart from small variations.[107]

The searcher checked the ship's cargo against the cockets and, if he found it correct, allowed incoming goods to be landed. For outward-bound ships, the searcher delivered the cockets cancelled and a bill of discharge to the purser, once he was satisfied that all the goods on board had been customed.[108]

At approximately half-way through the accounting year, often at Easter, a 'view of account' (*visus compoti*) was held at the Upper Exchequer. The King's Remembrancer ordered the sheriffs to summon the collectors to appear in person at the Upper Exchequer with their rolls of particulars and an estimate was made of how matters stood between the collectors and the Exchequer. The total amount which the collectors ought to have received was recorded and against this was set the total paid into the Exchequer, special assignments paid out of the customs, and the proportion of the collectors' fees and wages paid to that date. The 'view of account' concluded with the sum still owing or the surplus in the collectors' favour.[109]

Whilst the clerk appears to have discharged many, if not most, of the day-to-day duties of the London customs house in the later fifteenth century,[110] the collector remained officially responsible for all money collected and answered for it in person at the Exchequer. The procedure

---

to be observed between 1480–1 and 1507, e.g. woad and salt (Cobb, 'Books of Rates', *op. cit.*, 5–6).

[106] The merchants gave the collectors letters of obligation promising subsequent payment of their customs dues. The collectors sometimes used these letters to satisfy creditors of the crown who had tallies assigned on the customs (Harriss, 'Fictitious Loans', *op. cit.*, 189).

[107] See below, p. xliv.

[108] Schanz, *op. cit.*, II, 359–60; *C.C.R. 1422–9*, 429, and see above, p. xxiii.

[109] Mills, 'Collectors', 194–5; Gras, 142. Surviving original London 'views of account' are usually small pieces of parchment on which these details are given, together with the number of membranes of the collectors' 'Particulars', which suggests that these had actually been produced for examination in the Exchequer (E.122/73/39; 79/8; 114/6; 163/6).

[110] See the declaration of Richard Hill, clerk of Ralph Bukberd, one of the London collectors of tunnage and poundage, in which the clerk accounted to the collector for

at the final audit of a customs account was the same as that for any other 'foreign account'.[111] First, a definite day was appointed for the audit and the sheriffs were instructed to distrain the collectors and controllers to appear at the Upper Exchequer on that day. It would appear that in the late fifteenth and early sixteenth centuries the collectors, controller and surveyor usually appeared in person and that permission to appear by attorney was granted only in exceptional circumstances. Delivery of the particular accounts (when recorded) was usually said to have been made by the customs officials by their own hands.[112] Notes on the accounts also indicate that when the account ended at Michaelmas the London customs officials generally delivered the particulars into the Upper Exchequer in the November following. On entry into the court the collectors swore a solemn oath on the Black Book of the Exchequer of Receipt that they would render true accounts of their receipts and expenditure. Then they were assigned to a particular auditor in open court to prevent collusion with an auditor of their own choice. The auditor, 'worse than a demon unless propitiated with great gifts', was supposed to check each account in detail.[113] It was frequently noted that the collector's account had been checked against the accounts of the controller and surveyor.[114] When the details had been checked, the totals of the various customs and subsidies received were entered at the foot of the collector's account.[115] The totals were then declared before

---

more than £17,000 which he had collected between 1506 and 1509, with allowances for the money which he had already paid to the collector, assignments from the customs, goods licensed for export customs free, payment of the fees and wages of the controller, surveyor, various clerks and waiters, and ending with the balance paid over in the presence of other customs officials (E.122/165/4).

[111] Mills, 'Collectors', 195–6. The stages through which such an account passed in the Exchequer and the bribes which (allegedly) had to be paid to the Exchequer official encountered at each stage are described in a satirical poem attributed to John Bell, a controller and collector of customs in Boston and adjacent ports, 1389–1420. This shows that procedure in the early fifteenth century was similar to that described by Thomas Fanshawe in *The Practise of the Exchequer Court* (1572). The fees which collectors of customs and others had to pay to Exchequer officials were regulated by an ordinance of the Council of 1456 (C. H. Haskins and M. D. George, 'Verses on the Exchequer in the Fifteenth Century', *E.H.R.*, XXXVI (1921), 58–67).

[112] See below, p. 75 and E.122/194/24; 78/6–8; 79/12; 80/1 etc.

[113] Haskins and George, *op. cit.*, 59. The surviving collectors' accounts often bear marginal annotations in the auditor's hand, such as 'cloth without grain, denizen' (or alien), 'wax of Hanse merchants', 'value alien' (where goods were subject to an *ad valorem* duty), '*per breve*' (where there was a licence to export free or at a reduced rate) (E.122/194/19, 22; 80/2).

[114] The Petty Custom controlment of 1480–1 was 'examined with the rolls of the surveyor and the customers' (see below, p. 75). Marginal annotations on the collector's account may indicate discrepancies between it and the other accounts, e.g. 1502–3, '123 pieces of raisins, 124 by controller', 'pouches, pouchrings by controller', 'not in controlment' (E.122/80/2). Notes, corrections and totals at the foot of each membrane are often in one hand.

[115] That these totals were entered on the account in the Exchequer and not in the port is shown by the fact that in many cases they follow a note of the delivery of the account into the Exchequer. Also the totals are often in an Exchequer hand in contrast to that of the account (E.122/162/1; 79/9, 12, 17; 194/18). From 1471 the totals are sometimes entered on a small membrane attached to the account (E.122/194/19; 79/12, 17; 80/2).

one of the Barons who, if satisfied, would signify his approval, which might be recorded on the account.[116]

Usually the controller's and surveyor's part in the audit finished with the completion of the checking of the account, although the controller might be called on to testify concerning some special item of expenditure.[117] Proof of expenditure, however, lay almost entirely with the collectors who produced tallies recording payments of cash receipts into the Exchequer of Receipt, royal writs for payments ordered to be made to individuals, and receipts in the form of indentures showing that the payments had been made. The collectors also claimed their allowances for wages and office expenses. When the auditing Baron was satisfied a summary 'account' (*compotus*) was drawn up comprising the 'head' of the particular account specifying the names of the collectors, the type of custom and the period covered by the account, and the 'foot' of the particulars giving the totals of customs received or due. The details of payments and allowances were then entered on the account and a balance was struck, a clerk writing '*et quietus est*' or '*et debet*' on the account.[118] The completed account was inspected by the two Remembrancers.[119] It was then forwarded to the Clerk and the Controller of the Pipe for enrolment on the Enrolled Customs Accounts.[120] Here the Clerk made a final check of tallies, writs, receipts and allowances before he entered the account on the Enrolled Customs Account under the eye of the Controller. Debts remaining on the account were entered on the Pipe Rolls as was the *quietus* of the collectors when the debt was finally discharged.[121] Payment of 'rewards' to the collectors, controller and surveyor appears usually to have been made at the completion of the audit[122] until the end of the fifteenth century when such payments became a fixed charge on the collectors' accounts.

The Reliability of the Particular Accounts

The two main factors which affected the reliability of the accounts were, firstly, the extent to which the customs officials discharged their duties conscientiously and honestly and, secondly, how far merchants considered it worthwhile to attempt to evade payment of customs. Both of these partly depended on the degree to which the Crown attempted to enforce the laws relating to the customs. As has been seen, the clerks appear to have discharged most of the day-to-day duties in the London customs system of the later fifteenth century, but the collectors retained

---

[116] See '*proba(tur)*' entered against the totals in the 1507–8 wool account (E.122/79/17).

[117] *Chaucer Life-Records, op. cit.*, 225, 266–7.

[118] Thus, *pace England's Export Trade*, 4, it would appear that these summaries were made in the Exchequer and not sent up from the ports. Examples survive amongst the K.R. Accounts, E.122/78/1; 79/1; 73/13; 79/16.

[119] A memorandum of the total amount owed by the collectors and the allowances claimed was entered in the 'Status et visus compotorum' section of the Memoranda Rolls, e.g. Lord Treasurer's Remembrancer's Memoranda Roll 21 Edw. IV, E.368/254; 'Status et visus compotorum' Trinity 21 Edw. IV ms.4–5.

[120] Mills, 'Collectors', 195–6.

[121] *Chaucer Life-Records, op. cit.*, 267–8.

[122] P.R.O. Exchequer, Issue Rolls, E403/827 A m.5; 839 ms.6–7; 848 ms.6–7.

the ultimate responsibility for collecting and accounting for the customs.[123] Prosecutions of London customs officials were not very numerous during the reign of Edward IV and there would appear to have been none for non-residence in their posts.[124] The most serious charges came in 1481 when the collectors of tunnage and poundage were accused of allowing a Genoese merchant to land 100 bales of woad not assessed for custom. They produced pardons but were dismissed from office.[125] There is evidence that at the beginning of Edward IV's reign, London customs officials were being bribed or 'entertained' by the mercers.[126]

Early in Henry VII's reign the controller of wool custom was fined £100 for non-residence and the deputy searcher was twice fined for engaging in trade, but there would appear to have been no subsequent prosecutions for such offences.[127] During the reign there were some nine prosecutions for deceits and concealments perpetrated by London customs officials. The most serious case was that of the collectors of petty custom, Robert Fitzherbert and Williame Galle, who failed to account for their receipts between 1494 and 1496.[128] In the latter part of the reign heavy fines were imposed on a number of customs officials for offences allegedly committed in office and these included William Curteis, one of the London collectors of tunnage and poundage, who, in March 1506, paid 500 marks for a pardon and was dismissed from office.[129] Altogether there were 12 prosecutions of London customs officials out of 125 for the whole kingdom during Henry VII's reign.[130] Since London was by far the busiest port and the one which could be most easily supervised by the Treasurer of the Chamber and his subordinates,[131] the evidence does not suggest an unusual degree of negligence

---

[123] See above, p. xxvi.

[124] Based on a survey of the Repertories to the Memoranda Rolls (P.R.O. Exchequer, K.R. Memoranda, Repertory Rolls, Ind. 7040) with a more detailed examination of some of the Rolls. Five collectors were charged with not taking the required securities from merchants (E.159/240, Recorda, Hil. 3 Edw. IV, rot. 25; 241, Recorda, Easter 4 Edw. IV, rots. 14, 16; 249, Recorda, Mich. 12 Edw. IV, rot. 40). The searcher William Baldry was pardoned for failing to render an account for forfeited goods (E.159/248, Recorda, Hil. 11 Edw. IV, rot. 2).

[125] E.159/257, Recorda, Hil. 20 Edw. IV, rots. 7, 10; *C.P.R. 1476–85*, 232, 269.

[126] In 1463, 6½d. was spent 'for drynke with the customers and sercheours' and in the following year £1 0s.2d. 'for a dyner made to the under tresorer, customers, sercheours and others of our felaship to be frendly in customeng of our wares and especially that it should not be opened at the watersyde'. In 1464, also, the collectors of tunnage and poundage were given £10 'by thavys of the Felaship to be frendly in the same' (Mercers' Company, Wardens Accounts, 1391–1464, fos. 205r., 208v.). I am indebted to Miss Heather Creaton for these references.

[127] Guth, 229–30. I am greatly indebted to Dr. Guth for allowing me access not only to his thesis but also to his manuscript table of penal cases on the Memoranda Rolls 1485–1509.

[128] Cobb, 'Cloth Exports', *op. cit.*, 603.

[129] Edmund Dudley's Book of Debts (B.L. Lansdowne MS.127, f. 17v.); E.159/284, Recorda, Michaelmas and Hilary 21 Hen. VII.

[130] Guth, 230–1.

[131] The King's Chamber appears to have exercised close supervision of the customs from the 1480s onwards through Sir Reginald Bray, the undertreasurer of England, and Sir

or corruption on the part of London customs officials at this time.

The incentives for merchants to seek to evade payment of customs do not appear very great in the late fifteenth century. Poundage on imports and exports represented only five per cent on the (low) customs valuation of denizens' goods and six and a quarter per cent (including petty custom) on aliens' goods. The duty on cloth ranged from approximately two per cent for denizens to six per cent for aliens. Only the duties on wool represented a substantial burden of some 25 per cent for denizens and 33 per cent or more for aliens, but wool was a bulky commodity which was difficult to smuggle undetected.[132] In addition, the increase in the number of customs officials (particularly waiters) in the port of London at this time made detection more probable and wholesale bribery more expensive. Nevertheless, some merchants, particularly London mercers, appear to have attempted to evade the customs (or to make reduced payments) whenever they could. Some 312 actions for alleged customs evasion in the port of London were brought in the Exchequer Court during the reign of Edward IV. In more than a third of the cases (123) the informers can be identified as customs officials, mostly searchers, their deputies or servants. In 96 cases (all in the last five years of the reign) the information was brought by the King's Attorney and in the remaining cases by private individuals.[133] Between 1461 and 1470 there were 167 cases but in the year of the readeption of Henry VI and the seven years following (1470–78) there was a marked falling off with only 24 cases in all. A substantial increase occurred in the last five years of the reign (1478–83) with 121 cases of which 104 were concentrated in the period between Trinity 1478 and Easter 1480. It is, perhaps, significant that 1478 was the year of the appointment of the first surveyor of customs in the port of London, although similar officials had been appointed in other ports from 1471.[134]

In the Trinity Term of 1478, 36 actions were brought by the King's Attorney against merchants of several companies for importing a variety of goods (especially madder, but also linen, flax, furs, hops, nails, kettles, oars and wax) allegedly without payment of poundage.[135] A year later the King's Attorney laid 14 informations against a prominent mercer, John Marchall, for customs evasion on a great variety of imports to the value of £2,500. All the offences were said to have taken place between 1466 and 1471, which suggests, after such a lapse of time, that an example was being made of Marchall.[136]

Whilst the actions were in progress against Marchall, the Court of the

---

John Heron, the Treasurer of the Chamber (W. C. Richardson, *Tudor Chamber Administration 1485–1547* (Baton Rouge, 1952), 123–4).

[132] *England's Export Trade*, 22–3.

[133] P.R.O. Exchequer, K.R. Memoranda, Repertory Rolls, Ind. 7040.

[134] Ross, *op. cit.*, 384.

[135] E.159/255, Recorda, Trinity 18 Edw. IV, rots. 4–33. The highest valuation of a consignment was 100 marks, and most were considerably less.

[136] There were also three charges of exporting coin from Sandwich to Flanders during the same period. Marchall produced pardons for the offences (E.159/256, Recorda, Trinity 19 Edw. IV, rots. 4–14).

Mercers' Company in July 1479 complained of harsh treatment from the customs officials but they were advised by one of their Wardens to comply quietly with the customers' demands.[137] In September the Merchant Adventurers recorded in the minutes of their Court, with an air of injured innocence, that the king had been 'straungely enformed how the Marchauntes of this his citie shulde embesell gretely his subsidie' and that consequently, on his orders, the Mayor had summoned the Wardens of the Adventurers and informed them that the king was determined that the merchants should pay the subsidy (of poundage) according to statute, and that every merchant should render upon oath a true bill of content of his goods.[138]

Fearing that they might be sued in the Exchequer for arrears of subsidy, the Adventurers sent deputations to treat with the king and the Council but, in December, it was reported that the king was adhering to his demand for £2,000 for the arrears although the envoys had been authorised to offer only 500 marks.[139] In the same month, nine mercers were charged with customs evasion, all the alleged offences involving small quantities of linen recently imported, apart from one cargo valued at £1,500 dating back to 1473.[140] At the same time the Merchant Adventurers were lobbying the queen, Lord Hastings, Earl Ryvers and the Marquess of Dorset amongst other notables, to intercede with the king on their behalf. In January 1480 the king informed a deputation that he was prepared at the instance of the queen to reduce the £2,000 fine by 500 marks and the Adventurers appointed a committee to devise ways for raising the money.[141] The fine was subsequently reduced further to 2,000 marks of which £1,000 was to be paid immediately, the Wardens being under bond to the king for payment of the remaining 500 marks. In return the king agreed to grant a pardon for all offences relating to the subsidy.[142]

Edward IV, however, continued to harbour suspicions of the Adventurers and in April 1480 it was reported at an assembly that he was greatly moved and displeased 'by straunge informacion' that the Company 'of symple and froward disposicion' would not appoint any ships to go to the Easter Market at Bergen-op-Zoom. The king was said to be threatening to withdraw his acceptance of 2,000 marks and insist on payment of the subsidy arrears in full. A delegation to the king apparently succeeded in satisfying him of the Adventurers' good intentions and at the same time took the opportunity to present complaints about Hanseatic privileges.[143] Later in the same month charges (in addi-

---

[137] *Acts of Court*, 116–18.
[138] *Ibid.*   [139] *Ibid.* 119–23.
[140] E.159/256, Recorda, Mich. 19 Edw. IV, rots. 30–34.
[141] *Acts of Court*, 125–6. A scale of contributions was agreed: £40 from each alderman, 40 marks from each warden, £20 from previous wardens and 20 marks from the rest of the livery (*ibid.* 127).
[142] *Ibid.* 127–9.
[143] *Ibid.* 136–7. Political troubles in Brabant would appear to have kept English merchants away from the market at this time (N. J. M. Kerling, 'Relations of English merchants with Bergen op Zoom 1480–1481', *Bulletin of the Institute of Historical Research*, XXXI (1958), 136).

tion to those held over from the previous Michaelmas Term) were brought in the Exchequer Court against 28 mercers for offences involving, chiefly, the import of linen (with small quantities of other goods), allegedly without payment of poundage. All the offences were said to have taken place on 27 July 1479.[144] In May the Court of the Adventurers was informed that the Chancellor was displeased that the merchants had not sought to obtain their pardons and that he was threatening to return the bill which promised pardon to the king and to instruct the Chief Baron to proceed with sentencing the offenders.[145] All but seven of the mercers charged then produced pardons and in the remaining cases only one judgment (a fine of 8s.) is recorded, the others being adjourned without conclusion.[146] For the remainder of the reign the number of London customs cases dwindles, the highest recorded being seven in Hilary Term 1481.[147]

Some 230 actions for alleged customs evasion in the port of London were brought in the Exchequer Court during the reign of Henry VII. These amounted to about a fifth of the actions brought for the country as a whole.[148] The informers in almost all the cases relating to the port of London were customs officials, particularly the searchers, but there were also private informers operating under crown patronage.[149] Between 1485 and 1495 there were some 64 cases, but more than double that number (132) in the following decade with a marked falling off after 1505. Most notable were the ten cases prosecuted by the King's Attorney in 1497 against Hanse merchants for importing uncustomed goods (mostly silk) to the value of £1,657.[150] In most smuggling cases, however, the goods were valued at less than £10.

In addition to the straightforward cases of customs evasion, actions were brought (under specific statutes) alleging the illegal export or import of particular commodities. Most numerous of these in Edward IV's reign were the 40 actions for the export of staple goods (principally pewter and hides) to places other than Calais.[151] There were seven actions concerning thrums (pieces of waste thread or yarn) exported contrary to statute.[152] Fourteen actions were brought in Hilary Term 1463 alleging failure by merchants to give customs officials security that they would bring back silver plate in return for exported wool.[153]

---

[144] E.159/257, Recorda, Easter 20 Edw. IV, rots. 8–11.

[145] *Acts of Court*, 137.

[146] The pardons were for all offences committed before 24 January 1480. The entry of 47 pardons on the Patent Roll includes the names of 25 mercers whose cases do not appear on the Memoranda Rolls (*C.P.R. 1476–85*, 243–4).

[147] E.159/257, Recorda, Hilary 20 Edw. IV, rots. 7–13.

[148] Guth, 142.

[149] *Ibid.* 130–2.

[150] E.159/273, Recorda, Hilary 12 Henry VII, rots. 46–7.

[151] Contrary to the statute of 8 Hen. VI c.17. There were only five such cases in Henry VII's reign (Guth, 215).

[152] 8 Hen. VI, c.23. There were at least 13 such actions for the port of London under Henry VII. Dr. Guth points out that exports of thrums and horses were sometimes recorded in the customs accounts despite statutory prohibitions (Guth, 213).

[153] Contrary to 14 Edw. III, stat. I, c.21, 480 Staplers obtained pardons in November 1505 for alleged offences against this statute (Hanham, *op. cit.*, 245).

There were also five cases concerning the unlicensed export of coin.[154]

During Henry VII's reign further statutes were introduced prohibiting trade in specific commodities. A statute of 1489 banning the export of wool purchased in certain specified shires led to 19 actions in the port of London.[155] Three separate statutes banning the import of silk and sarcenet cloths, ribbons and laces led to at least 14 actions for the port of London, the goods involved being valued at from £20 to £300.[156] The statute of Richard III's parliament banning the import of diverse manufactured articles led to only one action (in 1508) concerning goods imported from Flanders and this was dismissed at the personal wish of the king.[157] Two 'navigation acts' of 1485 and 1489 which restricted the import of Gascon wines and Toulouse woad to English ships only, led to at least 24 actions in the port of London.[158] Some 20 actions concerning the port of London resulted from the statute of 1487 which required merchants to obtain certificates for goods customed in one port and then shipped to another English port, for production to the officials at the latter (to prevent smuggling under the guise of coastal trade) and also that goods should be entered in the customs books in the name of the owner (not the shipper or agent).[159]

Whilst the level of enforcement of general and specific customs laws thus varied considerably throughout the two reigns, it would seem clear that the peak period of customs prosecutions by the crown was between 1478 and 1480 with a considerable degree of enforcement also from 1461 to 1470 and 1495 to 1505. Even at its peak, however, the amount of customs evasion revealed would not appear to have been so great as to invalidate the evidence of Particular Accounts concerning general trends in overseas trade.

The overseas trade of London in the later years of Edward IV
Whilst stricter enforcement of the customs laws from 1478 onwards may have led to some increase in the proportion of trade recorded in the accounts, there are firm grounds for believing that there was a real boom in London's overseas trade in the later 1470s and early 1480s. Political factors undoubtedly played an important part in the boom, especially the Treaty of Utrecht of 1474 which brought to an end six years of conflict with the Hanseatic League during which time only Cologne merchants maintained trading relations with England.[160] After 1474 the enrolled petty custom figures for miscellaneous alien imports and exports distinguish between the trade of the Hanse and that of all other aliens, presumably because compensation of £10,000 conceded to the Hanse was to be remitted from their customs payments. From a

---

[154] There were 52 such cases in Henry VII's reign, most of which related to London (Guth, 220).
[155] Guth, 207–8.
[156] *Ibid.* 208–9.
[157] I Ric. III c.12; Guth, 212–13.
[158] I. Hen. VII c.8, 4 Hen. VII c.10; Guth, 210–12.
[159] 3 Hen. VII c.8.; Guth, 204–5.
[160] M. M. Postan, 'The Economic and Political Relations of England and the Hanse (1400–1475)', in Power and Postan, 134–7.

total value of £7,908 in 1475–6, the Hanse miscellaneous trade in the port of London rose rapidly, especially after the re-admission of Cologne merchants to the Hanse and to the Steelyard in 1478, to reach a total value of £22,181 in 1480–1.[161] At the same time the value of the miscellaneous trade of other aliens which stood at £18,454 in 1475–6 rose to slightly less (£21,563) than the Hanse total in 1480–1.[162] There was a further small rise in Hanse miscellaneous trade in 1481–2 (£22,534) but then a small decline in the years immediately following with an even steeper decline in general alien trade after 1481.[163] The figure for denizen and non-Hanseatic alien merchandise valued for poundage also reached a record level (£124,000) in 1480–1, falling a little in the following year.[164]

The Treaty of Picquigny and its commercial counterpart, agreed in January 1476, which abolished certain dues paid by English merchants, appears to have given some stimulus to the Anglo-Gascon wine trade so that imports of non-sweet wine into London in 1480–1 reached 3,770 tons, the highest total for nearly thirty years (622n.).[165]

Monetary factors gave a boost to Anglo-Burgundian trade in the 1470s. The Burgundian mints, assisted by debasements of the coinage in 1467 and 1474, were attracting considerable quantities of silver to Antwerp from South Germany. As their main return cargo, the German merchants eagerly sought for the cloth which English merchants brought to the Brabant fairs since they were excluded from the Hanseatic territories and from Flanders.[166] London's annual broadcloth exports (thus heavily concentrated on Brabant) exceeded 40,000 for the first time in 1480–1. Out of a total of 40,074 cloths, 22,384 were exported by denizens, 14,079 by Hanseatic merchants and 3,611 by other aliens. London's share of total cloth exports appears to have been some 60 per cent in the years 1478–81, falling to about 55 per cent in the three following years.[167] The wool trade which had suffered from continual bans on credit sales and from bullionist regulations, until the late 1470s, revived a little when normal credit transactions were again allowed and

---

[161] E.356/22, ms.36–8.

[162] This figure, however, does not include the growing trade of Castilian merchants who, under a treaty of 1466, were exempt from petty custom on general imports and exports (Wendy R. Childs, *Anglo-Castilian Trade in the later Middle Ages* (Manchester, 1978), 53–5).

[163] E.356/22, ms.38–40.

[164] Power and Postan, 346.

[165] Out of 8,327 tuns for the whole country (M. K. James, *Studies in the Medieval Wine Trade* (Oxford, 1971), 47–8, 58, 112–14). In the early fourteenth century some 20,000 tuns of Gascon wine had been imported annually into England (J. L. Bolton, *The Medieval English Economy 1150–1500* (1980), 290).

[166] J. H. Munro, 'Monetary Contraction and Industrial Change in the Late-Medieval Low Countries, 1335–1500' in N. J. Mayhew (ed.), *Coinage in the Low Countries (880–1500)* (BAR International Series, 54, 1979), 118.

[167] These figures exclude cheaper cloths such as Welsh friezes and 4,669 cloths which left London on carts mostly bound for Southampton. 3,948 of these belonged to alien (mostly Italian) merchants (Cobb, 'Cloth Exports', *op. cit.*, 604–5).

London's exports reached 7,216 sacks (all denizens' wool) in 1480–1 (**598–604**).[168]

Woollen cloth was by far the most important commodity exported from London in the 1480s with raw wool occupying very much a secondary position, whilst other exports were in decline or of relatively small significance.[169] Thus, a London petty custom account of 1420–1 records exports of a great variety of manufactured articles: of metal such as daggers, knives, buckles, basins, plates, brass pots and pans, chafing-dishes, fonts, holy water stoups, razors and shears, and of leather such as bags, purses, gloves, girdles, points and buckets, with comparatively few imports of such articles.[170] By 1480–1 the situation was almost completely reversed. Apart from cloth, the only manufactured items exported in significant quantities were pewter pots and other pewter vessels (**243** *passim*) with some items of brass such as candlesticks (**527**) and kettles (**446, 475, 487**), whilst there were substantial imports of small manufactures. The most important raw materials exported, apart from wool, were tin and lead, the trade in which was mostly recorded in the name of Edward IV's licensee, Alan de Monteferrato (**622n.**).[171] The remaining exports were chiefly agricultural products such as butter, cheese, bacon, salt meat, grain (mainly wheat), tallow, candles, calfskins and rabbit skins.

In return, in the 1480s alien merchants imported into London vital raw materials such as iron, osmund, steel, copper, tar, resin, wax, hemp, flax and dyestuffs. Also imported were small quantities of calamine (**30, 82**), the zinc ore found in the valley of the Meuse, which was used in the making of brass. Imports of tin-glass or bismuth (**178, 183**) suggest that it was used a century earlier in pewter manufacture than had formerly been thought.[172]

The most conspicuous imported manufactured commodity in the 1480–1 account is linen of various origins and qualities including, from the Low Countries, Flemish, Ghentish, Hainault, Brabant, Holland and

---

[168] This was out of a total of 11,382 sacks for the whole country. London's exports fell to 4,133 sacks in 1481–2 (*England's Export Trade*, 68). In comparison, at the high point in some years of the 1350s over 40,000 sacks were exported (Bolton, *op. cit.*, 294, 299).

[169] At a rough valuation of £2 per cloth and £6 per sack of wool, London's cloth exports in 1480 were worth about £80,000 and wool exports about £43,000.

[170] Gras, 452–514. By 1438–9, however, a considerable variety of cheap manufactured goods was being imported from the Baltic and the Netherlands, although not on the scale of 1480–1. In 1438–9, apart from cloth, the only manufactured goods exported in quantity were pewter vessels (J. L. Bolton, *Alien merchants in England in the reign of Henry VI, 1422–61* (unpublished B.Litt. thesis, Oxford, 1971), 123–33).

[171] London's tin exports were in decline at this period although the trade was growing at Southampton and other ports. Pewter exports were at a low ebb generally. Tin and pewter exports were regularly recorded separately from the general trade in the Enrolled Customs Accounts, 1478 onwards (J. Hatcher, *English Tin Production and Trade Before 1550* (Oxford, 1973), 119, 130–1, 168); J. Hatcher and T. C. Barker, *A History of British Pewter* (1974), 76).

[172] Calamine was already being imported into England in the early fourteenth century (T. H. Lloyd, *Alien Merchants in England in the High Middle Ages* (Brighton, 1982), 156). For bismuth cf. 'by the later sixteenth century English pewterers were adding bismuth (tin-glass) to fine pewter to produce a harder and more durable alloy' (Hatcher and Barker, *op. cit.*, 224–5).

Zeeland linen and, from Germany, Osnabruck and Herford in West-phalia, Brunswick, Hanover and soultwich linen. It would appear that at least 420,000 ells (about half a million yards) of linen, together with other articles of linen such as sheets, table-cloths, napkins and towels, were imported by alien merchants in 1480–1.[173] There must also have been large imports of linen by denizen merchants in the same year.[174] Cologne, and other, linen thread was imported in considerable quanti-ties. Fustian, the cloth from South Germany and Italy made of a mixture of cotton and flax, appears frequently in the 1480–1 account in the names of Hanseatic merchants, as does Cologne silk.

Battery, beaten plate made from a mixture of copper and lead or tin, and articles made from it such as basins, pots, kettles, candlesticks and frying pans, formed a substantial import via the Brabant fairs from the centres of its production at Dinant, Namur, Liège and Cologne.[175] Another conspicuous type of metal-ware imported was armour of all descriptions, from complete suits ('complete harness', **82, 89, 121, 129, 139**) and horse armour (**93, 114, 121**) to separate pieces: habergeons (**24, 58** *passim*), brigandines (**15, 93** *passim*), sallets (**93, 94** *passim*), bevors (**114, 139**), breastplates (**58, 114, 187**), corslets (**94, 114**), vam-braces (**85, 89, 93, 139**), leg-harness (**85, 89** *passim*) amongst others. References to imports of guns, gunstones and gunpowder (**150, 173, 176, 181**) illustrate the growth of newer forms of armaments.

The import of cloth-making tools such as distaffs (**23, 178–9**), wool-cards and combs (**4, 20** *passim*), spindles and spindle-whorls (**23, 93, 183**), shuttles (**17, 20** *passim*), teazles (**1, 20** *passim*) and cloth-shears (**45, 178** *passim*) emphasises the vigour of the English cloth industry at this time and its decline in Flanders.

The 1480–1 account records a brisk trade in books, more than 900 being imported by alien merchants, unfortunately with a no more pre-cise description than 'diverse histories', apart from five which are specifically called 'printed' (**144**). Nearly 400 of these were in the name of Peter Actoris, a native of Savoy, afterwards Stationer to Henry VII (**1, 23** *passim*). For readers, alien merchants imported some 30 gross of spectacles and 26½ gross of spectacle cases (**17, 26, 30** *passim*) which were probably the products of the, by then, well-developed spectacle industry in the Low Countries.[176]

The influx of large quantities of small manufactured wares from over-seas was causing concern by the early years of Edward IV. An Act was passed in 1464 allegedly to satisfy the 'piteous complaints' of the artifi-cers and handicraftmen and women of London and other towns con-

---

[173] Worth some £5–10,000. Considerable quantities of linen had been imported into London since the later fourteenth century, largely from Westphalia (Vanessa Harding, *The Port of London in the Fourteenth Century. Its topography, administration and trade* (Unpublished Ph.D. Thesis, St. Andrews, 1983), 202–5).

[174] See above, p. xxxi, for the many customs cases involving the import of linen by London mercers, and denizen imports recorded in the customs accounts for 1465–6 and 1487–8 (E.122/78/7; 194/18).

[175] Bolton, *The Medieval English Economy, op. cit.* 278.

[176] Michael Rhodes, 'A Pair of Fifteenth-Century Spectacle Frames from the City of London', *The Antiquaries Journal*, lxii, pt. 1 (1982), 65–6.

cerning the 'grete multitude of dyvers chafferes and wares, perteyning to their Craftes and occupations, beyng full wrought and redy made to the sale' which were being imported by denizens and aliens with the result that 'aswell housholders as journey men, Servauntes and Apprentizes in grete nombre, at this day be unoccupied, and lyve in grete ydelnes, poverte and ruyne'. For which reasons it was ordained that from the following Michaelmas no denizen or alien merchant should import, on pain of forfeiture, a wide range of manufactures including woollen bonnets, laces, ribbons, saddles, stirrups, spurs, locks, hammers, pincers, dice, tennis balls, points, purses, gloves, girdles, shoes, knives, daggers, shears for tailors, playing-cards, pins, rings, chafing-dishes, sacring-bells, hats, brushes and wool-cards.[177]

A similar Act was passed in 1484, this time (it was said) at the petition of various crafts such as the girdlers, pointmakers, pinners, pursers, glovers, cutlers, goldbeaters, painters, saddlers, cardmakers and coppersmiths. The prohibited goods enumerated in this Act are much the same as in 1464, with the addition of such luxuries as painted glasses, painted images, beaten gold and silver 'wrought in papers for Payntours' and holy-water stoups. This time, at least, such frivolous items as dice, playing-cards and tennis balls escaped condemnation.[178] There is little evidence that the Crown was concerned to enforce the ban on these imported manufactures despite the damage they may have inflicted on English crafts. More serious attempts were made, however, during Henry VII's reign, to enforce the Acts banning imports of silk cloths, ribbons and laces.[179]

The Acts of 1464 and 1484 have been described as dealing with 'trivial matters',[180] but the petty custom account of 1480–1 and earlier accounts show that these Acts did not exaggerate the enormous variety of miscellaneous manufactures which were being imported. Native craftsmen appear to have had good reason to fear the scale of these imports: for example, in 1480–1, 28,600 leather, latten, wire, thread and silk girdles were imported into London by aliens, and more than 46,000 knives and daggers of various sorts (folding, pen, standing, pot, ivory, painted and paring knives). This supports the view that the profits of the expanding cloth trade were giving people in general more spending power and that the area where demand was growing most rapidly was that for cheaper goods for the mass market. What English industry could not supply (if the gilds did not allow the production of lower quality goods) was made up by low-grade foreign imports.[181] Whereas Dr. Thirsk's mid-sixteenth century yeomen, peasants, labourers and servants with cash to spend wanted 'a brass pot for the kitchen shelf, a colourful pair of striped stockings or a knitted Monmouth cap',[182] their late fifteenth counterparts sought imported straw hats or St. Omer hats (**1**, **24** *passim*),

---

[177] *Rot. Parl.* V, 506–7. [178] *Stat. Realm*, ii, 495–6.
[179] See above, p. xxxiii.
[180] J. R. Lander, *Government and Community, England 1450–1509* (1980), 26.
[181] Bolton, *The Medieval English Economy*, *op. cit.*, 266, 273, 282, 286, 319.
[182] J. Thirsk, *Economic Policy and Projects. The Development of a Consumer Society in Early Modern England* (Oxford, 1978), 8.

Nuremburg mirrors (**23, 37** *passim*), imitation pearls (**93**) and chalcedony (**27, 28** *passim*) and mistletoe beads (**26, 27** *passim*).

Evidence for the routes taken by London overseas trade in the 1480s is largely indirect. Unfortunately, unlike many of the Bristol accounts, the London Particular Accounts do not specify the destination or provenance of ships in the port and one has therefore to rely on the evidence of the nature of the cargoes, the nationality of merchants (where this is given or can be deduced) and the home ports of the ships. Even this latter detail is frequently omitted from the accounts but the 1480–1 account specifies home ports more frequently than any other surviving London account of the period.

Of 224 ships (including three found only in the Butler's Account) recorded as entering the port of London in 1480–1, 82 were English, 28 of Brabant and 39 of Zeeland, 11 Dutch, 7 Flemish, 17 Hanseatic, 20 French, 7 Portuguese, 5 Spanish, 1 Venetian galley and 7 unidentified. This very much underestimates the number of Spanish ships since, as mentioned previously, Castilian merchants did not pay petty custom.[183] Ships importing wine and other goods belonging to denizen merchants only also are not recorded.[184]

Of 215 outgoing ships recorded in 1480–1, 74 were English, 17 of Brabant and 24 of Zeeland, 6 Dutch, 4 Flemish, 15 Hanseatic, 14 French, 8 Portuguese, 21 Spanish (in this case fully recorded because Castilian merchants paid cloth custom), 1 Venetian galley and 31 unidentified.[185] The fact that fewer outgoing ships are recorded than incoming is partly due to the omission from the Petty Custom account of the wool fleets which sailed in December 1480 and July and September 1481 with over 7,000 sacks of wool (**598–604**).[186] About 60 per cent of the English ships belonged to London, the remainder coming largely from the east coast (Boston, Lynn and Yarmouth) and the south and west (Weymouth, Fowey, Saltash and Dartmouth). The Brabant ships belonged to Antwerp and Bergen-op-Zoom and the Zeeland ships to Arnemuiden, Middelburg, Flushing and Reimerswaal. The proportion of Antwerp and Bergen ships appears to have increased since the mid-fifteenth century over those from ports nearer the mouth of the Scheldt.[187] English, Spanish and Portuguese ships bulk larger in the

---

[183] See above, n. 162. Some 30 Spanish ships importing goods of Spanish merchants only are recorded in the tunnage and poundage account of 1487–8 (E.122/78/7).

[184] The London tunnage and poundage account of 1487–8 records some 80 ships importing wine, fish, salt and miscellaneous goods of denizen merchants only, with a further 15 carrying goods of denizen and Spanish merchants only (E.122/78/7).

[185] In contrast in 1390–1, 443 ships were recorded in the Petty Custom account as entering the port of London and 357 as leaving. Dr. Harding believes the total number of ships entering in this year (allowing for those with exempt cargoes) was probably 550–600 (Harding, *op. cit.*, 262–3). There is evidence, however, that English merchant ships increased very considerably in size in the fifteenth century (D. Burwash, *op. cit.*, 96–7, 100).

[186] Between July 1478 and Michaelmas 1479, 117 ships left London with 7,057 sacks of wool (Power, 'The Wool Trade', in Power and Postan, 42–3).

[187] See the analysis of shipping in the port of London in the surviving accounts between 1438 and 1466 (Marie-Rose Thielemans, *Bourgogne et Angleterre 1435–1467* (Brussels, 1966), 314–17).

1480–1 account than previously with fewer Dutch and Flemish ships. The Dutch ships belonged to Dordrecht, Holland, Leiden, Purmerend, Gouda and Leek, and the Flemish to Ostend and Sluis. The French ships were all from northern French ports: Calais, Dieppe, Guérand, Le Conquet, Harfleur, Caen, Rouen and Réville.

There can be no doubt from the evidence of the 1480–1 account and elsewhere that, by this time, trade was heavily concentrated on the London–Brabant (especially Antwerp) axis. The author of the 'Libelle of Englyshe Polycye' had boasted in the 1430s that English merchants bought more at the Brabant fairs than all other nations, exchanging their cloth for mercery, haberdashery and grocery.[188] Since that time, exclusion from other markets increasingly drew English merchants to Brabant.[189] In addition, by the middle of the fifteenth century, tidal surges had opened up the southerly channel of the Honte (western Scheldt) as far as Antwerp and the eastern Scheldt to Bergen-op-Zoom so that direct access to both ports became possible for larger ships. Bulk cargoes continued, however, frequently to be transhipped into barges at Arnemuiden (the 'quay' of Antwerp) as well as Middelburg which was also regarded as Antwerp's outport.[190] A branch from the great medieval road between Cologne and Bruges ran north-west to Antwerp, and this was the route taken by the Cologne merchants and the South Germans bringing their silver and copper from Central Europe and purchasing English cloth.[191] By the 1480s English cloth imports into the Brabant Fairs were being compared to an 'immense flood tide'.[192]

The four great Brabant Fairs were the Pask or Easter Mart of Bergen-op-Zoom which opened on Maundy Thursday and was followed immediately by the Sinxten or Whitsun Mart at Antwerp, and the Bamis Mart at Antwerp (starting in late August) which was followed with scarcely a break by the Cold Mart at Bergen (starting in late October). In the fifteenth century each fair lasted at least six weeks and the four fairs covered (with overlap) a minimum of 22 weeks in the year.[193] Since the fairs occurred in two almost continuous periods and the two towns were only 30 miles apart, it is difficult to say precisely whether any ship or group of ships in the port of London was setting out to, or returning from, Antwerp as distinct from Bergen. However, some 20 English, Brabant, Zeeland and Dutch ships which left London between 16 November and 9 December (**277–318** *passim*) with cloth, rabbit-skins, salt meat, tallow, candles, pewter and beer were probably bound for the Cold Mart.[194] Twenty ships which left between 9 and 30 April (**442–83**

---

[188] Sir George Warner (ed.), *The Libelle of Englyshe Polycye* (Oxford, 1926), 26–8.
[189] See above, p. xxxiv.
[190] Ralph Davis, 'The Rise of Antwerp and its English Connection, 1406–1510' in D. C. Coleman and A. H. John (eds.), *Trade, Government and Economy in Pre-Industrial England* (1976), 4.
[191] *Ibid.* 11–12; S. T. Bindoff, 'The Greatness of Antwerp' in G. R. Elton (ed.), *The New Cambridge Modern History*, vol. II *The Reformation* (Cambridge, 1958), 52–3.
[192] Munro, *op. cit.*, 118.
[193] Bindoff, *op. cit.*, 55–6.
[194] Troubles in the Low Countries had kept the English merchants away from the Easter Mart of 1480. A treaty signed on 18th October 1480 by John Pickering on behalf of the

passim) were probably bound for the Easter Mart[195] and 14 between 4 and 30 June for the Whitsun Mart (**498–520** *passim*) but the largest concentration of outgoing shipping occurred between late July and late September (**541–96** *passim*) when some 50 ships with the heaviest shipments of cloth by denizen merchants (as many as 70 consignments on one ship) left, probably for the Bamis Mart, thus emphasising Antwerp's greater importance than Bergen. The Hanse merchants in London had their own ship, the *Mary* of the Steelyard, which made six round trips (probably to Brabant) in the course of the year, exporting cloth and agricultural products and returning with a variety of miscellaneous goods in the names of Hanse and other alien merchants (**1, 40, 88, 114, 150, 177, 243, 317, 398, 471, 503**). Eight English and Brabant ships made three (in some cases four) round trips during the year.[196]

Of the incoming ships, 20 English, Brabant, Dutch and French vessels are recorded on 13 November 1480 with a great variety of Hanse and alien merchants' goods, coming probably from the Cold Mart (**20–39**). A special fleet of five ships from the Dutch port of Purmerend came in on 27 December with cargoes of fresh eels (**49–53**). Seventeen ships arrived on 7 March, seemingly between markets (**82–98**), 20 between 1 and 14 June probably from the Easter Mart (**136–55**) and 31 of all nationalities on 21 July with Hanseatic and miscellaneous wares, probably from the Whitsun Mart (**167–96**).

Apart from the 'Mary of the Steelyard', it seems probable that most of the cargoes of the Hanseatic ships (whose homeports were Hamburg and Danzig) were traded directly between the Baltic and England, and not through the fairs, since (apart from some miscellaneous wares picked up on the way) these ships brought in the Baltic goods (timber, pitch, tar, ashes, wax, furs, stockfish, osmund and flax) in the names of Hanse merchants only (**10, 13, 32, 125–6, 168–70, 197, 199**) and exported cloth, pewter and candles, again in Hanse names (**290, 293, 425, 440, 502, 566–7, 574, 576**). Dr. Veale has pointed out an interesting reversal in the Anglo-Hanseatic fur trade at this time in that a small group of Hanse merchants exported 138,000 rabbitskins in 1480–1, a trade which continued to increase until the end of the century, whilst the import of Baltic squirrel skins into England was in decline.[197] The names of 30 Hanse merchants appear regularly in the 1480–1 account, some of whom such as the Questenbergs, Greverodes and Blitterswicks of Col-

Merchant Adventurers and by the lord and town officials of Bergen-op-Zoom gave the English merchants more privileges than ever before in the town. They were allowed to use a special quay where transport was available, to have rooms and stores at a fixed rent and a space for meeting in the market place. The Cold Mart began on 26 October 1480 and may have continued until Christmas (Kerling, *op. cit.*, 136–7).

[195] The Easter Mart probably began on 19 April 1481 and continued to the end of May (*ibid.* 138).

[196] The ships of Anthony Brabander of Middelburg, Peter Jacobson of Arnemuiden, Peter Menger of Antwerp, Clais Thorn of Arnemuiden, Cornelius Nese of Middelburg, John Wodeles of London, William Tabbard of Boston and Thomas Coys of London.

[197] E. M. Veale, *The English Fur Trade in the later Middle Ages* (Oxford, 1966), 158–9, 177.

ogne and John Salmer of Dinant had been leading merchant families in London from at least the middle of the century.[198]

The French ships, apart from those of Calais which participated in the Brabant trade (**17, 36, 90, 313, 571**), were mostly from the Seine region (Harfleur, Rouen and Dieppe: **46, 67, 70, 80, 99, 104, 166**) or Brittany (Guérande and Le Conquet: **29, 64, 193**), importing wheat, apples, nuts, salt, millstones, fish and woad and exporting cloth, pewter, lead, brass, copper, tar, pitch and candles (**237, 311, 360, 368, 392, 484–5, 492, 497, 544**). The Gascon wine trade which, as has been mentioned, had enjoyed a limited revival since 1475, is not recorded in the Petty Customs Account. The Butler's Account of 1480–1, however, shows alien merchants' wine being brought in by ships of London, Plymouth, Holland, Brittany, the Seine, Spain, and Venice (**605–22**).

London, as Dr. Childs has demonstrated, was the centre of the growing English trade with Castile in the 1480s, encouraged by commercial privileges granted and maintained by Edward IV even when Castile was in alliance with France. The ships came mainly from San Sebastian in the province of Guipúzcoa and Bilbao, both on the north coast, and Cadiz in the south. Unfortunately, due to customs exemption, the iron, wine, Toulousan woad and oil which Spanish merchants imported are not recorded in the 1480–1 account but some 3,000 cloths which they exported in 20 of their own ships (**262–3, 319–593** *passim*) and in 12 others (**368, 428, 455–588** *passim*) and in carts to Southampton, are in the account. The Spaniards exported a greater proportion of cloth dyed in grain or half grain than did other alien merchants. Dr. Childs estimates that in 1480–1 Spanish imports into the whole kingdom were worth £6,880 and exports £6,274. In addition, at least 20–30 London merchants were actively engaged in trade with Spain at this time.[199]

Portuguese imports in ships of Viana (**14, 101, 107**) and Oporto (**15, 16**) are more fully recorded than the Spanish, with some 300,000 oranges and sugar and cork amongst other items. In return the Portuguese took cloth, pewter, calfskins and tallow (**288, 303, 324, 327, 446, 464, 581**).

The Italian trade, although in decline in the later fifteenth century, was still considerable in the 1480s. The sole Italian ship to visit the port of London in 1480–1, the Venetian galley of Bernard Bondymer, was one of a fleet of three which had arrived at Southampton in February 1481, the other two going on to Flanders. Bondymer's galley brought to London a cargo of spices, wine, soap, expensive cloths, carpets, silk, glasses and other luxuries to the value of over £6,000. More than half of this (in value) was in the names of three merchants, Maryn' Monsenego, Anthony Bavarino and Alewiso Contarini. The remaining importers were mostly crew members, from the patron or commander and his counsellors, to the mate, crossbowmen, purser, bow and stern oarsmen and other sailors, all detailed in the account (**156, 619**). Bondymer's galley exported some 550 cloths and £750 worth of pewter, calfskins, cotton russet and tin (**588**). In addition, some 150 carts left London for

[198] Bolton, *The Medieval English Economy*, *op. cit.*, 310.
[199] Childs, *op. cit.*, 61–3.

Southampton with 3,500 cloths in the names of Genoese, Venetian, Florentine, Luccan and other alien merchants and 500 cloths of denizen merchants, most of which were probably for export to Italy.[200]

Genoese merchants used ships of Cadiz (**12, 200**), Bilbao (**43**), Oporto (**16**) and Fowey (**198, 201**) to import £4,650 worth of woad, alum, Spanish grain, sugar, dates, raisins and paper. Florentine merchants used ships of Oporto (**15**) and London (**47–8**) to import £700 worth of sugar. Cloth in the names of Genoese and Florentine merchants went out in Spanish and Portuguese ships in return (**262, 324, 327, 489, 556**) and they are also to be found involved in the trade with Brabant (**56, 130, 305, 498, 573, 577**). Amongst the aliens, the Italian trade would appear to have ranked next in value to the Hanseatic at this time.

The boom of the late 1470s and early 1480s was short lived. Harvests in England were bad between 1481 and 1483 and then only average until the abundance of the 1490s and this almost certainly affected trading activities in general.[201] In Flanders and Brabant too there was a crushing famine in the years 1481–2.[202]

General unrest in the Burgundian territories between 1482 and 1492 and, in particular, the Flemish revolt against the Archduke Maximilian in 1484, with raids from Bruges and Sluis on shipping, made passage of the Scheldt and Honte towards Antwerp insecure. Armed convoys were provided for the cloth fleets bound for the Brabant Fairs but, at times, English merchants deserted Antwerp for Middelburg.[203] For a time the trade of the Brabant Fairs suffered and, after 1482, denizen cloth exports from London declined more conspicuously than those of the Hanse and other aliens. By the late 1480s, however, Antwerp (siding with Maximilian) had recovered its trading position,[204] but a further setback came with Henry VII's prohibition of trade with the Burgundian territories in 1493. Exceptionally, the Spanish trade with England continued to increase at this time even when Castilian merchants lost most of their commercial privileges under the treaty of Medina del Campo in 1489.[205] It was not, however, until 1496, with the conclusion of the Intercursus Magnus, that London's cloth trade again reached the level of the 1480s and it was in the first decade of the sixteenth century that the sustained increase began which reached its peak in the middle of the century.[206]

The early 1480s thus constituted a high point in London's overseas trade in the fifteenth century. The London Petty Customs Account of 1480–1, in recording much of this trade, provides detailed evidence of

---

[200] Cobb, 'Cloth Exports', *op. cit.*, 604.
[201] W. G. Hoskins, 'Harvest Fluctuations and English Economic History 1480–1619', *Agricultural History Review*, xii (1964), 31.
[202] H. van der Wee, *The Growth of the Antwerp Market and the European Economy* (The Hague, 1963), II, 96–8.
[203] *Ibid.* 96–8, 103, 105.
[204] *Ibid.* 103–4; Davis, *op. cit.*, 14.
[205] Childs, *op. cit.*, 55.
[206] *England's Export Trade*, 6, 141; Cobb, 'Cloth Exports', *op. cit.*, 605; van der Wee, *op. cit.*, 123.

the developing consumer society of the time which contrasts with the general picture of urban decline and lack of population growth in the later fifteenth century.

The Controller's Account of Petty Custom, 1480–1

The account (P.R.O., E.122/194/25) consists of 27 parchment membranes each some 20 cms. wide by 93 cms. long, except for membrane 11 which is 47 cms. long and membrane 27 which is 36 cms. long, all tied together at the head in Exchequer style. The bulk of the account appears to be written in one small, neat, bastard hand but some membranes (3, 11d, 27) are written in a similar but larger, more upright hand in which there are also insertions elsewhere (e.g. **208–10, 473**). Since the controller had only one clerk it is impossible to say whose the second hand might have been unless it was that of the controller himself. At the foot of the face each membrane except the last are the initials T.F. (Thomas Fowler) indicating that the controller had checked the account.[207] The notes of audit are in other hands (**215**). The account was carefully compiled with a few alterations or corrections mainly to valuations (noted in round brackets in the edited text, **26, 61, 63** *passim*). It appears to have been written up in the usual manner from bundles of bills of content and cockets with each ship's cargo consolidated under one heading and one date.[208] In order to consolidate each ship's cargo and separate it from others the account must have been written up some days or even weeks in arrears of the actual loading and unloading. The greater part of the entry for the incoming Venetian galley (**156**) shows clear signs of having been copied from a bill of content provided by the purser since it lists the crew and merchants (from Andrew Caruse to Treviso de Luderyn') in alphabetical order by first name. The other merchants on the galley, including those with the most valuable cargoes, are not entered alphabetically, indicating that they made their own declarations to the clerk. The language of the account is what has been called 'the patois of the custom house',[209] dog Latin with many English and some French words used for commodities, when there was no common Latin equivalent.

Merchants in the account are described either as Denizen, Alien or Hanse with a few other categories of those with special exemptions such as Breton, of Veere and 'Spanish of Guipúzcoa'.[210] The name of the master and the name and homeport of incoming ships are recorded in the 1480–1 account and the latter detail appears more frequently in this

---

[207] This also happens in Fowler's surviving accounts for 20 November 1477 – 13 July 1478 (E.122/194/23 first membrane only) and 9 April – 24 July 1483 (E.122/73/41 and 162/5) but not in his account for Michaelmas 1472–3 (E.122/194/20). The 1483 account is written in a hand similar to that of 1480–1 but the 1472–3 and 1477–8 accounts are in different hands.

[208] See above, p. xxv. There are a few exceptions to this consolidation, e.g. nos. **386, 395, 387, 410**.

[209] Gras, 561.

[210] The customs' officials appear to have used 'of Guipúzcoa' as a general term for Castilian since they even applied it to Cadiz in southern Castile, (**262**, John Cameo) whereas Guipúzcoa is a northern province.

account than in almost any other surviving later fifteenth century London customs account. The homeports of outgoing ships are not recorded in the account but, where known, have been added (in square brackets) in this edition.

The most distinctive feature of the 1480–1 account (as of the other surviving petty custom and tunnage and poundage Accounts between 1473 and 1495) is that it records a large number of carts leaving London laden with cloth for export from Southampton and other outports. This was in accordance with a provision of the Tunnage and Poundage Act of 1472 which laid down that, in order to prevent frauds in the packing of cloth for export, cloths were to be packed in the presence of the collectors of customs and that custom and subsidy were to be paid in the port where they were packed whether or not the cloths were to be taken to another port for shipment overseas. This provision remained in force until it was repealed by Act in 1495. The result is a unique record for this period of the traffic in cloth between London and its outports.[211]

The parallel Surveyor's Account of Petty Custom, 1480–1 (E.122/194/24) consisted of 29 membranes (one of which has been lost) each some 20 cms. wide by 75 cms. long. It is written in a rougher hand than that of the Controller's Account with corrections in a second hand. Ships' names and homeports are much less frequently given in the Surveyor's than in the Controller's Account. Each ship's cargo is less regularly consolidated under one heading and date than in the Controller's Account. The order of the entries varies between the Controller's and Surveyor's Accounts indicating that they were compiled independently. There are a number of small differences in detail between the accounts (the variations in the Surveyor's Account are shown in this edition preceded by an *S* and in square brackets) but these do not affect the overall picture of trade which each presents. In general the Surveyor's Account gives the impression of having been less carefully compiled than the Controller's.

Thomas Fowler or Fuller is recorded on the Enrolled Customs Accounts as controller of petty custom from Michaelmas 1472 to Michaelmas 1474 and from Easter 1477 to 22 August 1485. Between Michaelmas 1474 and 25 March 1475 there was stated to be no controller and from 26 March 1475 to Easter 1477 the controller was Thomas Stockton.[212] Fowler's appointment as controller is not recorded on the Patent Roll until 29 October 1476.[213] In 1478 Fowler was receiving a 'reward' of £20 per annum and this became the regular amount paid to the controller.[214] On 12th February 1482 Fowler, called 'king's servant' and controller, was licensed to buy and sell merchandise and on 1 March 1484, as Thomas Fuller, he was re-appointed controller.[215] On 17

[211] Cobb, 'Cloth Exports', *op. cit.*, 602–3. The Southampton Brokage Books record carts entering the town from London with cloth but without details of merchants and quantities.

[212] E.356/22, ms.34–40.

[213] *C.P.R. 1467–77*, 592.

[214] See above, p. xxii.

[215] *C.P.R. 1476–85*, 252, 421. He was again licensed to buy and sell (R. Horrox and P. W. Hammond, eds., *British Library Harleian Manuscript 433* (1979), I, 202).

September 1485 Thomas Fuller, almost certainly the same man, was appointed collector of the subsidy and aulnage of cloths for sale and of tunnage and poundage and on 23 November following he was licensed to buy and sell and import and export merchandise.[216] As a collector of tunnage and poundage Fuller would have received an annual reward of £66 13s.4d., considerably more than as controller of petty custom.[217] Fuller had ceased to be collector of tunnage and poundage by 29 June 1486.[218]

More than one Thomas Fowler or Fuller is referred to in records relating to London during this period.[219] The most likely candidate for the controller, since he is described as 'king's servant', is the Thomas Fowler named in 1472 as yeoman of the Crown.[220] In 1475, Thomas Fowler, one of the ushers of the king's chamber, led a contingent of one man-at-arms and 20 archers on Edward IV's expedition to France.[221] If this was the same man as the controller it would help to explain the gap in the latter's service as controller between Michaelmas 1474 and Easter 1477. In May 1476 Fowler, the usher of the chamber, received a pardon for all offences in which he is described as 'late of Buckingham and late escheator in the counties of Oxford and Berkshire and Bedford and Buckingham'.[222] Other pardons of 1484 and 1486 also call him 'late sheriff of Bedford and Buckingham'.[223] By 1484 Fowler was being described as an esquire of the body and was granted custody of the manor of Bekley, Oxon., and the office of Steward of the towns and lordships of Buckingham, Hakmersham, and Brikell, Bucks.[224] Thomas Fowler was sheriff of Bedford and Buckingham again in 1487–8 and M.P. for Buckingham in 1495. He is said to have died in 1496.[225]

---

[216] *C.F.R. 1485–1509*, no. 82; *C.P.R. 1485–94*, 46. William Stafford had been appointed controller of Petty Custom on 21 September 1485 (*ibid.* 83).

[217] See above, p. xxii.

[218] See *Materials for a history of the Reign of Henry VII, op. cit.*, I, 476 where he is described as 'late collector'.

[219] Thomas Fowler, a mercer, was one of the company chosen to ride to meet Edward IV on his return from France in 1475 and to receive Edward V in London in 1483. He was one of wardens of the Mercers' Company in 1485–6 (*Acts of Court*, 88–90, 147, 288–93).

[220] *Rot. Parl.* VI, 16. A Fowler, probably the same man, had been amongst the king's supporters imprisoned by the Lancastrians in 1470 (D. A. L. Morgan, 'The King's Affinity in the Polity of Yorkist England', *Transactions of the Royal Historical Society*, 5th ser. XXIII (1973), 11n.). He may also have been the Thomas Fowler, stockfishmonger, formerly of London and Oxford, also of Buckingham and Beckley, pardoned in 1472 (C.67/49, m.24).

[221] T. Rymer, *Foedera* (The Hague, 1741), V, pt. III, 56. Fifty household officials provided contingents for the expedition (J. R. Lander, 'The Hundred Years War and Edward IV's 1475 Campaign in France' in A. J. Slavin, ed., *Tudor Men and Institutions* (Louisiana State University Press, 1972), 95).

[222] *C.P.R. 1467–77*, 583–4.

[223] C.67/51, m.20; 53, m.15. He was sheriff in 1478–9 and 1483–4, for which latter year he was granted £70 (Horrox and Hammond, *op. cit.*, I, 96).

[224] *C.P.R. 1476–85*, 391, 429.

[225] J. C. Wedgwood, ed., *History of Parliament. Biographies of the Members of the Commons House 1439–1509* (1936), 352–3. It is possible that not all the references given here relate to the same man.

William Weston was appointed surveyor of Petty Custom and Tunnage and Poundage on 19 November 1480 with a fee of 100 marks per annum for himself and £10 for his clerk and served until April 1483.[226] In 1477–8 Weston had been sheriff of Surrey and Sussex with a fee of £40.[227] He obtained a pardon for all offences in office in March 1484.[228] Weston was probably a mercer.[229]

EDITORIAL METHOD

Form of the Calendar. The Calendar is intended to reproduce all significant material from the original manuscript. The order of the heading for each ship or cart has been re-arranged so as to place the date first instead of last (as in the manuscript), otherwise the word order of the original has been preserved. The words '*de*' before each merchant, '*pro*' before commodities and '*prec(ium)*' before each valuation have been omitted. Certain designations of merchants (e.g. alien) and certain weights and measures have been abbreviated, *see* List of Abbreviations. Each entry is given a serial number (in bold type) and the names of ships are in italics. Obscure words for which no translation can be offered are placed in inverted commas. Where a word is unusual or its meaning is open to more than one interpretation, the original spelling is given between inverted commas and in round brackets immediately after the translation offered. Significant variants taken from the parallel Surveyor's Account are placed, preceded by *S*, in square brackets after the calendar version and (except for names) in inverted commas if the original spelling of the Surveyor's Account is reproduced. Details of merchants' trades, domicile or nationality, which have been obtained from sources other than the Petty Custom Account, have not been inserted in the Calendar but are in the General Index. Footnotes have, in general, been used to offer explanations of obscure commodities and other words where these occur once only but in other cases such explanations have usually been incorporated in the Glossary. Other footnotes are given for merchants and ships only in cases where the additional information is relevant to this particular Customs Account. The use of square brackets indicates editorial additions.

Names of persons, places and ships. The original spelling of surnames has been retained but marks of suspension have been given only when a final syllable is clearly missing. Christian names have been translated from the Latin and English forms have been standardised but unusual foreign spellings, e.g. 'Albright' (for Albert) have been retained. Place names are given in their modern form but unusual original spellings are given, in round brackets, immediately after the modernised versions

---

[226] *C.P.R. 1476–85*, 225; E.356/22, ms.38–9.

[227] P.R.O. Warrants for Issues, E.404/76/3/21.

[228] C.67/51, m.20.

[229] Velvet for the king's robes and other precious cloths were bought for Henry VII's Coronation from 'William Weston, that was custumer' (*Materials for a history of the Reign of Henry VII, op. cit.*, II, 9–11). There are many references to William Weston, mercer, in the *Acts of Court*, 147, 200, 223 *passim*.

xlvi

and all manuscript forms are given in the General Index. The original spelling of ships' names has been preserved.

Weights and measures. These have been converted, where possible, into meaningful and recognizable units. The 1507 Book of Rates (printed in Gras) and the treatise 'the noumbre of weyghtes' throw light on the content of some of the weights and measures found in the manuscript. 'C.' and 'M.', the 'hundred' and 'thousand', may be measures of weight – either decimal or the hundred-weight of 112 lbs. – or of number, of varying quantity, e.g. a 'hundred' of stockfish contained 120. Valuations in the Account sometimes establish which type of weight or measure was being used, but since there is only a total valuation for each merchant's cargo it is frequently not possible to determine which 'hundred' or 'thousand' was intended in any particular case. Weights and measures have therefore been converted to decimal where the matter is not in doubt, but 'C.' and 'M.' have been retained in all other cases (with the most likely meaning given in the Glossary).

PETTY CUSTOMS ACCOUNT 1480–1

(P.R.O., E.122/194/25)

[m.1] 'Controlment of Thomas Fowler, controller of the petty custom of the Lord King in the port of London in the time of Henry Davers and Robert Fitzherbert collectors of the said petty custom, from the feast of St. Michael in the 20th year of King Edward IV, to the same feast then next following' [29 Sept. 1480 – 29 Sept. 1481].

[IMPORTS]

1. 2 Oct. From the ship of Lubert van Boke called *Mary* of the Steelyard[1] ('Styleyerd')

Peter Auctoris,[2] A, 1 chest with 32 vols. diverse histories, 12 pcs. coarse lawn [*S* linen], 3 pcs. cottons, 2 mantles miniver, £20

Edward Johnson, A, 1 hhd. 1 firkin with 4 doz. white skins, 30 doz. gloves, 2 grs. pen knives, 2 grs. folding knives, 10½ grs. knives, 1 doz. leather pouches, 3 grs. black bag rings, 3½ grs. bags, 6 grs. latten buckles, 1 grs. thread laces, 14 [*S* 4] lbs. bead strings, ½ doz. 'standyng' knives, 3 doz. bags for children ('pueris'), £12

Godfrey Willyam, A, 38 dog-stones, £12 13s.4d.

Henry Frankenberch,[2] A, 1 chest with 44 vols. diverse histories and other small books, 3 doz. red skins, £12

Laurence Gryll, A, 3 bales madder, £6

Stephen Wanne, A, 1 maund with 51 [*S* 41] ticks, 6 doz. and 3 napkins, 1 pc. Brabant linen cloth cont. 36 ells, 1 pc. Flemish linen cloth cont. 20 ells, £10 6s.8d.

Bartholomew Claysson, A, 1 brl. and 1 fardel with 21 pcs. Holland linen cloth cont. 493 ells, 2 doz. napkins, 3 doz. shears for tailors, 2 furs coarse miniver, £11 13s.4d.

Peter Wolf, A, 1 brl. with 12 marks of shears, 6 marks 6 doz. barbers' shears, 18 tailors' shears, 1 grs. 'button' locks,[3] 1 grs. small locks, 2 doz. hammers, 5 doz. compasses, 500 clasps, 4 doz. pouches, 58s. [*S* 58s.4d.]

Michael Harrys, A, 1 small fardel with 2 doz. skins cordwain, 5 doz. sheepskins, 26s.8d.

John Vandermaste, A, 1 hhd. with 30 doz. pins, 26½ doz. lbs. Oudenarde thread, 8 doz. pouches, 1½ doz. barbers' pouches, £8 6s.8d.

Hans Culle, H, 1 dry vat with 11,000 grey skins, £91 13s.4d.

Lambert Rotard, H, 4½ vats steel, £27

John Salmer, H, 3 bales 1 'bascheron' battery, £40

Henry Lathuson, H, 3 rolls Hainault ('Henegoys') linen cont. 1,900 ells, 12 C. loose ('lose')[4] stockfish, £51

1

Gerard van Grove, H, 1 pack Cologne thread, £13 6s.8d.

Hans Swalyngburgh, H, 4½ lasts loose stockfish, £40 10s.

Arnold van Stalle, 1 roll Osnabrück linen cloth, £12

William Grenewolt [*S* 'Grewold'], H, 1 roll 'Hertford'[5] linen cloth cont.
1½ rolls, 2 brls. ashes [*S* pot ashes], £18 6s.8d.

Hans Stut, H, 1 straw of wax weight 3 quintals

Tylman van de Mere, A, 3 hhds., 1 brl. [*S* 3 pipes] with teazles, 7 pcs.
Holland linen cloth cont. 126 ells, 2 pairs sheets, £11 13s.4d.

Peter Bylle, A, 1 hhd. with 8 doz. St. Omer hats ('Sertomerhattes')[6] [*S*
'Sentomers hattes'], £4

[1] The Hanseatic factory in London containing the Hansards' Guildhall and wharf.

[2] For Peter Auctoris (Actoris) and Henry Frankenberch, the most important alien
traders in books at this period, see N. J. M. Kerling, *Caxton and the Trade in Printed
Books* (reprinted from *The Book Collector*, Autumn, 1955), and E. Armstrong,
'English purchases of printed books from the Continent, 1465–1526', *E.H.R.*, xciv
(1979), 273–8.

[3] ? Door catches, cf. 'door button by which the door is fastened or closed' (S. W.
Beck, *The Draper's Dictionary* (1886), 37).

[4] ? Not packed in barrels.

[5] ? Herford, Westphalia: see **2** below.

[6] The manufacture of felt hats flourished at St. Omer during the fifteenth century
(*Mémoires de la Société des Antiquaires de la Morinie*, xvi (1879–81), 589–90).

2. 2 Oct. From the ship of John Goldesburgh called *John Remyngton*
[of London]

Albright Falland, H, 1 straw of wax weight 10 quintals

Henry Bevyr, H, 2 rolls Herford and Osnabrück linen cloth,[1] £24

Arnold van Stalle, H, 2 rolls Herford and Osnabrück linen cloth, £24

William Grenevolt, H, 2 rolls cont. 2½ rolls Osnabrück, £30

Hans Stut, H, 1 straw of wax weight 8 quintals

Peter Cray, A, 1 hhd. with 3 doz. pipes, 10 doz. stirrups, 18 bits, 6 doz.
spurs, 4 grs. buckles, 15 grs. thread laces, 19 lbs. Cologne thread, 5
pcs. Bord Alexander, 2 doz. latten girdles, 1 grs. combs, 12 lbs. hair,
2 doz. rolls of gold, £7 16s.8d.

[1] From the valuations in the 1507 Book of Rates each 'rowle' of Herford ('Har-
ffordes') and Osnabrück cloth should have contained 1,200 ells (Gras, 699, 701).

3. 2 Oct. From the ship of William Spryng called *Christofer* of
Colchester

William Scapehuson, H, 1 straw of wax weight 12 quintals

Arnold van Stalle, H, 2 rolls Herford and Osnabrück linen cloth, £24

4. 2 Oct. From the ship of John Bullehawte called *Mary* of Rouen

Laurence Fabyan, A, 10 millstones, 8 pouches with 80 doz. wool-cards,
180 ells canvas, 3½ brls. turpentine, 4 grs. papers[1] of points, £34

Peter Larate [*S* Larett], A, 3 puncheons with 36½ doz. brushes, 7 small
cases soap weight 14 C. lbs., 2 pcs. canvas linen cloth cont. 80 ells, 1
small fardel with 3½ doz. brushes, £11

John Boret [*S* Barett], A, 1 hhd. with 3 grs. playing-cards, 3½ grs.
combs, 1 doz. tailors' shears, 3 doz. barbers' shears, 4½ doz. brushes,

1½ doz. pouch rings, 4 doz. razors, 15 lbs. violet powder,[2] 2 doz. wooden ('treen') gold weights, 40s.

[1] Paper packets or bundles, cf. 'ten papers or bundles of silk' (K.R. Memoranda Roll, 11 Hen. VII, E.159/272, Recorda, Michaelmas, m.6).

[2] ? Sugar perfumed by mixing with essence of violet (W. Heyd, *Histoire du Commerce du Levant au moyen age* (Leipzig, 1923), ii, 692).

5. 2 Oct. From the ship of Ellis Arnold called *Kateryn* of London
William Scapehuson, H, 2 straws of wax weight 24 quintals
James Falke, A, 1 dry vat with 5 C. lbs. flax, 50s.
John Gyles, A, 50 reams brown paper, 15 red hides, 2 masts of gold skins, £6 13s.4d.
Anthony Kele, A, 1 pipe with 5,000 balls,[1] 50s.
Cornelius Smyth, A, 1,000 cruses, 33s.4d

[1] Probably tennis balls, which were rated 20s. the thousand in 1582 (Willan, *Rates*, 6).

6. 2 Oct. From the ship of David Williamson called *Mary* of Rotherhithe ('Redereth')
James Warre, A, 1 maund with 8 pcs. Ghentish linen cloth cont. 200 ells, 50s.

7. 2 Oct. From the ship of John Pache called *Anne* of Colchester
William Grenewolt, H, 2 lasts soap, £12
Arnold van Stalle, H, 1 roll Herford linen cloth, £12

8. 5 Oct. From the ship of Richard Simonis called *Rikmans* of Queenborough
William Scapehuson, H, 1 straw of wax weight 10 quintals
Tylman Barkys, H, 1 straw of wax weight 10 quintals
George Tak, H, 7 sacks flax, £10 10s.

9. 7 Oct. From the ship of Hugh Noldson called *Christofer* of Bergen-op-Zoom ('Barowe')
James Williamson, A, 3 M. garlic, 3 brls. herring, 500 pavingstones, 1 pipe with 5,000 balls, £13 16s.8d.
John Cornelys, A, 2 remnants Brabant linen cloth cont. 30 ells, 13s.4d.

10. 14 Oct. From the ship of Godfrey Wrede called *George* of Hamburg
Gerard Lesbern, H, 3 straws of wax weight 27 quintals
Herman Plough, H, 2 straws of wax weight 22 quintals
William Scapehuson, H, 6 wide ('magn' bond'') [S brls.] sturgeon, 23 narrow ('parv' bond'') brls. sturgeon, 1 dry vat with 6 C. lbs. linen yarn, £37
2 straws of wax weight 19 quintals
Tylman Barkys, H, 1 straw of wax weight 10 quintals
Hans Culle, H, 5 straws of wax weight 48 quintals
Hans Stutte, H, 4 straws of wax cont. 40 quintals
Albright Falland, H, 3½ lasts train oil of small girth,[1] 3 lasts pitch, 3 packs, 1 fardel pickling linen cloth cont. 30 C. ells, £61

3

5 straws of wax cont. 42 quintals

Hans Swalyngburgh, H, 3 packs soultwich linen cloth cont. 36 C. ells, £54

Henry Lathuson, H, 5 lasts 4 brls. osmund, 300 wainscots, 1 pack flax, 1½ lasts salt fish, 4 vats copperas, 1 pack stockfish, M. loose stockfish, 5 weys glass, 7 packs soultwich linen cloth cont. 7 M. 3 C. ells, 8 packs pickling linen cloth cont. 8 M. 7 C. ells, 1 pack narrow linen cloth cont. 1,400 ells Hainault ('Henoud'),[2] 1 roll Brunswick cont. 800 ells, 4½ rolls Hainault, £336 16s.8d.

2 straws, 1 pc. wax weight 22 quintals

Said master, H, 2 lasts 4 brls. osmund, 50 wainscots, ½ last pitch, 2 boards for shoemakers, 18 lbs. flax, 8 packs pickling linen cloth cont. 7 M. 7 C. ells, ½ rolls Hainault cont. 450 ells, 2 bolts cont. 40 ells narrow linen cloth, £93

Hans Hosterberche, H, 4 lasts stockfish, 4 lasts tar, 3 lasts pitch, 3 narrow brls. train oil, 2 lasts osmund, 3 narrow brls. sturgeon, ½ 'bascheron' battery, 1 pack pickling linen cloth cont. 12 C. ells, 1 pack soultwich cont. 14 C. ells, 8½ rolls Hainault cont. 3,950 ells, 2 packs pickling linen cloth cont. 24 C. ells, £200 10s.

½ straw of wax cont. 7 quintals

Henry Fryk, H, M. 7 [*S* 6] C. loose stockfish, £16

---

[1] i.e. in narrow barrels, usually twelve barrels to the last.

[2] *Smit, 1150–1485*, 1308, gives 'Henaud' as an alternative form of 'Henegowen' (Hainault).

11. 14 Oct. From the ship of Robert Wodeles called *Mary* of London

John Kele, A, 2 M. garlic, 2,000 paving-tiles, 1 bag cont. 1,000 balls, £8 10s.

Anthony Kele, A, 2 brls. nails, 1 basket cont. 8 C. lbs. packthread, 1 pack cont. 5 C. lbs. flax, £10 10s

12. 21 Oct. From the ship of John Camachio called *Sancta Maria* of Cadiz

John Spynell', A, 24 bales 10½ butts dates, 5 tuns 6 sorts large raisins, £78

Jeronimo Imary, A, 12 bales gum, 1 bale grain of Seville weight 280 lbs., £26

Gabriel Furnarius, A, 622 bags [*S* 450 bags 172 sacks] alum, 290 bales woad, 64 bales writing paper, 2 butts oil, £727 16s.8d.

John Baptista Gentyll', A, 100 bales woad, £66 13s.4d.

Paul Larka, A, 6 cases sugar, £12

Barnabas Centuryon [*S* Senturion] A, 103 bales woad, £68 13s.4d.

13. 26 Oct. From the ship of Caspar Boke called *Christofer* of Hamburg

Said master, H, ½ last tar, 50 wainscots, 30s.

William Scapehuson, H, 2 straws of wax cont. 28 quintals

Henry Lathuson, H, 3 lasts 2 brls. tar, 4 vats 8 brls. copperas, 5 lasts 8 C. loose stockfish, 3 firkins sturgeon, 1 roll Hainault linen cloth, 1 fardel 'Niperfeld'[1] linen cloth cont. 300 ells, 1 chest with 100 ells Hainault, £98 3s.4d.

Albright Falland, H, 10½ packs flax, £20
1 straw of wax cont. 10 quintals

Gerard Lesborn, H, 2 packs flax, £7

Lambert Rotard, H, 2 lasts osmund, 3 lasts loose stockfish, 1 last salt fish, 1 roll Hainault [*S* 'Hennovers'] linen cloth, £54
3 straws of wax weight 24 quintals

Herman Plough, H, 1 straw of wax weight 11 quintals

Hans Hosterberche, H, 26 C. loose stockfish, 5 lasts 11 brls. ashes, ½ roll Hainault [*S* 'Hennovers'] linen cloth cont. 600 ells, £38

[1] ? Nivelles, Brabant which had a linen industry, see Oskar de Smedt, *De Engelse natie te Antwerpen in de 16ᵉ eeuw* (Antwerp, 1950, 1954), 383.

14. 3 Nov. From the ship of Digo Founs called *Sanctus Spiritus* of Viana
Said master, A, 2,000 ropes of onions, 42 doz. cork, £6 13s.4d.

[m.1d.]

15. 6 Nov. From the ship of Alvery Yenes called *Tres Magos* of Oporto

Alexander Portinarius, Peter Vase, Peter Andrewe and Dygo Yenes, As, 308 cases sugar of which 30 cases are powdered sugar,[1] 96 brigandines, 9 C. 29 bowstaves, £531 13s.4d.

Gerald Yenes, A, 16 bowstaves, 5s.

Said master, A, 1 case sugar, 40s.

John Fons, A, 1 hhd. honey, 13s.4d.

[1] *S* Alexander Portinarius, 256 cases sugar (30 cases powdered),
Peter Vase, 12 cases sugar, Peter Andrew, 10 cases sugar,
Dygo Yenes, 30 cases sugar, 9 C. 39 bowstaves.

16. 7 Nov. From the ship of John Stephyns called *Sanctus Spiritus* of Oporto

Stephen Justynyan' and Frank Justynyan', As, 971 bales woad, £647 6s.8d.

Raphael Lomelyn' and Nicholas Lomelyn', As, 477 bales woad, 270 bags alum, 1 fardel Spanish grain weight 50 lbs., £590 10s.

Cosma Spynell', A, 296 bales woad, £197 6s.8d.

Paul Larca, A, 111 bales woad, £74

John Ambrose Nigron', A, 50 bales woad, £33 6s.8d.

Gabriel Furnarius, A, 190 bales woad, £126 13s.4d.

Said master, A, 3 hhds. 2 brls. oil, 1 case sugar, 20 'russe pell' pro bowers',[1] 1 pipe grain of Portugal weight 150 lbs., £15 15s.

John Bapista Gentyll', A, 46 bales woad, £30 13s.4d.

Baptista de Aurea, A, 88 bowstaves, 40s.

Martin Rodkyns [*S* Roderigus], A, 4,000 farts of Portugal ('fart' de Portingale'),[2] 6s.8d.

Peter Gonsalvus, A, 2 C. cork, 33s.4d.

[1] ? Red skins for bowyers. An archer was most likely to wear a skin on his left forearm as a guard or a larger piece as a kind of apron.
[2] A ball of light pastry, a 'puff' or sweetmeat (*O.E.D.*) 'Fertes with other subtilties'

were served with 'Ipocras' at Archbishop Warham's enthronization feast in 1504 (J. Leland, *Collectanea*, ed. T. Hearne (1770), 24).

17. 8 Nov. From the ship of John Marcus called *Grace Dewe* of Calais

Martin Johnson, A, 1 chest with 18 grs. knives, 14 doz. pen knives, 2 doz. shuttles, 9 grs. musk-balls, 5 doz. key-bands, 7 grs. spectacle cases, [*S* 1 grs. bells,] 36 lbs. bristles, 24 lbs. latten wire, 11 grs. glass beads, 12 grs. wooden beads, 4 doz. 'coppyn' hats, 6 pcs. and remnants Brabant linen cloth cont. 204 ells, £12

18. 11 Nov. From the ship of John Mathew[1] called *Christofer* of Dordrecht

Said master, A, 5 brls. mackerel, 13s.4d.

[1] Mathewson: see **605** below.

19. 13 Nov. From the ship of John Benyfeld called *Kateryn* of Benfleet

Henry Lathuson, H, M. loose cropling stockfish, £5

Matthew Blyterswyke, H, 4 sacks litmus, £4.

20. 13 Nov. From the ship of Luke Countman called *Le Belle* of Antwerp

Gerard Lesbern, H, 1 sack feathers, 30s.

John Sewyk, H, 1 hhd. with 5 C. lbs. aniseed ('agnes sede'), £4 3s.4d.

Matthew Blyterswyke, H, 4 sacks litmus, £4

Cornelius Smyth, A, 1,400 cruses, 46s.8d.

John Kele, A, 3 sacks flax, 400 bunches garlic, £5 16s.8d.

Armewes Somvile, A, 2 maunds 4 pipes 1 brl. with 1,600 fullers' handles[1] [*S* 'fullers tesell cum hand'], 20,000 teazles, 4 pcs Tournai fustian, 6½ grs. small purses, 1 grs. small coffers, 6 doz. pen-cases, 1½ doz. key-bands [*S* 'kai thongs'], ½ doz. manacles, 4 grs. buttons and 'pailes',[2] 500 thimbles, 4 pairs cappers' shears,[3] 10 pairs knives, 13 grs. laces, 100 clarions, 9 ells Flemish linen cloth, £7

John Wylbek, A, 1 brl. with 4½ doz. wool-cards, 50 doz. knives, 2 doz. daggers, 3 doz. 10 pairs hatters' cards,[4] 2,000 wooden beads, 200 'cole' glasses [*S* 'close glassis'], 3 pairs wool-combs, 4 doz. wire, £4 15s.

Peter Wolf, A, 1 basket with 11 C. 26 lbs. fustic, £4

Martin Johnson, A, 1 basket with 9½ doz. small forcers [*S* 'cofers'], 400 bunches garlic, 56s.8d.

Said master, A, 55 wainscots, 4 fulls of kettles, 33s.4d.

Arnold Howell, A, 1 small basket with 2 C. lbs. frying pans, 5 pairs shuttles, 5 narrow shuttles, 26s.8d.

[1] 'A number of teasels were put into a small frame, having crossed handles, eight or ten inches long. Being fitted with the thistle-heads, it formed a tool not unlike a horse curry-comb'. This tool was used to raise the nap on the surface of cloth. (A. Ure, *The Philosophy of Manufactures* (3rd ed., 1861), 192–3).

[2] ? spangles (cf. 'pailles', Cotgrave's *Dictionary*).

[3] Cap-makers' shears.

[4] Toothed instruments used to raise a nap. Men's hats were made of a foundation of

wool felted together, upon which was laid beaver down or other fine fur to produce a nap (Ure, *op. cit.*, 190).

21. 13 Nov. From the ship of Michael de Mere called *Christofer* of Antwerp

Henry Berebrewer, A, 2 sacks hops, 1 hhd. with 2 feather-beds, 1 pc. Brabant linen cloth cont. 24 ells, 3 kettles, 1 tick, 2 dripping [*S* 'rosting'] pans, £5 18s.

John Johnson, A, 5 maunds 1 basket with 2,000 drinking glasses, 800 cruses, £5

Gerard Sconborowe, A, 1 sack hops, 30s.

22. 13 Nov. From the ship of Thomas Coys called *Petyr Stokker* of London

Roger van Feld, H, 1 pack Herford linen cloth cont. 3 rolls, £45

Henry Lathuson, H, 3 M. [*S* 'lose'] titling stockfish, £7 10s.

23. 13 Nov. From the ship of Copyn Welle called *Trinite* of Antwerp

Henry James, A, 1 basket with 15 reams white paper, 6 pcs. dornick linen cloth cont. 62 ells, 3 pcs. tuke cont. 36 ells, 3 doz. Oudenarde thread, 1 doz. blue thread, 5 pcs. Brabant linen cloth cont. 168 ells, 51 reams brown paper, £10 3s.4d.

John Kele, A, 5 sacks hops, 1 pipe cont. 3,000 balls, ½ C. lbs. flax, 1 sack packthread cont. 4 C. lbs, £11 5s.

Cornelius Claysson, A, 2 baskets with 50 doz. felt hats, 30 doz. 'copyn' hats, £3 16s.8d.

John Welbek, A, 1 pipe with 5 doz. brushes, 12 doz. brooches, 2 doz. pouches, 6 doz. mirrors, 6 doz. card-boards, 2 great glasses, 3 bundles brooms, 36s.8d.

Cornelius Johnson, A, 2 vats with 2,000 balls, ½ C. [*S* '½ pack'] brushes, £6 10s.

James Falke, A, 2 hhds. with 24 grs. jet ('kole') beads, 48s.4d.

Michael Harrys, A, 300 cruses, 1 small basket with 7 doz. drinking glasses, 12s.

Cornelius Smyth, A, 1,200 cruses, 1 basket with 4 'faas' drinking glasses, 2 doz. pint bottles, 1,500 whorls, 8 doz. distaffs, £3

John Vandermaste, A, 1 basket 1 brl. with 87 doz. 'copyn' hats, 7 grs. pin-cases, 20 doz. playing-cards, 1½ doz. pouches, ½ doz. leather laces, £5 10s.

Peter Segir, A, 1 corf with 27 doz. 'copyn' hats, 20 pairs shuttles, 43s.4d.

Peter Auctorys, A, 1 chest with 29 vols. diverse histories, £9 5s.

Henry Frankenberch, A, 1 hhd. with 41 vols. diverse histories, £14

James Frise, A, 2 sacks flax, 1 sack hemp, 1 pipe with 6,000 balls, 1 basket with 4½ doz. 'yperlinges',[1] 4 red hides, 1 harness barrel[2] with 4½ grs. wooden beads, 16 lbs. flax, £10

Laurence Tyman, A, 1 pipe 1 small brl. with 6 grs. pouches, 18 grs. wire girdles, 4 grs. tucking hooks, 6½ grs. pouch rings, 3 grs. wire girdles, 4 grs. thread laces, 3½ doz. daggers, 18 grs. knives, 1 grs. leather girdles, 5 doz. locks, 24 doz. 'copin' hats, £21

Martin Johnson, A, 1 case combs, 1 dry vat 1 basket with 29 grs. Nuremberg ('Norburgh') mirrors, 6 grs. glass beads, 11 doz. 'copyn' hats, 150 lbs. latten basins, 3 fulls of kettles, 3 grs. glass beads, 15 sums of nails, 5 doz. pouches, £7

Anthony Kele, A, 1,000 cruses, 1 sack with 1,200 balls, 45s.4d.

Frank Mathewe, A, 1 small chest 1 hhd. with 400 spice-cakes, 500 'scone Jesus', 1½ doz. 'Jesus de box' [*S* '500 scone Jesus in box'],[3] 1 doz. looking ('locked') glasses, 3½ doz. small pouches, 2 doz. whistles, 1½ reams painted paper, 36s.8d.

John van Osse, A, 1 basket with 21 doz. 'copyn' hats, 10s.

Matthew Falk, A, 4,000 pavingstones, 300 white stones, 58s.4d.

Matthew Bliterswyke, H, 4 sacks litmus, £4

Roger van Feld, H, 2 vats Cologne woad, £13 6s.8d.

George Tak, H, 3 bales madder, £6

[1] ? Cloth of Ypres or coverlets: cf. Willan, *Rates*, 34.

[2] A barrel in which to pack armour (*Manners and Household Expenses in England*, ed. T. H. Turner (1841), 217, 401).

[3] ? Scones stamped with the figure of Christ, as bakers often stamped their finest (pandemain) loaves (C. A. Wilson, *Food and Drink in Britain* (1973), 241). *S* omits '1½ doz. Jesus de box'.

24. 13 Nov. From the ship of William Cornyssh called *Nicholas* of London

Charles Harryesson, A, 1 brl. with 18 habergeons, 18 gorgets, £5 8s.

John Vandermaste, A, 1 bale with 36 reams wrapping ('spendable') paper, £3

Martin Johnson, A, 1 dry vat with 5½ grs. locks, 4 grs. razors, 7 grs. small bells, 5½ doz. writing tables, 10 doz. puppets[1] ('popett'), 4 grs. wire girdles, 4½ grs. latten rings, ½ grs. latten bells, 6,000 awl blades, 2 grs. compasses, 3 doz. needles, 1 grs. spurs, 2 grs. wooden beads, £10 6s.8d.

Luke Nekar, A, 1 pipe with 27 doz. St. Omer hats, 2 doz. swords, £15 13s.4d.

Stephen Branche, H, 1 basket with 9 pcs. broad busk, 15 pcs. narrow [*S* busk], 10 pcs. Holland linen cloth cont. 260 ells, £23 10s.

Gerard Lesbern, H, 1 straw of wax weight 9 quintals

Arnold van Stalle, H, 1 chest with 24 pcs. Holland linen cloth cont. 587 ells, 4 pairs balances, £23

Anthony Odindale, H, 3 bales madder, £6

Tylman Barkys, H, 1 pack linen cloth with 24 pcs. Osnabrück cont. 20 C. ells, 36 pcs. minsters cont. 18 C. ells, 34 pcs. Brabant and Holland cont. 900 ells, £84 10s. (£65 *del.*)

William Grenewolt, H, 1 maund with 30 pcs. Holland linen cloth cont. 1,000 ells, £36

[1] Children's dolls, cf. 'puppets or babies for children' (Willan, *Rates*, 48).

25. 13 Nov. From the ship of Stephen Cripse called *Julyan* of Gravesend

John Welbek, A, 1 chest with 5 pcs. Flemish linen cloth cont. 162 ells, 2 doz. 10 painted cloths, 20 doz. mirrors, 3 doz. pouches, 3 pairs balances, 8,000 pins, 1 [*S* 2] doz. small coffers, 2 doz. daggers, 10,000 glass beads, 3 grs. points, 12½ doz. playing-cards, 1 doz. mittens with gloves, 2 doz. pouches, 8 lbs. blue thread, 2 doz. candlesticks, £7

Peter Wolf, A, 2 sacks hemp, 3 brls. slip, ½ C. 13 lbs. filings [*S* 'of iron'], £3 8s.6d.

James Laurans, A, 1 small basket with 2 doz. balls, 6 doz. bodkins, 6 doz. pen-cases and ink-horns, 12 doz. knives, 6 lbs. bristles, 5 small cross-bows, 26s.8d.

26. 13 Nov. From the ship of Richard Dockyng called *Martyn* of London

Tylman van de Mere, A, 1 basket with 20 pcs. broad busk cont. 600 ells, 12½ pcs. Brabant linen cloth cont. 560 ells, 5 pcs. Holland cont. 70 ells, 4 pcs. Holland cont. 65 ells, £24 13s.4d.

William Codde, A, 1 hhd. with 7 grs. 6 doz. 7 bags, 6½ grs. bag rings, 12 doz. terrets, 6 grs. tucking hooks, 4 grs. leather girdles, 3 grs. latten girdles, 18½ grs. latten buckles, 12 doz. copper gold, 10 doz. writing tables, 17 [*S* 12] doz. mirrors, 7 doz. pouches, 6 grs. hatbands, 2 grs. trumpets, 6 lbs. 'casch' [*S* 'craissh']¹ brushes, 6 quires painted paper, 4 doz. gloves, 6½ doz. hatbands, £14

Cornelius Johnson, A, 1 chest with 12 grs. leather laces, 4 grs. thread laces, 24 doz. mails, 6 grs. leather girdles, 3 doz. brushes, £8 18s.

James Falke, A, 1 hhd. with 4 C. lbs. flax, 40s.

James Bolle, A, 1 chest with 15 grs. playing-cards, 6 grs. wire girdles, 1 basket with arrow-root ('cowe and calfe'),² 2 sacks flax, £8 15s.

Edward Johnson and Anthony Gylbert, As, 1 dry vat with 4 grs. pins, 1 doz. lbs. bristles, 1 doz. 'stringyng yern', 1 grs. mistletoe ('mistell') beads,³ 3 grs. small pouches, 4 grs. bags, 4 doz. 'hert',⁴ 1 tick, 2 pairs sheets, 1½ doz. running glasses,⁵ £8 3s.4d. (£3 16s.8d. *del.*)

Peter Segir, A, 1 hhd. with 7 doz. St. Omer hats, 1 sack hemp, £3 16s.8d.

Peter Wolf, A, 1 basket with 40 fulls of kettles, 8 doz. felt hats, 14 grs. 10 doz. latten buckles, £6 16s.8d.

Martin Johnson, A, 2 bales paper, 2 cases combs, 2 brls. white plate, 1 basket with 20 lbs. bristles, 2 grs. spectacles, ½ grs. locks, 2 lbs. string thread, £6 15s.

John Johnson, A, 1 brl. with [*S* 100] lbs. bristles, 1 fardel with 20 ells diaper, 15 ells diaper towelling, 40 ells Holland linen cloth, 1 hart ('hert') skin, 53s.4d.

Arnold Howell, A, 1 sack hemp, 30s.

Luke Neckar, A, 1 hhd. with 3 doz. caskets, 1 great forcer, 26s.8d.

John Sevik, H, 1½ packs soultwich linen cont. 18 C. ells, £27

Matthew Blyterswyke, H, 2 small brls. with 100 lbs. bristles, 33 doz. mistletoe beads, 1,400 thimbles, 550 graters, 27 doz. latten rings, £4

Peter Capper, A, 1 maund with 15 yds. diaper, 5 doz. diaper napkins, 3 pcs. Flemish cont. 140 ells, 2 pcs. Brabant cont. 70 ells, 2 pcs. Flemish cont. 72 ells, 2 remnants Brabant and Flemish cont. 22 ells [*S* 13 ells Brabant, 9 ells Flemish], 1 quilt, £6 16s.8d

9

¹ ? A manger or stable (*Middle English Dictionary* under 'cracche').

² A nutritious starch prepared by crushing the corms of the arum maculatum (T. B. Groves, 'On Portland Arrow-Root', *Pharmaceutical Journal and Transactions*, xiii (1853), 60–1).

³ The hardened white berries of mistletoe used as beads (*Middle English Dictionary* under 'mistel').

⁴ ? Ornaments or pieces of jewellery in the shape of a heart (*Middle English Dictionary* under 'herte' 1c).

⁵ Hour-glasses used in navigation for keeping the watches and timing the courses sailed (*Rye Shipping Records 1566–1590*, ed. R. F. Dell (Sussex Record Society, 1966), 148).

[m.2]

27. 13 Nov. From the ship of Robert Walcok called *Leonard* of London

James Bolle, A, 1 hhd. with 28 grs. boxwood ('box') beads, 1½ grs. imitation chalcedony ('counterfet calcedons'), 3 grs. wire girdles, 9 grs. glass beads, 13 grs. small glass beads, £3 1s.8d.

William Codde, A, 1 small basket with 2 grs. mistletoe beads, 16 grs. 7 doz. knives, 6 cases pot knives, 2 chess boards, 1 doz. spouts, 1 doz. 'chasyng' balls, 24 lbs. counters, £4 10s.

Edward Johnson and Anthony Gylbert, As, ½ brl. filings, 1 chest with 400 white sheepskins, 17 grs. papers of points, 8 grs. leather laces, 8 doz. red skins, 23 grs. girdles, 10 doz. latten girdles, 10 grs. playing-cards, £8 19s.

Peter Segyr, A, 1 basket with 60 doz. 'copyn' hats, £3 10s.

Peter Wolf, A, 2 brls. with 24 sums patten nails and 80 sums patten nails, £6 2s.

James Falke, A, 1 basket 1 brl. with 52 doz. hammers, 6 doz. fire-irons, 4 grs. jet beads, 4 doz. salt-cellars, 2 doz. cruets, 12 doz. cards, £3 10s.

Arnold Howell, A, 1 sack hemp, 30s.

Gerard van Grove, H, 1 pack Cologne thread, £13 6s.8d.

Arnold van Stalle, H, 1 small pack linen cloth with 45 pcs. Holland linen cloth cont. 1,000 ells, £40

28. 13 Nov. From the ship of John Roke called *Julyan* of London

James Bolle, A, 1 hhd. with 8 grs. latten buckles, ½ grs. imitation chalcedony, 4 grs. compasses, 1 grs. marking irons, 6 doz. annulets, 600 irons for weavers, 8 doz. locks, 5 grs. wire girdles, ½ grs. copper rolls, 6 grs. knives, 1,500 thimbles, 1 grs. spurs, 4 grs. Nuremberg ('Norbour') [*S* 'Norborgh'] locks, 2 doz. stirrups, ½ grs. locks, 2 grs. laces, £9 5s.

Peter Conteryn and Augustine Gracia, As, 1 bale with 38 pcs. [*S* cloth] imitation Arras ('counterfet Araas'),¹ 1 pc. Holland linen cloth cont. 56 ells, 1 cat fur, 2 diaper towels, 1 coarse diaper table-cloth, £30

John van Armesbery, H, 1 fardel with 3 bales fustian, £40

Gerard van Grove, H, 1 fardel with 3 bales fustian, £40

Hans Culle, H, 1 fardel with 2 bales fustian, £26 13s.4d.

Matthew Hynkylman, H, 1 pack linen cloth with 46 pcs. hastrey ('haustr'),² cont. 16 C. ells linen, 5 pcs. busk and Osnabrück, £43 15s.

Arnold van Stalle, H, 1 pack with 4 pcs. broad busk, 3 pcs. narrow busk, 79 pcs. Holland cont. 1,718 ells, £72 15s.4d.

John Russynthorp, H, 12 brls. white and black plate, 1 brl. latten plate, 1 chest with 14 doz. Paris thread, £46

William Scapehuson, H, 1 straw of wax weight 11 quintals

Albert Falland, H, 1 straw of wax weight 10 quintals

Hans Stut, H, 1 straw of wax weight 10 quintals

Peter Syber, H, 1 fardel with 2 bales fustian, £26 13s.4d.

Matthew Bliterswyke, H, 2 packs Cologne thread, £26 13s.4d.

John Questynburgh, H, 1 fardel with 28 pcs. minsters cont. 8 C. 12 ells, 34 pcs. Holland cont. 940 ells, 6 pcs. coarse Holland cont. 211 [*S* 1,211] ells, £54 10s.

Lambert Rotard, H, 6 brls. steel, £36

[1] Arras in Artois was noted for its rich tapestry fabric (*O.E.D.*).

[2] Cf. 'Hastrey clothe called browne hastrey the C elles xxxs.' (Gras, 699). In 1479 'Haustar' or 'halftar' cloth was imported from Brabant to make sheets (Alison Hanham, *The Celys and their world* (Cambridge, 1985), 212).

29. 13 Nov. From the ship of Dennis Vesyall called *Laurens* of Guérande ('Gerrand')

John Labi and Dennis Vesyall, As, 60 weys Bay salt, £40

Philibord [*S* Philpott] Archer, A, 2 hhds. with 600 lampreys, 1 pc. canvas linen cloth cont. 30 ells, £6 13s.4d.

30. 13 Nov. From the ship of John Capp called *Volantyne* of London

Edward Johnson, A, 1 hhd. with 15 grs. knives, 1 grs. daggers, 18 pot knives, 2½ grs. gloves, 2 boots of calaber fur, 10 [*S* 2] doz. latten rings, 1 grs. bags, £9 10s.

Henry Jamys, A, 1 chest with 24 pcs. Brabant cont. 771½ ells, 1 doz. lbs. blue thread, ½ ream paper, 9 pouches, 4 pairs knives, £12 16s.8d.

James Bolle, A, 1 hhd. with 24 doz. pins, 5 grs. knives, 1 grs. small rolls copper, 6,000 awl blades, 3 grs. thread laces, 2 doz. stirrups, ½ grs. locks, 5 grs. boxwood beads, ½ grs. chalcedony, ½ grs. spurs, £7 3s.4d.

John Vandermaste, A, 1 hhd. with 23 doz. spurs, 1½ doz. bits, 4 grs. knives, 20 doz. pins, 1 pc. tapestry cont. 9 yds., 8 grs. pen-cases and ink-horns, 8½ doz. piercers, ½ doz. leather cushions, 9 doz. pouches, £9 18s.

Henry Frankenberch, A, 1 hhd. with 126 vols. diverse histories, 3 pcs. Holland linen cloth cont. 80 ells, £14

Peter Auctoris, A, 1 chest with 67 vols. diverse histories, £10 3s.4d.

James Falke, A, 2 hhds. with 8 grs. small coffers, 5 grs. razors, 4 doz. balances, 3 doz. bags, £6 15s.

Anthony Kele, A, 2 sacks flax, 1 sack hemp, £4 10s.

Paul van Malder, A, 1 small basket with 2 reams 8 books painted [? paper],[1] 4 painted cloths, 3 doz. pins, 2 doz. small images, 2 doz. parchment images, 1 grs. 'parket'[2] images, 53s.4d.

Luke Neckar, A, 1 basket with 22 [*S* 12] doz. St. Omer hats, 1 doz. caskets, 9 doz. 'coppyn' hats, 1 small fardel with 9 doz. gloves, 1 doz. hatters' cards, 1 small brl. with C. lbs. filings, £6

John Demayn, A, 2 brls. calamine ('calmyn'), 26s.8d.

John Claisson, A, 27 dog-stones, 1 corf with 250 budge skins, 1 box with

2 doz. spectacles, £13 10s.

Roger van Feld, H, 1 pack with 18 C. ells Herford [*S* linen cloth], £36 (£18 *del.*)

Hans Culle, H, 1 fardel with 2 bales fustian, £26 13s.4d.

John van Armysbery, H, 1 fardel with 2 packs Cologne thread, £26 13s.4d.

Ingilbright Sevenek, H, 1 fardel with 2 packs Cologne thread, £26 13s.4d.

John van Stralen, H, 1 fardel with 2 packs Cologne thread, £26 13s.4d.

---

[1] The 1558 Book of Rates has 'paynted books' but this may be an error for 'printed' (Willan, *Rates*, 68 n.).

[2] ? Plaster, cf. 'parget' meaning plaster or roughcast (*O.E.D.*).

31. 13 Nov. From the ship of Anthony Welle called *Christofer* of Bergen-op-Zoom

John van Scalstreate, A, 1 chest with 1 doz. large painted cloths, 20 small painted cloths, £3 10s.

Peter Johnson, A, 1,500 cruses, 50s.

Michael Harrys, A, 6 dog-stones, 30s.

32. 13 Nov. From the ship of Clays Bylle called *Maria* of Danzig

Herman Overcamp, H, 10 lasts 3 brls. tar, 6 brls. pitch, 16 bundles iron,[1] 15 pcs. copper plate cont. ½ mease, 19 wide brls. sturgeon, 7 lasts ashes, 4½ packs flax, 9 C. bowstaves, 2 C. clapholt, 1 qr. wainscots, 1 nest of counters, 4 C. lbs. flax, 1 nest of coffers, 4 bundles whiting ('merlyng'), ½ C. sail thread, £94 15s.

4 [*S* small] pcs. wax weight 1½ quintals

Hans Culle, H, 4 sacks flax, 1 last 2 brls. pitch, 1 last 2 brls. osmund, £11 16s.8d.

1 straw of wax weight 7 quintals

Herman Plough, H, 2 packs flax, 1 last train oil in wide brls., 6 lasts osmund, £44

James van Werd, H, 1 pack flax, 1 last train oil in wide brls., 1 last 2 brls. osmund, £20 13s.4d.

1 straw of wax weight 12 quintals

Matthew Peltez, H, 1 last osmund, £4

2 straws of wax weight 20 quintals

Gerard Lesbern, H, 2 lasts 2 brls. osmund, 4 packs flax, 1 last 10 brls. sturgeon in wide brls., £46 13s.4d.

3 small pcs. wax weight 4½ quintals

Matthew Hynkelman, H, 1 straw of wax weight 9 quintals

William Scaphuson, H, 1 pack with 14 C. ells spruce canvas, £23 6s.8d.

Albert Falland, H, 4 packs flax, 14 brls. osmund, 23 narrow brls. train oil, 2 meases 15 [*S* pcs.] copper cont. 1½ [*S* 3½] meases, £78

2 straws of wax weight 22 quintals

Tylman Barkys, H, 3 packs flax, 2 lasts 4 brls. osmund, £21 6s.8d.

Hans Stutte, H, 4 lasts train oil in wide brls., 7 narrow brls. train oil, 3½ lasts osmund, 5 packs flax, 9 brls. sturgeon, 3 C. bowstaves, 3 packs [*S* cloth] canvas cont. 3,000 ells, 1 brl. with 43 doz. wooden mazers ('maser trees'), £160 5s.4d.

¹ Cf. 'iron called fagot iron the bundle cont. 5 C.' (Willan, *Rates*, 35).

33. 13 Nov. From the ship of John Yoman called *Trinite Bull* [of London]

James Falke, A, 2 brls. 1 maund with 80 lbs. bristles, 2 grs. spectacle cases, 2 doz. needles, 12 marks of shears, 31 dickers razors, 2 C. lbs pans, 6 grs. jet beads, £8 10s.

James Bolle, A, 1 chest 1 hhd. with 8 doz. pins, 2½ grs. spurs, 12 grs. boxwood beads, 2 grs. glass beads, 1 doz. latten holy-water stoups, 1 grs. glass beads, 15 grs. leather laces, 10 grs. thread laces, 25 doz. pins, 3 doz. small pouches, 3 grs. boxwood beads, 4 leather pouches, £14

Edward Johnson, A, 1 hhd. with 20 grs. knives, 12 caskets, 3½ grs. pouches, £8 6s.8d.

Lewis Bonvis, A, 1 fardel with 2 pcs. baudekin, 3 pcs. tawny satin, 2 pcs. red and black satin cont. 184 braces, 1 pc. taffeta cont. 38 braces, £27

Frank Mathew, A, 1 hhd. with 8 reams 17 quires painted paper, 1½ doz. stained cloths, 485 coverings for pots, 4 pouches, 4 ivory glasses, 2 doz. small coffers, 6 ivory paxbreds, 6 doz. knives, 1 doz. whistles, 5 cases of imagery, 2 doz. pieces,¹ 6 doz. tin cruets, ½ doz. daggers, 2 doz. leather girdles, 3 grs. harp strings, 14 doz. 'Jesus',² 1 doz. small candlesticks, 100 iron 'stickyng' candlesticks, 16 coffers, 1 box with toys ('japes'), £7 3s.4d.

John van Armysbery, H, 1 fardel with 3 bales fustian, £40

Hans Culle, H, 1 fardel with 2 bales fustian, £26 13s.4d.

Gerard van Grove [*S* John Greverard], H, 1 pack hastrey linen cloth cont. 41 pcs. cont. 13 C. ells, £32 10s.

Stephen Branche, H, 3 bales madder, £6

John Russinthorp, H, 1 fardel wth 3 bales fustian, 1 small coffer with 10 pcs. lawn, £50

John Salmer, H, 1 basket battery, £10

Arnold van Stalle, H, 1 pack linen cloth with 33 pcs. Osnabrück cont. 5 [*S* 2] rolls, 3 pcs. narrow busk, 18 pcs. Holland cont. 444 ells, £42 6s.8d.

Roger van Feld, H, 1 pack Cologne thread, £13 6s.8d.

Gerard van Grove, H, 1 fardel with 3 bales fustian, £40

John van Strawlyn, H, 1 fardel with 2 bales fustian, £26 13s.4d.

Everard Southerman, H, 1 maund with 21 pcs. hastrey cont. 15 C. 5 ells, 3 pcs. minsters cont. C. ells, 2 pcs. Brabant cont. 96 [*S* 50] ells, 32 pcs. Holland cont. 773 ells, £71 13s.4d.

John van Derbesen, H, 1 basket with 26 pcs. Holland linen cloth cont. 618 ells, 22 pcs. hastrey cont. 11 C. 6 ells, 10 pcs. narrow busk, 4½ C. tavelon shanks, £63 3s.4d.

Peter Syber, H, 1 fardel with 3 bales fustian, £40

Herman Slotkyn, H, 1½ packs Cologne thread, £20

[m.2d.]

Matthew Blyterswyke, H, 1 fardel with 2 bales fustian, 1 pack Cologne thread, £40

Anthony Odyndale, H, 1 brl. with 27 clouts Cologne silk, 27 bundles 'calle'[3] silk, 15 pcs. camlet, £180 13s.4d.

Lambert Rotard, 7 brls. steel, £42

[1] ? Chess-men.
[2] Figures or representations of Christ.
[3] Silk for making cauls (Willan, *Rates*, 54n.).

34. 13 Nov. From the ship of Henry Fryse called *Margret Stokker*

John Dancell, A, 1 hhd. 1 chest with 27 doz. glasses, 7 doz. pouches, 22 pouches with rings, 23 doz. single caps, 9 [*S* doz.] double caps, 15 doz. small purses, 2 fardels cont. 65 doz. brushes, 1 tun 1 pipe with teazles, £15 10s.

Henry Frankenberch, A, 12 vols. diverse histories, 20s.

James Larans [*S* Laurens], A, 1 small basket with 300 pomegranates, 10s.

Charles Harryesson, A, 2½ bundles brushes, 20s.

Adrian Naes, A, 2½ brls. wine lees, 1 brl. filings, 6s.8d.

Michael Wynde, A, 1 chest 2 small baskets with 5 remnants Brabant cont. 60 ells, 4 painted cloths, 20 lbs. flax, 32s.

Peter Cray, A, 1 brl. with 1 [*S* 2] grs. knives, 8½ grs. thread laces, 6 grs. silver paper, 6 caps, 12 grs. latten buckles, £6

Isabella Bronell, A, 1 basket 1 sack with 3 pcs. Flemish linen cloth cont. 41 ells, 6 doz. points, 8 doz. thread laces, 2,000 pins, 1 lb. twine, 3 doz. hats, 32 lbs. flax, 36s.8d.

Adrian Naes of Veere,[1] A, 1 dry brl. 1 chest 2 fardels 1 maund with 3 feather-beds, 8 old pillows, 4 old cloths, 1 spit, 10 doz. knives, 25 iron pins [*S* 1 doz. pins,] 7½ doz. pouches, 1 doz. 4 pairs cards, 23 doz. shirts, 9 pcs. buckram, 11 pcs. Holland cont. 183 ells, 25 pcs. Brabant cont. 92 ells, 1½ C. stockfish, 4 kettles, 1 [*S* old] brass pot, 3 coverlets, £17 3s.4d.

Gerard Lesbern, H, 4½ packs flax, £12

8 pcs. wax weight 10 quintals

Matthew Hynckylman, H, 1 pack with 36 pcs. soultwich cont. 17 C. 59 ells, £26 5s.

John van Derbeson, H, 4 brls. steel, £24

Herman Plough, H, 1 brl. cont. 3,000 grey skins, £25

Frank Savage, H, 1 frail 1 'bascheron' 1 basket battery, £30

George Tak, H, 1 brl. with 5 pcs. Holland cont. 113 ells, 5 pcs. tuke, 2 pcs. cottons, £7 13s.4d.

John van Armysberyn, H, 2 fardels with 5½ packs Cologne thread, £53 6s.8d.

Henry Lathuson, H, 4 lasts 6½ C. loose stockfish, 3 rolls hannovers, £82 10s.

William Grenewolt, H, 1 brl. pot ashes, 1 pack with 20 C. ells soultwich, £30 3s.4d.

[1] The merchants of Veere had been granted the same customs privileges as the Hansards on account of the aid which they and their lord, Henry of Borselle, had given to

Edward IV in recovering the kingdom in 1471 (*C.C.R. 1468–76*, 233–4).

35. 13 Nov. From the ship of Simon Pecheford called *Mary Floure*

John Fox, A, 1 small basket with 200 [*S* drinking] glasses, 2 brls. slip, 10s.

Peter Wolf, A, 1 chest with 2 grs. 8 doz. knives, 8½ doz. white and black rings, 1 doz. [*S* tin] candlesticks, 8 doz. mirrors, 2 lbs. 6 ozs. white coral, 7 doz. gold pipes, 1 grs. spurs, 14 ozs. amber, 1 pc. coarse Holland cont. 20 [*S* 25] ells, 100 budge skins, 3 great grs. laces, 2 grs. spectacles, 6 stocks of mirrors, 13 bundles [*S* doz.] mistletoe, 12 lbs. stable ('cressh') brushes, 2 grs. latten girdles, 2,400 [*S* 3,400] chalcedony, 3 grs. cards, 20 lbs. ginger, 1 grs. latten tucking hooks, 6 doz. pouches, 4 doz. small pouches, 3 grs. musk-balls, 4 grs. sugar loaves, 1 pouch, 1 small knife, £22 10s.

Peter Auctoris, A, 1 chest with 60 vols. diverse histories, £10

Derek Ketylhode, A, 2 stone pots with 7 glasses, 7½ lbs. broken latten, 3 lbs. stable brushes, 5 pincers, 5 copper pans weight 5½ lbs., 8s.4d.

Anthony Odindale, H, 1 pack Cologne thread, 2 bales madder, £17 6s.8d.

Matthew Hynkelman, H, 1 pack with 46 pcs. hastrey cont. 14 C. 54 ells, 3 pcs. minsters cont. C. ells, 4 pcs. Osnabrück [*S* cont. C. ells], £40 10s.

Hans Stut, H, 1 straw of wax weight 12 quintals

Gerard Lesbern, H, 2 straws of wax weight 16 quintals

John Greverod, H, 1 fardel with 2 bales fustian, 1 sack onion seed weight 2 C. lbs., £28 13s.4d.

Arnold van Stalle, H, 1 pack with 4 pcs. hastrey cont. C. 65 ells, 8 pcs. broad and narrow busk, 69 pcs. Holland cont. 1,612 ells, £72 16s. 8d.

Peter Syber, H, 1 fardel with 3 bales fustian, £40

Herman Slotkyn, H, 1 fardel with 2 packs Cologne thread, £26 13s.4d.

Matthew Blyterswyk, H, 1 fardel with 2 bales fustian, £26 13s.4d.

Gerard van Grove, H, 1 bale fustian, £13 6s.8d.

Herman Plough, H, 1 straw of wax weight 10 quintals

John van Armysbery, H, 1 fardel with 2 bales fustian, 2 packs Cologne thread, £53 6s.8d.

John Salmer, H, 1 frail of battery, £10

George Tak, H, 1 pack with 36 pcs. Holland cont. 902 ells, 16 [*S* pcs.] narrow busk, £46

Ingilbright Sevenek, H, 2 packs Cologne thread, £26 13s.4d.

William Scapehuson, H, 1 pack with 10 C. lbs. candle-wick, £5
2 straws of wax weight 20 quintals

John Questinburgh, H, 1 fardel with 82 pcs. Brabant cont. 1,938 ells, 10 pcs. Holland cont. 266 ells, £43 13s. 4d.

Hans Culle, H, 1 pack with 4 bales fustian, £53 6s.8d.
1 straw of wax weight 14 quintals

Everard Sowtherman, H, 1 pack with 28 pcs. broad busk, 36 pcs. narrow [*S* busk], 4 pcs. broad white busk, 1 pc. Brabant cont. 30 ells, £41 13s.4d.

Albert Falland, H, 1 straw of wax weight 11 quintals

Lambert Rotard, H, 6 brls. steel, £36

John Russynthorp, H, 2 fardels with 110 pcs. Brussels cont. 2,200 ells, £44

Tylman Barkys, H, 1 maund with 23 pcs. Osnabrück, 22 pcs. minsters cont. 3 rolls, £42

36. 13 Nov. From the ship of John Bawdewyn called *Barge* of Calais

William Scapehuson, H, 2 straws of wax weight 21 quintals

John Questinburgh, H, 1 fardel with 2 bales fustian, £26 13s.4d.

Hans Culle, H, 1 pack with 4 bales fustian, £53 6s.8d.
   1 straw of wax weight 12 quintals

Peter Syber, H, 1 fardel with 3 bales fustian, £40

Albright Falland, H, 1 straw of wax weight 11 quintals

John van Armesbery, H, 1 fardel with 4 bales fustian, £53 6s.8d.

John Russynthorp, H, 1 fardel 1 brl. with 60 pcs. Ghentish Holland cont. 1,800 ells, £45

Matthew Blyterswyke, H, 1 fardel with 3 bales fustian, £40

John Greverod, H, 1 brl. with 3½ doz. lbs. Cologne thread, 1½ doz. small coffers, 4 great writing tables, 26s.8d.

John van Strawlyn, H, 1 last soap, 1 pack 2 brls. with 21 bundles caul silk weight 42 lbs., 6 clouts Cologne silk weight 24 lbs., £44

37. 13 Nov. From the ship of William Tabbard called *Maria* of Boston

James Fryse, A, 1 chest with 6 grs. cards, 1½ grs. worsted laces, 2 grs. thread laces, ½ doz. swords, 6 grs. buckles, 2 doz. lamps, 2½ [S 6½] grs. wire girdles, 4 grs. leather girdles, 23 lbs. hair, 2,000 awl blades, 10 grs. wooden beads, 18 doz. pins, 1 grs. 7 doz. pouch rings, 1 grs. 7 doz. knives, 2 doz. daggers, 3 doz. wallets ('pauteners'), 80 doz. worsted corses [S girdles], £16

James Falke, A, 1 hhd. with 16 doz. Nuremburg mirrors, C. lbs. flax, 4 grs. spectacle cases, 6 grs. pen-cases, 6 grs. ink-horns, £3 6s.8d.

Stephen Justynyan and Frank Justynian, As, 2 small pipes with Seville grain weight 260 lbs., £13

Arnold van Stalle, H, 1 pack with 7 pcs. hastrey cont. 174 [S 183] ells, 4 pcs. broad busk, 3 pcs. narrow busk, 84 pcs. Holland cont. 1,988 ells, £74 14s.

John Questynburgh, H, 1 fardel with 2 bales fustian, 1 pack Cologne thread, £40

Hans Stutte, H, 1 straw of wax weight 10 quintals

Gerard van Grove, H, 1 fardel with 3 bales fustian, 1 pack Cologne thread, £53 6s.8d.

John van Armysbery, H, 1 fardel with 2 packs Cologne thread, 3 fardels with 6 bales fustian, £106 13s.4d.

Peter Syber, H, 2 fardels with 4 bales fustian, £53 6s.8d.

John Russynthorp, H, 1 fardel with 2 bales fustian, 1 fardel with 76 pcs. and remnants cont. 1,933 ells [S Holland], £84 13s.4d.

John Greverod, H, 1 fardel with 2 bales fustian, £26 13s.4d.

John van Derbeson, H, 1 pack with 25 pcs. hastrey cont. 748 ells, 12 pcs. Holland cont. 75 ells, 13 pcs. Brussels cont. 213 ells, 12 pcs. narrow busk, 2 boards of shanks, £48

George Tak, H, 1 roll Osnabrück linen cloth, £12

John Salmer, H, 1 corf 1 frail 1 pipe battery, £30

Arnold van Stalle, H, 1 roll Osnabrück linen cloth, £12

William Grenewolt, H, 1 basket with 68 pcs. and remnants Holland cont. 703 [*S* 1,703] ells, £40

Hans Culle, H, 1 great vat 1 small dry vat with 18,000 calaber [furs], £75[1] (£13 10s. del.)

Roger van Feld, H, 2 packs with 24 C. ells soultwich, 900 ells [*S* narrow] linen cloth, 12 pcs. Holland cont. 300 ells, £68 5s.

William Scapehuson, H, 2 straws of wax weight 22 quintals

Lambert Rotard, H, 6 brls. steel, £36

1 straw of wax weight 8 quintals

Frank Savage, H, 1 frail battery, £10

[1] Corrected in another hand.

38. 13 Nov. From the ship of John Pyper called *Christofer* of Brightlingsea ('Brikelsey')

John Kele, A, 1 sack hemp, 1 sack flax, £3

James Falke, A, 1 chest with 26 doz. bags, 12 doz. playing-cards, £3 8s.4d.

Cornelius Smyth, A, 1 sack flax, 30s.

[m.3]

39. 13 Nov. From the ship of Cornelius Johnson called *Christofer* of Leiden ('Legh')

John Kele, A, 1 sack hemp, 30s.

40. 1 Dec. From the ship of Lubert van Boke called *Mary* of the Steelyard

John Evyngar, A, 1 sack hops, 30s.

Edward Johnson and Anthony Gilbert, As, 1 brl. filings, 2 brls. with 24 grs. knives, 86 doz. [*S* diverse] knives, 10 grs. buckles, 1½ grs. gloves, 1 grs. [*S* and 24 doz.] pouches, 12 doz. hooks, 6 caskets, 4 lbs. ivory combs, 2 lbs. [*S* small] ivory knives, 22 [*S* 32] doz. pins, 1 grs. [*S* painted] knives, £22

Henry Fryk, H, 10 lasts loose stockfish, £100

John van Derbeson, H, 4 brls. steel, £24

James van Werd, H, 2½ lasts white herring, £10

Tylman Barkys, H, 4 lasts ashes, £4

41. 1 Dec. From the ship of John Hamond called *Gabryell* of London

Peter la Par, A, 3 bales combs, £3

42. 4 Dec. From the ship of John Stephenis called *Nicholus* of Fowey

Vasco Fernandus, A, 7 sorts figs and raisins, 1,500 oranges, 56s.8d.

43. 13 Dec. From the ship of John Somelso called [*S Sancta*] *Maria* of Bilbao

Anthony de Serro, A, 1,143 bales woad, £762

Stephen Justynyan', A, 82 sacks alum, 80 bales woad, £114 162s.8d.

Paul Larka, A, 86 bales woad, £57 6s.8d.

Raphael Lomelyn' and Nicholas Lomelyn', As, 10 bales woad, 1 bale paper, £7 13s.4d.

44. 18 Dec. From the ship of Michael Dyke called *Blak George* of Ostend

Michael Lanke, A, 1 last white herring, 1 last salt fish, £8

45. 18 Dec. From the ship of Cornelius Moche called *Barbara* of London

Said master, A, 9 brls. salt fish, 1 brl. with mirrors, £3 15s.

John Dedekker, A, 1 small fardel with 1,000 kid skins [S for gloves], 54 doz. gloves, £5

Michael van Prate, A, 1 sack hemp, 1 chest 1 fardel 1 small basket with diverse remnants coarse Flemish cont. 140 ells, 10 doz. mirrors, 6 doz. pouches, 12 rolls buckram, 20 daggers, 9 doz. shoes [S for children], 8 books of painted paper, 1,000 imitation chalcedony, 30 [S small] ivory combs, 2 doz. shanks, 24 pcs. steel, 5 small anvils, 170 ells coarse canvas, C. packthread, 12 lbs. blue thread, 2 frying pans, 2,000 buckles, 1 grs. [S whip] cord, 20 doz. flowers of horn and silk ('floures de horne et sylk'), 8 pairs knives, £10 1s.8d.

Lewis van Dermers, A, 1 brl. with 2,500 teazles, 900 handles [S for fullers], 8 old shearmen's shears, 36s.8d.

Arnold van Stalle, H, 15 doz. and 5 red skins, £10

46. 22 Dec. From the ship of William Labye called *Mighell* of Dieppe

John Elyot, A, 1 case combs, 11 pouches with 9 doz. 8 pairs wool-cards, 2 doz. standishes, 1 pair standing knives, 26 reams paper, 5 grs. tin rings, 6 doz. latten 'agnus dei', 3 tin paxbreds, 3 doz. playing-tables, 20 lbs. violet powder, 3 brls. apples, 13 doz. 7 brushes, 8 qrs. walnuts, £28

John de Lapomery, A, 1 pipe 1 puncheon 1 basket 1 small case with 40 reams paper, 14 grs. playing-cards, 12 grs. thread laces, 6 grs. combs, 4 doz. small glasses, 6 daggers, 2 doz. knives, 2 hangers, 3 grs. tin rings, 1 doz. small shears, 1 grs. glasses, 6 spear-heads, 36 reams paper, 1 grs. [S latten] gold weights, £12 6s.8d.

Alan Hamond, A, 1 puncheon with 3 playing-tables, 1 bag tablemen, 1 grs. gold weights, 1 doz. gimlets, 1 doz. knives, 4 doz. razors, 2½ doz. barbers' stones, 4 doz. glasses, 1½ doz. bells, 3 grs. combs, 2½ doz. pipes, 1 doz. horse-combs, 1 doz. playing cards, 4 grs. points, 2½ grs. leather laces, 2 doz. leather girdles, 26s.8d.

47. 22 Dec. From the ship of John Goldesburgh called *John Remyngton* of London

John de Barde, A, 50 cases sugar, £83 6s.8d.

48. 22 Dec. From the ship of Thomas Horne called *Thomas* of London[1]

John de Barde, A, 50 cases sugar, £83 6s.8d.
Frederick Pryoll, A, 17 [*S* great] brls. raisins of Corinth, £40

¹ See also below, **609**.

49. 27 Dec. From the ship of Simon Cappis called *Fryday* of Purmerend ('Premerend')
Said master, A, 6 brls. stub-eels, 4 brls. kive and 3 brls. pimpernol eels, 18 brls. white herring, 2 brls. pimpernol, £23 6s.8d.
John Petirson A, 1 brl. stub-eels, 1 brl. kive and 2 brls. pimpernol eels, £4
Said master, A, fresh¹ eels, £53 6s.8d.

¹ i.e. not salted.

50. 27 Dec. From the ship of Clays Lowson called *Gabriell* of Purmerend
Said master, A, 2 lasts white herring, 1 last salt fish, 8 brls. stub-eels, 3½ brls. kive and 3 brls. pimpernol eels, £30 16s.8d.; fresh eels, £60

51. 27 Dec. From the ship of Simon Johnson called *Barbara* of Purmerend
Said master, A, 4 brls. stub-eels, 2 brls. kive eels, £8 13s.4d.; fresh eels, £33 6s.8d.

52. 27 Dec. From the ship of John Petirson called *Sanctus Petrus* [*S* Sanctus Spiritus] of Purmerend
Said master, A, [*S* 50] fresh eels, £21

53. 27 Dec. From the ship of James Floresson [*S* Florenson] called *Sanctus Andreas* of Purmerend.
Said master, A, 2 brls. stub-eels, 5 brls. kive eels, 2 brls. pimpernol, £9 13s.4d.; fresh eels, £24

54. 30 Dec. From the ship of James Ratesburgh called *Burnet* of London
Gerard van Grove, H, 1 pack Cologne thread, £13 6s.8d.
Matthew Bliterswyke, H, 2 bales madder, £4

55. 30 Dec. From the ship of Lambert Williburchen called *Christofer* of Flushing
Peter Peresson, A, 6 lasts 3 brls. herring, 2 lasts salt fish, 3 small brls. salt fish, 50 brls. onions, 500 paving-tiles, 80 bunches garlic, 300 cruses and pots, £35

[m.3d.]
56. 2 Jan. From the ship of Thomas Ketton called *Mary Dawbeney*¹
Gerard van Grove, H, 1 pack Cologne thread, 2 bales madder, £17 6s.8d.
Henry Lathuson, H, 3 lasts loose stockfish, £30
Edward Johnson, A, 1 firkin green ginger weight 30 lbs., 2 hhds. with 2

doz. lbs. string thread, 4 pcs. fustian, 80 doz. pouches, 9 grs. knives, 1,300 thimbles, 12 lbs. stable brushes, 3 grs. latten trumpets, 12 lbs. troy weights, 1 doz. squirts, 6 doz. writing-tables, 9 doz. snuffers, 6 doz. compasses, 2 grs. razors, 1 grs. small locks, 6,000 clasps, 4 papers of laces, 2 doz. latten cranes, 1,400 bells, 2 doz. stirrups, 800 bodkins, 500 small glasses, 1 tapestry coverlet, 1 grs. annulets, 2 small forcers, 28 doz. gloves, 1½ grs. folding knives, 2 doz. latten girdles, 7½ doz. leather [?girdles], 4½ doz. bits, 12 doz. spurs, 5,000 brigandine nails, 12½ doz. feathers for hats, 12 standing pot knives, 12 doz. pen knives, £22 3s.4d.

Henry James, A, 1 basket with 12 doz. red hides, 4 quilts, 19 pcs. narrow busk cont. 630 ells, 16 pcs. broad busk cont. 560 ells, 12 leather cushions, £22 15s.

Deryk Oldekyrk, A, 1 brl. with 3 doz. mirrors, 33s.4d.

John Petirson, A, 2 brls. stub-eels, ½ brl. kive eels, 3½ brls. pimpernol eels, 3½ brls. white herring, £7 13s.4d.

Clays Lowson, A, 2 brls. stub-eels, 2 brls. kive, £5 6s.8d.

Gabriel Furnarius, A, 1 brl. with 90 lbs. caddis, £3

¹ See also below, **610**.

57. 2 Jan. From the ship of Walter Johnson called *Jamys* of Gouda ('Tregowe')

Cornelius Vandebrille [*S* Vandrebell], A, ½ last white herring, 3 brls. salt fish, 2½ brls. salmon, 1 brl. mackerel, 50 wainscots, 300 paving-tiles, £7

58. 2 Jan. From the ship of Clais Thorn called *Julyan* of Arnemuiden ('Armewth')

John Russinthorp, H, 2 bales madder, 1 fardel with 3 corses of Oudenarde thread cont. 28 doz., £9

Gerard van Grove, H, 1 pack Cologne thread, 2 bales madder, £17 6s.8d.

Matthew Bliterswyke, H, 2 bales madder, £4

Arnold van Stalle, H, 1 pack with 57 pcs. Holland cont. 1,142 ells, 1 pc. Osnabrück, £46

Matthew Hynkylman, H, 1 pack with 35 pcs. soultwich, 30 pcs. pickling, £22 10s.

William Scapehuson, H, 3 straws of wax weight 36 quintals

John Questynburgh, H, 3 bales madder, £6

George Tak, H, 6 bales madder, £12

Tylman Barkys, H, 1 bale madder, 40s.

1 straw of wax weight 9 quintals

Roger van Feld, H, 1 maund with 4 rolls Herford linen cloth, £48

Gerard Lesbern, H, 1 sack feathers, 1 fardel with 10 C. ells soultwich, £16 10s.

Henry Fryk, H, 3 lasts 3 C. loose stockfish, £33

Hans Hosterberch, H, 2 lasts loose stockfish, £20

John van Derbeson, H, 8 bales madder [*S* £16], 1 last osmund [*S* £4], £20

Simon Johnson, A, 16 brls. stub-eels, 8 brls. kive eels, £34 13s.4d.

John Claysson, A, 6 lasts 2 brls. salt fish, ½ last stub-eels, £34 13s.4d.

Clays Lowson, A, 1 last 2 brls. stub-eels, 6 brls. kive, 2 brls. pimpernol, 17 brls. salt fish, £36 6s.8d.

Gerard Matysson, A, 6 lasts salt fish, £24

Simon Coppe, A, 6 brls. stub-eels, 7 brls. kive, £16

Edward Johnson, A, 1 brl. with 4 doz. pouches, 5 grs. knives, 5 grs. bullions, 6 lbs. blue thread, 1 habergeon, 1 brl. plate [S breastplate], 6 red hides, 56s.8d.

James Bolle, A, 1 chest with 14 grs. playing-cards, £3 5s.

James Floresson, A, 2 brls. stub-eels, 5 brls. kive, 6½ brls. pimpernol, £12 13s.4d.

John Petirsson, A, 14 brls. stub-eels, 6½ brls. kive eels, £29 16s.8d.

Bernard van Utreth, A, 1 fardel with 17 vols. diverse histories, 46s.8d.

59. 2 Jan. From the ship of Anthony Brabander called *George* of Middelburg

Hans Culle, H, 1 straw of wax weight 12 quintals

Arnold van Stalle, H, 4 bales madder, 3 brls. oil, £10

Albert Falland, H, 1 straw of wax weight 11 quintals

Matthew Hynkylman, H, 1 pack with 47 pcs. soultwich cont. 12 C. ells, £18

James van Werd, H, 1 straw of wax weight 12 quintals

George Tak, H, 3 bales madder, £6

Tylman Barkys, H, 5 bales madder, £10

1 straw of wax weight 9 quintals

Roger van Feld, H, 4 vats Cologne woad, £26 13s.4d.

Gerard Lesbern, H, 3 bales madder, 1 sack feathers, 4 C. bowstaves, £15 10s.

1 straw of wax weight 11 quintals

John Salmer, H, 1 'bascheron' 2 frails battery, £30

Hans Hosterberch, H, 1 last stockfish, 2 lasts titling stockfish, £15

Willian Grenewolt, H, 4 brls. with saltpetre weight 16 C. 24 lbs. [S 14 lbs.], £37 16s.8d.

Hans Stut, H, 1 straw of wax weight 12 quintals

John van Derbeson, H, 7 bales madder, 4 brls. steel, £38

Clays Gerardson, A, 5 lasts salt fish, 2 lasts 4 brls. herring, £29 6s.8d.

Simon Johnson, A, 3½ lasts salt fish, 1 last 9 brls. herring, £21

Clays Lowson, A, 8 brls. stub-eels, 1 brl. kive, 8 brls. salt fish, £17

John Petirson, A, 2 brls. stub-eels, 1 brl. kive, £4 6s.8d.

60. 2 Jan. From the ship of William Racheford called *Thomas* of London

Henry James, A, 1 firkin green ginger weight 50 lbs., 1 brl. 1 basket with 27 red hides, 12 brushes, 87 pillows, 8 quilts, 1½ grs. Flanders lace, 20 lbs. [S packing] thread, 4½ doz. sheets, £14 10s.

John Kanys, A, 1 maund with 23 reams paper, 3,000 awl blades, 5 lbs. packthread, 3 gorgets, £3 5s.

Peter Segir, A, 1 pipe with 4,000 balls, 1 sack hemp, £3 10s.

Martin Johnson, A, 1 dry vat with 48 grs. Nuremburg mirrors, £3 3s. [*S* 4d.*]

Thomas Johnson, A, 1 pipe with 13 grs. ink-horns, 6 grs. pin-cases, 10 grs. spectacles, 2 doz. pouches, 2 gilt cases, 13 doz. knives, 43s.4d.

Martin Coppyn, A, 1 brl. white herring, 6s.8d.

61. 13 Jan. From the ship of John Demure called *Margret* of Dieppe[1]

Said master, A, 4 qrs. wheat, 4 qrs. rye, 4 qrs. barley, 14 pcs. figs, £5

John Muet, A, 16 qrs. wheat, 16 qrs. rye, 16 qrs. barley, £10 13s.4d.

John Blank, A, 16 qrs. barley, 53s.4d.

John Augo, A, 16 qrs. barley, 53s.4d.

William de la Plase, A, 1 tun 1 pipe 1 hhd. weight ('pois') of iron, 28 lbs. saffron, 15 brls. filbert nuts, £15

Colin Dele, A, 16 qrs. wheat, £5 6s.8d.

William Richard, A, 61 qrs. wheat, £20 6s.8d.

William Gardyn, A, 16 qrs. maslin, 53s.4d.

[m.4]

John Doblet, A, 16 qrs. wheat, 16 qrs. maslin, 16 qrs. barley, £10 13s.4d.

Gyon Carpenter, A, 2½ doz. wool-cards, 13s.4d. (6d. *del.*) [*S* 12s.6d.]

John Bussher, A, 2 pcs. figs and raisins, 5s.

[1] See also below, **611**.

62. 17 Jan. From the ship of Michael Elyng called *Blak George* of Ostend

Peter Clene, A, 8 brls. shotten herring, 4 brls. herring, 8 brls. salt fish, 1 brl. pimpernol eels, ½ C. salt fish, £6 10s.

63. 12 Feb. From the ship of John Bargeman called *Christofer* of Reimerswaal ('Remersale')

Said master, A, 40 skives teazles, 2 bales madder weight 14 C. lbs., 1 basket with 48 [*S* 36] doz. felt hats, 400 bunches garlic, 1,000 paving-tiles, 2 brls. mackerel, £9 13s.4d. (45s. *del.*)

John Skywyng [*S* Skillyng] A, 90 skives teazles, 45s.

64. 12 Feb. From the ship of John Cossyance called *Mighell* of Le Conquet

Anthony Grace, A, 49 brls. salmon, £32 13s.4d.

65. 13 Feb. From the ship of Ecbord Jacobson called *Christofer*

John Johnson, A, 8½ lasts salt fish, ½ last white herring, 6½ brls. 4 kilderkins [*S* firkins] herring, £37 13s.4d.

66. 13 Feb. From the ship of Isbrand Albright called *Petir Owtotey*

John Johnson, A, 9 lasts 9 brls. salt fish, £39

67. 15 Feb. From the ship of Robinet Dearte called *Kateryn* of Dieppe

Said master, A, 86 [*S* 96] qrs. wheat, 8 qrs. filbert nuts, £33 6s.8d.

22

68. 15 Feb. From the ship of Cornelius Selander called *George* of Bergen-op-Zoom

Said master, A, 10 brls. herring, 50 wainscots, 2,000 pavingstones, 2 sacks flax, £8 13s.4d.

James Williamson, A, 1 pipe with 5,000 balls, 1 sack flax, 1 sack hemp, £5 10s.

Leonard Yemanson, A, 3 lasts 4 brls. white herring, 24 oars, £13 16s.8d.

John Evingar, A, 2 sacks hops, 500 Flanders scouring stones,[1] £3 6s.8d.

Lambert Rotard, H, 13½ brls. sturgeon, ½ [*S* 1½] brl. olives, £11 10s.

---

[1] Cf. 'brickstones called flaunders tiles to scoure with' (Willan, *Rates*, 10).

69. 17 Feb. From the ship of Philip Gerrard called *Mary* of London

Alexander Portinarius, A, 1 fardel with 2 cloths w.g., £24

70. 20 Feb. From the ship of Dennis Furner called *Maria* of Harfleur

Nicholas Tabbard, A, 1 small fardel with 6 doz. knives, 24 doz. combs, 3 doz. razors, 2 doz. spectacles, 4 grs. points, 3 doz. balances, 3 doz. knives, 3 pairs shears, 20s.

Robert Dod, A, 15 tuns Caen-stone, 1 pipe with apples, 53s.4d.

Robert Catelan, A, 1 pipe with filbert nuts, 1 small bag with 200 ells canvas, 50s.

Peryn Mayewe, A, 1 tick, 3s.4d.

71. 20 Feb. From the ship of Lambert Willibrod called *Christofer* of Flushing

Peter Person, A, 10 lasts white herring, 10 brls. [*S* salt] codsheads, £41 13s.4d.

Said master, A, 2½ brls. 2 firkins white herring, 10s.

72. 20 Feb. From the ship of Peter Johnson called *Anthony* of Flushing

Hugh Jacobson, A, 11 lasts 8½ brls. white herring, 2 firkins 1 brl. codsheads, £45 13s.4d.

73. 21 Feb. From the ship of Ollard Claysson called *Christofer* of Flushing

Said master, A, 1 last 6½ brls. 3 firkins white herring, £5 6s.8d.

Bartholomew Johnson, A, 9 lasts 4 brls. salt fish [*S* 9 lasts herring, 4 brls. salt fish], £37 6s.8d.

74. 21 Feb. From the ship of Coppyn Person called *Fastelawyn* of Flushing

Said master, A, 6 lasts white herring, £24

Coppyn Andreson [*S* Andrianson], A, 9 lasts herring, 1 brl. codsheads, £36 3s.4d.

George Roo, A, 2 lasts white herring, £8

75. 22 Feb. From the ship of Coppyn Bonvir [*S* Bonvise] called *James* of Flushing

Said master, A, 9½ brls. 3 firkins white herring, 33s.4d.

76. 22 Feb. From the ship of Leonard Everad called *Kateryn* of Benfleet

Romayn Botshayn, A, 1 last white herring, £4

77. 25 Feb. From the ship of Peter Jacobisson called *Trego* of Arnemuiden

Clays Bromer, A, 3 lasts herring, £12

John Johnson, A, 3 brls. stub-eels, 2 brls. kive eels, £7

James Williamson, A, 1 sack flax, 1 sack hemp, £3

John Claysson, A, 23 brls. salt fish, £7 13s.4d.

Henry James, A, 1 chest with 15 pcs. Ghentish Holland cont. 390 ells, 6 doz. lbs. white and blue thread, 5 lbs. saffron, 6 coverlets, 5 doz. cushion-cloths, 17 pcs. tuke, £22 18s. [*S* £22 18s.4d.]

John Henrikson, A, 16 brls. salt fish, £5 6s.8d.

Gerard von Grove, H, 3 bales madder, 3 packs Cologne thread, £46

Albright Falland, H, 6 C. bowstaves, £12

1 straw of wax weight 11 quintals

Hans Stut, H, 2 straws [*S* of wax] weight 19 quintals

Arnold van Stalle, H, 11 brls. cork, 1 pack with 29 pcs. hastrey cont. 725 ells, 2 pcs. Osnabrück cont. C. 8 ells, 82 pcs. Holland cont. 1,650 ells, £56

Matthew Bliterswyke, H, 2 bales madder, £4

Lambert Rotard, H, 6 brls. steel, £36

John Salmer, H, 1 frail 1 'bassheron' 1 basket battery, £30

Roger van Feld, H, 2 bales madder, 1 basket with 10 pcs. broad busk, £10 13s.4d.

James van Werd, H, 4 bales madder, £8

William Scapehuson, H, 1 straw of wax weight 11 quintals

Hans Culle, H, 1 straw of wax weight 10 quintals

Everard Southerman, 1 maund with 2 rolls Osnabrück, 2½ rolls Herford cont. 3 rolls, 2 painted cloths, £60 13s.4d.

John Greverod, H, 8½ brls. steel, 2 fardels with 7 sacks hemp, £61 10s.

John van Derbeson, H, 5 bales madder, 2 lasts osmund, £18

Hans Hosterberch, H, 2 lasts 7 C. loose stockfish, £27

William Grenewolt, H, 1 roll Herford linen cloth cont. 1 roll 2 C. 1 qr. 4 ells, £14 6s.8d.

John Russyngthorp, H, 6 brls. cork, £3

78. 25 Feb. From the ship of Simon Mellar called *Maria* of Lynn

Everard Southerman, H, 4 bales madder, £8

John Salmer, H, 2 frails 1 basket battery, £30

Roger van Feld, H, 1 maund with 2½ rolls 10 ells Herford, £30

Tylman Barkys, H, 1 pack linen cloth with 64 pcs. broad busk, 50 pcs. narrow busk, £67 13s.4d.

Arnold van Stalle, H, 1 chest with 49 pcs. Holland cont. 1,077 ells, £26 16s.8d.

Henry Jamys, A, 1 chest 1 fardel with 14 reams [*S* white] paper, 14 doz. lbs. white and blue Cologne thread, C. 25 lbs. flax, 16 pcs. broad busk, 16 [pcs.] narrow busk cont. 1,210 ells, 3 pcs. tuke, £24

79. 28 Feb. From the ship of John Gole called *Kateryn* of Caen,
Thomas de Done, A, 2 baskets with 18 [*S* 8] reams paper, 15 grs. combs,
1½ doz. tailors' shears, 10 doz. playing-cards, 6 doz. gold weights, 8
doz. scissors, 2 grs. oil of spikenard, 29 bales dishes ('dic') [*S* 'dys'], 6
doz. knives, 2 doz. mirrors, 4 pairs latten balances, 6 lbs. violet
powder, 55s.

80. 3 Mar. From the ship of William Muget called *Kateryn* of Harfleur
John Demayle, A, 18 tuns Caen-stone, 8 ticks, £4

81. 5 Mar. From the ship of Henry Maryer called *Christofer* of
'Lothury'[1]
Said master, A, 7 pcs. Ghentish [*S* Breton] linen cloth cont. 70 yds., 30s.

  [1] ? Locquirec, dep. Finistère, Brittany.

82. 7 Mar. From the ship of Robert Bigg called *Volantyn* of London
Peter Actorys, A, 1 chest 1 vat with 69 vols. diverse histories, £12
John de Mayn, A, 6 brls. calamine, £4
John Kele, A, 2 lasts oil, 1 pipe with 5,000 balls, £18 10s.
James Bolle, A, 2 hhds. with 10 grs. purse-wire, 6 grs. musk-balls, 3
    doz. small coffers, 1 grs. imitation chalcedony, 4 grs. thread laces, 4
    grs. wire girdles, 8 grs. hatbands, 10 grs. thread girdles, 2 doz. clasps,
    5 grs. mistletoe beads, 2 grs. mirrors, 6 doz. paxes, 2 grs. spectacle
    cases, 40 doz. pins, 2 grs. pen-cases, 1 grs. pin-cases, 1 grs. jet beads,
    £10
Anthony de la Hay, A, 1 pipe with 4 complete harness, 1 brl. with 30
    pairs wool-cards, 1 bottom of a basin, 1 brl. wine lees, 1 brass pot, ½
    brl. with C. lbs. filings, £10 13s.4d. [*S* 8d.]
Edward Johnson, A, 2 hhds. with 12 doz. spurs, 6 doz. gardbraces, 18
    bits, 8 grs. pouches, 18 grs. knives, 6 doz. black rings, 9 doz. gloves,
    24 red hides, £10 6s.8d.
Albright Johnson, A, 1 sack hemp, 1 sack flax, 1 chest with 11 pcs.
    Brabant linen cloth cont. 204 ells linen, 40 lbs. flax, £8 6s.8d.
Anthony Kele, A, 2 sacks flax, £3
John Druet [*S* Drewett] A, 36 lbs. blue thread, 20s.
Goswyn Rodinkerk, H, 5 bales madder, £10
Andrew Petirson, A, 3 sacks flax, £4 10s.

83. 7 Mar. From the ship of Ellis Arnold called *Kateryn* of London[1]
John Dancell, A, 1 chest 1 tun with 6 doz. mirrors, 30 doz. small glasses,
    2 doz. swords, 80 doz. small glasses, 6½ doz. coloured skins, 7 tapestry
    coverlets, £12 10s.
Nicholas de Boke, A, 1 vat 1 pipe with 40½ doz. wool-cards, £12 8s.4d.
Peter van Oustyn, A, 1 small chest with [*S* 4] great painted cloths, 5 [*S* 1]
    small painted cloths, 2 doz. Spruce skins,[2] 1 pc. Flemish linen cloth
    cont. 40 ells, 2 pcs. Flemish cont. 80 ells, 51s.10d.
Lewis van Demersse, A, 1 pipe with teazles, £3
Maryn Monsenego, A, 1 chest cinnamon weight 131 lbs., £10
Andrew Petirson, A, 3 sacks flax, £4 10s.[3]

84. 7 Mar. From the ship of Richard Dockyng called *Martyn Baldry* of London
Cornelius Joosson, A, 3 sacks hemp, 1 hhd. with 6 grs. spurs, £8 5s.
Peter Segir, A, 2 baskets with 100 doz. 'coppyn' hats, £5 16s.8d.
James Bolle, A, 2 hhds. with 3 grs. small coffers, 1½ grs. locks, 3 grs. compasses, ½ gross marking irons, 2 doz. clasps, 20 grs. Nuremburg mirrors, 1 pipe with 6,000 balls, 2 sacks flax, £10 5s.
Edward Johnson, A, 1 bale paper, 2 chests with combs, 1 chest with 12 grs. leather laces, 6 grs. pen-cases, 6 grs. spectacle-cases, 6 grs. pin-cases, 3 doz. 'coppyn' hats, 46 papers of points, £11 8s.4d.
Arnold Howell, A, 2 sacks hemp, £3
Thomas Johnson, A, 1 case combs, 1 dry vat 1 corf 1 brl. with 300 doz. Nuremburg mirrors, 32 doz. pipes, 2 grs. thimble cases, 14 doz. small pouches, 3 doz. great pouches, 1 grs. locks, 2½ grs. shears, 80 marks of scissors, £4 13s.4d [*S* £4 12s.10d.]
John Kele, A, 4 sacks hemp, £6
Margaret Claysson, A, 1 sack flax, 30s.

[m.4d.]
85. 7 Mar. From the ship of Cornelius Johnson called *Christofer* of Bergen-op-Zoom
Said master, A, 2,000 pavingstones, 26s.8d.
John Bungawe, A, 1 fardel 1 brl. with 2 old napkins, 28 gorgets, 3 pairs vambraces, 2 pairs leg-harness, 1 helmet, ½ doz. half-vambraces, 2 pcs. diaper napkins cont. 37 ells, 1 old towel, £7 16s. [*S* £7 15s.10d.]
Cornelius Joosson [*S* Johnson], A, 1½ packs brushes, 2 pipes with 8,000 balls, £5 10s.
Andrew Petirson, A, 350 bunches garlic, 2 brls. with 3,200 balls, 55s.
Albright Johnson, A, 1 vat with filbert nuts, 8s.4d.
Martin Johnson, A, 1 brl. with 36 papers of pins, 8 grs. spectacles, £5 3s.4d.

86. 7 Mar. From the ship of Michael Mer called *Christofer* of Antwerp
John Evingar, A, 3 sacks hops, 200 pavingstones, £4 13s.4d.
Paul Godfraye, A, 2 sacks hops, £3
John Kele, A, 5 sacks hops, £7 10s.
Walter Reynold, A, 3 brls. 3 pipes wine lees, 1 pipe with 400 spice-cakes, 1 brl. slip, 33s.4d.
Edward Johnson, A, 6 brls. slip, ½ brl. filings, 1 sack hemp, 35s.
Henry Jamys, A, 1 vat with 4,600 balls, 100 bundles brown paper, £5
Martin Johnson, A, 2½ lasts herring, £10
Thomas Johnson, A, 1 sack hops, 1 maund with 160 doz. straw hats, 6 doz. pillows, £4 13s.4d.

87. 7 Mar. From the ship of Peter Menger called *Petir* of Antwerp
John Kele, A, 7 sacks hops, £10 10s.

Anthony Kele, A, 1,500 cruses, 3 sacks hops, ½ last herring, £8 10s.
Said master, A, 9 brls. white herring, £3
Martin Johnson, A, 2½ lasts white herring, £10
Elizabeth Wolf, A, 7½ brls. 10 firkins pimpernol eels, £4
Thomas Johnson, A, 3 sacks hops, 1 maund with 40 [*S* 140] doz. straw
  hats, £6 16s.8d.
John Vandermaste, A, ½ pack brushes, 10s.
Peter Wolf, A, 2 chests with 400 foot ('fote') glasses,[1] £3
George Tak, H, 2 sacks hemp, £3

  [1] ? Glasses with stems and feet.

88. 7 Mar. From the ship of Lubert van Boke called *Maria* of the
  Steelyard
Tylman Barkys, H, 10 lasts ashes, 3 lasts 10 brls. tar, £13 16s.8d.
Gerard Lesbern, H, 1 straw of wax weight 11 quintals
Henry Lathuson, H, 6 brls. [*S* lasts] salt fish, 2 lasts stockfish, £22
Lambert Rotard, H, 6 brls. steel, ½ last herring, £38
Stephen Branche, H, 1 last salt fish, £4

89. 7 Mar. From the ship of John Brasse called *Christofer* of
  Bergen-op-Zoom
John Bungawe, A, 1 pipe with 6 complete harness, 2 pairs leg-harness, 1
  doz. pairs half-vambraces, ½ [*S* 1½] doz. vambraces, £19 18s.
James Williamson, A, 1 sack flax, 30s.
Thomas Johnson, A, 400 bunches garlic, 26s.8d.
Martin Johnson, A, 1 sack hemp, 1 small basket with 6 doz. 'coppyn'
  hats, 2 grs. small locks, 7 doz. annulets, 17 grs. pin-cases, 1 doz. pairs
  shuttles, 16 pairs sheets, £4 10s.
Arnold Howell, [*S* A], 1 brl. with C. lbs. packthread, 6 pcs. coarse
  narrow canvas cont. 100 [*S* 150] ells, 26s.8d.
John Ratte, A, 1 brl. with 120 mirrors, 13s.4d.

90. 7 Mar. From the ship of John Bawdewyn called *Barge* of Calais
John Kele, A, 12 brls. nails, £24
John Vandermaste, A, 2 baskets with 62 [*S* 162] doz. straw hats, £10
  3s.4d.
John Salmar, H, 2 'bassherons' battery, £20
John Russinthorp, H, 1 brl. with 95 bundles caul silk, 26½ clouts Cologne
  silk [*S* weight 297 lbs.], 1 dagger, 2 pairs knives, £405
Goswyn Rodinkerk, H, 6 bales madder, £12
Frank Savage, H, 2 'bassherons' battery, £20
William Grenewolt, H, 1 maund with 1 roll Herford linen cloth, 6 pcs.
  Holland cont. 159 [*S* 109] ells, £15
John Greverod, H, 6 bales madder, 1 brl. with 4 doz. 7 barbers' basins,
  120 [*S* 110] small basins, 1 doz. pcs. girth-webs [*S* for horses], £24
  3s.4d.
John van Armysbery, H, 4 bales madder, £8

91. 7 Mar. From the ship of Robert Alcok called *Leonard* of London

James Falk, A, 1 hhd. 1 brl. with 20 grs. jet beads, 1½ grs. gloves, 2 grs. wooden beads, 600 awl hafts and graving hafts, £4 10s.

Andrew Petirson, A, 1 sack flax, 30s.

Edward Johnson, A, 2½ sacks hemp, 350 sheepskins, £4 8s.4d.

Martin Johnson, A, 1 sack hemp, 1 hhd. with 10 grs. ink-horns, 4 grs. 9 doz. spurs, 4 grs. 'pere'[1] glasses, 3 grs. pin-cases, 2½ doz. 'coppyn' hats, £5 8s.4d.

Margaret Claisson, A, 1 pipe with 22 pcs. Brabant cont. 300 [*S* 342] ells, 1 tick, 10 lbs. flax, 24 lbs. yarn, 1 sack flax, £11

Adrian Pere, A, 1 bag with 7 pcs. and remnants Holland cont. 82 ells, £6

[1] ? Pouring glasses. Cf. 'peer or pere: to pour' (*O.E.D.*).

92. 7 Mar. From the ship of James Holland called *Christofer* of Holland

Cornelius Joosson [*S* Johnson], A, 1 vat with 6,000 balls, £3

James Bolle, A, 1 hhd. with 12 grs. thread girdles, 2 grs. thread laces, 16 doz. papers of pins, 2 doz. clasps, 4 doz. lbs. counters, 1½ gross locks, 1 grs. copper gold, 1 grs. imitation chalcedony, 2½ grs. knives, 500 pack-needles, 4 grs. harp-strings, 3 pouches, 2 grs. jet beads, 4 grs. pen-cases, 6,000 sail-needles, [*S* 6 grs. ink-horns], £7 13s.4d.

Albright Johnson, A, 3 pipes filbert nuts, 3 brls. herring, 33s.4d.

Thomas Johnson, A, 1 dry vat with 13 grs. ink-horns, 28 [*S* 38] doz. gilt pin-cases, 16 grs. jet beads, 3½ grs. pen-cases, 26s.8d.

Gerard Lesbern, H, 1 straw of wax weight 10 quintals

93. 7 Mar. From the ship of Thomas Koys called *Petir Stokker* of London[1]

John Dancell, A, 1 chest with 31 doz. single caps, 10 doz. double caps, 23 swords, 18 pairs cappers' shears, 4 daggers, 13 doz. gipsers with rings, 22 doz. coloured skins, 60 doz. knives, £17 16s.8d.

Peter Segir, A, 1 chest 1 basket 1 pipe 1 firkin with 8 doz. 2 [*S* 10 doz.] St. Omer hats, 6 brushes, 2 C. lbs. filings, 7 doz. blue thread, 5½ doz. hatters' cards, 6 pairs wool-cards, 4 sums nails, 14 doz. skins, 2 painted cloths, 14 doz. St. Omer hats, 2 grs. gloves, 10 hatters' stocks,[2] £20 13s.4d.

Nicholas de Boke [*S* Boll], A, 1 maund with 204 doz. and 3 straw hats, 36s.8d.

Marcello Maures, A, 2 chests with 2 C. 40 [*S* 14] lbs. flax, 82 lbs. [*S* linen] yarn, 1 cupboard, 18 swords, 8 caskets, £3 10s.

John de Vase, A, 1 brl. with 2 diaper table-cloths, 1 pc. Flemish linen cloth cont. 34 ells, 1 doz. napkins, 1 doz. weavers' brushes, 12 lbs. yarn, 3 lbs. twine, 14 ells canvas, 1 painted cloth, 2 candlesticks, 5 shuttles, 53s.4d.

Paul Couper, A, 2 pipes with 8,000 teazles, 1 hhd. with 3,000 spindles, 2 doz. cards, 24 doz. knives, £3

Griffen van Rye, A, 1 dry vat with 1 painted table, 12 great glasses, 50 lbs. turnsole, 3 doz. painted cloths, 3 pcs. cypress [cloth] cont. 120 ells. Flemish, 14 pcs. Bord Alexander, £11 6s.8d.

George Roo, A, 2 pipes 1 vat with 20 pairs leg-harness, 18 mail gorgets,

3 doz. 4 pairs splints, 8 pairs mail sleeves, 8 pairs gussets, 18 habergeons, 12 pairs vambraces, 2 pairs cuirasses, 15 pairs brigandines, 14 sallets, 1 armour for a horse's neck, 19 swords, 36 sallets, 5 pairs splints, 1 chamfron, 1 gorget, £25 3s.4d.

Giles Malet, A, 1 brl. with 8 doz. brushes, 11 latten whips, 3½ doz. bonnets, 2 doz. gloves, 2 grs. points, 1 doz. playing-cards, 1 grs. silk points, 1½ doz. gipsers, 10 doz. wooden combs, 4 ozs. silk, 8 doz. flat laces, 8 doz. knives, 36 imitation pearls, 12 doz. wooden beads, £3

¹ See also **614**.
² ? Block or mould on which a hat is shaped.

94. 7 Mar. From the ship of John Yoman called *Trinite Bole* [of London]

James Falk, A, 1 sack hemp, 1 hhd. with 6 grs. mirrors, £4 10s.

Cornelius Joosson, A, 2 hhds. with 6 grs. ink-horns, 14 grs. pen-cases, 28 grs. glass beads, 9 lbs. string thread, 4 doz. balances, 9 grs. thread laces, 26 doz. mirrors, 8 doz. cruets, 6 [*S* doz.] paxes, 2 grs. [*S* rolls] copper gold, 1 doz. latten wire, 4 doz. small balances, 2 grs. spectacle-cases, 8,000 imitation chalcedony, £11 13s.4d.

Andrew Petirson, A, 2 sacks hemp, £3

James Bolle, A, 1 chest 2 hhds. with 12 grs. leather laces, 12 grs. knives, 2 grs. flax brushes, 12 grs. pin-cases, 4 grs. bodkins, 12 lbs. latten wire, 2 doz. clasps, 4 doz. thimbles, 1 doz. lbs. counters, 3 doz. annulets, 1 grs. locks, 25 lbs. curtain rings, 1 grs. imitation chalcedony, 4 grs. wire girdles, 6 grs. knives, 5 grs. bone beads, 10 grs. thread girdles, 3 lbs. beaten ('bet') copper, 1 grs. razors, 7 doz. writing tables, 5 grs. thread laces, 4 [*S* 3] grs. mistletoe [? beads], 8 doz. papers of pins, 1 grs. copper gold, 6 doz. sallets, 6 doz. gorgets, 7 grs. Nuremburg mirrors, £24 15s.

Edward Johnson, A, 1 chest 1 hhd. with 1 doz. painted cloths, 3 [*S* doz.] coverlets, 1½ doz. hanger blades, 3 doz. boxes, 1 doz. latten crosses, 19 doz. latten girdles, 3½ doz. hearts, 6 doz. 9 swords, 4 grs. girdles, 3 grs. pouches, 6 doz. pen knives, 5,000 brigandine nails, 4 doz. thread, 8 doz. flax brushes, 10 doz. red lasch, 15 caskets, 5 doz. gardbraces, 22 doz. [*S* grs.] knives, 3½ grs. pouches, 2 grs. gloves, ½ doz. bonnets, 2 [*S* doz.] balances, 3 doz. sheepskins, 1 grs. buckles, 4 lbs. copper wire ('filum'), 6 doz. black rings, 4 lbs. steel, £20 [*S* £19 19s.6d.]

John Fox, A, 5 brls. slip, 2 brls. with 20 doz. drinking glasses, 20s.

John Kele, A, 4 sacks hemp, 4 brls. nails, 1 basket with 180 doz. straw hats, £21

John Vandermaste, A, 2 baskets with 100 doz. straw hats, 16 corslets, 12 gorgets, £19

Peter Wolf, A, 1 chest with 2 doz. painted cloths, 19 doz. 5 lbs. Cologne thread, 5 grs. spectacles, 9 doz. 4 daggers, 4 doz. pen-cases, 2 great grs.¹ thread laces, 30 doz. bags, £14 16s.8d.

Walter Reynold, A, 5 brls. slip, 10s.

Joos Swarfeld, A, 1 small basket with 8 doz. pins, 100 bodkins, 2 papers of points, 20s.

John Questynburgh, H, 6 bales madder, £12

Roger van Feld, H, 2 bales madder, 1 pack with 30 pcs. hastrey cont. 753 ells, 9 pcs. Holland cont. 242 ells, 6 pcs. Brabant canvas cont. 150 ells, £33 6s.8d.

Peter Syber, H, 1 pack Cologne thread, £13 6s.8d.

[*S* Anthony Kele, A, 3 sacks canvas, £4 10s.

Martin Johnson, A, 1 chest 1 brl. with 4 grs. razors, 16 grs. red beads, 2 doz. lbs. latten wire, 1 doz. lbs. stable brushes, 6 doz. sacring bells, 7 grs. pen-cases, 3 doz. 'coppyn' hats, 18 grs. Nuremburg mirrors, 60 doz. ells coarse caddis, 4 grs. thread laces, 13 doz. daggers, 2 grs. knives, 7 lbs. blue thread, £10]

John Salmer, H, 2 frails 1 'bassheron' 1 basket 1 bale basins, £50

Goswyn Rodynkerk, H, 5 bales madder, £10

[m.5]

Frank Savage, H, 1 frail 1 'bassheron' battery, £20

Matthew Bliterswyke, H, 3½ brls. steel, £21

Hans Stut, H, 50 pcs. copper plate cont. 1½ meases, £18

William Grenewolt, H, 1 maund with 2 rolls 2 C. 36 ells [*S* 2 rolls cont. 2 C. 26 ells] Herford linen cloth, £28

Gerard Lesbern, H, 1 straw of wax weight 10 quintals

John van Armysbery, H, 3 bales madder, £6

Arnold van Stalle, H, 1 fardel with 15 pcs. narrow busk, 12 pcs. broad busk, 2 vats woad, £28 16s.3d.

Stephen Bramshe, H, ½ last osmund, 40s.

Lambert Rotard, H, 6 brls. steel, £36

Anthony Odyndale, H, 1 pack Cologne thread, £13 6s.8d.

John Greverod, H, 5 bales madder, £10

    [1] Twelve gross the great gross.

95. 7 Mar. From the ship of William Tabbard called *Mary Boston* [of Boston]

Albright Johnson, A, 2 sacks with 2,200 straw hats, £3 6s.8d.

John Kele, A, 2 pipes with 13,000 balls, £6 10s.

John Questinburgh, H, 3 bales madder, 1 brl. with 17 clouts Cologne silk, £62 13s.4d.

Roger van Feld, H, 1 pack Herford and Osnabrück linen cloth cont. 2 rolls 2 C. 40 ells, £28

Peter Syber, H, 1 pack Cologne thread, £13 6s.8d.

John Salmer, H, 2 'bassherons' 2 frails 1 pipe battery, £50

John Russyngthorp, [H], 1 pack with 99 pcs. buckram, 37 pcs. Hainault cont. 1,385 ells, 26 pcs. Flemish cont. 513 ells, 9 doz. shop sheets ('shop shet'),[1] 3 pcs. barras [*S* canvas] cont. 73 ells, £79 6s.8d.

Goswyn Rodynkerk, H, 1 pack Cologne thread, 1 pack with 33 pcs. broad busk, 12 pcs. narrow busk, £41 6s.8d.

Frank Savage, H, 2 frails battery, £20

Gerard van Grove, H, 2 packs Cologne thread, £26 13s.4d.

William Grenewolt, H, 1 roll [*S* 1 C.] 1 qr. Osnabrück linen cloth, ½ roll Herford, £18 13s.4d.

Hans Stut, H, 1 straw of wax weight 10 quintals

George Tak, H, 1 pack with 48 pcs. broad busk, 58 pcs. narrow, £61

John van Armysbery, H, 1 pack Cologne thread, 4 bales madder, £21 6s.8d.

Lambert Rotard, H, 6 brls. steel, £36

Arnold van Stalle, 5 bales madder, £10

John Greverod, H, 8 bales madder, 1 fardel with 6 pcs. narrow busk, £19

[1] ? Packing sheets. Cf. 'old sheets called packing sheets the doz.' (1545 Book of Rates, Bodleian 8°C 23 Jur.).

96. 7 Mar. From the ship of Walter Adrianson called *David* of Antwerp

Martin Johnson, A, 1 maund with 179 doz. straw hats, 1 maund with arrow-root, £5 6s.8d.

Anthony Kele, A, 2 brls. nails, 2 sacks hops, 1 pipe with 4,000 [*S* 5,000] balls, £9

Arnold Howell, A, 1 sack hemp, 6 pairs kempsters' combs, 33s.4d.

Thomas Johnson, A, 1 dry vat with 40 doz. pins, 24 doz. bags, 5 grs. latten buckles, 1 remnant Holland linen cloth cont. 11 ells, 4 grs. [*S* 3 grs.] 4 doz. locks, £4 8s.4d.

Cornelius Smyth, A, 2,000 cruses, 200 glass bottles, 2 sacks hops, £7 6s.8d.

John Kele, A, 12 sacks hops, 600 pavingstones, C. double plates, £22

Andrew Petirson, A, 600 cruses, 26s.8d.

John Evingar, A, 2 sacks hops, £3

Everard Johnson, A, 2 sacks hops, 1 basket with 6½ doz. 'yperlyng', £4 6s.8d.

Cornelius Claysson, A, 1 basket with 60 doz. 'coppyn' hats, £3

John Vandermaste, A, ½ pack brushes, 1 small basket with 2 doz. sallets, 1 corslet, £4 13s.4d.

Henry James, A, 1 fardel with 6 doz. lbs. blue thread, 1 kip gold skins, 48s.4d.

97. 7 Mar. From the ship of John Cappe called *George Cobham*

Anthony Kele, A, 6 brls. oil, £4

John Kele, A, 1 last oil, 2 dry pipes with 10½ doz. sallets, 2 doz. steel bonnets, 7,000 balls, £26

John Fox, A, 5 brls. slip, 10s.

John van Rodenberch, A, 1 maund with 8 doz. painted cloths, 50s.

John Bungawe, A, 1 maund with 55 [*S* 255] doz. straw hats, £12 16s.8d.

John Salmer, H, 2 'bassherons' 1 frail 1 basket battery, £40

John Russynthorp, H, 1 fardel with 20 pcs. Hainault cont. 834 ells, 4 pcs. Flemish cont. 93 ells, 4½ pcs. fustian, £28 10s.

John Questynburgh, H, ½ pack Cologne thread, 1 pack with 32 pcs. broad busk, 31 pcs. narrow busk, £43 10s.

Goswyn Rodynkerk, H, 7 bales madder, 1 pack with 23 pcs. broad busk, 23 pcs. narrow busk, £40 16s. 8d.

Gerard van Grove, H, 1 pack Cologne thread, £13 6s.8d.

Hans Stut, H, 1 straw of wax weight 10 quintals

John van Armysbery, H, 3 bales madder, 1 pack Cologne thread, £19 6s.8d.

Arnold van Stalle, 5 bales madder, £10

Lambert Rotard, 6 bales 'mad' [*S omits*] steel, £36
John Greverod, H, 1 pack with 5 pcs. Hainault cont. 200 ells, 85 pcs.
hastrey cont. 2,670 ells, 21 pcs. broad busk, £86 10s.

98. 7 Mar. From the ship of Cornelius Nese called *Mathew* of
Middelburg
Lewis Fox, A, 1 brl. with 20 pairs wool-cards, 4 lbs. wire, 7 ells. Flemish
linen, 30s.

99. 19 Mar. From the ship of Coleyn Garry called *Mighell* of Rouen
John Kyng [*S* Ryng], A, 30 qrs. wheat, 12 qrs. pippins, 12 qrs. apples, 30
brls. walnuts, 12 wicker bottles, £15 13s.4d.
Said master, A, 1 ship's cable, 20s.

100. 19 Mar. From the ship of Robert Monk called *Mary* of London
John Kele, A, 3 brls. nails, 1 brl. oil, 1 basket 1 pipe with 6 C. lbs.
packthread, 7,000 balls, £12 6s.8d.
William Codde, A, 1 hhd. ½ brl. with 12 grs. leather girdles, 7 qrs.
pouches, 6½ [*S* 5½] doz. bags, 6½ grs. latten buckles, 1 grs. cruets, 3 grs.
small salt-cellars, 24 doz. copper gold, 8½ grs. hatbands, 3 grs. girdles
with aglets, 6 grs. dog-hooks, 3½ grs. [*S* 3 grs. 9 doz.] knives, £10
6s.8d.
Frank Savage, H, 1 pipe battery, £10

101. 19 Mar. From the ship of Peter Fernandus called *Maria de Lawe* of
Viana
Vasco Petrus [*S* Perus], A, 200 doz. cork, 100,000 oranges, 3 doz.
Portuguese skins, £45 6s.8d.
Alfonso Yanes, A, 700 lampreys, £11 13s.4d.

102. 19 Mar. From the ship of William White called *Christofer Howard*
of London.
John Kele, A, 1 pipe with 7 doz. archers' sallets, 2 doz. sallets, C. lbs.
flax, 3½ brls. nails, £17 10s.
William Codde, A, 1 hhd. with 24 cases with knives, 1 doz. mirrors, 7
grs. 1 doz. bag rings, 38 grs. 10 doz. knives, 9 grs. 3 doz. leather
girdles, £13 10s.
Peter Wolf, A, 1 brl. with 33 doz. bags, 5 doz. red lasch, 6 doz. pen
knives, 6 small shears, 6½ grs. hooks, 5 grs. 4 doz. knives, 2 sacks
hemp, £10 8s.4d.
William Grenewolt, H, 1 small bag. with 40 timbers lettice, £13 6s.8d.

103. 20 Mar. From the ship of Laurence Burdon called *Blithe* of
London
John Dancell, A, 1 small chest with 14½ doz. double caps, 16 doz. single
caps, 3 doz. [*S* red] leather skins, 6 mirrors, £9
John Welbek, A, 1 chest 1 fardel 3 brls. with 7 doz. 4 painted cloths, 43
doz. mirrors, 3 tables with images, 22 small coffers, 22 cases for
distaffs ('rokk'),[1] 3 doz. hatters' cards, 7 doz. pouches, 17 papers with

blue thread, 1 doz. wool-cards, 11 doz. basan [*S* 'besel'] leather, 3 doz. brushes, 4 doz. ink-horns, 1 tick, 1 case with 1 image of the Blessed Mary, 2 doz. mirrors, £15 16s.8d.

Armes Dassomvile, A, 1 brl. with 4 doz. 2 [*S* 2 doz. 4] cappers' shears, 4 doz. key-bands, 2 doz. coopers' irons,[2] 1,000 nails, 4 doz. pack-needles, 5 grs. buttons, 13 doz. knives, 2½ doz. daggers, 4 sallets, 6 habergeons, 10 grs. [*S* thread] laces, 10 lbs. raw thread, 1 coverlet, 500 teazles, 4 doz. forcers, £5 16s.8d.

Henry Frankenberch, A, 1 fardel with 13 pcs. buckram, 1 pc. coarse [*S* Holland] linen cloth cont. 20 ells, 12 [*S* 22] doz. mistletoe beads, £3 3s.4d.

[1] Rock: a distaff (*O.E.D.*).
[2] ? the mark or sign, made of iron, with which each cooper was bound, by ordinance, to mark all the barrels he made (C. Elkington, *The Coopers and their Craft* (1933), 18).

104. 20 Mar. From the ship of Cardynawte Avice called *Gylmet* of Rouen

Richard Fabyan, A, 8 qrs. wheat, 1 puncheon 1 hhd. with 18 doz. 11 pairs wool-cards, £6 10s.

105. 24 Mar. From the ship of Thomas Cotton called *Christofer* of London

Simon Johnson, A, 1 brl. kive eels, 20s.

106. 24 Mar. From the ship of William Philpott called *Clement* of London

William Grenewolt, H, 1 bag with 50 timbers lettice, 6 sacks hops, 10 lasts ashes, £35 13s.4d.

Lambert Rotard, H, 5 lasts ashes, £5

Peter Segir, A, 1 chest with ½ doz. St. Omer hats, 18 daggers, 13 doz. Brussels leather, 3 small coffers, 2 'karks' [*S* caskets], 53s.4d.

Armes Dassomwile, A, 1 pipe 1 brl. with 3,000 teazles, 2 pcs. Flemish linen cloth cont. 62 [*S* 42] ells, 6 caskets, 1 coarse harness, 2 sallets, 2 gorgets, 1 steel bonnet, 120 ells diaper, 12 skives teazles, £5 13s.4d.

107. 29 Mar. From the ship of Dewgo Vyncenty called *Saynt Saveour* of Viana

Gonsalvo Fernando, A, 70,000 [*S* 77,000] oranges, 165 doz. cork, 500 lampreys, 1 pipe train oil, 6 cases sugar, 5 doz. Portuguese skins, 4 sacks bays, 20 ends iron [*S* weight] 4 C. lbs., £59 8s.

108. 31 Mar. From the ship of John Pytman called *Gabriell* of St. Osyth

John Vandermaste, A, 1 hhd. with 38 doz. pins, 4½ grs. knives, 3 doz. pouches, £6 13s.4d.

109. 2 Apr. From the ship of Thomas Bett called *Kateryn Charles* of London[1]

Peter Dalgay, A, 6 pipes Toulouse woad, 4 bales 2 hhds. 1 coffer combs, 1 coffer with glass, £46 10s.

[1] See also below, **615**.

[m.5d.]

110. 2 Apr. From the ship of Thomas Andrew called *Thomas Fyncham* of London

Raymond Kery, A, 6 pipes Toulouse woad, £30

Peter Dalgay, A, 1 corf with combs, 50s.

111. 3 Apr. From the ship of John Heyns called *Mary Neewe Condy*

Francis Fornandus, A, 400 lampreys, 40 sacks litmus, 40 doz. cork, 3 [*S* 4] doz. Portuguese skins, 1 sack bays, 50 lbs. wax, £37 8s.4d.

Gonsalvus Rodrecus [*S* Roderigus], A, 300 lampreys, 10,000 oranges, 40 doz. cork, 6 doz. Portuguese skins, £14 6s.8d.

Andrew Alvolus, A, 40 doz. cork, 10,000 oranges, 5 doz. Portuguese skins, 350 [*S* 300] lampreys, £14 10s.

112. 3 Apr. From the ship of Fouse de Vase called *Porte de St. Mary*[1]

Fournant Deanus, A, 60,000 oranges, 400 lampreys, 6 pipes oil, 1 sort of figs and raisins, 6 sacks litmus, £44

[1] ? Puerto de Santa Maria, Cadiz prov., S.W. Spain.

113. 10 Apr. From the ship of Ferot de la Crosse called *Margret* of Réville ('Ryvell')

William Hamond, A, 20 millstones, 24 small millstones, £10

Said master, A, 4 doz. buckets, 3 doz. earthen chafing-dishes, 3s.4d

114. 14 Apr. From the ship of Lubert van Boke called *Mary* of the Steelyard

Lambert Rotard, H, 6 lasts ashes, £6

Henry Bevir, H, 11 lasts 11 brls. salt fish, 2 rolls cont. 2½ rolls Herford, £78

Henry Lathuson, H, 2 lasts loose stockfish, 1 pack with 10 C. ells soultwich, £35

Roger van Feld, H, 1 pack with 31 pcs. broad busk, 33 pcs. narrow [busk], £37 3s.4d.

James Frise, A, 2 hhds. with 10 doz. 5 gorgets, 4 doz. 9 gussets, 4 doz. 10 mail aprons, 1 [*S* mail] habergeon, 4 doz. sallets, 2 'yperling', £17 [*S* £16 18s.]

Peter Craye, A, 1 firkin green ginger weight 80 lbs., 3 firkins treacle weight 5 C. 14 lbs., 4 doz. 9 glass bottles, 1 pipe 1 brl. with 5 corslets, 11 breastplates, 11 brigandines, 15 pairs gussets, 2 habergeons, 3 gorgets, 1 pair mail sleeves, 1 mail hood ('capron'), 5 doz. splints, 1 mail brace, 1 pair gardbrace, 6 plates for horses' heads, 2 helmets, 4 sallets, 4 plate bevors, 6 sums nails, 2,400 buckles, 4 shoulder-plates, 4 arm plates, 2 leg-harness, 14 pairs old gloves, 1 doz. rests, 4 grs. buckles, 2½ grs. latten buckles [*S* bells], 2 grs. 'prage' knives, 8 doz. spurs, 2 doz. stirrups, 1 grs. wooden combs, 1½ grs. silver paper, 10 doz. girdles, 1,000 beads, 8 girdles, 30 doz. razors, 3 pcs. lawn, 1 doz. [*S* tabor] pipes, 1 grs. silver [*S* thread] laces, 1 habergeon, £28 3s.4d.

115. 14 Apr. From the ship of Cornelius Nese called *Mathew* of Middelburg

Said master, A, 2 pokes hops weight 7 C. 14 [*S* 7 C. 24] lbs., 40s.
James Frise, A, 1 basket with 9½ doz. 'yperling', 5 sacks hops, £10 3s.4d.
John Sewyk, H, 10 lasts ashes, £10

116. 14 Apr. From the ship of Peter Alfonso called *Sesio* of Portugal
Said master, A, 60,000 oranges, 10 cases sugar, 80 pcs. figs, 190 quarters
figs, 4 sacks bays, 800 lampreys, 18 doz. Portuguese skins, 48 doz.
cork [*S* 40 doz. cork, 8 doz. cork for slippers], 80 sacks 14 [*S* 4] small
sacks litmus, £134 6s.8d.

117. 14 Apr. From the ship of Anthony Brabander called *George* of
Middelburg
Henry Lathuson, H, 2 lasts 9 C. 1 qr. loose stockfish, 1 pack pickling
cont. 10 C. ells, £39
William Grenewolt, H, 20 lasts ashes, 2 lasts soap, £28
Gerard Lesbern, H, 1 last sturgeon in wide [brls.], £12
George Tak, H, 2 sacks hemp, 2 frails battery, £23
Tylman Barkys, H, 13 lasts ashes, £13
Lambert Rotard, H, 5 brls. steel, ½ last ashes, £30 10s.
Coryn Gisbright, A, 2 fardels 1 poke with 100 doz. split skins ('splitt')
for hats, 32 doz. double hats, 500 doz. children's hats, 30 lbs. thread
for hats, 200 ells coarse Holland, 100 doz. single hats, £7 13s.4d.
Edward Johnson, A, 1 hhd. 1 brl. with 32 doz. pins, 20 doz. spurs, 10
doz. pouches, ½ doz. latten rings, 6 doz. brigandine nails, 4 doz. bits, 4
bills, £7
John Monys, A, 1 chest 2 firkins with 6 doz. swords, 6 lbs. oil of
spikenard with 1,000 glasses [*S* 'tothem'], 16 daggers, 8½ grs. knives, 4
grs. girdles, 6 doz. daggers, 2 grs. single feathers, 3 doz. 4 double
feathers, 10 doz. gloves, 2½ grs. pouches, 21 [*S* 31] coarse mail sleeves,
7 mail flaps [*S* 'flappetts'], 13 coarse gorgets, 60 [*S* 4] lbs. bristles, 1
casket, £22

118. 14 Apr. From the ship of Peter Menger called *Petir* of Antwerp
Matthew Falk, A, 2½ doz. 'yperling', 5 brls. slip, 28s.4d.
James Frise, A, 7 sacks hops, £10 10s.
Edward Johnson, A, 17 brls. slip, 2 firkins filings, 36s.8d. [*S* 36s.]
Anthony Kele, A, 2 sacks hops, 1 sack flax, £4 10s.
John Evingar, A, 5 sacks hops, £7 10s.
Said master, A, 600 [*S* white] pavingstones, 20s.
John Giles, A, 100 bundles black paper, 58s.4d.

119. 14 Apr. From the ship of Cornelius Bremer called *Christofer* of
Arnemuiden
Said master, A, 1,500 pavingstones, 20s.
Lyon de Loo, A, 1 brl. with 40 purses, 40,000 pins, 23s.4d.
Gerard Lesbern, H, 4 sacks hops, £6

120. 14 Apr. From the ship of Peter Jacobisson called *Trego* of
Arnemuiden

John Petirson, A, 6 lasts salt fish, £24

John Claisson, A, 21 brls. salt fish, £7

James Frise, 2 baskets with 19 doz. 4 'yperling', 3 sacks hops, £11

Edward Johnson, A, 1 chest with 2½ doz. caskets, 1 doz. pot knives, 8 lbs. copper wire, 3½ grs. [*S* 3 grs. 1 doz.] gloves, 14 doz. [*S* 6 doz. 8] swords, 18 doz. latten girdles, 7 doz. iron rings, 10 doz. sheepskins, 12½ grs. knives, 3 grs. 8 doz. pouches, £16 20d.

Christofer Johnson, A, 18 brls. salmon, £12

Martin Baker, A, 1 maund with 12 doz. red skins, 100 coarse white skins, 3 remnants Brabant linen cloth cont. 36 ells, 1 windlass for a cross-bow, 8 pairs cords, 2 lbs. thread for cross-bows, 2 trusses for cross-bows, 56s.8d. [*S* 55s.]

John Evingar, A, 1 sack hops, 30s.

Albright Falland, H, 1 fardel with 100 timbers lettice, £33 6s.8d.

William Grenewolt, H, 22 lasts ashes, £22

Gerard Lesbern, H, 9 lasts 2 brls. ashes, £9 3s.4d.

Henry Lathuson, H, 3 lasts 5½ C. loose stockfish, £36

Matthew Hynkylman, H, 2 lasts 18 casks loose stockfish, £20

Tylman Barkys, H, 10 lasts ashes, £10

Hans Stut, H, 1 small fardel with 34 [*S* 24] timbers lettice, £11 6s.8d.

121. 18 Apr. From the ship of John Vanderwode called *Mary* of Malines ('Mallyng')

Griffyn van Rye, A, 1 brl. with 2 doz. painted cloths, 1 doz. mirrors, 2 doz. small coffers, 50s.

Bernard Harrysson, A, 1 brl. with 2 doz. hatters' cards, 9 latten chafing dishes, 1 basin, 1 ewer, 1 habergeon, ½ doz. candlesticks, 1½ doz. pouches, 8 brls. wine lees, 45s.

John Dancell, A, 2 chests with 2½ doz. single bonnets, 10 double bonnets, 9 doz. knives, 10 daggers, 10 doz. coloured skins, 2 complete harness, 2 head-plates for horses, 177 pcs. 18 rolls buckram, 9 small coffers with 4 doz. bonnets, £24 13s.4d.

Derik Oldekyrk, A, 1 chest 1 brl. with 13 [*S* 3] pcs. Brabant linen cloth cont. 353 ells, 3½ doz. gorgets, 5 doz. hatters' cards, 1 pc. raw Brabant cont. 30 ells, 34 pcs. buckram, 10 pcs. camlet, 12 pcs. Holland cont. 180 ells, £33 6s.8d. [*S* £33 8s.4d.]

Marcello Moris [*S* Mawrys], A, 3 pokes hops weight 10 C. 21 lbs., 1 brl. orchil, 1 brl. saltpetre weight 36 lbs., £4 15s.

William Grenewolt, H, 30½ lasts ashes, £30 10s.

122. 26 Apr. From the ship of Clays Thorn called *Julyan* of Arnemuiden

John Claysson, A, 8 lasts 11 brls. salt fish, 15 C. staplefish, £50 13s.4d.

James Harrisson, A, 1 brl. with 3½ doz. wool shuttles, 5 doz. linen shuttles, 16s.8d. [*S* 26s.8d.]

Arnold Howell, A, 1 sack flax, 30s.

Jose Swarfeld, A, 1 small brl. filings, 1 bag with 7½ doz. pins, 1 doz. pouches, 3 doz. candle-snuffers, 36s.8d.

Matthew Hynkylman, H, 3 M. loose stockfish, £30

William Grenewolt, H, 30 lasts ashes, £30
Stephen Bramshe, H, 1 last stockfish, 14 brls. salt fish, £14 13s.4d.

123. 28 Apr. From the ship of Henry Stork called *Kateryn* of Hamburg
Said master, H, 8 brls. salmon, 1 brl. salt fish, £5 13s.4d.
John Simondison, A, 2 brls. salt fish, 1 brl. salmon, 5 couples of ling [*S* fish] 26s.8d.

124. 13 May. From the ship of James Walterson [*S* Wilbordson] called *Jamys* of Arnemuiden
Walter Derikson, A, 1 great sack with 50 doz. split skins for hats, 50 doz. double hats, 100½ doz. single hats, 600 doz. hats for boys, 4 lbs. thread for hats, £6
Deryk Marcheson, A, 2 sacks with 100 doz. split skins for hats, 80 doz. single hats, 600 doz. children's [*S* boys'] hats, 8 [*S* 1] lbs. thread for hats, £5 8s.4d. [*S* £5 6s.8d.]
John Stawte, A, 1 poke with 12 doz. children's [*S* boys'] hats, 14 doz. double hats, 1 lb. thread for hats, 6s.8d.
James Harriesson, A, 3 brls. with 2 old feather-beds, 6 old pillows, 1 coverlet, 1 pair sheets, 1 remnant brown linen cloth cont. 33 ells, 40s.

[m.6]
125. 13 May. From the ship of Henry Kaster called *George* of Hamburg
Henry Lathuson, H, 11 lasts 3 brls. tar, 4 lasts 9 brls. pitch, 400 wainscots, 1½ lasts osmund, 12 vats copperas, 3 vats 2 packs flax, 5 sacks feathers, 7 weys 30 sheaves glass, 1 pack 'Niperfeld' linen cloth cont. 14 C. ells, 4 packs pickling cont. 4 M. 5 C. ells, 2 C. oars, £175 10s.
2½ straws of wax weight 6 quintals
Herman Plough, H, 1 straw of wax weight 12 quintals
Gerard Lesbern, H, 3 packs flax, £12
William Scapehuson, H, 1 straw of wax weight 10 quintals
Tylman van Howell, H, 3 lasts train oil in wide [brls.], £36
Albright Falland, H, 1 mease of copper cont. 1½ meases, £18
1 straw of wax weight 10 quintals
Hans Swalyngburgh, H, 1 pack with 12 C. [*S* ells] pickling, £12
Hans Culle, H, 4 packs flax, £16
2 straws of wax weight 21 quintals
Said master, H, 4 C. 3 qrs. wainscots, 4 lasts ashes, 1 last pitch, 11½ lasts tar, 2½ C. stockfish, 2 packs narrow linen cloth cont. 100 ells, 2 small fardels with 4 pcs. cont. 300 ells 'forlaken',[1] 2 pcs. coarse Holland cont. 30 ells, £34
2 small pcs. wax weight 1 quintal
Hans Stut, H, 1 mease of copper cont. 1½ meases, £18
2 straws of wax weight 16 quintals
Hans Hosterberche, H, 2 rolls Hannover linen cloth, 1 last pitch, £25

[1] Voorlaken, cloth made from the first crop of wool (*Smit, 1485–1585*, p. 1527).

126. 17 May. From the ship of Gaspar Boke called *Mary* of Hamburg

William Scaphuson, H, 1 straw of wax weight 10 quintals
Hillibrand van Vuno, H, 1 straw of wax weight 10 quintals
Tylman van Howell, H, 3 lasts train oil in wide brls., £36
  1 straw of wax weight 13 quintals
Hans Culle, H, 6 packs flax, 1 brl. 1 small basket with 51 timbers coarse
  grey, 50 timbers lettice, £53 8s.4d.
  5 straws of wax weight 55 quintals
Said master, H, 300 wainscots, 1 vat 2 packs flax, 100 small trays, ½ roll
  Hannover linen cloth, 2 pcs. narrow linen cloth cont. 50 ells, £26
  8s.4d.
  2 small pcs. wax weight 1 quintal
Gerard Lesbern, H, 3 packs flax, £12
Albright Falland, H, 2 meases of copper cont. 2½ meases, 2½ packs flax,
  £34
  1 straw of wax weight 12 quintals
Hans Swalyngburgh, H, 1 pack with 13 C. ells soultwich, 1 pack cont. 12
  C. ells pickling, £31 10s.
Hans Hosterberche, H, 3 packs [S lasts] loose stockfish, 2 weys 1 qr.
  glass, ½ roll Hannover [S Herford] linen cloth cont. 4 C. ells, £40
  6s.8d.
Henry Lathuson, H, 2 [S 12] vats 2 brls. copperas, 4 vats flax, 10½ lasts
  tar, 4 sacks feathers, 2½ lasts osmund, ½ C. oars, 3 packs pickling cont.
  33 C. ells, 1 pack 'Niperfeld' cont. 9 C. ells, 2 packs soultwich cont. 24
  C. ells, 1 pack with 8 C. ells soultwich and 4 C. ells Hannovers, 2
  packs pickling cont. 24 C. ells, 2½ rolls Hannovers cont. 9 C. ells, 1
  fardel with 3 C. ells Hannovers, £238 10s.4d.
  1 straw of wax weight 16 quintals
Matthew Hynkylman, H, 200 wainscots, 27 C. loose stockfish, 1 small
  roll Hannover linen cloth cont. 4 C. ells, 1 chest with 2 pcs. Hamburg
  linen cloth cont. 100 ells, £40
Herman Plough, H, 1 straw of wax weight 8 quintals
Tylman Barkys, H, 1 straw of wax weight 11 quintals
Eggard Meir, H, 3 packs flax, 1½ lasts osmund, 2½ packs with 22 C. [S
  ells] pickling, 100 ells 'ulsom',[1] ½ roll 'ulsom', 1 pack soultwich cont.
  10 C. ells, £60 6s.8d.
  ½ straw of wax weight 6 quintals
Hans Stut, H, 3 packs flax, 1 mease of copper cont. 1 [S 2] meases, £30
  5 straws of wax weight 53 quintals
George Tak, H, 3 lasts stockfish, 1 roll Hannovers, 1 pack soultwich
  cont. 8 C. ells, 200 ells 'lemagois',[2] 1 small [S fardel] with 2 C. ells
  soultwich, C. ells Hannovers, £63

[1] Ülzen, Hanover prov. N.W. Germany.
[2] ? Limoges, Haute-Vienne dep., France. Limoges when applied to textiles usually
indicates a type of embroidery, blue or same colour as ground. I am indebted for this
information to Mr. J. Nevinson.

127. 18 May. From the ship of Cornelius Frank called *Saresyn* of Sluis
Said master, A, 14 [S 4] pcs. resin, 2,000 Flanders' tiles,[1] 6 bundles rods,
56s.8d.

William Grenewolt, H, 7 lasts ashes, £7

[1] See above, **68** n.

128. 18 May. From the ship of Robert Monk called *Mary* of London
Gerard Skynner, A, 14 brls. salt fish, 8 brls. gull-fish, 5½ C. salt fish, £11
10s.

129. 21 May. From the ship of William Bircham called *Mari* of
Greenhithe
John Gerem, A, 1 maund with 1 doz. complete harness, 5 pairs brigandines, 1 doz. sallets, 1 doz. narrow splints, 4 pairs leg-harness, 4
leather coverings for sallets, £38

130. 21 May. From the ship of John Spryng [*S* Springham] called
Kateryn of London
Lewis Fondemars, A, 1 pipe with teazles, 23s.4d.
Gabriel Furnarius, A, 1 pipe grain of Spain weight 3 qrs., £4 5s.
John Welbek, A, 1 hhd. with 1 old pair brigandines, 1 pair mail sleeves,
5½ doz. leather of diverse colours, 4 painted cloths, 3 doz. brushes,
20s.

131. 23 May. From the ship of William Philpot called *Clement* of
London
John Elyot, A, 8 millstones, 12 panniers of glass, 2 mounts of plaster, 1
puncheon vine shoots ('vyn' graffes'),[1] 3 tin crosses, £18 16s.8d.

[1] The ash from burnt vine shoots was used to make a medical plaster (A. Evans (ed.),
Pegolotti (Francesco Balducci), *La Pratica della Mercatura* (Cambridge, Mass., 1936),
430).

132. 23 May. From the ship of Cornelius Jacobisson called *Mary* of
Faversham
Marcello Maurys, A, M. salt fish, £10

133. 24 May. From the ship of Roger Higgys called *Mary Elwyn* of
Plymouth[1]
Janynet Gascoigne, A, 4 pipes Toulouse woad, £20
Jordan Pictz, A, 22 pipes 14 sacks cont. 64 measures Toulouse woad,
£180

[1] See also below, **618**.

134. 28 May. From the ship of James Rattesburgh called *Burnet* of
London
John Kele, A, 6 brls. nails, 1 dry vat with 8 doz. archers' sallets, 5½ doz.
steel bonnets, 4 steel bonnets, 38 lbs. flax, £21 15s.
Peter Segir, A, 1 basket with 60 doz. straw hats, 8 doz. 6 St. Omer hats,
1 doz. swords, 5 [*S* 1] grs. spurs, £10
James Lode, A, 3 brls. salmon, 1 brl. salt fish, 46s.8d.
Tyse Selly, A, 1 pipe with 3 panes of shanks, 300 budge skins, 3 timbers
coarse mink, 300 shanks, 5 timbers lettice, 4 remnants Brabant linen

cloth cont. 110 ells, 3 doz. 2 papers of blue thread, 1 pc. bocasin, 16 pcs. buckram, 1 old feather-bed, 2 pairs sheets, £18

Matthew Hynkelman, H, 1 straw of wax weight 10 quintals

Frank Savage, H, 2 frails battery, £20

Matthew Bliterswyke, H, 1 fardel with 3 bales fustian, £40

John van Strawlyn, H, 1 small fardel with 9 clouts Cologne silk, £30

John Salmer, H, 1 basket 1 'bascheron' battery, £20

Gerard van Grove, H, 2 bales madder, £4

135. 30 May. From the ship of Robert Johnson called *John* of Yarmouth

Oliver Bonewik, A, 2 brls. herring seam, 1 sack hemp, 12 candlesticks, 1 full of kettles, 1 cupboard with 6 remnants Flemish linen cloth cont. 30 ells, 1 doz. cushion cloths, 2 doz. knives, £4 6s.8d.

136. 1 June. From the ship of William Surdyvale called *Christofer* of London

John Carbrowe, A, 1 last pitch and tar, 18 spears, 6 hammers, 5 staves, 43s.4d.

137. 2 June. From the ship of Cornelius Moch called *Barbara* of London

William Grenewolt, H, 12 lasts ashes, 6 sacks hops, 12 pipes oil, £69

Collard Carlys, A, 1 pipe with teazles, 10 pouches, 33s.4d.

138. 2 June. From the ship of Cornelius Johnson called *Christofer* of Bergen-op-Zoom

James Brokare, A, 1 sack flax, 1 sack hemp, 1 pipe with 5,000 balls, £5 10s.

John Giles, A, 1 small fardel with 10 [*S* 2] pcs. broad busk, 13 pcs. narrow busk cont. 898 ells, £12 13s.4d.

Peter Wolf, A, 2 sacks hemp, 1 corf 1 hhd. with 1 doz. red skins, 1,600 balls, £5

Cornelius Selander, A, 1 sack flax, 1 bag flax cont. C. lbs., 1,500 cruses, 2,000 paving-tiles, 3 brls. tar, £5 16s.8d.

Gerard Lesbern, H, 2 bales madder, 2 sacks hops, £7

Arnold van Stalle, H, ½ last cork, 1 basket with 1 roll Herford linen cloth, £14

John Sewyk, H, 13 brls. tar, 23s.4d.

139. 2 June. From the ship of Robert Bigg called *Valentyn* of London

John Bungowe, A, 1 pipe 2 hhds. 1 sack with 6 complete harness, 18 pairs leg-harness, 10 pairs vambrace, ½ doz. sallets, 3 mail faulds, 1 pair gauntlets, 8 pairs brigandines, 1 bevor, 7 doz. pairs 4 pcs. flanchards, 5 doz. mail faulds, 10 doz. 7 [*S* pcs.] mail gorgets, ½ doz. mail sleeves, 6 doz. straw hats, 2 brls. wine lees, ½ doz. swords, 2 candlesticks, 7 chafing-dishes, 1 staff, £41 15s.

Peter Wolf, A, 1 brl. with 19 doz. 3 pairs knives, 19 doz. small bags, 6 doz. red skins, 1 grs. spectacles, 6 doz. spurs, 1,000 awl blades, 45s.

Anthony Kele, A, 4 sacks hemp, £6

John Kele, A, 5 sacks hops, £7 10s.

[m.6d.]

Edward Johnson, A, 1 chest 1 basket with 3 doz. daggers, 300 hafts, 8 doz. compasses, 100 pipes for candles [*S* candlesticks], 6 doz. small pouches, 6 doz. candle snuffers, 3 doz. mirrors, 7 grs. bells, 200 crosses, 10 doz. latten signets, 3 grs. wooden beads, 3,000 small beads, 3 grs. locks, 2 grs. razors, 15 doz. red lasch, 2 grs. flax brushes, 1,200 white sheepskins, 2 doz. lbs. thread, 8 brls. wine lees, £10 10s.

Laurence Tyman, A, 1 sack hemp, 1 basket 1 hhd. with 28 doz. caddis webs, 1 grs. worsted laces, 4 doz. needles, 2 grs. graters, 4½ doz. daggers, 5 doz. knives, 9 doz. pouches, 20 marks of shears, 24 doz. pins, 5½ doz. black rings, 1 doz. black leather, 1½ grs. compasses, 1 doz. red hides, 14 doz. black and red leather [*S* hides], £9 16s.8d.

Peter Segir, A, 1 basket with 80 doz. straw hats, 2 doz. swords, £5

John Cabare, A, 1 hhd. with 2 complete harness, 5 pairs leg-harness, 5 pairs brigandines, 6 sallets, 4 vambrace, 4 flanchards, 2 falls, 18 pairs [*S* plate] stirrups, 1 steel skull, 1 gorget, 15 swords, £10 16s.8d.

Lewis Aufan, A, 1 brl. with 17 mirrors, 4 lbs. thread, 6 small books, 2,000 bone beads, 1 small box, 1 old feather-bed, 2 images, 12 lbs. pineapple kernels, 33s.4d.

Peter Actoris, A, 1 chest with 40 vols. diverse histories, £7 10s.

John van Andwarp, A, 1 chest with 2 old feather-beds, 13 cushion cloths, 4 bench-covers, 40s.

Peter Caffer, A, 1 brl. with 7 grs. Flanders lace, 2 coverlets of tapestry work, 1 remnant Holland cont. 12 ells, 2 remnants Brabant cont. 30 ells, 4 pillows, 5 C. lbs. iron, £5 16s.8d.

Peter Mathewson, A, 2 sacks hemp, £3

George Loys, A, 1 brl. with 400 budge skins, 400 shanks, 12 furs of wild cat, 200 goatskins, 1 pc. Brabant linen cloth cont. 24 ells, 2 cushions, £8

Stephen Bramsche, H, 2 rolls Herford, 2 bolts Osnabrück cont. 63 ells, £24 10s.

Arnold van Stalle, H, 3 rolls Herford linen cloth cont. 4 rolls, £48

Tylman van Howell, H, 1 straw of wax weight 10 quintals

Matthew Hynkelman, H, 1 brl. with 76 timbers coarse grey, £19
1 straw of wax weight 6 quintals

Anthony Odyndale, H, 1 brl. with 34 bundles caul silk, 1 bundle Cologne silk, £116 13s.4d.

Matthew Bliterwike, H, 3 bales fustian, £40

John Russynthorp, H, 14 brls. white and black plate, 1 brl. latten plate, £16

John van Strawlyn, H, 1 brl. with 21 clouts Cologne silk, £70

Frank Savage, H, 1 frail battery, £10

140. 2 June. From the ship of Cornelius van Stonebarowe called *Valantyn* [of] Bergen-op-Zoom

John Bargeman, A, 73 skives teazles, 36s.8d.

James Brokare, A, 1 sack flax, 1 sack hemp, £3

Andrew Petirson, A, 2,000 cruses, 1 pipe with 3,000 [*S* 4,000] balls, £5 5s.

John Giles, A, 2 sacks 2 pokes hops, £5

John Harrys, A, 2 baskets with 460 doz. straw hats, £11 10s.

John Malyns, A, 1 small chest 1 brl. with 9 grs. tucking hooks, 30 grs. thread laces, 3½ grs. girdle hooks, 4½ grs. hooks, 9 doz. hair laces, 2 doz. key-bands, ½ doz. small pouches, 25 grs. thread points, 18 pencases, 40 doz. shears, 6½ grs. wire girdles, 4 lbs. blue thread, 16 doz. knives, £3 16s.8d.

James Falk, A, 2 cases combs, 40s.

Arnold van Stalle, H, ½ last cork, 1 basket with 1 roll Herford [*S* Hannovers], £14

Gerard Lesbern, H, 2 bales madder, 2 sacks hops, £7

John Sewik, H, 13 brls. tar, 21s.8d.

141. 2 June. From the ship of John Brasse called *George* of Bergen-op-Zoom

Arnold van Stalle, H, 1 roll Osnabrück linen cloth, £12

Stephen Bramsche, H, 1 basket with 19 pcs. Holland cont. 450 ells and 22 [*S* ells], £12 [*S* £11 13s.4d.]

Matthew Bliterswyke, H, 2 bales madder, £4

Dorothea Selyk, A, 1 bag with 3 pcs. fustian, 2 pcs. buckram, 4 pcs. Bord Alexander, 4 pillows, 33s.4d.

John Claysson, A, 11 cradles of glass, 2 sacks hemp, £14

Andrew Petirson, A, 1,000 cruses, 30s.

Paul Housman, A, 1 dry vat with 1 feather-bed, 6 cushions, 2 pairs sheets, 1 couch-bed, 20s.

Peter Capper, A, 3 brls. cork, 20s.

John Verbrake, A, 11 lasts ashes, £11

142. 2 June. From the ship of Henry Wilburchen called *Mary* of Flushing

Said master, A, 3 lasts herring, 4 C. salt fish, £8

143. 2 June. From the ship of George Brasse called *Bere* of Bergen-op-Zoom

Gerard Lesbern, H, 2 sacks hops, £3

James Brokare, A, 1 basket with 22 doz. straw hats, 1 small brl. green ginger weight 60 lbs., 1 sack flax, £3 3s.4d.

John Cobare, A, 2 sacks hops, £3

Andrew Petirson, A, 2 baskets with 180 doz. straw hats, £4 16s.8d.

John Harrys, A, 2 baskets with 460 doz. straw hats, £11 10s.

James Falk, A, 1 basket with 4,000 balls, 40s.

John Verbrake, A, 4 brls. ashes, 1 maund with 26 frying-pans, 16s.8d.

144. 2 June. From the ship of Nicholas Jacobisson called *Mary Knyght* of Middelburg

John Bungowe, A, 35 brls. wine lees, £5 3s.4d.

Frank Justynyan and Augustine Justynyan, As, 18 bales woad, £12
Said master, A, 2 sacks hops, 2,000 paving-tiles, £4 6s.8d.
John Kele, A, 2 sacks hemp, £3
Peter Segir, A, ½ pack brushes, 1 corf with 30 doz. 'copyn' hats, 40s.
Peter Walkyn, A, 1 hhd. 1 fardel with 6 pcs. and remnants Brabant linen
cloth cont. 140 ells, 5 printed ('prentyd') books, 23 quires printed
('prented') [*S* painted] papers, 9 painted cloths, £6 6s.8d.

145. 8 June. From the ship of Masse Storey called *Blak Bark* of Ostend
Said master, A, 24 C. white herring, 20s.

146. 14 June. From the ship of Roger Bernard called *Mary* of London
Lewis van Demers, A, 51 skives teazles, 1 pipe with teazles, 56s.8d.
Bonyfas Sambre, A, 1 fardel with 3 furs of grey, 3 furs of miniver, 100 [*S*
tawed] lambskins, 150 budge shanks, 40 hare skins, 2 old furs of lamb,
£5 6s.8d.

147. 14 June. From the ship of Peter Jacobson called *Trego* of
Arnemuiden
Anthony Odindale, H, 1½ packs Cologne thread, £20
William Grewolt, H, 18½ C. salt staplefish, 8 brls. salt fish, £21 3s.4d.
Stephen Bramsh, H, 1 roll Herford linen cloth, £12
Lambert Rotard, H, 4 brls. steel, £24
Henry Bevir, H, 2½ rolls Herford, ½ roll Osnabrück, £36
Matthew Hynkylman, H, 1 maund with 1 roll Herford linen cloth, £12
William Scapehuson, H, 1 straw of wax weight 12 quintals
Tylman van Howell, H, 2 straws of wax weight 24 quintals
John Questynburgh, H, 8 bales madder, £16
John Salmer, H, 1 frail 1 'bassheron' 3 baskets battery, 1 small brl.
copper weight 4 C. 40 lbs., £54 6s.8d.
Gerard Lesbern, H, 2 vats woad, £13 6s.8d.
Matthew Bliterswyk, H, 5 bales madder, 4 sacks hemp, £16
Roger van Feld, H, 1 pack with 3 rolls 80 ells Herford, 4 C. ells
Osnabrück, 2 C. ells soultwich, £47 16s.8d.
John van Armysbery, H, 1 fardel with 2 bales fustian, £26 13s.4d.
Peter Syber, H, 2 fardels with 5 bales fustian, £66 13s.4d.
Ingilbright Sevenek, H, 1 pack Cologne thread, £13 6s.8d.
Arnold Johnson, A, 24 dog-stones, £6
William Danyell, A, 2 cupboards, 6s.8d.
Leonard Sowlyn, A, 5 brls. slip, 16s.8d.
James Falk, A, 1 hhd. 1 brl. with 12 grs. mistletoe [? beads], 4 grs.
imitation mistletoe [? beads], 4 sums card nails, 1½ grs. small pouches,
5 grs. purses, 5 sums lath-nails, 1 sum red nails, 8 clouts of awl blades,
6 clouts of pack-needles, 1½ grs. locks, 10 doz. [*S* imitation] mistletoe
[? beads], £5 6s.8d.
William Codde, A, 1 hhd. 1 basket with 1 doz. copper crosses, 8 doz.
small tin bottles, 6 grs. leather girdles, 4 grs. 3½ doz. pouches, 5 doz.
red skins [*S* leather], 4 grs. 1 doz. knives, 3 doz. latten rings, 6 doz.
iron rings, 7 doz. writing tables, 5½ grs. latten girdles, 4 grs. Jews'

harps ('Jue harpes'), 2 doz. [*S* latten] squirts, 12 lbs. stable brushes, 2½ grs. bead-stones, 4,000 glass beads, £13 13s.4d.

Edward Johnson, A, ½ brl. filings, 14 small dog-stones, 2½ lasts mustard querns, 1 hhd. with 22 pot knives, 3 doz. coffers, 6½ grs. 2 doz. knives, 4 doz. sheepskins, 9 doz. spurs, 6,000 latten nails, 1 grs. small pouches, 1 grs. gloves, 3½ grs. pouches, 5 [*S* 6] doz. rings, £13 16s.8d.

Peter Segir, A, 1 brl. filings, 1 chest with 4 doz. 8 caskets, 15 doz. basan skins [*S* leather], 3 doz. hatters' cards, £6

Lewis van Demers, A, 1 pipe with teazles, 23s.4d.

John Kele, A, 3 pipes with 12,000 balls, 2 sacks flax, 2 sacks hops, 6 brls. nails, £28 10s.

Gerard Hegwold [*S* Hogwolt], A, 1 [*S* chest] with 1 doz. red skins, 5 timbers lettice, 1 painted cloth, 23 timbers grey, 1 bundle thread laces, 1 lb. ginger, £8 15s.

[m.7]

148. 14 June. From the ship of Giles van Gente called *Jamys* of Reimerswaal

Said master, A, 3,000 bricks, ½ C. white salt, £3 [*S* £4]

149. 14 June. From the ship of Henry Brete called *Clement* of Ostend

Baltasar Edgare [*S* Odgar], A, 22 C. salt staplefish, 2 M. herring, 10 [*S* salt] ling fish, £22 13s.4d.

150. 14 June. From the ship of Lubert van Boke called *Mary* of the Steelyard

Stephen Bramsche, H, 1 roll Herford linen cloth, £12

Lambert Rotard, H, 8½ brls. steel, £51

Hans Stut, H, 1 straw of wax weight 8 quintals

Matthew Hynkylman, H, 1 straw of wax weight 8 quintals

William Scapehuson, H, 2 guns, £4
    1 straw of wax weight 11 quintals

Albright Falland, H, 1 straw of wax weight 10 quintals

Tylman van Howell, H, 1 straw of wax weight 11 quintals

Tylman Barkys, H, 1 straw of wax weight 11 quintals

John Salmer, H, 1 'bascheron' [*S* 1] basket battery, £20

Roger van Feld, H, 1 pack Herford linen cloth cont. 3 rolls, 11 pcs. soultwich cont. 3 C. ells, £40 10s.

John Russyngthorp, H, 1 tun oil, £4

Henry Lathuson, H, 1 great brl. osmund, 10s.

Frank Savage, H, 1 frail battery, £10

Edward Johnson, A, 14 dog-stones, £3 10s.

Arnold Johnson, A, 24 dog-stones, £6

151. 14 June. From the ship of William Petyte called *Christofer* of Weymouth

Gerard van Grove, H, 4 bales fustian, 1 pack Cologne thread, £66 13s.4d.

John Stakylhuson, H, 1 dry vat with 22 clouts Cologne silk, 67 bundles caul silk [*S* silk for cauls], £296 13s.4d.

Anthony Odyndale, H, 1 pack Cologne thread, 1 brl. with 27 clouts Cologne silk, 44 bundles caul silk, £250

John Questynburgh, H, 1 pack Cologne thread, £13 6s.8d.

John van Armysbery, H, 4 fardels with 6 bales fustian, 2 packs Cologne thread, £106 13s.4d.

John Salmer, H, 1 'bascheron' 4 baskets battery, £50

Matthew Bliterswyk, H, 2 bales fustian, 1 sack hemp, £28 3s.4d.

Peter Syber, H, 4 fardels with 8 bales fustian, 1 pack Cologne thread, £120

Ingelbright Sevenyk, H, 2 packs Cologne thread, £26 13s.4d.

Lambert Rotard, H, 6½ brls. steel, £39

John van Strawlyn, H, 1 pack Cologne thread, £13 6s.8d.

152. 14 June. From the ship of John Goldesburgh called *John* of London

Derek Heer [*S* de Heyr], A, 2 vats with 7,000 teazles, 3 doz. caskets, 3 pcs. Holland cont. 46 [*S* 66] ells, 1½ doz. shirts, 13 doz. knives, 1 doz. daggers, 18 pouches, 2 table-cloths, 2 pairs cappers' shears, 3 [*S* 4] doz. 'dressyng' pins, 2 forcers, 3 doz. beads, 1½ doz. mirrors, ½ doz. small coffers, 18 doz. points, £5 3s.4d.

Frank Justynyan, A, 1 brl. Spanish grain weight 33 lbs., 33s.4d.

153. 14 June. From the ship of Robert Alcok called *Leonard* of London

James Bolle [*S* Falk], A, 1 hhd. 1 brl. with 12 doz. brushes, 6,000 glass beads, 4 doz. imitation mistletoe [? beads], 1½ grs. razors, 1 bag [*S* with] bells, 2 doz. needles, 1 grs. locks, 4 grs. spectacles, 3 doz. wooden beads, 44 doz. glass beads, £3 13s.4d.

154. 14 June. From the ship of John Wodeles called *Thomas Basset* of London

John Questynburgh, H, 1 fardel with 2 packs Cologne thread, £26 13s. [*S* and 4d.]

Gerard van Grove, H, 1 pack Cologne thread, £13 6s.8d.

John van Armysbery, H, 4 fardels with 6 bales fustian, 2 packs Cologne thread, £106 13s.4d.

John Salmer, H, 1 'bascheron' 1 frail 1 pipe 2 baskets battery, £50

Gerard Lesbern, H, 1 straw of wax weight 11 quintals

Peter Syber, H, 4 fardels with 8 [*S* 7] bales fustian, £106 13s.4d.

Ingelbright Sevenek, H, 2 packs Cologne thread, £26 13s.4d.

Lambert Rotard, H, 5 brls. and 6 half brls. steel, £48

John van Strawlyn, H, 1 pack Cologne thread, £13 6s.8d.

John Kele, A, 5 brls. nails, £10

155. 14 June. From the ship of Robert Johnson called *Martyn* of Middelburg

John Semoye, A, 1 dry vat with 12 pairs old sheets, C. lbs. flax, 7 [*S* diaper] table-cloths and towels, 1 quilt, 2 pillows, 1 feather-bed, 2 curtains, 43s.4d.

156. 14 June. From the galley of Bernard Bondymer[1] [of Venice]

Andrew Caruse 'q^d' (? quodam: for a certain)[2] Jane, A, 1 bag with 1 bushel sponges, 6s.8d.

Alesio Summa for George, A, 1 brl. soap, 13s.4d.

Alesio de Catero for Damyan [*S* crossbowman], A, 1 bag pepper weight 100 lbs., £4

Allegreto de Catero, crossbowman ('balastrer'), A, 1 chest soap weight 4 [*S* 3] C. lbs., 1 small chest soap weight C. lbs., 1 carpet, 53s.4d.

Andrew George Peron, 'iuratte',[3] A, 200 'trumpe'[4] glasses, 500 sponges, £3 6s.8d.

Beasio de Lago for Drago, A, 2 carpets, 1 brl. oil, 3 pcs. camlet, 2 brls. succade weight C. lbs., 150 'trumpe'[4] glasses, 2 chests soap weight 12 C. lbs., £15 15s.

Beasio Dulcimo [*S* de Dulcenio] for Nicholas, A, 1 chest soap weight 3½ C. lbs., 46s.8d.

'Comito'[5] [*S* of the galley], A, 1 chest with 150 lbs. stavesacre, 1 small bag coloquintida, 4 brls. succade weight 2 C. lbs., £6

Dominico de Bodna for Stephen, A, 60 pcs. soap weight C. lbs., 1 brl. soap, 1 bag setwall weight 12 lbs., 100 bocals, 40s.

Damyan Pastrovichio for Luke, A, 1 brl. soap, 1 bag with 50 pcs. soap, 2 carpets, 40s.

Damyan Pastrowichio for Ralph, crossbowman, A, 2 brls. oil, 12 carpets, £9 6s.8d.

Dymytrio de Sancto George for Novello, 1 chest soap weight 5 C. lbs., 1 brl. treacle weight ½ C. lbs., 120 'trumpe'[4] glasses, 5 standishes, £5

Francis de Catero, 'palomber',[6] A, 1 brl. oil, 13s.4d.

Francis de Meseo, gentleman, A, 4 pcs. camlet, 1 fardel silk ('seda') weight 30 lbs., 7 carpets, £18 13s.4d.

George Dantyvery for Nicholas, A, 1 brl. orpiment weight 2 C. lbs., 33s.4d.

George de Sancta Maria for Ralph, A, 3 carpets, 3 small cypress coffers, 28 standishes, 15 mazers, 473 bocals, 1 chest soap weight 6 C. lbs., 150 sponges, 1 brl. oil, £10

George de Camsa for Furio, 2 branches coral with 1 silver coral [*S* silver shell], 3 pairs small coral beads, 1 lb. latten thimbles, 1 great sack with sponges, 1 brl. oil, 5 carpets, 1 brl. succade weight 40 lbs., 2 chests pepper weight 1,000 lbs., 1 chest pepper weight 400 lbs., 1 fardel silk weight 16 lbs., £67

George Caruse, crossbowman, A, 1 chest soap weight 5 C. lbs., 1 chest pepper weight 100 [*S* 50] lbs., £5 6s.8d.

George de Sancto George for Nadale, A, 2 pcs. camlet, 4 carpets, 100 powder-boxes [*S* of painted wood], 1 bag pepper weight 240 lbs., 1 chest soap weight 6 C. lbs., £18

George de Scutery for Sancte, A, 1 bag with 100 sponges, 1 brl. treacle weight C. [*S* ½ C.] lbs., 1 chest soap weight 6 C. lbs., £5 5s.

George de Lago, 'previour'[7] [*S* 'purner'], A, 1 brl. oil, 170 bocals, 1 chest 1 great brl. soap weight 15 C. 1 qr. 12 lbs. [*S* and 1 great brl. soap weight 2½ C.], 1 brl. raisins of Corinth, 1 chest with glasses, 1 small chest with knives, £16

George de Catero for Dimitrio Penose, A, 1 chest soap weight 3 C. lbs., 2 bags frankincense weight C. lbs., 3 pcs. long [*S* camlet], 2 pcs. [*S* short coarse] camlet, £10

George de Jara [*S* for] crossbowman, A, 1 chest soap weight 6 C. lbs., 2 bags soap weight 2 C. lbs., 1 brl. succade weight C. lbs., £7

John de Bodna for Ralph, A, 2 apes, 40s.

John de Antivery for Pero, A, 1 brl. oil, 13s.4d.

John de Luderyn' for Dimitrio, 1 brl. treacle weight ½ [*S* 1] C. lbs., 18s.4d.

John Camsa, 'sotto',[8] A, 2 bales dates, 1 great chest with 4 C. lbs. dates, 3½ C. lbs. soap, 1 bag silk weight 25 lbs., £18 13s.4d.

Jeronimo de Poela for George, A, 1 brl. oil, 13s.4d.

John Sebemco, crossbowman, A, 20 bocals, 200 boxes citronade, 1 sack with 600 sponges, 1 brl. treacle weight ½ C. lbs., £3 16s.8d. [*S* £3 6s.8d.]

John de Asdryna for Stephen, A, 1 small bag glass beads cont. 500, 10s.

John Masarachio for Nicholas, A, 2 hens ('gallin'), 13s.4d.

John de Squetery, red ('rosso')[9] crossbowman, A, 1 chest soap weight 5 C. lbs., 1 bag pepper weight 12 lbs., £3 15s.

John de Monte Famul, 'comito',[5] A, 2 small brls. treacle weight 40 lbs., 13s.4d.

John de Bodna, gunner ('bombardere'), A, 1 [*S* great] brl. oil, 13s.4d.

John Bombarder, A, 1 chest with 11 pcs. camlet, 2 pcs. fine says, 10,000 needles, 1 pc. 'kateram' weight 3 lbs., 3 carpets, 17 [*S* 14] kips gold skins, £26 13s.4d. [*S* £23 13s.4d.]

Luke de Bodna for Ralph, A, 1 brl. oil, 1 chest soap weight 5 C. lbs., £4

Luke de Catero for Ralph, A, 3 chests 1 case soap weight 16 C. lbs., 12 carpets, 1 brl. green ginger weight 25 lbs., 5 pcs. camlet, 1 brl. succade weight C. lbs., 4 brls. raisins of Corinth, 1 brl. oil, 180 bocals, 20 nests of cypress coffers, 100 sponges, 100 'trumpe'[4] glasses, £34 10s.

Lazaro de Seta for Paul, A, 1 brl. oil, 1 brl. treacle weight ½ C. lbs., 1 bag. pepper weight [*S* 1½ C.], 60 bocals, 1 carpet, £8 10s.

Luke de Squetery for Paul, A, 1 brl. oil, 1 brl. succade weight 25 lbs., 1 fardel silk weight 12 lbs., £5

[m.7d.]

Leonard Purveour, A, 1 firkin raisins of Corinth, 10s.

Michael de Sancta Maria for Jane, A, 1 box with 50 pomanders, 31 [*S* 21] carpets, 2 brls. prunes, 1 great sack with sponges, 2 brls. [*S* 1 small brl.] prunes weight 1 qr., 1 chest pepper weight 500 lbs., 10 sugar-loaves weight 80 lbs., 1 doz. nuts, 60 standishes, 3 coffers, 30 pcs. 2 brls. soap, 100 boxes citronade, 1 chest soap weight 5 C. lbs., £45 7s.6d.

Michael de Sancta Maria, 'palomber',[6] A, 1 brl. treacle weight C. lbs., 1 brl. oil, 1 great brl. soap weight (blank in MS), £3 13s.4d.

Michael Deantivery for Pero, A, 1 brl. oil, 1 brl. treacle weight 50 lbs., 200 sponges, 1 chest soap weight 5 C. lbs., £5 10s.

Maryn' de Sancto Georg' for Novello, A, 1 balet pepper weight 300 lbs., 150 bocals, 27 nuts, 2 [*S* 1] small pc. brazil weight 16 lbs., 100 'trumpe'[4] glasses, £15

Mononyn' de Candia, counsellor ('homine de consilio'),[10] A, 1 chest with glasses, 26s.8d.

Nicholas Maserachio for Ralph, A, 10 carpets, 1 chest pepper weight 250 lbs., [S drinking glasses], 7 pcs. camlet, 100 nuts, 4 boxes turbith weight 20 lbs., 3 boxes sarcocolla weight 30 lbs., 1 chest soap weight 4 C. lbs., 2 small barrels 1 bag orpiment weight 1½ C. lbs., 1 doz. files, ½ lb. coral, 60 copper rings with stones, 100 bocals, 3 brls. oil, £36

Nicholas Caruse for Jane [S James], A, 1 brl. oil, 13s.4d.

Nicholas de Squetery for Andrew, A, 2 chests with [S diverse] glasses, 150 lbs. pepper, £20

Nicholas de Crayna for George, A, 2 brls. oil, 1 brl. confections weight 75 lbs., 1 chest soap weight 2 C. lbs., £4 [S £3 18s.4d.]

Nadale de Sancto Georgio for Nadale, A, 5 carpets, £3 6s.8d.

Novello de Sancta Maria for Jane, A, 7 carpets, 1 brl. succade weight 25 lbs., 1 fardel silk weight 6 lbs., 1 chest pepper weight 400 lbs., £23

Nadale de Lago for Nicholas, A, 1 brl. oil, 13s.4d.

Nicholas Daldamo for Andrew, A, 1 fardel silk weight 6 lbs., 28 lbs. pepper, 1 brl. oil, £3 13s.4d.

Nadale Sosina for George, A, 1 brl. oil, 1 carpet, 1 sack with 300 sponges, 1 chest soap weight 4 C. lbs., £5

Nadale de Antyvery for Nicholas, A, 1 brl. oil, 13s.4d.

Nicholas Sosyna for Damyan, A, 60 'trumpe'[4] glasses, 1 bag with 13 nuts, 1 bag pepper weight 200 lbs., £8

Nicholas Caruse, crossbowman, A, 1 chest soap weight 6 C. lbs., 1 brl. oil, 1 bag pepper weight 250 lbs., 180 [S 80] bocals, £15

Novello Compano, A, 4 old gilt girdles, 1 chest soap weight 4½ C. lbs., 1 butt lemons, £5

Nicholas de George, crossbowman, A, 1 brl. succade weight C. lbs. [S ½ C.], 2 boxes turbith weight 4 lbs., 2 boxes aloes weight 4 lbs., 50s.

Novello de Sancta Maria for Dimitrio, A, 1 brl. soap, 2 fardels silk weight 40 lbs., £14

Novello de Antyvery for Ralph, A, 1 brl. oil, 42 [S C.] bocals, 1 bag pepper weight 250 lbs., 5 pcs. sendal, 6 carpets, 1 chest soap weight 5 C. lbs., 1 brl. succade weight C. lbs., £25

Nicholas Somma for Martin, A, 1 great brl. capers, 1 brl. oil, 1 brl. green ginger weight 40 lbs., 8 pcs. camlet, 1 fardel silk weight 20 lbs., 23 carpets, 1 ape, 100 sponges, 1 chest pepper weight 300 lbs., [S glasses and citronade], 1 brl. treacle weight [S 50 lbs.], 1 brl. orpiment weight 40 lbs., 1 brl. coloquintida weight 40 lbs., £48 [S £51]

Nicholas de Castello Novo for George, A, 1 bag soap weight 1 qr., 3s.4d.

Nicholas de Antivery for Pero, A, 1 brl. raisins of Corinth, 100 bocals, 50s.

Nicholas de Catero de la Porta, A, 1 small bale pepper, £25

Nicholas Maserachio, 'portulat',[11] A, 1 fardel silk weight 60 lbs., £20

Nicholas de Sancta Maria for Andrew, A, 1 fardel silk weight 12 lbs., 1 small brl. succade weight ½ C. lbs., 1 chest soap weight 3 C. lbs., £6 10s.

Novello de Lago for Drago, A, 1 bag soap weight ½ [S 1½] C. lbs., 20s.

Paul Lago for Nadale, A, 1 pc. camlet, 1 chest pepper weight 300 lbs., 1 chest soap weight 5 C. lbs., 100 bocals, £16 16s.8d.

Pero [*S* Peter] de Squtery for Sancte, A, 1 carpet, 1 brl. succade [*S* weight] 75 lbs., 1 brl. treacle weight [*S* 50] lbs., 1 brl. oil, 1 chest soap weight 6 C. lbs., £7 8s.4d.

Primo de Squtery for Andrew, A, 1 brl. succade weight 25 lbs., 8s.4d.

Pero de Sancte Leo Grobissa, A, 1 brl. raisins of Corinth, 1 brl. oil, 1 brl. treacle weight 60 lbs., 1 bag with 300 sponges, 1 chest soap weight 5 C. lbs., 18 standishes, £8 5s.

Pero [*S* de] Sosina for Novello Supissa, A, 2 brls. raisins of Corinth, £4

Pero de Bodna for Novello, A, 50 bocals, 1 chest prunes weight 5 C. lbs., 1 chest pepper weight 450 lbs., 2 [*S* 1] hhd. prunes, £26

Ralph de Sancto Nicholo, crossbowman of the galley of George,[12] A, 1 brl. prunes, 1 small brl. succade weight 25 lbs., 1 chest with 1 bag silk weight 7 lbs., 1 box coral weight 6 ozs., 2 lbs. ribbons, 3 carpets, 7 standishes, 3 C. lbs. soap, 2 carpets, £10 13s.4d.

Ralph de Sancto George for Mark, A, 1 brl. treacle weight $\frac{1}{2}$C. lbs., 16s.8d.

Ralph de Monte Pusillo for Jane, A, 2 carpets, 20 standishes, $\frac{1}{2}$C. apples, 1 brl. oil, 1 small chest with shears and beads, 1 chest soap weight $4\frac{1}{2}$ C., £6 11s.8d.

Ralph de Sosina for Nicholas, A, 1 brl. oil, 1 brl. treacle weight 20 lbs., 20s.

Ralph Pastrowichio for Pero, A, 1 brl. oil, 13s.4d.

Ralph Caruse for Jane [*S* James], A, 1 brl. oil, 13s.4d.

Ralph de Bodna for Michael, A, 1 brl. oil, 1 brl. treacle weight 25 lbs., 21s.8d.

Ralph de Sancto Nicholo for Nicholas, A, 1 small chest prunes weight 2 C. lbs. 1 qr., 36s.8d.

Ralph Campano for Pero, A, 310 bocals, 30s.

Ralph Patrovichio for George, A, 1 brl. soap, 13s.4d.

Stephen Caruse for Jane, A, 80 copper rings with stones, 12 carpets, 100 'trumpe' glasses,[4] 1 lb. coral, 1 great grs. thimbles, 4 boxes turbith weight 17 lbs., 4,000 brigandine nails, 6 doz. files, 100 nuts, 1 qr. enamel, £18 16s.8d.

Stephen de Lago for Michael, A, 5 long pcs. camlet, 5 carpets, 2 brls. oil, 1 small sack with 100 sponges, 1 brl. succade weight $\frac{1}{2}$ C. lbs., 1 ape, 130 bocals, 2 chests pepper weight 600 lbs., 1 chest soap weight $4\frac{1}{2}$ [*S* 6] C. lbs., £44 13s.4d.

Stephen de Sancto Nicholo for Damyan, A, 1 bag with 1 mark of shears, 1 brl. with glass beads and shears, 1 bag soap weight 3 qrs., 5 glass pots, 1 griffin's egg ('grypes hegg'),[13] £3

Stephen Cateryn', A, 1 cloth sack with 40 carpets, 17 pcs. camlet, £43 13s.4d.

Stayo de [*S* Monte] Nigro for Damyan, A, 1 brl. treacle weight C. lbs., 33s.4d.

Sancto Malapero, gentleman, A, 6 carpets, 1 chest with 19 pcs. camlet, £23

Trevaso de Luderyn' for 'producuno' [*S* dicuno], A, 2 brls. soap,

26s.8d.

Angelo de Nicholo, purser ('skryven'),[14] A, 1 butt 21 bales dates, £30 13s.4d.

Nicholas de Angelo, assistant purser ('skryvenelle'),[15] A, 3 chests with glasses, 11½ brls. enamel weight 2 C. 30 lbs., 1 small fardel silk, £50

Nicholas de Sosina for Damyan, A, 1 fardel with 12 lbs. [S silk], 10 lbs. cloves, 1 carpet, £5 6s.8d.

Allegreto de Jara, A, 1 fardel with 7 [S 11] long pcs. 1 remnant camlet, £14

Ralph de Sancto Georgio for George, A, 2 sacks with 200 sponges, 120 bocals, 340 'trumpe'[4] glasses, 1 brl. succade weight 25 lbs., 1 bag pepper weight 325 lbs., 2 chests soap weight 9 C. lbs., £23

Nicholas de Sosina for Damyan, A, 1 carpet, 6s.8d.

Peter Pastrovichio for Nadale, A, 300 [S 450] bocals, 1 chest pepper weight 400 lbs., £17 15s.

Said patron[16] [S Bernard Bondemer, patron of the galley], A, 4 bales pepper [S weight 120 lbs.], 3 brls. cloves, 2 cases cinnamon [S weight 32⅓ lbs.], 34 cases soap [S weight 45 lbs.], £267

Nicholas Dedo, A, 1 brl. frankincense, 4 balets brazil, 1 chest with 20 [S 10] pcs. camlet, 1 pc. black satin, 1 pc. green satin [S 1 pc. satin cont. 22 yds., 1 pc. old satin cont. 18 yds.], 2 pcs. narrow says, 4 pomanders, £70

Francis Nave [S Novo], A, 4 small cases soap weight 8 C. lbs., £5 6s.8d.

Damyan de Catero for Novello, A, C. 90 bowstaves, 1 chest 1 bag pepper weight 450 lbs., £20

Maryn' Monsenego, A, 1 remnant cloth of gold cont. 10 yds., 3 bales ginger, 1 brl. nutmegs, 67 bales pepper, 7 brls. cloves, 5 cases cinnamon, 2 brls. mace, 1 bale sanders, 1 bale carpets [S cont. 31], £2,425

Laurence Lorydan', A, 1 fardel with 16 [S 6] carpets, £10 13s.4d.

Alewiso Conteryn', A, 2 cases cinnamon, 19 [S 9] bales pepper, 6 brls. cloves, 2 bales brazil, 3 bales silk, 1 chest with 21 pcs. long camlet, 1 case with 26 doz. Cyprus kerchiefs, £920

Jeronimo Teople [S Typolo], A, 1 box borax weight 8 lbs., 1 case powdered sugar, 28 cases Messina sugar, 1 brl. mace, 6 brls. green ginger, 4 bales silk weight 300 lbs., £218

Damyan de Nigron', A, 1 bale pepper, £30

Anthony Bavaryn', A, 5 bales silk weight 300 lbs., 1 bale indigo [S cont. 80 lbs.] 2 bales brazil weight M. 50 lbs., 34 butts raisins of Corinth, 1 brl. mace, 8 [S 7½] bales pepper, ½ bale cloves, 1 case cinnamon, 5 M. 8 C. 56 bowstaves, £812

Benedict Bonvise, A, 2 brls. oil, 2 brls. 3 qrs. 1 butt [S ¼ butt] raisins of Corinth, 4 cases soap, 1 fardel silk weight 25 lbs., 1 brl. with 19 kips gold skins, £31 6s.8d.

Stephen Fesaunt, A, 1 bale silk weight 25 lbs., £8 6s.8d.

George Trevesan, A, 1 [S case] cassia fistula weight 147 [S 127] lbs., 1 case euphorbium weight 2 C. lbs., 3 bales silk weight 150 lbs., £54

John de Barde, A, 1 fardel with books, 20s.

Cosma Spenell', A, 9 bales Moorish wax weight 34 C. lbs., £68

50

John Ambros de Nygron', A, 2 bales silk weight 100 lbs., £33 6s.8d.

Nicholas Lomelyn', A, 29 bales almonds weight 3 M. 8 C. lbs., £43 10s. (£29 *del.*)

John Andrew Sene, A, 17 [*S* 7] cases soap, £28 6s.8d.

Paul Fustaryno, A, 60 carpets, £40

[1] The 1480 fleet of three Venetian state galleys, including that of Bernard Bondymer, had entered Southampton on 12 February 1481. After staying there for more than three months Bondymer's galley left for London and the other two for Flanders (*The Port Books of Southampton for the Reign of Edward IV, 1469–1481*, eds. D. B. Quinn and A. A. Ruddock (Southampton, 1937–8), II, xxix).

[2] Hereafter calendared simply as 'for'. It seems probable that this and subsequent entries indicate that Italian merchants were handling merchandise on behalf of certain members of the crew or other merchants.

[3] ? The 'padrone giurato' who was in command of the personnel on board the galley between the bow and the mainmast (C. Manfroni, 'Cenni Sugli Ordinamenti Delle Marine Italiane Del Medio Evo', *Rivista Marittima* (Rome, 1898) 473, 485). Cf. 'Tamiso Peron Jurato' of the galley of Baley Trevisan at Southampton in 1481 (*The Port Books of Southampton for the Reign of Edward IV*, op. cit. 193).

[4] ? Flared or trumpet-shaped glasses, a common shape for Venetian goblets.

[5] The mate who was in command of the personnel on board between the stern and the mainmast (C. Manfroni, loc. cit.).

[6] Palombaro: a sailor charged with mooring the galley and keeping watch on the mooring rope (A. Jal, *Glossaire nautique* (Paris, 1848), 1119).

[7] ? Prodiere (Venetian 'proviere'): an oarsman who rowed and steered at the bow (G. Bertoni, *Dizionario di Marina Medievale e Moderno* (Rome, 1937), 686–7).

[8] Probably for 'sotto comito' the second mate (Jal, op. cit., 1370).

[9] 'Rosso' was a term used to describe a soldier of the free corps, each of whom wore a red cape or surcoat (A. Guglielmotti, *Vocabolario Marino e Militare* (Rome, 1889), 1523).

[10] Each galley had a counsellor, an experienced man who, subject to the authority of the captain or patron, gave orders regarding matters of navigation and kept the charts and portolanos (Manfroni, loc. cit.; Jal, op. cit. 503).

[11] Portolato: an oarsman who set the stroke for the others; also, a stern oarsman (Jal, op. cit., 1208; M. E. Mallett, *The Florentine Galleys in the Fifteenth Century* (Oxford, 1967), 202).

[12] The galley of Alowisus George, patron, which had reached Southampton in company with that of Bernard Bondemer (*The Port Books of Southampton for the Reign of Edward IV*, op. cit. xxix).

[13] The egg of the Griffin or vulture, also a cup or vessel made of a similar (? ostrich) egg (*Middle English Dictionary*).

[14] The purser was a quasi-public official who paid the crew and also kept accounts of all merchandise loaded and unloaded (Manfroni, loc. cit.).

[15] The assistant purser kept account of the amount spent on food on the galley (ibid. 487).

[16] The commander of galley. Each galley was leased by the senate to the nobleman who was the highest bidder, provided that the latter was a capable person of proper age and with reliable financial backers. The patron had to recruit and pay the necessary officers and crew and follow the senate's instructions for the voyage. He received payments from the merchants for their board and freight charges on goods exported and imported and also traded on his own account (ibid. 472–3, 484; F. C. Lane, *Venice and History* (Baltimore, 1966), 45–52).

[m.8]

157. 22 June. From the ship of Thomas Cotton called *Christofer* of London

Joys van Aysshe, A, 3 pipes 1 hhd. with 5 pcs. 4 rolls buckram, 4 pcs. treillis, 2 pcs. Flemish linen cloth cont. 80 ells Flemish, 9 pcs. and remnants coarse Holland cont. 129 ells, 1 doz. weavers' spools, 12 doz. spectacles, 12,000 card heads, 18 pairs wool-cards, 6 caps, £12

158. 2 July. From the ship of Donas Petirson called *Petir* of Ostend
Said master, A, 16 C. salt staplefish, £16

159. 5 July. From the ship of Anthony Brabander called *George* of Middelburg
James Falk, A, 1 hhd. 1 brl. with 3,500 [*S* 2,500] balls, 20 sums patten-nails, 48s.4d.
Anthony de la Hay, A, 2 sacks hops, 1 hhd. with 8 doz. 2 'Falland' flanchards, 8 doz. 2 gorgets, £7 3s.4d.
Henry Holander, A, 1 sack 1 basket with 10 doz. knives, 6 doz. shears, 6 doz. spectacles, 6 doz. spectacle-cases, 2 kettles, 2 brass pots, 3 candlesticks, 1 remnant coarse canvas cont. 8 ells, 26s.8d.
Anthony Kele, A, 1 brl. nails, 40s.
Henry Williams, A, 1 bag with 4 remnants coarse Holland cont. 40 ells, 2 pcs. Holland cont. 60 ells, 43s.4d.
Bartholomew Spilman, A, 2 sacks hemp, 1 maund with 10 C. lbs. packthread, 20 quilts, 2 doz. tapestries, £18 6s.8d.
Henry Bevir, H, 2 rolls Herford linen cloth, £24
Herman Swarte, H, 13 cases glass, £13
Albright Falland, H, 1 straw of wax weight 10 quintals
Gerard Lesbern, H, 1 straw of wax weight 8 quintals
Tylman van Howell, H, 1 straw of wax weight 10 quintals
William Scapehuson, H, 2 packs candle-wick, £8
    1 straw of wax weight 10 quintals
John Salmer, H, 1 'bassheron' 1 basket 1 small 'cropp' of battery, £23
Lambert Rotard, H, 5½ brls. steel, £33
John Greverod, H, 6½ brls. [*S* steel], 1 brl. 1 bale 1 basket 1 bag with 68 pcs. Constance ('custans') buckram,[1] 3 doz. pcs. cottons, 2 pcs. imitation Paris [? cloth], 60 pcs. buckram, 11 pcs. broad busk, 4 pillows, £57 6s.8d.
Hans Stut, H, 1 straw of wax weight 8 quintals

[1] The region to the north of Lake Constance was important for the production of linen cloth.

160. 5 July. From the ship of Copyn Andrewson called *Fastelaven* of Flushing
Said master, A, 3 M. salt staplefish, £30
Peter Andrewson, A, 2 M. salt staplefish, £20
Bartholomew Johnson, A, 1 pipe with dry haddock, 6s.8d.

161. 5 July. From the ship of Dennis Mathew called *Mawdelyn* of Bergen-op-Zoom
William Grenewolt, H, 3 small fardels with 50 timbers lettice, 1 timber 30 skins mink, 2 furs of leopard wombs, £19 6s.8d.
Anthony de La Hay, A, 1 brl. with 4 doz. 4 mail flanchards, 2 gorgets,

£3 10s.

162. 5 July. From the ship of Lambert Williambrodson called *Christofer* of Flushing
Peter Person, A, 2 M. salt staplefish, £20
Bartholomew Johnson, A, 2 M. salt staplefish, £20
Nicholas Angelo, A, 1 chest with 8 small brls. enamel weight 2 C. lbs., 20 crystal drinking glasses, 500 glass beads, £8

163. 5 July. From the ship of Edmund Johnson called *Jamys* of Flushing
Coppyn Passe, A, 18 C. salt staplefish, 1 qr. dry coal-fish, 100 drinking pots, 100 earthen crocks, 4 C. lbs. resin, £18 13s.4d.
Cornelius Bussher, A, 1 quartern white salt, 48 bundles flax, 10 pillows, 100 earthen crocks, 56s.8d.

164. 16 July. From a certain boat coming from Rochester
John Skrynket, A, 55 bundles rods of osier, 6s.8d.

165. 16 July. From the ship of Cornelius Nese called *Christofer* of Middelburg
William Standfast, A, 1 last train oil in narrow brls., £8
Lambert Jacobson, A, 1 dry brl. with 3 pcs. Brabant linen cloth cont. 72 ells, 1 pc. Holland cont. 24 ells, 46s.8d.
Said master, A, 4½ pokes flax, 46s.8d.
John Clays, A, 1 small corf with 1 doz. [*S* dagger] sheaths, 3 doz. 3 wooden combs, 2 doz. 3 girdles, 17 pairs wooden beads, 4 [*S* 3] latten girdles, 14 [*S* 13] small mirrors, 11 doz. leather and thread laces, 18 [*S* 17] doz. leather and thread points, 5 doz. long laces, 1 lb. brooches, 10 pinpillows, 2 purses, 6 coverings for distaffs, 2 doz. small knives, 6 small pouches, 6 spoons, 1 small chest, 13s.4d.
Said master, A, 1½ ton weight iron, 1 narrow brl. train oil, ½ last cork, 50 wainscots, 2 pokes hops, £8 10s. [*S* iron and train oil val. £3 10s., the rest £5]
William Bocher, A, 3 sacks 4 pokes hops, 1 brl. with 36 doz. pins, 1 doz. lbs. blue thread, 4 lbs. packthread, £12 3s.4d.

166. 18 July. From the ship of Robert Dearte called *Kateryn* of Dieppe
Nicholas de Sancto Mores, A, 40½ brls. ½ hhd. salmon, 17 pipes Gascon, Rochelle, French and Portuguese woad of Caen,[1] 18 scarlet bonnets, 2 grs. knives, 2 doz. gloves, 2 pipes 1 small case glass, 2 small fardels with 2 pcs. canvas cont. 40 ells, 4 small pcs. strait linen cloth cont. 40 ells, [*S* 1 pc.] diaper towelling, £55 6s.8d.

[1] Woad was associated with Caen in the later fifteenth century as it was frequently shipped there for England: cf. *Overseas Trade of Bristol*, 274, 286.

167. 21 July. From the ship of Christian Coffyn called *Blak Barge* of Ostend

Said master, A, C. salt fish, 20s.

168. 21 July. From the ship of Hans Hagen called *Christofer* of Hamburg

Peter Ecksted, H, 4½ packs flax, £8

2 straws of wax weight 20 quintals

Herman Plough, H, 2 straws of wax weight 21 quintals

Hans Hosterberch, H, 22 C. loose stockfish, 1 vat with saltpetre weight 14 C. lbs., 2 rolls Hannover linen cloth cont. 3 rolls, £84

Gerard Lesbern, H, 1 pack candle-wick [*S* val. £4], 8 weys 21 sheaves glass, 1 pack soultwich cont. 14 C. ells, 1 pack pickling cont. 10 C. ells, [*S* 1 pack 'Niperfeld' cont. 6 C. ells], £50

Matthew Hynkylman, H, 3 M. loose stockfish, £30

1 straw of wax weight 10 quintals

Lambert Rotard,[1] H, 3 packs flax, 1½ lasts osmund, 1 vat 1 mease copper cont. 2 meases, 1 great C. clapholt, 2 lasts pitch, £47

1 straw of wax weight 11 quintals

Hans Stut, H, 2 straws of wax weight 18 quintals

William Scapehuson, H, 3 packs candle-wick, 1 pack with 4 C. stockfish, 6 C. lbs. yarn, £23

Henry Luthuson, H, 650 wainscots, 12 vats 13 brls. copperas, 1 vat saltpetre weight 12 C. lbs., 9 sacks feathers, 3 brls. sturgeon, 16½ weys glass, 7 packs pickling cont. 7 M. 3 C. ells, 5 packs 7 pcs. soultwich cont. 5 M. ells, 1 pack 'Niperfeld' cont. 6 [*S* 7] C. ells, 3½ rolls Hannovers, 1 vat with 145 timbers coarse grey, 50 lbs. brown thread, 1 pack cont. 2 C. ells pickling, 10 C. ells soultwich, £335 8s.4d. [*S* £318 8s.4d. to 'grey', remainder £17]

Said master, H, 2 brls. sturgeon, 2 packs soultwich cont. 14 C. ells, 6 pcs. pickling cloth cont. 2 C. ells, £25

Hans Cull, H, 4 straws of wax weight 44 quintals

George Tak, H, 2½ lasts loose stockfish, 1½ rolls Hannovers, 1 fardel with 2 C. ells Osnabrück linen cloth, £47

[1] *S* puts this entry under **170**, ship of Hans Rutyng.

169. 21 July. From the ship of Clays Bartoles called *George* of Danzig

Herman Plough, H, 3 packs flax, 1 pack flax and candle-wick, 7 brls. tar, 7 brls. ashes, 2 lasts train oil in wide brls., 1 mease copper cont. 1½ meases, £59 3s.4d.

1 straw of wax weight 10½ quintals

James van Werd, H, 14 [*S* 4] brls. tar, 1½ packs flax, 1 mease copper [*S* plate] cont. 1½ meases, 1 small pack spruce canvas cont. 6 C. ells, £31 3s.4d.

1 straw of wax weight 12 quintals

Gerard Lesbern, H, 2 packs flax, 12 wide brls. train oil, 3 meases copper cont. 4 meases, £68

2 straws of wax weight 20 quintals

Peter Eksted, H, 2 packs flax, 100 wainscots, 1 great C. clapholt, 1 last train oil in wide brls., 1 last bowstaves, 7 brls. osmund, 1 pack spruce canvas cont. 13 C. ells, 1 small fardel with 6 timbers of ermines, 3 ropes amber, £63 6s.8d.

4 straws 5 pcs. wax weight 42 quintals

Roger van Feld, H, 6 packs flax, 2 lasts ashes, 10 wide brls. train oil, 10 brls. osmund, 1 nest of counters, £40 6s.8d.

4 straws of wax weight 36 quintals

Michael Gravelok, H, 4½ packs 1 qr. flax, 100 'borys'[1] flax, 14 nests of coffers, 2 nests [S of chests] with flax, 1 inkle chest,[2] 7 pullets, 4 lbs. amber, 6½ doz. playing-tables, 8 doz. red skins, 3 vats beer, 28 tuns rush oil, 9 brls. tar, 1 nest of counters, 1 shock of winnowing-fans ('wynnyng'), 2 shocks of soap boxes, 3 doz. boards for shoemakers, £46

1 brl. 1 pc. wax weight 6 quintals

Hans Molyner, H, 3½ packs flax, ½ last osmund, £10

1 straw of wax weight 10 quintals

Matthew Hynkilman, H, 45 pcs. broad copper, 86 pcs. split[3] copper cont. 4 meases, £36

I straw of wax weight 12 quintals

Lambert Rotard, H, 3 packs flax, 1 last osmund, 16½ wide brls. train oil, 1 last tar, 100 wainscots, £35 10s.

Herman Overcamp, H, 8½ packs flax and candle-wick, 14 brls. osmund, 2 wide brls. train oil, 14 brls. pitch, 14 brls. ashes, 6 C. bowstaves, 308 pcs. copper cont. 5 meases, £115

Hillibrand van Vuno, H, 14 brls. osmund, 2 lasts 4 brls. ashes, 2 meases copper cont. 3 meases, 3 packs flax, 14 brls. pitch, 2 packs spruce canvas cont. 16 C. ells, 25 bundles iron, £97 3s.4d.

2 straws of wax weight 18 quintals

Hans Stut, H, 6 packs flax, 2 lasts train oil in wide brls., 9 C. 24 bowstaves, 2 meases plate and split ('spliter')[3] copper cont. 2½ meases, 1 chest with 5 dickers spruce skins, 1 lb. amber, 6 bales flax, 1 counter, 1 vat beer, £99 10s.

6 straws of wax weight 60½ quintals

Hans Culle, H, 2 packs flax, 63 pcs. copper plate cont. 2 meases, £32

1 straw of wax weight 14 quintals

Henry Lathuson, H, 2 packs flax, ½ last osmund, 14 brls. ashes, £11 3s.4d.

Tylman Barkys, H, 1 mease copper plate cont. 1½ meases, 2 packs flax, 4 C [S 3 C.] 8 bowstaves, 1 fardel with 75 timbers lettice, £57

1 straw of wax weight 10 quintals

[m.8d.]

Nicholas Steyne, H, 3½ packs flax, 74 bales flax, 6 brls. pitch, 17 brls. tar, 1 nest [S counters], 4 inkle counters, 9 nests of coffers, 5 pullets, 3½ doz. playing-tables, 18 boards for shoemakers, 20 troughs ('trowes'), 7 shocks of soap boxes, 7 nests of chests, 4 inkle chests, 70 pepper querns, 15 shocks of trenchers, 12 bundles bast ropes, 4 red skins, 15 buck skins, 23 ells spruce linen cloth, 1 small bundle raw thread, 2 bundles candlewick, 1 small bundle sewing thread, 6 key-bands, 4 purses, 2 vats beer, 1 firkin spice-bread, 5 lbs. 4 ozs. amber, £46 13s.4d.

3 small pcs. wax weight 2 quintals

Said master, H, 3 packs flax, 1 last 4 brls. osmund, 2 lasts tar, 1 last
pitch, 100 clapholts, ½ mease copper, 8 bundles candle-wick, 2 pcs.
pickling cont. 1½ C. ells, 1 chest with 4 timbers squirrel, £29 13s.4d.
1 straw 2 pcs. wax weight 17 quintals

1. ? Bunches, cf. bos = bunch (Dutch).
2. Inkle, a linen tape or cloth, hence ? inkle chest, a linen chest.
3. Cf. 'coper spleten the barelle 23s.4d.' (Gras, 696).

170. 21 July. From the ship of Hans Rutyng called *Mighell* of Danzig

Herman Plough, H, 5 packs flax, 1 last train oil in wide brls., 19 brls.
osmund, 21 brls. tar, 3 meases copper cont. [S 4] meases, £88 20d.
2 pcs. wax weight ½ quintal

James van Werd, H, 1 pack flax, 1 mease copper plate cont. 2 meases,
£28
1 straw of wax weight 11 quintals

Gerard Lesbern, H, 2 packs flax and candle-wick, 2 lasts 4 brls. ashes, 3
meases copper, 20 pcs. copper plate cont. 4 meases, £58 6s.8d.
2 straws of wax weight 16 quintals

Peter Eksted, H, 4 packs flax, 21 brls. osmund, 22 brls. pitch, 1 dry brl.
with 50 timbers lettice, 56 timbers greywork, £60 6s.8d.
5 straws 6 pcs. wax weight 61 quintals

Roger van Feld, H, 5 [S 4] packs flax, 1 last osmund, 1 last pitch, 2 [S 3]
wide brls. train oil, 1 nest of counters, £29 [S £25]¹
4 straws 4 pcs. 2 chests wax weight 45 quintals

Hans Moliner, H, 1 pack flax, 9 brls. tar, 5 brls. osmund, £6 8s.4d.
3 straws of wax weight 32 quintals

Matthew Hynkelman, H, 90 pcs. copper plate [S cont. 3½ meases] 35
pcs. copper cont. 4½ meases [S 1 mease], 1 last osmund, 1 pack flax,
£62
1 straw of wax weight 11 quintals

Herman Overcamp, H, 5½ packs flax, 117 pcs. copper plate, 120 pcs.
copper cont. 7 meases, 14 brls. pitch, 6 lasts 5 brls. tar, 5 lasts 5 brls.
ashes, 14 brls. osmund, 60 bundles winnowing-fans, £118
5 pcs. wax weight 5 quintals

Tylman Barkys, H, 1 mease copper plate, 1 pack flax, 2 lasts 4 brls.
ashes, 1 brl. 1 fardel with 25 timbers grey, 3½ timbers beaver wombs, 1
timber mink, 56 timbers lettice, £50 6s.8d.
1 straw of wax weight 10 quintals

Hillibrand van Vuno, H, 14 brls. osmund, 4 packs flax, 4 lasts 8 brls.
pitch, 9 lasts 4 brls. ashes, 3 brls. 1 mease 15 pcs. loose copper cont. 3½
meases, 1 last train oil in wide brls., 1 pack spruce canvas cont. 10 C.
ells, £98 13s.4d.
2 straws of wax weight 18 quintals

Henry Lathuson, H, 1 pack flax, ½ last osmund, 14 brls. ashes, 30 pcs.
copper cont. ½ mease [S 'splytter'], £13 3s.4d.

Hans Stut, H, 3 packs flax and candle-wick, 2 lasts train oil in wide brls.,
6 C. 32 bowstaves, 14 brls. pitch, 12 brls. pot ashes, 3 meases copper
plate cont. 4 meases, 1 brl. beer, 1 dry brl. with 200 wooden mazers,
£100 (£89 15s. *del.*)

7 straws of wax weight 70 quintals

Said master, H, 300 wainscots, 2 great C. clapholt, 3 C. bowstaves, 1 nest counters, £19

George Moller, H, 7 packs flax, 2 lasts osmund, 3 meases copper cont. 4 meases, 3½ lasts pitch, 12 timbers lettice in 1 chest of Herman Over-camp, £91 10s.

1 small pc. wax weight ½ quintal

Hans Culle, H, 2 packs flax, 14 brls. pitch, 72 pcs. copper plate, cont. 3 meases, 1 dry vat with 150 timbers grey, 64½ timbers schönwerk ('skonewark'), 10 timbers lettice, 2 timbers 16 skins mink, £113

1 straw of wax weight 8 quintals

Luke Vynke, H, 23 chests 250 bales flax, 3½ packs flax, 6 nests of counters, 16 nests of coffers, 150 playing-tables, 50 boards for shoemakers, ½ shock 3 troughs, 8 shocks of soap boxes, 50 shocks of trenchers, 1 shock of cans, ½ last pitch, 4 brls. tar, 3 vats beer, 8 shocks of marline[2] ('merlyng'), 80 bundles winnowing-fans, 8 lutes, 1 shock of lutes for boys ('lutez pro pueris'), ½ shock [*S* ½ doz.] of blowers, 5 buck skins, 10 red skins, ½ shock of bast ropes, 1 lb. amber, 5 pullets, £46 3s.4d.

3 pcs. of wax weight 3 quintals

[1] *S* separate entry 'Roger van Feld, 1 pack flax, £4'.
[2] Cf. 'whipcorde the shock containing 60 bundles called merline the pound, 2d.' (Willan, *Rates*, 64).

171. 21 July. From the ship of Robert Johnson called *Mathew* of Middelburg

Said master, A, 1½ C. oars, £3

Peter Shipleger, A, 1 bag with 54 daggers, 33s.4d.

John Morse, A, 1 last ashes, 20s.

John Sontman, A, 1 poke hops, 20s.

Peter Eksted, H, 4 lasts pitch, 2 [*S* 2½] packs flax, £8

Roger van Feld, H, 6 lasts pitch, £6

172. 21 July. From the ship of Cornelius Johnson called *Christofer* of Bergen-op-Zoom

Cornelius Joosson, A, 2½ packs brushes, 1 pipe with 4,000 balls, 1 hhd. with 14 grs. glasses, 100 balls, 3½ doz. brushes, £4

Hugh Johnson, A, 1 sack hops, 1,500 pavingstones, 1 counter, 1 cup-board, ½ doz. [*S* small] presses, £3 10s.

173. 21 July. From the ship of John Bras called *George* of Bergen-op-Zoom

Matthew Falk, A, 3 brls. slip, 1 sack hops, 1,000 gunstones, 1 basket with 450 drinking glasses, 50s.

Adrian Johnson, A, 1 pipe with 8 pcs. Brabant linen cloth cont. 68 ells, 2 feather-beds, 20 lbs. hemp, 50s.

174. 21 July. From the ship of Robert Foster called *Volantyne* of London

Peter Actoris, A, 1 chest with 96 vols. diverse histories, £9

Edward Johnson, A, 1 hhd. with 6 doz. daggers, 6 pairs spurs, 8 doz.

gloves, 8½ grs. knives, 1 lb. copper wire, 1½ grs. 7 doz. pouches [*S* 1½ grs. 4 doz. pouches 2 grs. shoulder pouches], 6,000 latten nails, 22 pot knives, 2½ doz. caskets, 4½ doz. mirrors, 8 clouts of needles, 3 grs. razors, 8 dickers knives, 18 lbs. counters, 12 doz. locks, 2 doz. squirts, 8 doz. tables, 2 doz. brooch pins ('spang' tong'),[1] 6 doz. flax brushes, 400 mother of pearl crosses, 1 fardel with 24 red [*S* leather] skins, £15

Francis Mathewe, A, 1 roll with 2 doz. stained cloths, 28s.4d.

John Kele, A, 2 sacks hemp, £3

Cornelius Joosson, A, 1 chest with 14 grs. playing-cards, 1 painted cloth, £3

John Royear, A, 1 fardel with 2,400 Spanish budge, £24

Laurence Tyman, A, 1 basket 1 hhd. with 1 grs. bags, 8 lbs. wire thread, 2 pcs. tuke, 9 doz. bag rings, 3 grs. wire girdles, 3 doz. buckles, 2 grs. knives, 3 doz. daggers, 500 thimbles, 2 grs. pouches, 1½ doz. needles, 5 doz. coarse caddis, 5 grs. buckles, 7 doz. cards, 11 grs. girdles [with] aglets, 14 doz. pins, 8 grs. bells, 2 doz. red skins, 1 pc. Flemish linen cloth cont. 40 ells, 2 grs. laces, 4 doz. black leather, 9 doz. red skins, 4 C. [*S* and 1 qr.] white leather, 4 reams painted paper, £12 18s. [*S* and 4d.]

Cornelius Johnson, A, 1 basket with 5 doz. hawks' hoods ('cappis'), 1 lb. clavichord wire, 2 doz. wire ('wyron') candlesticks, 1 doz. nut-crackers, 1 doz. key-thongs, 1 doz. standing glasses ('stondynglas-sez'), 1 doz. holy-water stoups ('stock'), 16 doz. bells [*S* 'pell'], 4½ marks ironware, 9 gimlets, ½ doz. squirts, 500 buckles, 1 doz. small compasses, ½ grs. razors, 2 doz. locks, 2 doz. fire-irons, ½ grs. knives, 1 doz. chess-men, 9 doz. pipes, 40s.

Leonard van Lyer, A, 1 fardel with 100 budge skins, 26s.8d.

Matthew Hynkylman, H, 1 brl. with 16 pcs. Holland cont. 324 ells [*S* 424], £9 13s. 4d.

1 straw of wax weight 8 quintals

Hillibrand van Vuno, H, 2 straws of wax weight 20 quintals

Tylman Barkys, H, 1 maund with 3 rolls 2½ C. ells Herford, £41

Arnold van Stalle, H, 1 pack with 11 pcs. Brussels cont. 212 ells, 28 pcs. coarse Ghentish cont. 548 ells, 47 pcs. Holland cont. 11 C. 12 C. [*S* 1,112 ells], £45 13s.4d.

Everard Southerman, H, 1 fardel with 2 packs Cologne thread, £26 13s.4d.

[1] Spang: clasp, buckle, brooch, spangle (*O.E.D.*).

175. 21 July. From the ship of John Bargem[an] called *Julyan* of Reimerswaal

James Falk, A, 1 chest with 12 grs. playing-cards, £3

Peter Capper, A, 1 fardel with 6 doz. table-mats ('warnappis'),[1] 1 pc. diaper cont. 11 yds., 1 tapestry coverlet, 2 pcs. Flemish linen cloth cont. 34 ells, 30 bars [*S* 'barryoris'] iron weight 5½ C. lbs., £3 15s.

Martin Johnson, A, 1 sack flax, 30s.

John Evyngar, A, 3 sacks hops, £4 10s.

John Kele, A, 8 sacks hops, £12

Laurence Taylour, A, 1 sack with 300 'rolls for to make hats', 10s.
Said master, A, 1 basket with 20 doz. straw hats, 600 [*S* 6,000] paving-
tiles, £4 10s.

¹ Cf. gardnap: a round piece of wood or metal, a mat, or the like, placed under dishes
at table in order to protect the table-cloth (*O.E.D.*).

176. 21 July. From the ship of Luke Countman called *Bell* of Antwerp
James Falk, A, 2 sacks hemp, £3
Lewis van Demers, A, 100 skives teazles, 1 brl. with teazles, 56s.8d.
Matthew Walk, A, 3 brls. with 25 doz. drinking glasses, 33 stone pots, 1
    small basket with 6½ doz. compasses, ½ brl. nails, 3 brls. wine lees,
    1,500 gunstones, £3 3s.4d.
Anthony Kele, A, 1 sack flax, 30s.
Martin Johnson, A, 2 sacks hops, £3
Peter van Clefe, A, 5 sacks hops, 1 basket 1 brl. with 14 doz. dry plaice,
    4 doz. wool-cards [*S* 2 doz. wool-cards, 2 doz. small cards], 1 painted
    cloth, 1 doz. old shirts, 3 hair brushes, 1 lb. white thread, 30 lbs.
    packthread, £9 10s.
Henry Herysbek, A, 1½ C. frying and dripping pans, 1 hanger
    ('hangyll'), 20 fulls of kettles, 1 chest with 8 grs. playing-cards, 11 grs.
    small cards, 3 doz. 7 lbs. thread, 5 doz. shears, 11 lbs. aglets, 200
    thimbles, 1 table-cloth, £7 16s.8d.
Peter Wolf, A, 20 fulls of kettles, 1 corf with 18 stocks of mirrors, 6 doz.
    [*S* candle] snuffers, 1 doz. holy-water sticks, 4 doz. 2 daggers, 2
    bundles string yarn, 8 doz. hair brushes, 55s.
Said master, A, 1,000 pavingstones, 13s.4d.
Thomas Johnson, A, 3 sacks hops, 4 cases combs, £8 10s.
Gerard Lesbern, H, 3 sacks hops, £4 10s.

[m.9]
177. 21 July. From the ship of Lubert van Boke called *Mary* of the
    Steelyard
Roger van Feld, H, 2 straws of wax weight 18 quintals
Matthew Hynkylman, H, 4 nests of counters, £4
William Scapehuson, H, 1 straw of wax weight 11 quintals
Hillibrand van Vuno, H, 2 straws of wax weight 18 quintals
Gerard Lesbern, H, 1 straw of wax weight 10 quintals
Lambert Rotard, H, 10 brls. steel, £60
Tylman Barkys, H, 1 small fardel with 75 timbers lettice [*S* val. £25], 3
    bales madder [*S* val. £6], £31
John van Armysbery, H, 1 pack Cologne thread, £13 6s.8d.
Arnold Moldyke, H, 4 bales madder, 1 small fardel with 36 pcs. Holland
    cont. 756 ells, £35
William Grenewolt, H, 1 basket with 44 pcs. Holland cont. 1,009 ells,
    £25 3s.4d.
Anthony Odindale, H, 1 pack with 2½ bales fustian [*S* 2 bales Ulm
    ('hosmys')¹ fustian, ½ bale 'osborons'²], 19 pcs. treillis ('terlyson'),
    £38 3s.4d.
Peter Eksted, H, 1 straw of wax weight 10 quintals

Hans Culle, H 1 straw of wax weight 12 quintals

George Tak, H, 1 bale fustian, 1 bag with 3 pcs. taffeta, 28 wooden mazers, £17 16s.8d.

John Greverod, H, 7 bales madder, £14

Arnold van Stalle, H, 1 pack with 35 pcs. Holland cont. 802 ells, 32 pcs. narrow busk, £47 15s.

Hans Stut, H, 1 mease copper plate cont. 1½ meases, £18
1 straw of wax weight 8 quintals

Henry Lathuson, H, 2 vats saltpetre weight 14 C. lbs., £26 6s.8d.

Stephen Bramshe, H, 2 bales madder, £4

Conratte Boon, H, 1 fardel 1 pack 1 brl. with 9 pcs. Holland cont. 288 ells, 12 pcs. Brabant cont. 314 ells, 1 pc. diaper cont. 5 ells, 12 pcs. lawn, 12 pcs. coarse lawn, 36 ells Flemish linen cloth, 13 pcs. Burgundy ('burgeis') [*S* 'borgoyn'] [cloth], 1 grs. purses, C. lbs. flax, 2 small pcs. red [*S* 2 small pcs. wax, 6 red skins], 8 small painted cloths, £19 5s.

¹ Cf. 'holmys' fustian from Ulm (De Smedt, op. cit. 387).
² ? Augsburg, where fustian was manufactured (ibid.).

178. 21 July. From the ship of Coppyn Welle called *Trinite* of Antwerp

James Falk, A, 1 sack hemp, 2 brls. with 20 [*S* 30] marks ironware, 12 lbs. counters, 10,000 horn counters, £3 8s.4d.

James Fris, A, 2 sacks hemp, 1 sack flax, £4 10s.

Bartholomew Spylman, A, 1 basket with 8½ doz. 1 'iperlings', 400 white pavingstones, 3 pcs. and remnants Holland cont. 85 ells, 100 skives teazles, 2 doz. staves [*S* 'sawes'], 6 sacks hops, £20 15s.

Anthony Kele, A, 1 basket with 6 C. lbs. packthread, £3

Martin Johnson, A, 1 hhd. with 12 grs. Nuremburg mirrors, 8 grs. wooden beads, 10 grs. glass beads, 4 grs. locks, 5 grs. 'prage' knives, £3 18s. [*S* and 4d.]

Cornelius Smyth, A, 800 drinking pots, 6 fulls of kettles, 4 baskets with drinking glasses, 1 last pitch, 1 [*S* 6] lb. saffron, 200 wicker [covered] glass bottles, 3 bales mull-madder, 6 reams writing paper, £9 16s.8d.

Francis Mathew, A, 1 basket 1 roll 1 corf with 13 doz. crucifixes, 4 doz. knives, 6 doz. candle pipes, 1 painted book, 3 doz. rattles, 300 stone images, 20s.

John Gerrard, A, 1 basket with 600 sheep bells, 60 bundles dry plaice, 20s.

Frederyk Hegyle, A, 1 maund 1 brl. with 78 pcs. 'Osburn' (? Augsburg) fustian, 29 pcs. tuke, 1½ doz. playing-cards, 390 small graters, [*S* 380 key-bands], 88 silk girdles, £29 15s.

John Doyte, A, 1 hhd. 1 maund with 14 doz. pouches, 9 pairs knives, 4 C. dry plaice, £5

Henry Frankenberch, A, 1 pipe 1 hhd. with 240 [*S* 245] vols. diverse histories, £12 16s.8d.

John Kele, A, 1 pipe with 6,000 balls, 23 [*S* 13] cases glass, 3 sheaves iron, 1 basket with 9½ C. lbs. packthread, 14 ticks, 9 pcs. hastrey cont. 2¾ C. ells, 2 pcs. Brabant cont. 30 ells, C. lbs. flax, £27 10s.

Antonia Jamys, A, 1 basket with 2 old feather-beds, 4 doz. pillows, 4 doz. distaffs, 23s.4d.

John Welbek, A, 2 brls. 1 chest with 11 doz. sheets, 2 'fac'[1], 7 doz. glasses, 1 doz. glass bottles, C. lbs. feathers, 3 doz. straw hats, 10 mantles lamb, £3 18s. [*S* and 4d.]

Peter Wolf, A, 1 brl. with 11 grs. 4 doz. razors, £6 16s.8d.

William Stanfast, A, 7 bales madder, £14

Arnold Howell, A, 2 baskets with 40 doz. painted cloths, 3 doz. brushes, 5 pairs kempsters' combs, £3

Gerard Loy, A, 1 basket with 10 pcs. Brabant linen cloth cont. 240 ells, 36 pairs shearmen's shears, £10

William Codde, A, 1 basket with 2 feather-beds, 1 quilt, 5 doz. red skins, 26s.8d.

John Vandermaste, A, 4 bales paper cont. 72 reams, £7 3s.4d.

Thomas Johnson, A, 2 brls. with 60 lbs. bristles, 4½ grs. razors, 3 grs. Anthony's bells,[2] 23s.4d.

Cornelius Crowne, A, 1 pc. tin-glass weight 5 C. [*S* 100] lbs., £5

John Sewyk, H, 4 C. 1 [*S* 3] qr. stockfish, 1 pack pickling cont. 12 C. ells, £16 10s.

Roger van Feld, H, 4 vats Cologne woad, £26 13s.4d.

Simon Harrysson, A, 1 fardel with 11 pcs. Flemish linen cloth cont. 300 ells, £5 6s.8d.

[1] ? Fasculum: small vessel.

[2] A handbell, bell for a pig or the smallest church bell. St. Antony of Egypt was frequently depicted with a bell at his staff or round the neck of his accompanying pig. It was a privilege of the Hospitallers of St. Antony that their pigs could roam freely in the streets (O.E.D. *sub* 'tantony'; D. H. Farmer, *The Oxford Dictionary of Saints* (Oxford, 1979), 20).

179. 21 July. From the ship of Peter Menger called *Petir* of Antwerp

James Frize, A, 1 pipe with 708 doz. Nuremburg mirrors, 24 bundles [*S* wrapping] paper, £5 6s.8d.

James Falk, A, 2 sacks hemp, £3

Edward Johnson, A, 10 brls. slip, ½ brl. filings, 23s.4d.

John Gyles, A, 1 chest with 5,000 balls, 3 pcs. Flemish cont. 118 [*S* 107] ells, 1 pc. Brabant cont. 38½ ells, 1 doz. lbs. blue thread, 2½ doz. white thread, 9 wide brls. train oil, £11 6s.8d.

Martin Johnson, A, 1 brl. 1 small basket with 2 grs. 7 doz. spurs, 3 doz. 'coppyn' hats, 40 lbs. bristles [*S* hair], 50s.

John Paules, A, 1 chest with 1 pc. fustian, 1 pc. says cont. 12 ells, 1 remnant canvas cont. 12 ells, 20s.

Cornelius Smyth, A, 3 baskets with drinking glasses, 8 doz. distaffs, 1 sack hops, £3 6s.8d.

Peter van Clefe, A, 5 sacks hops, 4 brls. wine lees, 1 kettle, 3 small cloths, 1 bag flax cont. 2 C. lbs., £9 16s.8d.

Martin Wekard, A, 1 small chest with 2 doz. spectacles, 50 brushes, 30s.

Herman Herysbek, A, 2 sacks hemp, £3

John Kele, A, 5 sacks hops, £7 10s.

Peter Wolf, A, 1 chest with 350 foot glasses, 40s.

Said master, A, 600 [*S* 700] pavingstones, 200 Brabant stones ('braban-stone'),¹ 20s.

¹ ? Floor tiles. I am indebted for this suggestion to Dr. Derek Keene.

180. 21 July. From the ship of John Roke called *Julyan* of London
John Gerrard, A, 1 basket 1 hhd. 1 brl. with 2 feather-beds, 1 grs. spurs, 2 doz. splints, 1 doz. stirrups, 4 grs. buckles, 6 pcs. and remnants Flemish cont. 100 ells, 3 reams painted paper, 1,200 thimbles, 1 grs. glasses, 2 grs. knives, 2 doz. lbs. thread, 3 boxes bristles, 2 grs. black beads, 3 grs. razors, 2 doz. squirts, 12 lbs. stable brushes, 1 grs. sacring-bells, 1 doz. buckles, 1 lb. saffron, 3 marks ironware, 1 doz. needles, 2 grs. brushes, 7 grs. small bells, 7 painted cloths, £14 3s.4d.
John Kele, A, 9 brls. white and black plate, 1 brl. nails, £11
Peter Ekstede, H, 2 straws of wax weight 22 quintals
Hans Stut, H, 2 straws of wax weight 16 quintals

181. 21 July. From the ship of Clays Thorn called *Julyan* of Arnemuiden
Roger van Feld [*S* George de van Feld], H, 1 straw of wax weight 8 quintals
William Scapehuson, H, 2 packs candle-wick, £8
2 straws of wax weight 22 quintals
Matthew Bliterswyk, H, 3 bales madder, £6
Tylman Barkys, H, 1 straw of wax weight 12 quintals
John Questynburgh, H, 5 bales madder, £10
Gerard Lesbern, H, 2 straws of wax weight 26 quintals
Arnold van Stalle, H, 1 chest 1 pack with 23 pcs. Brussels cont. 465 ells, 23 pcs. Ghentish cont. 460 ells, 22 pcs. Holland cont. 516 ells, £32 3s.4d.
Peter Eksted, H, 1 straw of wax weight 10 quintals
Peter Syber, H, 1 pack Cologne thread, 1 fardel with 2 bales fustian, £40
John Russynthorp, H, [*S* 1] vat Cologne woad, £6 13s.4d.
Godard Slotkyn, H, 5 bales madder, £10
Ingilbright Sevenek, H, 1 fardel with 2 packs Cologne thread, £26 13s.4d.
John Greverod, H, 8 bales madder, £16
John van Derbeson, H, 1 pack Cologne thread, 1 small chest with 2 doz. 10 panes of shanks, £19
Arnold van Stalle, H, 1 small chest with 20 pcs. Holland cont. 554 ells, £13 13s.4d.
John van Strawlyn, H, 1 maund 1 vat with 46 pcs. broad busk, 9 pcs. narrow [*S* busk], 23 pcs. hastrey cont. 7 C. 108 ells, 30 [*S* 32] shearmen's shears, £65 8s.4d.
John van Armysbery, H, 1 fardel with 2½ packs Cologne thread, £13 6s.8d.
Frank Savage, H, 1 frail 1 'bassheron' battery, £20
Henry Bevir, H, 1 roll Hannover linen cloth, £12
Hans Stut, H, 2 meases split copper cont. 2½ meases, £30
Everard [*S* Gerard] Southerman, H, 1 straw of wax weight 10 quintals

Roger van Feld, H, 4 vats Cologne woad, £26 13s.4d.

James Falk, A, 1 hhd. 1 brl. with 20 grs. jet beads, 40 marks ironware, £4

Peter Segir, A, 1 basket with 30 [*S* doz.] 'copyn' hats, 30s.

Anthony Kele, A, 2 brls. nails, 1 sack flax, £5 10s.

John van Acon, A, 1 chest with 93 vols. diverse histories, £9 6s.8d. [m.9d.]

Deryk Spryng, A, 1 poke hops, 20s.

Alice Johnson, A, C. hemp, 1 small feather-bed, 12 glasses, 13 sheets, 12 cushion-cloths, 6 leather cushions, 12 skins for cushions, 6 leather pouches, 1 lb. blue and white thread, 1 painted cloth, 2 trivets, 1 pair tongs, 25s.

Adrian Williamson, A, 14 brls. wine lees, 3 doz. cards, 35s.

Bartholomew Spilman, A, 1 basket with 4 C. packthread, 4 doz. 'yperlings', 2 quilts, £4

Cornelius Johnson, A, 1 brl. with 1 [*S* 10] box bristles, 1,000 wimble ('wynnell') [*S* 'wymbull'] irons,[1] 2 doz. wimbles, 1 doz. tabor pipes, 4 [*S* 3] doz. locks, 10 doz. brushes, 2,000 glass beads, 1 grs. spectacles, 20 doz. mistletoe beads, 40s.

James Roye, A, 2 chests with 3 pcs. latten weight 8 lbs., 2½ grs. thread laces, 1 lb. say thread, 5 ells coarse lawn, 7 ells coarse Holland, 16 bags, 3½ doz. pins, 3 doz. beads, 2 grs. points, 1 doz. girdles, 2 doz. spectacles, 1 box with thimbles, 2 doz. combs, 12 ells ribbon, 3 small coffers, 2 sieves, 23s.4d.

Adrian Philip, A, 1 brl. 1 small fardel with 4 grs. small bells, 7 doz. small locks, 5 doz. cocks, 4 doz. snuffers, 3 doz. small tables, 1 grs. trumpets, 14 [*S* 4] grs. laces, 1 doz. small balances, 1 grs. ink-horns, 500 awl blades, 1,000 pack needles, 1 doz. gimlets, 2 doz. scissors, 3 lbs. curtain rings, 1 doz. sacring bells, 2 doz. pin-cases, 300 awl hafts, 1½ doz. shocks of glasses, 1 doz. flax brushes, 1 doz. glass beads, 1½ doz. squirts, 4 pcs. Brabant [*S* cont.] 58 ells, £3 3s.4d.

Hugh Florenson, A, 1 brl. with 350 black lambskins, 250 coarse budge skins, £4 5s.

Pero de Bodna, A, 1 brl. gunpowder weight 100 lbs., 1 brl. 1 basket with 13 pcs. Holland linen cloth cont. 298 ells, 1 grs. laces and points, 3 lbs. thread, 5 doz. pouches, 1 doz. copper spoons, £10 10s.

George de Lago, A, 1 roundel with 14 pcs. Holland cont. 336 ells, £7

Damyan de Sancto Nicholo, A, 1 brl. with 8 pcs. Holland cont. 192 ells, £4 16s.8d.

[1] ? shafts of wimbles or gimlets.

182. 21 July. From the ship of Clays Jacobisson called *Mary Knyght* of Middelburg

Said master, A, 2,000 paving-tiles, 400 white paving-tiles, 46s.8d.

James Falk, A, 2 bales combs, 2 small baskets with 700 sheepskins, 10 sums nails, £4

Cornelius Smyth, A, 100 wainscots, 40s.

John Evyngar, A, 1 qr. wainscots, 10s.

John Welbek, A, 1 chest with 3 grs. 3 cases knives, 2½ doz. painted cloths, 15 doz. glasses, 2 doz. pouches, 6 piercers, 5 tongs, 5 doz. balances, 500 glass beads, 6 lbs. say yarn, 1 grs. laces, 2 doz. [*S* single pouch] rings, 2½ doz. lbs. blue thread, 2 [*S* 3] doz. graters, 9 doz. irons, 1 pc. Flemish cont. 30 ells, 5 pairs sheets, 2 doz. brushes, 6½ doz. basan [*S* leather] skins, 9 grs. tinfoil, £8 18s. [*S* and 4d.]

Peter Wolf, A, 3 brls. linseed oil, 36s.8d.

Peter Johnson, A, 2 sacks hops, £3

Arnold Howell, A, 2 great and 2 small fulls of kettles, 2 old cloths, 4 pairs shuttles, 4 pcs. canvas cont. 108 ells, 36s.8d.

Henry Heuskyn, A, 1 maund with 2 old feather-beds [*S* and 1 feather-bed], 1½ doz. trowels, 25 pcs. black plate, 2 reams black paper, 2 kettles, 31s.8d.

Hillybrand van Vuno, H, 2 straws of wax weight 20 quintals

Stephen Bramsche, H, 2 bales madder, £4

Peter Eksted, H, 1 straw in 1 pipe and loose wax weight 8 quintals

John Sewyk, H, 8 lasts ashes, 1 small fardel with 6 pcs. Holland cont. 120 ells, £14

William Grenewolt, H, 1 pack with 3 rolls Herford linen cloth [*S* cont. 3 rolls], £36

183. 21 July. From the ship of Peter Jacobisson called *Trego* of Arnemuiden

James Fryse, A, 1 hhd. with 2 doz. 8 daggers, 2½ grs. thread laces, 6 doz. wire girdles, 11 doz. bag rings, 11 candlesticks, ½ C. lbs. bristles, 7 grs. knives, 5½ doz. pouches, 26 doz. pins, £10 11s.8d.

Bartholomew Spylman, A, 1 fardel with 27 pcs. [*S* 'Barowe'] canvas cont. 550 ells, £7 10s.

Edward Johnson, A, 1 chest with 10 doz. sheepskins, 7½ grs. pouches, 38,000 brigandine nails, 4½ lbs. copper wire, 4½ doz. swords, 2 grs. 3 doz. gloves, 6 grs. knives, 1½ grs. bag rings, £15

Cornelius Joosson, A, 1 chest 1 hhd. with 40 doz. pins, 10 grs. ink-horns, 9 grs. pen-cases, 6 grs. needle cases, 3 grs. spectacle ('brille') cases, 2½ grs. small glasses, 10 grs. boxwood beads, 2 grs. imitation chalcedony, 4 grs. small locks, 2 grs. small bags, £10

Antonia James, A, 2 brls. 1 corf with 10 [*S* 12] lbs. flax, 2 old feather-beds, 3 pillows, 1 doz. red laces, 1 doz. cushion 'leves' [*S* cloths], 7 pairs old sheets, 1 table-cloth, 1 diaper towel, 4 [*S* 2] chafing dishes, 14 candlesticks, 6 stone pots, 3 [*S* 300] spindles, 2 kettles [*S* weight 2 lbs.], 2 bolsters, 40s.

John Symondson, A, 1 pipe with 15 pcs. soultwich linen cloth cont. 39½ ells, 2 featherbeds, 3 coverlets, 33s.4d.

William Codde, A, 1 hhd. with 22 doz. gloves, 30,400 [*S* and 36 doz.] compasses, 10 doz. cruets, 2 doz. lamps, 2 grs. Jews' harps ('jue trumpes'), 23 cases knives, 2 doz. latten,[1] 38½ [*S* 37½] doz. backs, 1 doz. red skins, 5 grs. latten buckles, 4 doz. 9 daggers, 34 doz. rings, 10 grs. 7 knives, £15 8s.4d.

Matthew Hynkylman, H, 1 pack with 35 pcs. soultwich cont. 15 C. [*S* ells], 67 pcs. pickling cont. 11 C. ells, £33 10s.

Lambert Rotard, H, 6 brls. steel, £36

William Scapehuson, H, 2 straws of wax weight 24 quintals

Stephen Bramsche, H, 4 bales madder, £8

George Tak, H, 1 bale fustian, £13 6s.8d.

Matthew Bliterswyk, H, 1 pack with 43 pcs. hastrey cont. 9½ C. ells, 7 pcs. broad busk, 14 [S 7] pcs. narrow busk, £35 10s.

Tylman Barkys, H, 1 basket with 23 pcs. minsters cont. 5½ C. ells, 10 pcs. Herford cont. ½ roll, 47 pcs. Osnabrück cont. 2 rolls, 2 pcs. Holland cont. 52 ells, £45 10s.

Anthony Odyndale, H, 2 bales madder, 12 pairs shearmen's shears, 1 small fardel with 5 clouts caul silk, 4 lbs. Cologne silk, 1 lb. gold wire, 1 bale madder, £28 6s.8d.

Hyllibrand van Vuno, H, 1 dry vat with 3 [S 2] ticks, 2 habergeons, 2 pcs. buckram, 31 hand querns [S and 4 dog-stones], £10

John Questynburgh, H, 1 pack 1 basket with 26 pcs. broad busk, 32 [S pcs.] narrow busk, 3 pcs. Holland cont. 113 ells, 20 pairs shearmen's shears, £47 15s.

Gerard Lesbern, H, 4 packs flax, 3 bales madder, £22

1 straw of wax weight 9 quintals

William Grenewolt, H, 1 maund with [S 46 pcs.] Holland cont. 10½ C. 55 ells, £43 16s.8d.

1 pc. wax weight 3 quintals

Arnold van Stalle, H, 1 pack with 12 pcs. Brussels cont. 250 ells, 34 pcs. Ghentish cont. 712 ells, 39 pcs. Holland cont. 956 ells, £54 16s.8d.

Peter Eksted, H, 1 straw of wax weight 9 quintals

John Greverod, H, 2 sacks hemp, 1 pack 1 corf cont. 5 rolls Herford, £63

John Salmer, H, 1 frail 2 baskets battery, 1 pc. tin-glass, £31 13s.4d.

John Stakylhuson, H, 1 fardel with 21 clouts Cologne silk, 1 bundle caul silk, £73 6s.8d.

Roger van Feld, H, 1 pack with 2½ rolls Osnabrück, £30

Hans Stut, H, 2 meases copper plate cont. 3 meases, £36

1 straw of wax weight 11 quintals

Everard Southerman, H, 1 straw of wax weight 12 quintals

John van Strawlyn, H, 2½ packs Cologne thread, £13 6s.8d.

¹ Commodity omitted.

184. 21 July. From the ship of Thomas Joosson called *Petir* of Bergen-op-Zoom

Lewis Bonvis, A, 1 case 1 small fardel with 1 pc. velvet cont. 9 yds, 11 pcs. satin cont. 174 yds., 6 pcs. damask cont. 87 yds., 5 pcs. sarcenet cont. 79 yds., 12 pcs. baudekin, £83

Edward Johnson, A, 1 hhd. with 3 doz. daggers, 4 doz. compasses, 9 doz. candle pipes, 6 doz. candle-snuffers, 3 doz. mirrors, 11 grs. bells, 3½ grs. locks, 2½ C. white skins, 5 doz. sheepskins, 3 doz. running glasses, 2 doz. lbs. thread, 4 lbs. string thread, 1 grs. thread laces, 1 doz. red skins, £4 11s.8d.

John Gyles, A, 1 chest 1 basket with 25 pcs. Ghentish Holland cont. 598

ells, 1 remnant Holland cont. 12 ells, 4 kips gold skins, 1 doz. 2 lbs. blue thread, 10 [*S* 2] lbs. white thread, 12 doz. pillows, 3 feather-beds, 8 large red skins, 2 doz. leather cushions, £20 16s.8d.

Martin Johnson, A, 1 chest combs, 1 sack hops, 50s.

Anthony Kele, A, 2 sacks hemp, £3

John Hase, A, 7 baskets with 3 M. lbs [*S* white] iron plates, 2,000 sheep bells [*S* 'pell'], 4 C. lbs. kettles, 5 bands of kettles, 10 copper pans weight 4 C. lbs., £38

1 pc. wax weight 4 C. lbs.

Rowlond Forest, A, 1 small fardel with 16 quires painted paper, 54 [*S* small] papers of the Passion of Christ, 3 pcs. 1 remnant Brabant cont. 72 ells, 43s.4d.

Francis Mathewe, A, 1 roll with 18 painted cloths, 20s.

Andrew Rewe, A, 2 chests with 77 [*S* 177] vols. diverse histories, £13 10s.

John Kele, A, 12 sacks hemp, £18

James Bolle, A, 1 hhd. with 24 grs. boxwood beads, 1 brl. white and black latten plate [*S* 1 brl. latten plate, 7 brls. white and black plate], £14 3s.4d.

Cornelius Joosson, A, 1 fardel with 54 reams paper, 30 pcs. and remnants canvas cont. 500 ells, £9

John Welbek, A, 6 brls. soap, £4

Michael Roose, A, 1 maund with 7 [*S* 8] doz. red skins, 94 lbs. thread, 1½ grs. cards, 6 doz. gloves, £3 13s.4d.

[m.10]

William Standfast, A, 4 bales madder, 1 chest 1 brl. with 16 pcs. Gelder linen cloth cont. 4 C. ells, 9 pcs. buckram [*S* Brabant] cont. 305 [*S* 300] ells, 3 pcs. Hainault cont. 100 ells, 6 mirrors, 3 doz. Bruges thread, 11 grs. knives, 8 shearmen's shears, £32 16s.8d.

Arnold Howell, A, 1 sack with candle yarn weight 3 C. lbs., 20s.

Laurence Tyman, A, 1 sack hemp, 1 pipe 1 chest 1 basket 1 firkin with 3 doz. buckles, ½ grs. black rings, 1 grs. coarse caddis, 2 clouts of awl blades, 2 pcs. fustian, 2½ doz. needles, 3½ grs. thread laces, 5 grs. bells, 1,000 thimbles, 3 doz. daggers, 1 grs. wire girdles, 2 pcs. tuke, 2,000 bodkins, 4 doz. bags, 2 grs. knives, 1 grs. small coffers, 1 doz. latten rings, 3½ reams paper, 5 doz. pins, 2 grs. 8 doz. ribbons, 5 grs. girdles with aglets, 1½ grs. bag rings, 4 doz. pins, 4 grs. wire girdles, 1,200 chalcedony, 5 timbers calaber, 19 pcs. buckram [*S* Brabant] cont. 316 ells, £18 6s.8d.

Peter Wolf, A, 1 small chest with 2 grs. cypress coffers, 3 doz. dials, 1 grs. gold thread, 1 doz. cruets, 8 doz. padlocks, 2 bundles string thread, 2 grs. spectacle-cases, 46s.8d.

Peter Segir, A, 1 basket with 50 doz. 'coppyn' hats, 50s.

James Laurans [*S* Laurence], A, 2 doz. crossbows, 5 doz. shafts, 1 fardel with 6 doz. spectacles, 3 doz. locks, 11 doz. mirrors, 3 doz. pouches, 4 doz. hawks' hoods, 7 doz. knives, 3 doz. balances, 1 doz. bells, 2 lbs. weights, 4 doz. razors, 6,000 clasps, 500 ear-pickers, 7 lbs. aglets, 1 doz. compasses, 2 doz. barbers' mirrors, 1 lb. packthread, 6 doz. spectacle-cases, 11 doz. pen-cases and ink-horns, 6 doz. pin-cases, 8 doz. bodkins, 500 tucking hooks, 2 doz. hair brushes, 1 doz. scissors, 6 running-glasses, 40s.

Matthew Bliterswyke, H, 4 sacks hemp, £6

John Sewyk, H, 1 roll Brunswick linen cloth, £12

William Grenewolt, H, 1 pack Herford linen cloth cont. 2 rolls, £24

John Greverod, H, 10 bales madder, 10 bales alum, £30

Hans Stut, H, 1 straw of wax weight 8 quintals

Henry Bevyr, H, 1½ lasts train oil in wide brls., £18

185. 21 July. From the ship of John Yoman called *John* of London

James Bolle, A, 1 hhd. with 6 grs. thread laces, 6 grs. hatbands, 8 daggers, 3,000 thimbles, 18 grs. knives, 1 grs. marking irons, 3 grs. needle cases, 1 grs. spectacles, 30 marks of scissors, 1 doz. tailors' shears, 1 grs. pin-cases, £8

Peter Wolf, A, 1 brl. with 2 grs. 9 doz. razors, 2 doz. sacring-bells, 1 gross locks, 2,000 thimbles, 16 lbs. curtain rings, 4 grs. small bells, 1 lb. mortars, 19 clouts of needles, 1 clout of pack needles, 2 lbs. ivory combs, 1,000 jet ('geet') stones, 4 doz. mirrors, 4 grs. thread laces, 9 doz. hearts, 2 lbs. clavichord wire, 5 grs. 6 doz. spectacles, 1½ lbs. amber, 4,400 chalcedony, 5 grs. 6 [*S* 7] doz. knives, £18 16s.8d.

Peter Harryson, A, 1 brl. with 8 pcs. Holland cont. 165 ells, 6 ticks, 2 counters' tables, £4

Matthew Bliterswyk, H, 9 sacks hemp, £13 10s.

Anthony Odyndale, H, 2 bales fustian, £26 13s.4d.

John Questynburgh, H, 3 bales fustian, £40

Peter Eksted, H, 1 straw of wax weight 10 quintals

Peter Syber, H, 2 fardels with 5 bales fustian, £66 13s.4d.

John Russyngthorp, H, 1 brl. with 336 lbs. nutmegs, £16 16s.8d.

John Salmer, H, 1 brl. copper weight 6 C. lbs., £6

William Scapehuson, H, 3 straws of wax weight 36 quintals

John van Armysbery, H, 2 fardels with 4 bales fustian, 3 packs Cologne thread, £93 6s.8d.

Gerard van Grove, H, 2 packs Cologne thread, £26 13s.4d.

Henry Bevir, H, 2 rolls Herford linen cloth, £24

Hans Stut, H, 1 mease split copper, £12

1 straw of wax weight 10 quintals

186. 21 July. From the ship of John Wodelez called *Thomas Basset* of London

John Gyles, A, 1 chest with 26 [pcs.] Ghentish Holland cont. 733 ells, 1 pc. Holland cont. 49 ells, 5 [*S* doz.] lbs. blue thread, 3 grs. red laces, 1½ grs. thread laces, £16 3s.4d.

John Kele, A, 1 fardel with 147 pcs. Burgundy canvas cont. 2,200 [*S* ells], £26 13s.4d.

James Bolle, A, 1 chest 1 hhd. with 15 grs. Flanders-lace, 5 grs. spurs, 5 grs. wire girdles, 2 grs. imitation chalcedony, 3 grs. thread laces, 4 doz. balances, 10 grs. harp strings, 40 doz. pins, 20 grs. pen-cases [*S* 12 grs. ink-horns, 8 grs. pen-cases], 1 grs. spectacle-cases, 1 grs. locks, £18 6s.8d.

Peter Wolf, A, 1 chest with 14 pcs. Brabant linen cloth cont. 482 ells, 3 grs. mistletoe beads, 6 doz. daggers, 4 grs. 9 doz. bags, £15 3s.4d.

George Tak, H, 1 pack with 2½ rolls Hannover linen cloth, £30

Peter Eksted, H, 2 straws of wax weight 18 quintals

Hans Stut, H, 1 dry vat with 246 timbers calaber, £41

   1 straw of wax weight 10 quintals

187. 21 July. From the ship of William Petyte called *Christofer* of Weymouth

Edward Johnson, A, 1 brl. 1 small coffer with 13 breast-plates, 5 doz. splints, 8 doz. flax brushes, 1 visor, 20 grs. girdles, 1 doz. hangers, £6 11s.8d.

John Kele, A, 2 sacks hemp, 1 sack flax, 1 pipe with 6,000 balls, 4 brls. nails, £15 10s.

George Tak, H, 1 pack Hannover linen cloth cont. 2½ rolls, £30

Peter Eksted, H, 2 straws of wax weight 20 quintals

Matthew Blitterswyk, H, 1 pack with 49 pcs. hastrey cont. 15 C. 20 [*S* 70] ells, 24 pcs. broad busk, 13 pcs. narrow busk, £60 6s.8d.

John Russyngthorp, H, 1 brl. with 193 lbs. nutmegs, 8 clouts of Cologne silk, £37

William Scapehuson, H, 1 straw of wax weight 11 quintals

Gerard van Grove, H, 1 pack Cologne thread, £13 6s.8d.

Everard Southerman, H, 1 pack with 43 pcs. hastrey cont. 13 C. 18 ells, 36 pcs. Holland cont. 816 ells, £57 10s.

Hans Stut, H, 1 dry vat with 245 timbers calaber, £40 16s.8d.

   2 straws of wax weight 16 quintals

John van Strawly[n], H, 1 pack Cologne thread, 1 vat with 17 clouts of Cologne silk, £70

Roger van Feld, H, 1 pack with 3 pcs. Holland cont. 78 ells, 3 rolls Herford, £38 13s.4d.

Anthony Odindale, H, 2 packs Cologne thread, 2 bales madder, £30 13s.4d.

Goswyno Rodynkerk, H, 1 brl. with 63 bundles caul silk, 25 clouts of [*S* Cologne] silk, 5,000 [*S* teazle] tack needles, £294 3s.4d.

188. 21 July. From the ship of Richard Fyssh called *Gabriell* of St. Osyth ('S. Ossiis')

Peter Eksted, H, 1 straw of wax weight 9 quintals

Hans Stut, H, 2 straws of wax weight 18 quintals

189. 21 July. From the ship of William Tabbard called *Mary* of Boston

John Kele, A, 12 brls. nails, £24

Cornelius Smyth, A, 2 sacks hemp, 1 sack flax, £4 10s.

Henry Heuskyn, A, 1 brl. with 3 doz. lbs. white thread, 150 budge skins, 100 tavelon shanks, 1 tick, 2 furs calaber wombs, ½ grs. red laces, 2 papers of blue thread, 500 hose buckles, 2 pcs. Brabant cont. 48 ells, 5 clouts of pins, £7 3s.4d.

Peter Syber, H, 1 pack Cologne thread, 1 fardel with 3 bales fustian, £53 6s.8d. (£40 *del.*)

John Salmer, H, 1 pipe 1 frail battery, £20
Tylman Barkys, H, 1 straw of wax weight 12 quintals
William Scapehuson, H, 2 straws of wax weight 30 quintals
Tylman van Howell, H, 1 straw of wax weight 10 quintals
John Questynburgh, H, 1 fardel with 2 bales fustian, £26 13s.4d.
Henry Bevyr, H, 1 roll Herford linen cloth, £12
  1 straw of wax weight 11 quintals
Hans Stut, H, 1 dry vat with 250 timbers calaber, £41 13s.4d.
  1 straw of wax weight 12 quintals
Gerard Lesbern, H, 1 straw of wax weight 12 quintals
Lambert Rotard, H, 8 brls. steel, £48

190. 21 July. From the ship of Walter Culvercok called *Mary Gale* of Dartmouth
Herman Herisbek, A, 1 brl. latten plate, 1 dry brl. with 20 doz. pins, 2½ grs. beads, 2½ grs. pin-cases, 10 doz. padlocks, 2 doz. hair brushes, ½ doz. daggers, 1 grs. leather laces, 2½ grs. thread laces, 30 lbs. wire, 2 doz. clouts of needles, 5 grs. 9 doz. knives, £13 8s. 4d.
Peter John Grill, A, 1 pipe mace weight 175 lbs., £24 10s.
Andrew Giles, A, 1 fardel with 26 pcs. baudekin, 1 fur of martens, £26
John Kele, A, 9 brls. nails, £18
William Scapehuson, H, 3 straws of wax weight 34 quintals
Hillibrand van Vuno, H, 1 straw of wax weight 6 quintals
Matthew Hynkylman, H, 1 straw of wax weight 20 quintals
John van Armysbery, H, 1 fardel with 2 bales fustian, £26 13s.4d.
Hans Culle, H, 1 dry vat with 255 timbers grey, 3 [*S* 4] timbers beaver, £89
Henry Bevir, H, 1 roll Herford linen cloth, £12
  1 straw of wax weight 12 quintals
Henry Lathuson, H, 1 roll Brunswick linen cloth cont. 1½ rolls, £18 [m.10d.]
Hans Stut, H, 1 mease split copper cont. 1½ meases, £18
  1 straw of wax weight 8 quintals
Everard Southerman, H, 1 pack with 16 C. ells soultwich, £24
Gerard Lesbern, H, 1 straw of wax weight 10 quintals
Goswyn Rodynkerk, H, 2 bales fustian, 1 brl. with 18 bundles caul silk, £86 13s.4d.

191. 21 July. From the ship of Martin de Masket called *Maudelyn* of Leek ('Leket')
John Tebawde, A, 10 cases combs, 1 small balet with pipes, £30

192. 21 July. From the ship of Thomas Payn called *Petir Tate* of London
Peter Eksted, H, 1 dry vat with 75 timbers lettice, 112½ timbers calaber, 25 timbers grey, £52 3s.4d.
Hans Stut, H, 1 brl. with 10 timbers grey, 25 timbers lettice, 2 timbers mink, £14 13s.4d.

193. 21 July. From the ship of Thomas Titmer called *Mary* of Guérande

69

Prymos Verye, A, 48 millstones, 6 mustard stones, £26 13s.4d.

194. 21 July. From the ship of Cornelius Adryandson called *Barbara* of Middelburg
Gerard van Stonebarowe, A, 3 sacks 17 pokes hops, 1,000 paving-tiles [*S* pavingstones], £20 10s.

195. 21 July. From the ship of Cornelius Johnson called *Christofer* of Middelburg
Gerard van Stonebarowe, A, 6 sacks 14 pokes hops, £20

196. 21 July. From the ship of Cornelius Stonebarowe called *Valentyn* of Bergen-op-Zoom
John Kele, A, 5 sacks hops, £7 10s.
Cornelius Smyth, A, 700 drinking pots, 100 wainscots, £3 3s.4d.
Michael Malbrayn, A, 1 pipe with 3 feather-beds, 4 pcs. lawn, £3 3s.4d.
Arnold Howell, A, 1 sack hemp, 30s.
Gerard Loye, A, 1 basket with 6 pcs. Brabant cont. 125 ells, 41s.8d.
John Richard, A, 1 brl. with 9 pairs brigandines, 26 pairs gorgets, 61 splints, 8 habergeons, 4 pairs mail sleeves, 10 pairs flanchards, 10½ pairs mail sleeves, 10 mail falls, 2 sallets, 2 mail breeches, 5 Dutch gorgets, 3 [*S* 2] latten rings, £11 13s.4d.
Thomas Johnson, A, 4 bales madder, £8 [*S* 4 bales mull-madder, 40s.]

197. 28 Aug. From the ship of James Spisholt called *Reynold* of Danzig
Roger van Feld, H, 7½ lasts tar, 18 lasts 3 brls. ashes, 2 lasts 11 brls. pitch, 7 wide brls. train oil, 3 nests of counters, 500 wainscots, 2 great C. clapholt, 5 packs flax, £74 15s.
Hans Stut, H, 3 C. 8 bowstaves, £6
3 straws of wax weight 30 quintals
Herman Overcamp, H, 2 packs flax and candle-wick, 5 lasts 10 brls. tar, 5 lasts 10 brls. ashes, £15 13s.4d.
Peter Eksted, H, 4 packs flax, £16
3 straws of wax weight 30 quintals
Gerard Lesbern, H, 14 brls. osmund, 4½ packs flax, £16 13s.4d.
1 straw of wax weight 8 quintals
Tylman Barkys, H, 10 lasts ashes, 13 wide brls. train oil, 2 packs flax, 3½ lasts tar, £34 10s.
Herman Plough, H, 2 packs flax, 2 lasts 4 brls. tar, 2 lasts 4 brls. pitch, £12 13s.4d.
1 straw of wax weight 7 quintals
Matthew Hynkylman, H, 2 packs flax, 2 lasts 4 brls. pitch, 2 nests of counters, 2 nests of coffers, 7 shocks of trenchers, £13 6s.8d.
Hillibrand van Vuno, H, 1 straw of wax weight 8 quintals
Paul Kortume, H, 1 last pitch, 2½ lasts tar, 3 chests flax, 4 nests of chests, 2 pullets, 6 stools, 23 codfish, 2½ doz. pepper querns, ½ doz. rests, 14 bales flax, 40 nests of bits, 200 sheaths for swords, 2 ropes of amber, 60 [*S* painted] wooden platters, 2 counters, 1 fur of squirrel, £9 3s.4d.

198. 30 Aug. From the ship of Nicholas Barbour called *Kateryn* of Fowey

Laurence Grylle, A, 7 hhds. dates, £17 10s.

Nicholas Lomelyn', A, 30 bales dates each weighing 1½ C. lbs., £20

Jeronimo Imary, A, 1 bale Spanish grain weight 336 lbs., £16 16s.8d.

John Ambros de Nigron', A, 1 bale Seville grain weight 150 lbs., £8 8s.4d.

199. 30 Aug. From the ship of Datleff Salman called *Nicholus* of Hamburg

Ludeke Lowe, H, 48 lasts stockfish, 7 lasts salt staplefish, 22 brls. salt fish, 2 narrow brls. train oil, £434

200. 3 Sept. From the ship of John Chamachio called *Sancta Maria* of Cadiz

Frank Justynyan', A, 581 bales woad, £387 6s.8d.

Laurence Grylle, A, 30 bales woad, 17 small [*S* brls.] saltpetre weight 30 C. lbs., £54

Barnabas Centuryon, A, 178 bales woad, £118 13s.4d.

Gabriel Furnarius, A, 192 bales woad, £128

Anthony Salvage and Nicholas Lomelyn', As, 1 bale woad, 40 sacks alum each sack weight. 3 C. lbs., £30 13s.4d.

Peter John Grylle, A, 50 bales woad, £33 6s.8d.

John Ambros de Nigron', A, 2 C. 68 [*S* 2 C. 78] bowstaves, £4 10s.

Anthony de Sarro, A, 105 bales woad, £70

201. 3 Sept. From the ship of Robert Laverok called *Edward* of Fowey

Barnabas Centuryon, A, 26 tuns oil, 24 cases sugar, 1 bale grain of Portugal weight 100 lbs., £144

202. 3 Sept. From the ship of Peter Everdyk called *Jamys* of Middelburg

Ingyll' Huson, A, 250 wainscots, 1 pack flax, 1,000 paving-tiles, 5 lasts ashes, £14 13s.4d.

203. 3 Sept. From the ship of John Buk called *Mary Gaske* of Saltash

Anthony Salvage, A, 65 bales dates each weighing 1½ C. lbs., £60

Laurence Grille, A, 4 pipes 24 hhds. dates, £70

Nicholas Caretto, A, 1 pipe 5 brls. 40 bales dates, £64 10s.
  1 bale wax cont. 1½ quintals

Catayne Furner', A, 1 small sack Spanish grain weight 60 lbs., £3

204. 3 Sept. From the ship of Anthony Brabander called *George* of Middelburg

Said master, A, 4,000 paving-tiles, 4 brls. flax weight 2 C. lbs., 1 last 3 brls. tar, £4 18s.4d.

John Vandermaste, A, 1 basket with 2 C. lbs. packthread, 2 brls. white and black plate, 1 bale paper, 1 grs. spurs, £4 10s.

Henry Watkyns, A, 1 basket with 3 old feather-beds, 2 coverlets, 1 tick, 33s.4d.

James Fleet, A, 1 dry pipe with 21 images of the Blessed Mary, 24 [*S* small*] round cushions, £3 1s.8d.

Walter Richard, A, 6 small copper kettles, 1 elk skin, 1 brl. with 10 doz. 9 goat skins, 5 great elk skins, £3

Lambert Crome, A, 1 bag with 11 pcs. lawn, £5 10s.

Hugh Florens, A, 1 brl. with 5 pcs. Holland cont. 76 ells, ½ C. Irish lamb [? skins], 1 fur of 'bolt' wombs, 51s.8d.

John Clays, A, 2 bags with C. lbs. flax, 1 feather-bed, 16s.8d.

John Symson, A, 4 lasts ashes, £4

John Willyams, A, 1 brl. with 17 pcs. Zeeland [*S* linen cloth] cont. 104 ells, 45s.

John Duke, A, 1 basket with [*S* 2] sacks feathers, 4 ticks, 1 pc. diaper cont. 22 ells, 51s.8d.

Matthew Hynkylman, H, 4 vats flax, £16

Peter Eksted, H, 1 straw of wax weight 9 quintals

John Salmer, H, 2 'bassherons' battery, £20

John Sewyk, H, 1 last soap, 22 C. 1 qr. stockfish, £28

Roger van Feld, H, 3 rolls Herford, 1 pack flax, £40

Godfrey van Beston, H, 3 rolls Osnabrück linen cloth, £36

Hans Culle, H, 1 pack flax, £4

2 straws of wax weight 18 quintals

[m.11]

Herman Plough, H, 1 pack flax, £4

Henry Lathuson, H, 3 packs cont. 22 C. ells soultwich, 10 C. ells pickling, £43

William Scapehuson, H, 1 pack with candle-wick, £4

William Grenewolt, H, 2 packs flax, £8

Tylman Barkys, H, 1 hhd. with 82½ timbers grey [*S* £27 10s.], 9 firkins 16 octaves[1] dole [*S* stub] eels [*S* £6 16s.8d.], £34 6s.8d.

[1] The firkin was a quarter of a barrel and the octave presumably half this.

205. 3 Sept. From the ship of John Lokyngton called *Jesus* of London[1]

Harmews de Sondevile, A, 8 saws, 1 pipe 1 brl. with 300 eyelet pins, 2 doz. marking irons [*S* and 2 doz. souter's irons], 2 doz. key-bands, 2½ doz. butchers' irons, 1 doz. fishing and marking hooks, 3 doz. compasses, 1 doz. pincers, 2 doz. nutcrackers, 2 doz. patten knives,[2] 1 doz. dossals ('dusshels'), 3 coopers' axes, 5 cappers' shears, 1 habergeon, 5½ doz. brushes, 4 lbs. raw yarn, 3 bowyers' knives, 6 cheeses, 9 mirrors, 2,500 teazles, 1 doz. 3 painted cloths, 1 doz. paring knives, 19 worsted caps, 8 sewers' [*S* sawyers'] shears, 1 pc. Brabant cont. 34 ells, £5 15s.

Lewis van Demers, A, 4,500 teazles, 23s.4d.

John Dussher, A, 9 doz. skins of diverse colours, 1 chest with 5 doz. knives, 3½ doz. double and 6½ doz. single bonnets, 16 doz. skins of diverse colours, 16 coffers, 24 doz. pen-cases, 4½ doz. daggers, 5 pcs. Holland [*S* Hainault linen cloth] cont. 104 ells, £9 10s.

Tylman Barkys, H, 1 straw of wax weight 11 quintals

[1] See also **621** below.

[2] Knife used by pattenmakers to cut the wood for pattens.

206. 3 Sept. From the ship of Clays Henrykson called *Barbara* of Middelburg

Said master, A, 1,500 [*S* 2,500] paving-tiles, 3 bags feathers weight 1½ C. lbs., 25 boards for shoemakers, £3 11s.8d.

John Vandermaste, A, 1 hhd. with 6 doz. pouches, 3 doz. locks, 1 grs. playing cards, 3 grs. pen-cases [*S* 2 grs. pen-cases, 1 grs. ink-horns], 56s.8d.

William Keteler, A, 2½ lasts pitch, 150 wainscots, 1 basket with 2 C. 52 lbs. flax, £6 8s.4d.

John Demewre, A, 1 chest with 2 pcs. fustian, 1 remnant Flemish cont. 16 ells, 18 ells canvas, 12 lbs. flax, 2 lbs. yarn, 20s.

Nigel Berbruer, A, 1 pipe with 2 feather-beds, 1 pc. raw linen cloth cont. 28 ells, 30s.

Godfrey van Beyston, H, 6 sacks hemp, £9

John Salmer, H, 1 frail battery, £10

James van Werd, H, 2 lasts 11 brls. ashes, 3½ brls. 4 firkins sturgeon, £5 10s.

207. 3 Sept. From the ship of Robert Walcok called *Leonard* of London

James Falk, A, 1 hhd. with 3 grs. jet beads, 6 grs. imitation mistletoe [? beads], 1 grs. spurs, 10 grs. musk balls, 3 pcs. Holland cont. 54 ells, 1 sack hemp, £5 13s.4d.

Edward Johnson, A, 1 hhd. 1 brl. with 10 doz. rings, 1 grs. horse bits, 2 grs. 4 doz. spurs, 1 doz. coffers, 2 doz. [*S* and 8] pot knives, 1 [*S* doz.] sheep's leather, 2 grs. 2 doz. pouches, 6 doz. gloves, 1 grs. knives, £9 3s.4d.

Arnold van Stalle, H, 1 maund with 27 pcs. Holland cont. 587 ells, £23

Roger van Feld, H, 2 rolls Osnabručk, 1 roll Herford, £36

John Salmer, H, 1 frail battery, £10

Hans Culle, H, 1 straw of wax weight 10 quintals

Godfrey van Beyston, H, 2½ rolls Osnabrück, £12

Edward Johnson,[1] A, 1 hhd. 1 brl. with 10 doz. rings, 1 grs. horse bits, 2 grs. 4 doz. spurs, 1 doz. coffers, 2 doz. 8 pot knives, 1 doz. sheep's leather, 2 grs. 2 doz. pouches, 6 doz. gloves, 1 grs. knives, £9 3s.4d.

[1] Same entry as above, in another hand. Not repeated in *S*.

208. 10 Sept. From the ship of Michael Mayre called *Christofer* of Antwerp

John Giles, A, 100 bundles brown paper, £3 6s.8d.

Bartholomew Spylman, A, 100 pointels weld, 600 paving-tiles, 1 basket with 6½ doz. 'yperling', £6 16s.8d.

Matthew Lothewekeson, A, 18 [*S* 8] brls. slip, 36s.8d.

John Kele, A, 2 sacks flax, £3

Edward Johnson, A, 1 brl. with filings, 2 brls. with 6 doz. mail sleeves, 27 doz. pins, £6 16s.8d.

George Tak, H, 1 vat Cologne woad, £6 13s.4d.

John Salmer, H, 1 pipe 1 basket [*S* 'basheron'] battery, £20

Martin Johnson, A, 3 sacks hops, £4 10s.
John Vandermaste, A, 1 hhd. with 12 doz. brushes, 20s.

209. 17 Sept. From the ship of John Blowmeard called *George* of Bergen-op-Zoom
Andrew Petirson, ½ M. garlic, 40s.

210. 24 Sept. From the ship of George Bras called *Bere* of Bergen-op-Zoom
James Williamson, A, 3 M. garlic, 1 sack flax, £11 10s.
Said master, A, 50 earthen stew pots, 3s.4d.

[m.11d.]
211. 25 Sept. From the ship of John Turnour called *Thomas* of London
Frank Savage, H, 1 frail 1 'bassheron' battery, £20
Peter Eksted, H, 2 packs flax, £8

212. 25 Sept. From the ship of William Philpot called *Clement* of Ratcliff ('Redclyf')
Peter Eksted, H, 2 packs flax, £8
Gerard Lesbern, H, 4 lasts 8 brls. ashes, 14 brls. pitch, £5 16s.8d.
Bourghgat Bussher, A, 1 last herring, ½ last tar, ½ brl. herring, 60 round maple bowls, £4 15s.
Herman Stale, A, 150 wainscots, £3

213. 27 Sept. From the ship of Cornelius Nese called *Christofer* of Middelburg
Gerard Lesbern, H, 2 lasts 4 brls. pitch, 4 packs flax, 1 fardel cont. 1 qr. flax, £18 16s.8d.
Gysbright Martynson, A, 1 bag with 48 doz. split hats, 16s.8d.
John Williamson, A, 1 feather-bed, 5s.
Herman Plough, H, 3 lasts ashes, 21 [*S* 11] brls. pitch, £4 15s.
William Grenewolt, H, 10 lasts pitch, £10
Said master, A, 2 bags with 2 C. lbs. flax, 1 qr. wainscots, 33s.4d.

214. 27 Sept. From the ship of Hugh Jacobisson called *Christofer* of Flushing
Said master, A, M. salt fish, 5 C. bunches garlic, 4 weys Berflete[1] ('barflet') salt, 200 earthen stewing pots, 1 brl. salt fish, ½ last pitch, £17

[1] Fine quality salt for the table and dairy from either Berflete in Flanders or in Zealand (A. R. Bridbury, *England and the Salt Trade in the later Middle Ages* (Oxford, 1955), 116–17).

215. 27 Sept. From the ship of Cornelius Moche called *Barbara* of London
Michael Ciprian, A, 30 cases sugar weight 30 C. lbs., £45
Armews Somvyle, A, 2 pipes with teazles, 1 brl. soap, 1 small pack with 1 grs. gloves, 2 pairs sheets, 1 table glass, £4 13s.4d.

Said Michael Cyprian, A, 20 cases sugar weight 20 C. lbs., 5 cases broken sugar, £35

James Molen, A, 1 brl. with 19 doz. pouches, 5 spruce skins, £3 10s.

Stephen Blank, A, 1 brl. 1 bag with 1 pc. Flemish linen cloth cont. 18 ells, 50 pairs lasts for shoemakers, 6s.8d.

Nicholas Buke, A, 1 pipe 2 brls. with 34 doz. cards for wool, £8

Nicholas Riche, A, 1 pipe with 2 feather-beds, 20s.

John Badsard, A, 1 hhd. with 1,500 teazles, 10s.

John Dylle, A, 1 basket with 10 pcs. Holland linen cloth cont. 250 ells, £3 13s.4d.

Joys Clokemaker, A, 1 brl. 1 bag 2 vats with 12 doz. mirrors, 24 lbs. flax, 12 lbs. linen yarn, 2 feather-beds, 33s.4d.

Robert Waryng, A, 1 brl. 1 corf with 9 pcs. Flemish linen cloth cont. 200 ells [*S* 202], 1 pc. Holland cont. 23 [*S* 33] ells, 2 [*S* 1] table-cloths, 13 painted cloths, £4 5s.

Paul Coper, A, 2 chests 2 baskets with 5,000 teazles, 16 quires paper, 20s.

Said master, A, 8 C. scouring[1] tiles, 3s.4d.

[1] See above, **68**.

These 27 rolls the aforesaid controller delivered here by his own hands on the third day of November in the 21 year of King Edward IV and took oath.[1]

Examined with the rolls of the surveyor and customers.[2]

[1] In another (rougher) hand.
[2] In an Exchequer hand. *S* 'examined with the rolls of the controller and customers'.

[EXPORTS]

[m.12]

216. 30 Sept. In a cart of Peter Jamys going to Southampton[1]
Gabriel Furnarius, A, 3 bales with 43 cloths 20 yds. w.g.

[1] For the reason for the entry of outgoing carts and horses in the account see above p. xliv.

217. 30 Sept. In a cart of Peter Jamys going to Southampton
Gabriel Furnarius, A, 3 bales with 48 cloths 8 yds. w.g.

218. 30 Sept. In a cart of Peter Jamys going to Southampton
Gabriel Furnarius, A, 1 bale with 14 cloths 8 yds. w.g.

219. 30 Sept. On 10 horses of John Aryse going to the port of Bristol
Edward Brampton, D, 10 fardels with 50 cloths w.g.

220. 30 Sept. In the ship of Thomas Coys [of London]
William Jenk, D, 1 fardel with 4½ cloths w.g.
John Fysshare, D, 1 fardel with 2 cloths w.g., 27 pcs. double worsted
John Hawkyn, D, 1 fardel with 1 cloth, 16 yds. w.g.
William Weston, D, 1 fardel with 14 pcs. double worsted
Thomas Kelet, D, 1 fardel with 7 cloths w.g.
John Colet, D, 1 fardel with 2 cloths w.g.
Thomas Payn, D, 1 cloth w.g.
John Chambyr, D, 1 bale with 15 cloths w.g.
Andrew Rogerson, D, 1 fardel with 7 cloths w.g.
Peter Joye, D, 1 fardel with 9 cloths w.g.
William Wheteley, D, 1 fardel with 4 cloths w.g.
Edward Johnson, A, 1 brl. with 18 doz. [*S* lbs.] candles, 8 flitches bacon, £6 6s.8d.
John Benet, D, 1 cloth w.g.

221. 2 Oct. In a cart of William Notyngham going out to Southampton
Matthew de Catero, A, 1 bale with 12½ cloths w.g.; 200 goads Welsh straits [*S* cotton russet], £5[1]
George Greco, A, 1 fardel with 2 cloths 16 yds. w.g.

[1] For this and for similar entries below, the valuation applies only to the goods listed after the semicolon.

222. 2 Oct. In the ship of Cornelius Johnson
John Evingar, A, 12 pipes beer, £4
Herman Johnson, A, 20 pipes beer, £6 13s.4d.
Lambert Rotard, H, 9 pipes beer, £3

223. 2 Oct. In a cart of Richard Todde going to Southampton
Laurence Gryll', A, 3 bales with 47 cloths w.g.

224. 2 Oct. In a cart of Robert Todde going to Southampton
Laurence Gryll', A, 3 bales with 50 cloths 8 yds. w.g.

225. 3 Oct. In the ship of Laurence Johnson
Michael van Prat, A, 6 baskets with 6 weys rendered tallow ('cepi molton'),[1] 1 basket with 50 cheeses, £4
Cornelius Johnson, A, 15 pipes beer, 5 baskets with M. lbs. rendered tallow, 6 brls. with 64 doz. candles, £12
Deryk Oldekyrk, A, 12 pipes beer, £4
Michael Harryson, A, 4 pipes beer, 26s.8d.

[1] The tallow fat was melted in a pot and skimmed to remove impurities. It was then emptied through a sieve into a tub and was ready for use after standing for three hours (R. Monier-Williams, *The Tallow Chandlers of London* (1970), I, 35–6).

226. 4 Oct. In the ship of Laurence Legalowe
Said master, A, 5 fothers lead, £20

227. 4 Oct. In a certain barge going to Gravesend
Hans Swalyngborugh, H, 1 budget ('boget') with 6 bonnets of half grain, 6 bonnets w.g., 3 grs. points, £3

228. 5 Oct. In the ship of Thomas Grey
John Semer, D, 1 fardel with 1 cloth w.g.
John Stokare, D, 1 bale with 10 cloths w.g.
John Fynkyll, D, 3 fardels with 24 cloths w.g.
John Trewinard, D, 1 bale with 10 cloths w.g., 1 cloth in grain
Edward Fynkyll, D, 3 bales with 30 cloths w.g.
John Seman, D, 1 fardel with 8 cloths w.g.
William Cowper, D, 3 fardels with 18 cloths 8 yds. w.g.
Richard Alder, D, 1 bale with 10 cloths w.g.
Robert Leycrofte, D, 1 cloth w.g.
Thomas Screven, D, 1 bale with 17 cloths 8 yds. w.g.
Thomas Wattys, D, 1 bale with 12 cloths w.g.

229. 5 Oct. In a cart of William Spygot going to Southampton
Anthony Calvo, A, 2 bales with 24 cloths 10 yds. w.g.

230. 6 Oct. In a cart of William Spigot going to Southampton
Jasper Nigron', A, 3 bales with 49 cloths 16 yds. w.g.

231. 6 Oct. In a cart of Peter Jamys going to Southampton
Jasper Nigron', A, 3 bales 1 fardel with 42 cloths w.g.

232. 7 Oct. In a cart of William Spigot going to Southampton
Paul Parekerole, A, 1 bale with 14½ cloths w.g.

233. 7 Oct. In the ship of Cornelius Quatell [of Bergen-op-Zoom]

James Falk, A, 4 C. [*S* 4 M.] summer ('stages') rabbit-skins, 28s.

234. 7 Oct. In a cart of Peter James going to Southampton
Ralph de Cattero, A, 3 bales with 34 cloths w.g.

235. 11 Oct. In a cart of Peter Jamys going to Southampton
Raphael Lomlyn', A, 2 bales 1 fardel with 39½ cloths w.g.; 17 pcs. Welsh
straits, 4 rolls frieze, £8 6s.8d.

236. 11 Oct. In a cart of Robert Long going to Southampton
Ciprian Furnarius, D,[1] 1 fardel 1 roll with 12 cloths w.g.
Jeronimo Imary, A, 1 fardel with 6 cloths 10 yds. w.g.

[1] An esquire of the household, born in Genoa and granted letters of denization in 1475
(*C.P.R. 1467–77*, 518).

237. 12 Oct. In the ship of John Bulhawte [of Rouen]
Laurence Fabyan, [*S* D][1] 5 fothers 5 C. lbs. lead, 2 M. 5 C. lbs. rendered
tallow, 2 C. lbs. battery, 1 hhd. mustard seed, 6 brls. pitch, 1 hhd. 2
panniers with 400 lbs. candles, 12 cheeses, £32
Peter Laratt, A, 8 yds. cloth w.g.; 100 lbs. pepper, 1 hhd. with mustard
seed, 6 brls. pitch, £6

[1] Probably a mistake for alien, see **4** above.

238. 14 Oct. In a cart of William Johnson going to Southampton
Francis Molen, A, 3 bales with 32 cloths w.g.

239. 14 Oct. In a cart of Peter Jamys going to Southampton
Gabriel Furnarius, A, 3 bales with 48 cloths w.g.

240. 14 Oct. In a cart of Peter Jamys going to Southampton
Gabriel Furnarius, A, 3 bales with 49 cloths w.g.

241. 16 Oct. In a cart of John Rede going to Southampton
Anthony Calvo, A, 3 bales with 46 cloths 8 yds. w.g.

242. 242. 16 Oct. In a cart of Henry Cole going to Southampton
George de Sancta Maria, A, 2 bales with 18 cloths 16 yds. w.g.; 3 pcs.
Welsh straits, 33s.4d.
Michael de Catero, A, 1 bale with 13 cloths 8 yds. w.g.

243. 16 Oct. In the ship of Lubert van Boke [of the Steelyard]
Edward Johnson, A, 5 M. summer rabbit-skins, £5
Peter Wolf, A, 5 M. summer rabbit-skins, £5
John Salmer, H, 2 brls. with 12 C. lbs. pewter vessels, 1 brl. with 16 doz.
candles, £17
Anthony Kele, A, 15 [*S* 5] weys cheese, £6
Edward Johnson, A, 24 baskets with 19 weys rendered tallow, 8 brls.
with salt meat, £12
John Kele, A, 20 weys cheese, £8

Said master, A, 13 pipes beer, £4 6s.8d.

Tylman Barkys, H, 1 bale with 19 cloths w.g.; 400 goads Welsh straits, 2 vats with 90 doz. [*S* lbs.] candles, £17 16s.8d.

Hans Stut, H, 1 bale with 27 cloths w.g.; 30 goads Welsh straits, 20s.

Gerard Lesbern, H, 1 fardel with 6 cloths 6 yds. w.g.; 20 goads Welsh straits, 13s.4d.

244. 17 Oct. In a cart of William Spigot going to Southampton
Gabriel Furnarius, A, 3 bales with 46 cloths w.g.

245. 17 Oct. In a cart of William Spigot going to Southampton
Gabriel Furnarius, A, 3 bales with 49 cloths w.g.

246. 17 Oct. In a cart of William Spigot going to Southampton
Raphael Lomelyn', A, 3 bales with 46 cloths 8 yds. w.g.

247. 17 Oct. In a cart of William Spigot going to Southampton
Toremo Dore, A, 1 bale with 18 cloths w.g.

248. 19 Oct. In a cart of Peter Jamys
Jasper Nigron', A, 2 bales 1 fardel 2 rolls with 43 cloths 8 yds. w.g.

249. 20 Oct. In a cart of John Rede going to Southampton
Cosma Spenyll', A, 2 bales 1 fardel with 51 cloths 23 yds. w.g.

250. 20 Oct. In the ship of Thomas Eton going to Sandwich
John Sarro, A, 2 bales 1 fardel with 149 doz. tanned calfskins, 1 bale with 72 doz. tanned calfskins, £27 13s.4d.
Gabriel Furnarius, A, 420 doz. tanned calfskins, £42

[m.12d.]
251. 20 Oct. In a cart of John Bond going to Southampton
Laurence Gryll', A, 3 bales with 46 cloths 16 yds w.g.

252. 20 Oct. In a cart of John Boteler [*S* Butteler] going to Southampton
Laurence Gryll', A, 3 bales with 48 cloths 8 yds. w.g.

253. 20 Oct. In a cart of John Boteler going to Southampton
Laurence Gryll', A, 3 bales with 54 cloths w.g.

254. 20 Oct. In a cart of John Botler going to Southampton
Laurence Gryll', A, 1 bale with 16 cloths w.g.

255. 23 Oct. In a cart of Robert Rolff going to Southampton
Gabriel Furnarius, A, 3 bales with 35 cloths 8 yds. w.g.

256. 23 Oct. In the ship of Thomas Hikylman going to Sandwich
Gabriel Furnarius, A, 80 doz. tanned calfskins, £10

257. 24 Oct. In a cart of John Rede going to Southampton
Paul Larka, A, 4 fardels with 33 cloths w.g.

258. 24 Oct. In a cart of John Rede going to Southampton
Paul Larka, A, 3 bales 1 roll with 32 cloths 6 yds. w.g.

259. 24 Oct. In a cart of William Sellam going to Southampton
Paul Larka, A, 3 bales with 48 cloths 16 yds. w.g.

260. 24 Oct. In a cart of William Sellam going to Southampton
Paul Larka, A, 3 bales with 47 cloths 16 yds. w.g.

261. 24 Oct. In a cart of William Sellam going to Southampton
Paul Larka, A, 2 bales with 24 cloths 8 yds. w.g.

262. 25 Oct. In the ship of John Cameo ['Camacheo' *del.*] [of Cadiz]
Abraham Catell', A, 2 bales with 100 doz. tanned calfskins, £15
Frank Justinyan', A, 2 fardels with 20 cloths w.g.
Henry Rabet, D, 1 bale with 17 cloths 16 yds. w.g.
Richard Odyham, D, 1 bale with 20 cloths w.g.
John Tutsham, D, 1 bale with 12 cloths w.g.
William Spark, D, 3 bales with 54 cloths w.g.
Robert Henle [*S* 'Hendley'], D, 2 bales with 55½ cloths w.g.
Thomas Pynde, A, 2 bales with 36 cloths w.g.
Peter Bylbowe, man and merchant of the said province of Guipúzcoa,[1]
   Sp, 1 cloth w.g.
Peter Desavala of Guipúzcoa, Sp, 1 bale with 18 cloths 16 yds. w.g.
Said master of Guipúzcoa, Sp, 1 fardel with 7 cloths 8 yds. w.g.
Frank Deargomedo of Guipúzcoa, Sp, 1 bale with 11 cloths 8 yds. w.g.
Alfonso de Rota of Guipúzcoa, Sp, 1 cloth 8 yds. w.g.
John Martinus of Guipúzcoa, Sp, 1 bale with 8 cloths 8 yds. w.g.
Said master of Guipúzcoa, Sp, 1 bale with 20 cloths w.g., 7 yds. cloth in
   grain

   [1] Hereafter this is calendared simply as 'of Guipúzcoa'. In December 1474, in compensation for losses sustained from English attacks, Guipúzcoan merchants were granted 11,000 crowns (less 600 already paid) to be acquired by retaining half the customs chargeable on their goods in English ports. And in August 1476 this grant was amended to include the goods of all merchants of Castile and Léon in London, Sandwich, Southampton and Bristol (*C.P.R. 1467–77*, 480, 600).

263. 25 Oct. In the ship of John Debassorto
Martin Dordaydo of Guipúzcoa, Sp, 16 yds. cloth w.g.
Michael de Pontica of Guipúzcoa, Sp, 1 cloth w.g.
Michael de Lopean [*S* Lopyana] of Guipúzcoa, S, 4 rolls with 5 cloths 18
   yds. in grain
Alfonso de Lyon of Guipúzcoa, Sp, 2 fardels with 18 cloths 16 yds. w.g.
Peter Valedelede of Guipúzcoa, Sp, 1 bale with 13 cloths 8 yds. w.g., 1
   cloth 10 yds. in grain
Peter de Castro of Guipúzcoa, Sp, 4 bales 4 rolls 1 fardel with 46 cloths
   w.g., 5 cloths 10 yds. in grain

Peter Embeto of Guipúzcoa, Sp, 1 bale with 12 cloths 16 yds. w.g.
John de Bedua of Guipúzcoa, Sp, 13 yds. cloth w.g.
John Martinus of Guipúzcoa, Sp, 1 cloth 10 yds. w.g.
John Perus of Guipúzcoa, Sp, ½ cloth w.g.
John de Melebya of Guipúzcoa, Sp, 3 cloths 9 yds. w.g.
John Darnaro of Guipúzcoa, Sp, 22 yds. cloth w.g.
Martin Bono of Guipúzcoa, Sp, ½ cloth w.g.

264. 25 Oct. In a cart of John Rede
Lewis Gremaldo, A, 2 bales with 21 cloths 8 yds. w.g.

265. 26 Oct. In the ship of Saba de Sarrasto
Said master of Guipúzcoa, Sp, 17 yds. cloth w.g.
Martin Loprane of Guipúzcoa, Sp, 1 bale with 14 cloths 16 yds. w.g.
Peter Valedelede of Guipúzcoa, Sp, 1 fardel with 9 cloths 16 yds. w.g.
Peter Castro of Guipúzcoa, Sp, 3 bales with 41 cloths w.g.
Peter Embeto of Guipúzcoa, Sp, 1 bale with 12 cloths w.g.
Alfonso de Lyon of Guipúzcoa, Sp, 1 fardel with 9 cloths 16 yds. w.g.

266. 30 Oct. In the ship of Hugh Petirson
James Williamson, A, 1 pipe with 28 doz. [*S* lbs.] candles, 2 brls. with
  salt meat, 46s.8d.
John Stollard, A, 1 pipe 2 vats 1 brl. with 54½ doz. [*S* lbs.] candles, 4
  brls. with salt meat, 4 weys cheese, 18 flitches bacon, 1 vat with 3½ qrs.
  meal, 3 weys rendered tallow, 8 brls. honey, £15

267. 31 Oct. In a cart of John Hokare going to Southampton
Mark Stroce, A, 26 pcs. Welsh straits, £8 13s.4d.

268. 31 Oct. In the ship of Philip Betowe
Said master, A, 2½ lasts pitch, £5 16s.8d.

269. 6 Nov. In the ship of William Crose
Cosma Spenyll', A, 9 fothers 12 C. lbs. lead, £38 13s.4d.

270. 7 Nov. In a cart of William Spigot going to Southampton
Gabriel Furnarius, A, 3 bales with 41 cloths w.g.

271. 7 Nov. In a cart of William Spigot going to Southampton
Gabriel Furnarius, A, 3 bales with 38 cloths w.g.

272. 7 Nov. In a cart of William Spigot going to Southampton
Gabriel Furnarius, A, 2 bales with 25 cloths 16 yds. w.g.

273. 9 Nov. In the ship of William Wilson [*S* 'Willisson']
Peter Wolf, A, 8 M. summer rabbit-skins, £8
Thomas Wynnam, D, 2 bales with 25 cloths w.g.
Richard Eyryk, D, 1 bale with 10 cloths w.g.

274. 14 Nov. In a cart of Henry Cole going to Southampton

Frank Justinyan', A, 2 bales with 33 cloths 16 yds. w.g.

275. 15 Nov. In a cart of William Sellam going to Southampton
John Amberos, A, 3 bales with 40 cloths 8 yds. w.g.

276. 15 Nov. In a cart of William Sellam going to Southampton
Laurence Gryll', A, 2 bales with 30 cloths 16 yds. w.g.; 20 pcs. Welsh
straits, £5

277. 16 Nov. In the ship of Peter Mengyll [of Antwerp]
John Stakylhuson, H, 2 hhds. with salt meat, 1 hhd. with 50 doz.
candles, 2 baskets with 4 C. lbs. rendered tallow, £4 13s.4d

278. 16 Nov. In the ship of Thomas Gurley
Richard Henley, D, 1 fardel with 3 cloths 8 yds. w.g.

279. 16 Nov. In the ship of Michael de Meyre [of Antwerp]
John Salmer, H, 1 pipe 1 hhd. 4 brls. with 106 doz. candles, £5 6s.8d.

280. 16 Nov. In a cart of Thomas Arnold going to Southampton
Cosma Spenyll', A, 3 bales with 46 cloths w.g.

281. 16 Nov. In a cart of Thomas Spens going to Southampton
Cosma Spenyll', A, 3 bales with 45 cloths 16 yds. w.g.

282. 16 Nov. In a cart of Edmund Colsyll going to Southampton
John Kendall,[1] D, 3 bales with 42 cloths 16 yds. w.g.

[1] 1 November 1480, grant to John Weston, prior of the Hospital of St. John of
Jerusalem and John Kendall, Turcopolier of Rhodes, of a licence to export 320 cloths
in a ship called 'Le Marie' belonging to the order, then at Southampton, without
payment of subsidy (P.R.O. Treaty Roll C.76/164, m.6).

283. 16 Nov. In a cart of Edmund Colsyll [S 'Colshill'] going to
Southampton
John Kendall, D, 3 bales with 39 cloths w.g.

284. 16 Nov. In a cart of John Bedyll going to Southampton
John Kendall, D, 3 bales with 48 cloths w.g.

285. 16 Nov. In a cart of Peter Jamys going to Southampton
John Kendall, D, 2 bales with 30 cloths 16 yds. w.g.

286. 16 Nov. In a cart of John Bedyll going to Southampton
John Kendall, D, 2 bales with 50 cloths w.g.

287. 16 Nov. In a cart of John Rede going to Southampton
John Kendall, D, 2 bales with 50 cloths w.g.

288. 18 Nov. In the ship of John Stephyns [of Oporto]
Said master, A, 2 C. lbs. rendered tallow, 15s.

289. 20 Nov. In the ship of Thomas Bett [of London]
Thomas Wattys, D, 1 bale with 12 cloths w.g.
Charles Mountclare, D, 1 bale with 11 cloths w.g.

290. 20 Nov. In the ship of Jasper Boke [of Hamburg]
Gerard Lesbern, H, 1 bale with 11 cloths w.g.; 150 goads Welsh straits,
8 cheeses, £5
Hans Hosterberch, H, 2 bales with 46 cloths 21 yds. w.g.; 6 coverlets, 50
goads Welsh straits, 12 cheeses, £3
Henry Berch, H, 2 fardels 2 brls. with 14 cloths 11 yds. w.g.; 65
coverlets, 1 bench-cover, 12 doz. single bonnets, 12 cheeses, £13
6s.8d.
[m.13]
Frank Savage, H, 2 brls. with 12 C. lbs. pewter vessels, £16
Henry Lathuson, H, 3 bales with 81 cloths 4 yds. w.g.; 300 goads Welsh
straits [*S* cotton russet], 12 rolls frieze, £18
John Salmer, H, 1 bale with 10 cloths 16 yds. w.g.; 380 goads Welsh
straits, 1 pipe cont. 40 doz. candles, 2 brls. with M. 4 C. 3 qrs. pewter
vessels, £33 6s.8d.
Gerard Lesbern, H, 3 bales with 62 cloths w.g.; 500 goads Welsh straits,
£16 13s.4d.
Albert Falland, H, 1 bale with 10 cloths w.g.

291. 20 Nov. In the ship of John Matheuson [of Dordrecht]
John Evingar, A, 40 pipes beer, £13 6s.8d.

292. 23 Nov. In a cart of John Wyse going to Southampton
John Ambros, A, 3 bales with 50 cloths 16 yds. w.g.

293. 24 Nov. In the ship of Goddard Wrethe [of Hamburg]
Ingylbright Sevenek, H, 1 bale with 18½ cloths w.g.; 80 goads Welsh
straits, 53s.4d.
Matthew Hynkylman, H, 1 bale with 40 cloths w.g.; 80 goads Welsh
straits, 53s.4d.
Anthony Odyndale, H, 1 bale with 24 cloths w.g.; 60 goads Welsh
straits, 40s.
Henry Bevyr, H, 1 bale with 12 cloths w.g.; 60 goads Welsh straits, 40s.
Matthew Blytterswyke, H, 1 bale with 18 cloths w.g.; 80 goads Welsh
straits, 53s.4d.
William Scapehuson, H, 3 bales with 62½ cloths w.g.; 28 goads Welsh
straits, 20s.
John Questinburgh, H, 1 bale with 20 cloths w.g.; 429 goads Welsh
straits [*S* cotton russet], £14 6s.8d.
Henry Lathuson, H, 1 bale 1 fardel with 39 cloths w.g.
John Russenthorpp, H, 1 bale with 16 cloths 20 yds. w.g.; 94 goads
Welsh straits, 1 chest with 29 doz. [*S* lbs.] candles, £4 10s.
Hans Hosterborch, H, 1 bale with 13 cloths w.g.
Albert Falland, H, 1 bale with 25 cloths w.g.; 110 goads Welsh straits,
£3 13s.4d.

Tylman Barkys, H, 1 bale with 27 cloths w.g.; 50 goads Welsh straits, 33s.4d.

Arnold van Stalle, H, 1 bale with 20 cloths w.g.; 318 goads Welsh straits, £10 10s.

Arnold Moldyke, H, 2 brls. 3 kilderkins with 51 doz. candles, 53s.4d.

Henry Lathuson, H, 1 bale with 16 cloths w.g.

John Greverard, H, 1 bale with 20 cloths w.g.; 20 goads Welsh straits, 13s.4d.

Lambert Rotard, H, 1 bale with 13 cloths 5 yds. w.g.; 868 goads Welsh straits, £29

294. 24 Nov. In a cart of William Sellam going to Southampton
Gabriel Furnarius, A, 1 bale 2 fardels with 30 cloths w.g.

295. 24 Nov. In the ship of Richard Dockyng [of London]
James Bolle, A, 2 cases with 20 doz. candles, 2 brls. with salt meat, 1 chest with 10 pcs. Welsh straits, £5

George Hawkyn, D, 1 bale with 15 cloths w.g.

Robert Brown, D, 1 bale with 17 cloths w.g.

Peter Wolf, A, 10 blocks tin, £25

Anthony Gilbert, A, 5 M. summer rabbit skins, £5

William Donyngton, D, 1 bale with 28 cloths w.g.

John Benet, D, 1 bale with 21 cloths w.g.

Robert Brown, D, 1 fardel with 4½ cloths w.g.

Thomas Kyppyng, D, 1 fardel with 8 cloths w.g.

Ralph Bere, D, 1 fardel with 3 cloths w.g.

296. 27 Nov. In the ship of John Bawsak
Said master, A, 11 yds. cloth w.g.; 5 yds. Kendals, 2 yds. frieze, 3 tanned lambskins, 13s.4d.

297. 27 Nov. In the ship of William Smyth
William Isaak, D, 1 fardel with 4½ cloths w.g.

Robert Godwyn, D, 1 fardel with 2 cloths w.g., 1 pc. double worsted
Henry Vavaser [*S* Vavesour], D, 1 fardel with 3 cloths 16 yds. w.g.

298. 27 Nov. In the ship of Copyn Welle [of Antwerp]
John Evingar, A, 20 pipes beer, £6 13s.4d.

John Fryse, A, 17 [*S* 12] pipes beer, 5 brls. with salt meat, 3 brls. honey, £9

James Falke, A, 4 M. summer rabbit skins, £4

Peter Wolf, A, 4 M. summer rabbit skins, £4

John Salmer, H, 8 baskets with 16 C. lbs. rendered tallow, £6

Roger van Feld, H, 6 brls. with 60 doz. [*S* lbs.] candles, 1 hhd. with salt meat, £3 13s.4d.

James F[r]yse, A, 6 weys cheese, 3 brls. butter, 2 pipes with maslin meal, £4 10s.

Cornelius Smyth, A, 1 pipe 1 brl. with 50 doz. candles, 3 brls. honey, 2 brls. with salt meat, £5

Tylman van Demer, A, 12 brls. honey, 3 brls. with salt meat, £8
Martin Johnson, A, 3 hhds. 4 brls. with salt meat, 3 chests with 33 doz. candles, £4
Ralph Sent George, A, 1 fardel with 5½ cloths w.g.
Todero de Luka, A, 3 brls. with 36 doz. candles, 40s.
Said master, A, 3 pipes beer, 20s.

299. 28 Nov. In a cart of Henry Cole
Cosma Spenell', A, 2 bales 1 fardel with 45 cloths 16 yds. w.g.

300. 28 Nov. In the ship of Thomas Andrew [of London]
John Baxster, D, 1 fardel with 8 cloths w.g.

301. 29 Nov. In the ship of William Cornyssh [of London]
Matthew Hinkylman, H, 1 bale with 40 cloths w.g.; 40 goads Welsh straits, 26s.8d.
William Scapehuson, H, 1 bale with 30 cloths w.g.
John Questinburgh, H, 1 bale with 15 cloths w.g.; 160 goads Welsh straits, £5 6s.8d.
Tylman Barkys, H, 1 bale with 22 cloths w.g.; 20 goads Welsh straits, 13s.4d.
Paul Godfreye, A, 6 pipes beer, 40s.
Thomas Marchall, D, 1 bale with 17 cloths w.g.
Anthony Odindale, H, 1 bale with 18 cloths w.g.; 40 goads Welsh straits, 26s.8d.
Richard Chambir, D, 1 bale with 20 cloths w.g., 20 pcs. double worsted
Thomas Mayn, D, 1 fardel with 7 cloths 8 yds. w.g.

302. 29 Nov. In the ship of Henry Fryse
Ingilbright Sevenek, H, 1 bale with 17 cloths w.g.; 80 goads Welsh straits, 53s.4d.
Anthony Odindale, H, 1 bale with 18 cloths w.g.; 40 goads Welsh straits, 26s.8d.
Frank Savage, H, 2 brls. with 12 C. lbs. pewter vessels, £16
John Dosshare, A, 8 brls. 2 kilderkins honey, 8 baskets with M. C. 18 lbs. rendered tallow, 2 brls. with salt meat, £10
John Salmer, H, 2 pipes 6 brls. with 160 doz. candles, £8
William Grenewolt, H, 300 qrs. wheat, £100

303. 29 Nov. In the ship of Digo Fownse [of Viana]
Said master, A, 1 fardel with 1 cloth 8 yds. w.g.; 28 goads Welsh straits [*S* cotton russet], 13s.4d.

304. 29 Nov. In the ship of James Holand [of Holland]
Ingilbright Sevenek, H, 1 bale with 17 cloths w.g.; 80 goads Welsh straits [*S* cotton russet], 53s.4d.

305. 29 Nov. In the ship of John Yoman [of London]
Ingilbright Sevenek, H, 1 bale with 18 cloths w.g.; 82 goads Welsh straits [*S* cotton russet], 53s.4d.

Peter Wolf, A, 10 blocks tin, £25

Thomas Mayn, D, 1 bale with 15 cloths 8 yds. w.g.

John Salmer, H, 1 hhd. with 90 doz. candles, £4 10s.

Frank Savage, H, 1 fardel with 2 rolls frieze, 4½ rolls frieze, 400 goads Welsh straits, 2 brls. with 12 C. lbs. pewter vessels, £31

John Welbek, A, 4 pipes 1 hhd. 3 [*S* 2] brls. with salt meat, 4½ weys cheese, 7 brls. butter, 6 flitches bacon, 12 pipes beer, £12 13s.4d.

Laurence Tyman, A, 6 blocks tin, £15

Lewis Bonyvice, A, 9 baskets with 9 weys rendered tallow, £5

William Grenewolt, H, 2 bales with 29½ cloths w.g.; 60 goads Welsh straits [*S* cotton russet], 40s.

Tylman Vandemer, A, 1 bale with 46 pcs. Welsh straits [*S* cotton russet], £18

Peter Syber, H, 2 bales with 29 cloths w.g.; 166 goads Welsh straits, £8 13s.4d.

John Greverard, H, 1 bale with 19 cloths w.g.; 20 goads Welsh straits [*S* cotton russet], 13s.4d.

[m.13d.]

John van Armysbery, H, 1 bale with 15 cloths w.g.; 40 goads Welsh straits, 26s.8d.

William Martyn, D, 1 chest with 4 cloths w.g.

Albert Falland, H, 1 bale with 19 cloths w.g.; 222 goads Welsh straits, £7 10s.

John van Derbeson, H, 1 bale with 18 cloths w.g.; 80 goads Welsh straits, 53s.4d.

John Ebrall, D, 1 bale with 13 cloths w.g.

Michael Malbrayn, A, 12 doz. candles, 13s.4d.

James Falk, A, 1 pipe with 16 bushels maslin, 3 brls. with salt meat, 1 net ('reth'), 26s.8d.

George Tak, H, 1 bale with 15 cloths w.g.; 20 goads Welsh straits, 13s.4d. [*S* 23s.4d.]

John van Strawlyn, H, 1 bale with 18 cloths w.g.; 90 goads Welsh straits [*S* cotton russet], £3

Stephen Branche, H, 1 bale with 10 cloths w.g.; 305 goads Welsh straits [*S* 310 goads cotton russet], £10 13s.4d.

Roger van Feld, H, 1 bale with 16 cloths w.g.; 120 goads Welsh straits [*S* cotton russet], £4

John van Armysbery, H, 1 bale with 18 cloths w.g.; 80 goads Welsh straits, 53s.4d.

John Stakylhuson, H, 1 bale with 18 cloths 5 yds. w.g.; 40 goads Welsh straits, 1 hhd. with salt meat, 1 chest with 20 doz. candles, 53s.4d.

Matthew Blytterswyke, H, 1 bale with 14 cloths w.g.; 224 goads Welsh straits, £7 10s.

Gerard van Grove, H, 1 bale with 16 cloths w.g.; 20 goads Welsh straits, 13s.4d.

John Questinburgh, H, 1 bale with 17 cloths w.g.; 325 goads Welsh straits, £10 16s.8d.

Anthony Odindale, H, 1 bale with 14 cloths w.g.; 40 goads Welsh straits, 26s.8d.

Arnold van Stalle, H, 1 fardel with 9 cloths w.g.; 83 goads Welsh straits, 56s.8d.

John van Armysbery, H, 1 fardel with 5 cloths w.g.; 11 goads Welsh straits, 4 cheeses, 17 salt tongues, 13s.4d.

John Ebrall, D, 2 fardels with 9 cloths w.g.

Simon Smyth, D, 1 fardel with 7 cloths 16 yds. w.g.

Thomas Smyth, D, 1 fardel with 4 cloths w.g.

306. 29 Nov. In the ship of Robert Walcok [of London]
Thomas Smyth, D, 1 bale with 11 cloths w.g.

307. 29 Nov. In the ship of John Roke [of London]
Ingilbright Sevenek, H, 1 bale with 18 cloths w.g.; 80 goads Welsh straits, 53s.4d.

John Questinburgh, H, 1 bale with 17 cloths w.g.; 90 goads Welsh straits, £3

308. 1 Dec. In the ship of John Capp [of London]
Robert Southwode, D, 2 bales with 63 cloths w.g.

Roger Hevyn, D, 1 bale with 33 cloths w.g.

Thomas Bradburye, D, 1 fardel with 1 cloth w.g., 42 pcs. double worsted

Ingilbright Sevenek, H, 1 bale with 17 cloths w.g.; 80 goads Welsh straits, 53s.4d.

Roger Bonyfaunt, D, 1 bale with 33 cloths w.g.

Thomas Hore, D, 1 bale with 22 cloths w.g.

Richard Twig, D, 1 bale with 10 cloths w.g.

Robert Southwode, D, 1 bale with 30 cloths w.g.

John Crace, D, 1 bale with 30 cloths w.g.

John Fysshare, D, 1 bale with 20 cloths w.g.

John Colyns, D, 2 bales with 40 cloths w.g.

Roger Bonyfaunt, D, 1 bale with 13 cloths w.g.

John Chambyr, D, 1 bale with 30 cloths w.g.

Henry Cantlowe, D, 1 bale with 16 cloths w.g.

Nicholas Martyn, D, 2 bales with 36 cloths w.g.

John Rose, D, 1 bale with 14 cloths w.g., 58 pcs. double worsted, 4 pcs. single worsted

Robert Drayton, D, 1 bale with 16 cloths w.g.

John Stanley, D, 1 bale with 27 cloths w.g.

Thomas Lok, D, 1 fardel with 5 cloths w.g., 6 pcs. double worsted

Thomas Quadryng, D, 1 fardel with 6 cloths w.g.

William Redye, D, 1 fardel with 7½ cloths w.g., 6 pcs. double worsted

John Gose, D, 2 bales with 54½ cloths w.g.

William Clerk, D, 1 bale with 18 cloths w.g.

Richard Langton, D, 1 bale with 36 cloths w.g.

Peter Cristemas, D, 1 bale with 11 cloths w.g.

Thomas Lee, D, 1 bale with 22 cloths w.g.

John Fyssh, D, 1 fardel with 5 cloths w.g.

John van Armysbery, H, 1 bale with 19 cloths w.g.; 100 goads Welsh straits, 1 brl. with 12 cheeses, £3 13s.4d.

William Scapehuson, H, 1 bale with 17 cloths w.g.; 19 goads Welsh straits, 13s.4d.

Tylman Barkys, H, 1 bale with 18 cloths w.g.; 40 goads Welsh straits, 26s.8d.

William Whetewey, D, 1 bale with 23 cloths w.g.

Thomas Crewen, D, 1 bale with 10½ cloths w.g.

Stephen Jannys, D, 1 bale with 15 cloths w.g.

John Pellam, D, 2 bales with 52 cloths w.g.

John Ulsbye, D, 1 bale with 14½ cloths w.g.

Richard Eyryk, D, 1 bale with 15 cloths w.g.

Richard White, D, 1 bale with 24 cloths w.g.

John Pykton, D, 2 bales with 63 cloths w.g.

John Colet, D, 1 bale with 33 cloths w.g.

Hans Stut, H, 1 bale with 29 cloths w.g.; 25 goads Welsh straits, 16s.8d.

Thomas Kellet, D, 2 bales with 25 cloths w.g.

Richard Wethir, D, 2 bales with 37 cloths w.g.

Richard Laken, D, 1 fardel with 7 cloths 18 yds. w.g.

Ralph Bere, D, 1 bale with 15 cloths w.g.

John Benet, D, 1 bale with 9 cloths w.g.

William Sholdewell [S Choldwell], D, 1 fardel with 3 cloths w.g.

John Spilman, D, 1 bale with 10 cloths w.g.

Peter Siber, H, 1 bale with 18 cloths w.g.; 138 goads Welsh straits, £4 13s.4d.

John Russynthorp, H, 1 bale with 17 cloths w.g.; 90 goads Welsh straits [S cotton russet], £3

John Kyrkebye, D, 1 bale with 13½ cloths w.g.

Albert Falland, H, 1 bale with 25 cloths w.g.; 133 goads Welsh straits [S cotton russet], £4 10s.

Robert Squyer, D, 1 bale with 23 cloths 20 yds. w.g.

Thomas Stogye, D, 1 fardel with 4 cloths w.g.

Roger Bonyfaunt, D, 1 bale with 12 cloths w.g.

John Pekering, D, 1 bale with 11 cloths w.g.

John Rose, D, 1 fardel with 8 cloths w.g.

Edmund Talwyn, D, 1 bale with 14 cloths w.g.

Thomas Raven [S Rawyn], D, 1 bale with 15 cloths w.g.

Roger van Feld, H, 1 bale with 17 cloths w.g.; 110 goads Welsh straits, £3 13s.4d.

George Tag [S Tak], H, 1 fardel with 7 cloths w.g.; 8 goads Welsh straits, 6s.8d.

John Stakylhuson, H, 1 fardel with 7 cloths w.g.; 100 goads Welsh straits, £3 6s.8d.

John Russinthorp, H, 1 bale with 18 cloths w.g.; 90 goads Welsh straits, £3

Henry Frost, D, 1 fardel with 1 cloth w.g., 14 pcs. double worsted

John van Straulyn, H, 1 fardel with 7 cloths w.g.; 300 goads cotton russet, £10

309. 1 Dec. In the ship of William Tabbard [of Boston]

Robert Southwode, D, 3 bales with 87 cloths w.g.

Roger Hevyn, D, 1 bale with 33 cloths w.g.

Roger Bonyfaunt, D, 1 bale with 33 cloths w.g.

Ingilbright Sevenek, H, 1 bale with 17 cloths w.g.; 80 goads Welsh straits, 53s.4d.

William Scapehuson, H, 1 bale with 15 cloths w.g.; 180 goads Welsh straits, £6

John Crace, D, 1 bale with 30 cloths w.g.

John Colyns, D, 2 bales with 34 cloth 16 yds. w.g.

[m.14]

Nicholas Alwyn, D, 1 bale with 14 cloths w.g.

Henry Cantlowe, D, 1 bale with 10 cloths w.g.

Nicholas Martyn, D, 1 bale with 26 cloths w.g.

Richard Langton, D, 1 bale with 33 cloths w.g.

John Rose, D, 1 bale with 33 cloths w.g.

John Stanley, D, 1 bale with 32 cloths w.g.

Robert Drayton, D, 1 bale with 14 cloths w.g.

William Banknot, D, 1 bale with 21 cloths w.g., 4 pcs. double worsted

William Eton, D, 1 bale with 10 cloths w.g.

John Pellam, D, 1 bale with 30 cloths w.g.

John Questinburgh, H, 1 bale with 17 cloths w.g.; 50 goads Welsh straits, 33s.4d.

John Gose, D, 1 bale with 21 cloths 8 yds. w.g., 1 pc. double worsted

John Colyns, D, 1 fardel with 8 cloths w.g.

Thomas Bate, D, 1 fardel with 6½ cloths w.g.

Nicholas Morton, D, 1 bale with 16 cloths w.g.

John Collard, D, 1 bale with 10½ cloths w.g.

William Bentley, D, 1 fardel with 8 cloths w.g.

Roger Bonyfaunt, D, 1 bale with 11 cloths w.g.

Thomas Lee, D, 1 bale with 24 cloths w.g.

Stephen Jannys, D, 1 bale with 17 cloths 8 yds. w.g.

Roger Grove, D, 1 bale with 24 cloths w.g.

John Fysshare, D, 1 bale with 16 cloths w.g.

John Ulsbye, D, 1 bale with 31 cloths w.g.

Thomas Kyppyng, D, 1 bale with 32 cloths 8 yds. w.g.

Richard Jamys, D, 1 fardel with 3 cloths 16 yds. w.g.

Thomas Barnard, D, 1 bale with 15 cloths 16 yds. w.g.

Thomas Ward, D, 1 fardel with 9½ cloths w.g.

Richard White, D, 1 bale with 24 cloths w.g.

John Pykton, D, 1 bale with 31 cloths 6 yds. w.g.

Hans Stut, H, 1 bale with 25 cloths w.g.; 30 goads Welsh straits, 20s.

John Hosyare, D, 1 bale with 21 cloths. w.g.

William Ledys, D, 1 fardel with 3 cloths 8 yds. w.g., 3 pcs. double worsted.

John Salmer, H, 2 brls. with M. 2 C. lbs. pewter vessels, £16

William Jenk', D, 1 chest with 2 cloths w.g.

Matthew Bliterswyke, H, 1 bale with 18 cloths w.g.; 60 goads Welsh straits, 40s.

John Greverard, H, 1 bale with 19 cloths w.g.; 20 goads Welsh straits,

13s.4d.

Goswyn Redekyrk, H, 1 bale with 19 cloths w.g.; 80 goads Welsh straits, 53s.4d.

John Stakylhuson, H, 1 bale with 18½ cloths w.g.; 40 [*S* 60] goads Welsh straits, 1 chest with 21 doz. candles, 1 hhd. with salt meat, 6 doz. lbs. starch, £3

Alan Hubbard, D, 1 bale with 10 cloths w.g.

Peter Joye, D, 1 fardel with 8 cloths w.g.

Edward Brampton, D, 1 bale with 18 cloths w.g.

William Hayle, D, 1 bale with 18 cloths w.g.

Albert Falland, H, 1 bale with 25 cloths w.g.; 27 goads Welsh straits, £4 5s.

Peter Syber, H, 1 bale with 18 cloths w.g.; 118 goads Welsh Straits, £4

John van Strawlyn, H, 1 bale with 19 cloths w.g.; 60 goads Welsh straits, 40s.

Roger Bonyfaunt, D, 1 fardel with 4 cloths w.g.

Richard Langton, D, 1 fardel with 9 cloths w.g.

Robert Bryklysworth, D, 1 bale with 10 cloths w.g.

John Pykton, D, 1 bale with 24 cloths w.g.

Henry Cantlowe, D, 1 fardel with 5 cloths w.g.

Robert Squyer, D, 1 bale with 22½ cloths w.g.

Thomas Kelet, D, 1 bale with 25 cloths w.g.

John Fysshare, D, 1 fardel with 1 cloth w.g., 14 pcs. double worsted

John Crace, D, 1 fardel with 6 cloths w.g.

William Mannyng, D, 1 fardel with 4 cloths w.g.

John van Armysbery, H, 1 bale with 18 cloths w.g.; 80 goads Welsh straits, 53s.4d.

Roger van Feld, H, 1 bale with 15½ cloths w.g., 1½ cloths in grain, 3 cloths of half grain; 140 goads Welsh Straits, £4 13s.4d.

John van Derbeson, H, 1 bale with 16 cloths w.g.; 30 goads Welsh straits, 20s.

Hans Culle, H, 1 fardel with 5 cloths w.g.; 20 goads Welsh straits, 13s.4d.

John van Armysbery, H, 1 bale with 13 cloths w.g.; 30 goads Welsh straits, 20s.

John Russinthorp, H, 1 bale with 22 cloths w.g.; 135 goads Welsh straits, £4 10s.

Robert Boys, D, 1 fardel with 6 cloths w.g.

Thomas Callowe, D, 1 fardel with 3 cloths w.g.

John Fysshare, D, 1 fardel with 5 cloths w.g.

Walter Violet, D, 1 fardel with 2 cloths w.g.

John Collet, D, 1 fardel with 8 cloths w.g.

Thomas Bate, D, 1 fardel with 3 cloths w.g.

John Colet, D, 1 fardel with 5 pcs. double worsted

310. 1 Dec. In the ship of Henry Weye

Luke Valaryso, A, 1 bale with 40 doz. tanned calfskins, £6 13s.4d.

311. 1 Dec. In the ship of Denis Wesyall [of Guérande]

Said master, A, 59 pcs. brass weight 2 M. 3 C. lbs., 18 pcs. copper weight 4 C. 3 qrs. 20 lbs., £34

312. 1 Dec. In the ship of Robert Bygg [of London]
John Jamys, A, 11 pipes beer, £3 13s.4d.
Ingilbright Sevenek, H, 1 fardel with 1 cloth w.g., 2½ pcs. single worsted; 540 [*S* 640] goads Welsh straits, £21 6s.8d.
Geroff' Vanderhelstall, A, 1 hhd. with salt meat, 13s.4d.
Frank Mathew, A, 6 pipes beer, 40s.
John Demayn, A, 5½ weys cheese, 53s.4d.
Robert Fleccher, D, 1 fardel with 4 cloths w.g.
John Durham, D, 1 fardel with 2 cloths w.g.
Anthony de la Hay, A, 5 brls. with salt meat, 26s.8d. [*S* 26s.4d.]
Gerard Scalstret, A, 2½ brls. with 12 doz. candles, 13s.4d.
Goswyn Redekerk, H, 1 bale with 11 cloths w.g.; 15 goads Welsh straits, 10s.
John Gybbes, A, 24 doz. candles, 30 cheeses, 33s.4d.

313. 1 Dec. In the ship of John Bawdewyn [of Calais]
Richard Bryn, D, 1 bale with 18 cloths w.g.
Thomas Goldsmyth, D, 1 bale with 15 cloths w.g.
Thomas Lee, D, 2 bales with 44 cloths w.g.
John Millet, D, 1 fardel with 6 cloths w.g.
John Wode, D, 1 fardel with 8 cloths w.g.
Henry Halle, D, 1 bale with 33 cloths w.g.
Robert Drayton, D, 1 bale with 14 cloths w.g.
Roger Grove, D, 1 bale with 19 cloths w.g.
John Warner, D, 1 bale with 23 cloths w.g.
John Nawthan, D, 1 bale with 17 cloths w.g.
Roger Arnold, D, 1 bale with 29 cloths w.g., 8 pcs. double worsted
William Scapehuson, H, 1 bale with 9½ cloths w.g.; 360 goads Welsh straits, £12
Richard White, D, 1 fardel with 6 cloths w.g.
John Brampton, D, 1 bale with 12 cloths w.g.
Richard Langton, D, 1 bale with 36 cloths w.g.
William Bard, D, 1 bale with 13 cloths w.g.
Matthew Bliterswyke, H, 1 bale with 18 cloths w.g.; 60 goads Welsh straits, 40s.
John Greverard, H, 1 bale with 19 cloths w.g.; 20 goads Welsh straits, 13s.4d.
Goswyn Redekyrk, H, 1 bale with 18 cloths w.g.; 50 goads Welsh straits, 33s.4d.
Robert (Richard *del.*) Ryngbell, D, 1 bale with 14 cloths w.g.
Richard Wethir, D, 1 bale with 27 cloths w.g.
John Russinthorp, H, 1 bale with 16 cloths w.g.; 85 goads Welsh straits, 56s.8d.
William Sholdewell, D, 1 bale with 14 cloths w.g.
John Shylwyn, D, 1 bale with 18½ cloths w.g.
[m.14d.]

Ralph Bere, D, 1 bale with 21 cloths w.g.
Peter Joye, D, 1 fardel with 6 cloths w.g.
John Benet, D, 1 bale with 15 cloths w.g.
Thomas Kyppyng,[1] D, 1 bale with 18 cloths w.g.
William Hayle, D, 1 bale with 18 cloths w.g.
Robert Boys, D, 1 bale with 11 cloths w.g.
Roger Arnold, D, 8 cloths w.g.
John Spilman, D, 1 bale with 10 cloths w.g.
Nicholas Wylde,[1] D, 1 bale with 11 cloths w.g.
Thomas Kyppyng, D, 1 bale with 16 cloths w.g.
Robert Jakson, D, 1 fardel with 9 cloths w.g.
Edmund Talwyn, D, 1 bale with 15 cloths w.g.
John Baker, D, 1 fardel with 1 cloth 16 yds. w.g.
William Geffrey, D, 1 fardel with 3 cloths w.g.
John Paynter, D, 1 fardel with 2 cloths w.g.
Thomas Crosse, D, 1 cloth 8 yds. w.g.
John Salmer, H, 1 fardel with 3 cloths w.g.; 85 [*S* 500] goads Welsh straits, 4 pipes with 120 doz. candles, £22 13s.4d.[2]
Peter Syber, H, 1 bale with 18 cloths w.g.; 120 goads Welsh straits £4
John van Armysbery, H, 1 bale with 15 cloths w.g.; 40 goads Welsh straits, 26s.8d.
Arnold van Stall, H, 1 bale with 16 cloths w.g.; 238 goads Welsh straits, £8
Albert Falland, H, 1 bale [with] 25 cloths w.g.; 130 goads Welsh straits, £4 6s.8d.
John van Derbeson, H, 1 bale with 18 cloths w.g.; 55 goads Welsh straits, 36s.8d.
John Van Strawlyn, H, 1 bale with 18 cloths w.g.; 40 goads Welsh straits, 26s.8d.

[1] Entries for Thomas Kyppyng to Nicholas Wylde repeated, marg. 'vacat quia antea'.
[2] 56s.8d. *del.* '4 pipes... £22 13s.4d.' inserted here and in *S* in another hand.

314. 7 Dec. In the ship [*sic* for cart] of Peter Jamys going to Southampton
John Kendall,[1] D, 1 bale with 17 cloths w.g., 1 bale with 14 cloths w.g.

[1] See **282–287** above.

315. 7 Dec. In a cart of William Sellam going to Southampton
John Kendall, D, 3 bales with 43 cloths 22 yds. w.g., 2 cloths 22 yds. in grain

316. 7 Dec. In the ship of John Wilcok
William Isaac, D, 1 fardel 2 pipes with 13 cloths 8 yds. w.g.
Richard Isaac, D, 2 fardels with 23 cloths w.g.
John Kyrkbye, D, 1 fardel with 7½ cloths w.g.
Robert Godwyn, D, 2 fardels with 40 cloths w.g.
Richard Odyham, D, 1 bale with 20 cloths w.g.
William Herryot, D, 4 bales with 44 cloths w.g.
John Baylye, D, 2 bales 1 fardel with 27 cloths w.g.

Robert Basset, D, 1 bale with 20 cloths w.g.

317. 9 Dec. In the ship of Lubert van Boke [of the Steelyard]
Herman Plough, H, 4 pipes with salt meat, £4
John Salmer, H, 6 brls. with 72 doz. candles, £3 13s.4d.
Matthew Hynkylman, H, 1 bale with 16 cloths w.g.; 50 goads Welsh
straits, 33s.4d.
Stephen Branche, H, 1 bale with 310 goads Welsh straits, £10 6s.8d.

318. 9 Dec. In the ship of Luke Countman [of Antwerp]
Luke Nekare, A, 1 bale with 20 pcs. Welsh straits, £10

319. 9 Dec. In the ship of Anthony Grostiago
Peter Gumsalvo of Guipúzcoa, Sp, 1 fardel with 2 cloths 16 yds. w.g.
Peter Valedelede of Guipúzcoa, Sp, 2 bales with 29 cloths w.g.
John Martinus of Guipúzcoa, Sp, 1 fardel with 5 cloths w.g.
Alonso de Lyon, of Guipúzcoa, Sp, 1 fardel with 2 cloths 20 yds. in
grain, 13 yds. cloth of half grain, 4 cloths w.g.

320. 12 Dec. In a cart of Thomas Geffrey going to Southampton
Laurence Gryll', A, 3 bales with 40 cloths 16 yds. w.g.

321. 12 Dec. In a cart of John Rede going to Southampton
Thomas Pend', D, 3 bales with 42 cloths w.g.

322. 12 Dec. In the ship of Otys Code
William Heriot, D, 3 fardels with 24 cloths w.g.
Richard Odyham, D, 1 bale with 17 cloths 8 yds. w.g.
Thomas Bell, D, 1 fardel with 7 cloths 8 yds. w.g.
Robert Basset, D, 1 bale with 20 cloths w.g.

323. 12 Dec. In the ship of John Stephenis called *Nicholus* of Fowey
Robert Godwyn, D, 1 fardel with 2 cloths in grain, 2 cloths w.g.
Edward Brampton, D, 1 bale with 12 cloths w.g.

324. 12 Dec. In the ship of John Stephenis called *Sanctus Spiritus* of
Oporto
Lopo Alverus, A, 1 chest with 18 pcs. pewter vessels weight 21 lbs., 6
cushions, 13s.4d.
Said master, A, 1 fardel with 6 cloths 16 yds. w.g.; 4 coverlets, 51 pcs.
copper weight 2 M. lbs. 1 qr., 10 brls. pitch, £23
Alexander Portinarius, A, 4 fardels with 10 cloths 18 yds. w.g.; 40 pcs.
Welsh straits, 1 basket with C. 20 lbs. pewter vessels, £15
Alfonso Yanus, A, 1 fardel with 2 cloths w.g.; 6 yds. Welsh straits, 2
coverlets, 16s.8d.
John Stephyns, A, 1 cloth 16 yds. w.g.; 2 coverlets, 13s.4d.
Said master, A, 8 yds. cloth w.g.; 2 pcs. Welsh straits, 1 coverlet,
26s.8d.

325. 12 Dec. In a cart of John Rede going to Southampton

Cosma Spenyll', A, 2 bales with 25 cloths 16 yds. w.g.
John Spenyll', A, 1 fardel with 4 cloths 8 yds. w.g.

326. 12 Dec. In a cart of John Rede going to Southampton
John Baptista Gentyll', A, 3 bales with 45 cloths w.g.

327. 15 Dec. In the ship of Alvery Yanes [of Oporto]
Alexander Portinarius, A, 1 fardel with 3 cloths w.g.
Edward Brampton, D, 1 fardel with 5 cloths w.g.

328. 20 Dec. In the ship of John de Albustro [of San Sebastian]
Said John Albustro of Guipúzcoa, Sp, 1 cloth 8 yds. w.g.

329. 20 Dec. In a cart of Peter Jamys going to Southampton
Frank Justinian', A, 3 bales with 33 cloths w.g.

330. 20 Dec. In the ship of Michael Deke [of Ostend]
Richard Cok, D, 16½ yds. cloth w.g.
Said master, A, 3 doz. oars, 40s.

331. 23 Dec. In the ship of John Buk [of Saltash]
Thomas Stalbroke, D, 1 bale with 17 cloths w.g.

332. 2 Jan. In the ship of John Labye
John Lapomerye, A, 1 last soap, 4 C lbs. rendered tallow, £10 10s.
Gylwyn' Gordyn, A, 6 C. 12 lbs. rendered tallow, 2 brls. tar, 12 doz.
tanned calfskins, 2½ C. lbs. lead, £5 13s.4d.
John Borell, A, 1 cloth 16 yds. w.g.; 20 yds. Welsh straits, 12 doz.
candles, ½ C. lbs. 'vryas', 1 last pitch, 58s.

333. 8 Jan. In a cart of Peter Jamys going to Southampton
John Ambros, A, 1 bale with 18 cloths 8 yds. w.g., 7 fardels with 5 cloths
8 yds. in grain, 3 cloths 8 yds. of half grain

334. 10 Jan. In a cart of William Rede going to Southampton
Alexander Portinarius, A, 2 bales with 10 cloths 16 yds. w.g., 4 cloths in
grain, 6 cloths 8 yds. of half grain

335. 11 Jan. In a cart of William Sellam going to Southampton, to be
shipped in a certain galley
Luke de Monte Nigro, A, 1 fardel with 8 cloths 8 yds. w.g.; 1 pc. Welsh
straits, 6s.8d.

336. 11 Jan. In a cart of William Rede going to Southampton
Guy Mongona, A, 1 fardel with 2 cloths 8 yds. w.g.; 8 pcs. Welsh straits,
53s.4d.

337. 11 Jan. In a cart of Richard Marchall going to Southampton
Anthony Bavaryn', A, 3 bales with 45 cloths 8 yds. w.g.

338. 11 Jan. In a cart of Richard Marchall going to Southampton
Anthony Bavaryn', A, 3 bales with 39 cloths w.g.

339. 18 Jan. In a cart of Thomas Arnold going to Southampton
Allegreto de Jara, A, 3 bales with 36 cloths w.g.

[m.15]
340. 18 Jan. In a cart of William Sellam going to Southampton
Andrew Gylys, A, 1 fardel with 8 cloths 23 yds. w.g.; 6 pcs. single
worsted, 1 pc. Welsh straits, £4 10s.; and for the aforsaid 6 pcs. single
worsted [val. *del.*]¹

¹ Worsteds exported by non-Hanseatic aliens were liable both for *ad valorem* petty
custom and the specific duty imposed in 1347, hence the repetition (*England's Export
Trade*, 199).

341. 18 Jan. In a cart of John Rede going to Southampton
Andrew Gylys, A, 2 fardels with 5 cloths 16 yds. w.g.; 41 pcs. Welsh
straits, 2 pcs. single worsted, £20 10s.; and for the aforesaid 2 pcs.
single worsted

342. 26 Jan. In the ship of Michael Elyng' [of Ostend]
Peter Clayne, A, 2 pipes 4 brls. beer, 3 brls. with 30 doz. candles, 3 weys
rendered tallow, £4

343. 29 Jan. On three horses of John Gilbert going to the port of Bristol
Peter Valedelede of Guipúzcoa, Sp, 3 fardels with 10 cloths 8 yds. w.g.,
2 cloths 21 yds. in grain

344. 29 Jan. In the ship of Cornelius Moch [of London]
Giles Mase, A, 6 brls. with 66 lbs. candles, £3 6s.8d.

345. 30 Jan. In a cart of William Sellam going to Southampton
Luke Valarisa, A, 1 bale with 14 cloths w.g.

346. 5 Feb. In a cart of Peter Jamys going to Southampton
Lazaro de Pero, A, 1 fardel with 8 cloths 20 yds. w.g.; 2 pcs. Welsh
straits, 13s.4d.

347. 9 Feb. In a cart of William Sellam going to Southampton
Andrew Gylys, A, 1 bale with 11 cloths 8 yds. w.g.

348. 10 Feb. In a cart of William Hattyswell going to Southampton
Lewis Bonyvise, A, 1 bale with 11 cloths 20 yds. w.g.; 4 pcs. Welsh
straits, 26s.8d.

349. 14 Feb. In the ship of Nicholas Thorn' [of Arnemuiden]
Herman Johnson, A, 16 pipes beer, £5 6s.8d.
Lewis Bonevise, A, 29 baskets with 30 weys rendered tallow, £15
Edward Johnson, A, 10 pcs. tin, £25; 2 M. summer rabbit-skins, 40s.
John Kele, A, 6 brls. butter, 40s.

Luke Fons, A, 1 chest with 1 cloth w.g.; 3 coverlets, 2 cheeses, 26s.8d.

Ingylbright Sevenek, H, 1 bale with 20½ cloths w.g.; 17 goads Welsh straits, 13s.4d.

George Tak, H, 1 bale with 19 cloths w.g.; 21 goads Welsh straits, 13s.4d.

Albert Falland, H, 1 bale with 25 cloths w.g.; 80 goads Welsh straits, 53s.4d.

Roger van Feld, H, 1 bale with 25 cloths w.g.; 20 goads Welsh straits, 13s.4d.

Herman Overcamp, H, 1 maund with 4 M. 8 C. seasoned and M. summer rabbit-skins, £10 13s.4d.

John Van Strawlyn, H, 1 bale with 20 cloths w.g.; 30 goads Welsh straits, 20s.

Edward Johnson, A, 6 pipes beer, 40s.

Laurence Gylys, D, 1 fardel with 4 cloths 8 yds. w.g.

Matthew Blyterswyk, H, 1 bale with 14 cloths w.g.; 20 goads Welsh straits, 13s.4d.

Herman Plough, H, 1 bale with 31 cloths w.g.; 20 goads Welsh straits, 13s.4d.

Tylman Barkys, H, 1 bale with 17 cloths w.g.; 60 goads Welsh straits, 40s.

Henry Lathuson, H, 1 bale with 23 cloths 8 yds. w.g.; 50 goads Welsh straits, 33s.4d.

William Scapehuson, H, 1 bale with 16 cloths w.g.; 135 goads Welsh straits, £4 10s.

John Greverard, H, 1 bale with 20 cloths w.g.; 60 goads Welsh straits, 40s.

John Russynthorp, H, 1 bale with 12 cloths, 6 yds. w.g.; 20 goads Welsh straits, 13s.4d.

John van Derbeson, H, 1 bale with 20 cloths w.g.; 42 goads Welsh straits, 26s.8d.

Matthew Bliterswyk, H, 1 bale with 15 cloths w.g.; 20 goads Welsh straits, 13s.4d.

John Salmer, H, 2 brls. with 12 C. lbs. pewter vessels, £16

Arnold van Stalle, H, 1 bale with 16 cloths w.g.; 41 goads Welsh straits, 26s.8d.

Tylman Barkys, H, 1 bale with 10½ cloths w.g.; 40 goads Welsh straits, 26s.8d.

Hans Stut, H, 1 bale with 25 cloths w.g.; 1 maund with 4 M. seasoned and 2 M. summer rabbit-skins, £10

William Grenewolt, H, 1 bale with 12 cloths w.g.

Peter Syber, H, 1 fardel with 8 yds. cloth w.g.; 6,000 pins, 2 grs. points, 6s.8d.

Giles Gaunt, A, 1 brl. with C. qr. 14 lbs. pewter vessels, 40s.

Gerard Lesbern, H, 1 bale with 19 cloths w.g., 2 pcs. double worsted; 20 goads Welsh straits, 13s.4d.

Hans Culle, H, 1 bale with 27 cloths w.g.; 120 goads Welsh straits, £4

John Sewyk, H, 1 bale with 21 cloths w.g.; 1 roll frieze, 13s.4d.

Anthony Dupansell, A, 2 small brls. with C. 50 lbs. pewter vessels, 40s.

Albert Falland, H, 1 maund with 7 M. 8 C. [*S* 4 M. 8 C.] seasoned and 2 C. summer rabbit-skins, £9 16s.

350. 16 Feb. In a cart of Peter Jamys going to Southampton, to be shipped in a certain galley
Luke de Nigro, A, 1 fardel with 3 cloths 18 yds. w.g.
Said Luke, A, 3 cloths 20 yds. w.g.; 44 goads Welsh straits, 20s.

351. 17 Feb. In a cart of Henry Colyare going to Southampton
Allegreto de Jara, A, 1 bale with 11 cloths w.g.

352. 17 Feb. In a cart of Henry Cole going to Southampton
Lewis Bonyvise, A, 1 fardel with 4 cloths 16 yds. w.g.

353. 20 Feb. In a certain barge of Henry Smyth going to Gravesend
Adrian Muse, D, 1 bale with 12 cloths 6 yds. w.g.

354. 20 Feb. In the ship of Anthony Brabander [of Middelburg]
John Chambir, D, 1 fardel with 6 cloths 18 yds. w.g., 4 pcs. double worsted
George Tak, H, 1 bale with 18 cloths w.g.; 23 goads Welsh straits, 16s.8d.
Albert Falland, H, 1 bale with 25 cloths. w.g.; 105 goads Welsh straits, 1 maund with 5 M. 5 C. seasoned rabbit-skins, £14 13s.4d.
John Salmer, H, 2 brls. with 12 C. lbs. pewter vessels, 2 brls. with salt meat, £16 13s.4d.
Herman Overcamp, H, 1 maund with 4 M. 5 C. seasoned and 3 M. summer rabbit-skins, £12
Matthew Blyterswyk, H, 1 bale with 13 cloths w.g.; 17 goads Welsh straits, 13s.4d.
John Greverard, H, 1 bale with 19½ cloths w.g.; 100 goads Welsh straits, £3 6s.8d.
William Scapehuson, H, 1 bale with 42 cloths w.g.
John Russynthorp, H, 1 bale with 12 cloths w.g.; 20 goads Welsh straits, 13s.4d.
John van Derbeson, H, 1 bale with 17 cloths w.g.; 84 goads Welsh straits, 56s.8d.
Matthew Bliterswyk, H, 1 bale with 14 cloths 3 yds. w.g.; 20 goads Welsh straits, 13s.4d.
Hans Stut, H, 1 bale with 26 cloths w.g.; 1 maund with 4 M. seasoned and 2 M. summer rabbit-skins, £10
Gerard Lesbern, H, 1 bale with 22 cloths w.g.; 55 goads Welsh straits, 36s.8d.
Henry Lathuson, H, 1 bale with 35 cloths w.g.
John Chambr', D, 3 pcs. double worsted
John Evingar, A, 15 pipes beer, £5
Cornelius Brely, A, 1 fardel with 2 cloths 8 yds. w.g.; 4 brls. with 48 doz. 10 lbs. candles, 20 flitches bacon, £3 10s.
William Williamson, A, 1 pack with 18 yds. cloth w.g.

355. 21 Feb. In the ship of John Bargeman [of Reimerswaal]
John Brown, H, 34 pipes beer, 1 pipe vinegar, £12
Said master, A, 8 yds. cloth w.g.; 6 pcs. Welsh straits, 6 pipes beer, 1 brl. with 13 doz. candles, £5
Simon Williamson, A, 1 brl. with 16 doz. lbs. starch, 13s.4d.

356. 21 Feb. In the ship of James Doffyn
John Augo, A, 12 brls. 5 baskets with 31 C. 20 lbs. rendered tallow, 6 brls. pitch, 3 brls. with 35 doz. lbs. candles, 1 basket with C. 14 lbs. pewter vessels, £17
John Elyot, A, 1 cloth 22 yds. w.g.; 6 fothers 21 lbs. lead, 1 basket with 3 C. 1 qr. 15 lbs. copper, 23 brls. pitch, 2 C. lbs. rendered tallow, 12 lbs. candles, 2 yds. frieze, £32
Thomas Sylwey, A, 1 brl. with 2 C. 10 lbs. pewter vessels. 53s. 4d.

[m.15d]
357. 22 Feb. In a cart of William Johnson going to Southampton
John Spinell', A, 3 bales with 44 cloths 16 yds. w.g.

358. 22 Feb. In a cart of William Johnson going to Southampton
John Spinell', A, 3 bales with 50 cloths 10 yds. w.g.

359. 22 Feb. On four horses of Thomas Bishopp going to Plymouth
Ralph Astrye, D, 4 fardels with 12 cloths w.g.

360. 23 Feb. In the ship of Robert Dartye [of Dieppe]
Said master, A, 4 butts rumney, 3 brls. tar, 15 brls. pitch, 1 brl. with 10 doz. candles, £16 13s.4d.; 3 C. lbs. wax

361. 26 Feb. In the ship of Richard Grene
William Remyngton, D, 1 fardel with 2 cloths 14 yds. w.g.
John Jakys, D, 1 fardel with 6 cloths w.g.
Henry Neuman, D, 1 bale with 15½ cloths w.g.

362. 26 Feb. In a cart of John Brent going to Southampton
Lazaro de Pero, A, 1 fardel with 2 cloths 16 yds. w.g.
Bastean Michaell', A, 1 bale with 18 cloths w.g.

363. 27 Feb. In a cart of Richard [John *del.*] Rede going to Southampton
John Prioll', A, 1 fardel with 28 pcs. Welsh straits, cont. 550 goads, £13 6s.8d.
Luke Valarisa, A, 2 bales with 32 cloths 8 yds. w.g.

364. 27 Feb. In a cart of Richard Elyot going to Southampton
Laurence Mean, A, 3 bales with 51 cloths 8 yds. w.g.; 8 pcs. Welsh straits, 53s.4d.

365. 27 Feb. In a cart of Henry Colyare going to Southampton

Laurence Mean, A, 2 bales with 29 cloths w.g.
Bastyan Michaell', A, 1 bale with 16 cloths 8 yds. w.g.

366. 27 Feb. In the ship of Simon Coppys [of Purmerend]
Said master, A, 4 brls. with 2 M. 5 C. lbs. pewter vessels, £34 13s.4d

367. 27 Feb. In the ship of Roger Wilson going to Plymouth.
Ralph Astrye, D, 2 fardels with 15 cloths w.g.
Richard Odyam, D, 9 bales with 117 cloths w.g.
John Lokton, D, 2 bales with 21 cloths 8 yds. w.g.
John Tutsam, D, 1 bale with 10 cloths 16 yds. w.g.
Thomas Randyll, D, 1 cloth w.g.

368. 3 Mar. In the ship of Dennis Furner [of Harfleur]
Thomas Deodoney, A, 38 brls. pitch, 8 brls. tar, 1 brl. with C. 6 lbs.
   lead, 2 pipes with 30 bushels mustard, £10 3s.4d.
Anthony Course, A, 1 fardel with 20 yds. cloth w.g.;
   3 brls. with 19 lbs. pewter vessels, 2 basins, 2 ewers, 2 doz. candlesticks, 6 [*S* C. lbs.] pewter pots and vessels, 5 doz. salt ox tongues, £6
Robert Dort, A, 3 pipes with 1 last red herring, 4 brls. white herring, 2
   brls. pitch, 2 brls. tar, 2 cades red herring, 1 pc. worsted, £8; and for
   the aforesaid pc. of double worsted
Peter de Castro of Guipúzcoa, Sp, 4 fardels with 33 cloths, 8 yds. w.g.,
   1½ cloths in grain, 1½ cloths of half grain

369. 3 Mar. In a cart of William Johnson going to Southampton
Isuare Roys of Guipúzcoa, Sp, 3 bales with 47 cloths 16 yds. w.g.

370. 3 Mar. In a cart of William Johnson going to Southampton
Isuare Roys of Guipúzcoa, Sp, 2 bales with 33 cloths 16 yds. w.g.

371. 3 Mar. In a cart of John Yong going to Southampton
Isuare Roys of Guipúzcoa, Sp, 1 bale 2 fardels with 27 cloths 16 yds.
   w.g., 6½ cloths w.g.[1]

   [1] 'B' in marg. and in *S* also.

372. 3 Mar. On two horses of John Hasard going to Fowey
Thomas Randyll, D, 2 fardels with 7½ cloths w.g., 1 cloth 8 yds. in grain

373. 3 Mar. In the ship of Simon Johnson [of Purmerend]
Said master, A, 3 cloths w.g.; 2 rolls frieze, 26s.8d.

374. 3 Mar. In the ship of Clays Lowesson [of Purmerend]
Said master, A, 40 flitches bacon, 40s.

375. 7 Mar. In a cart of William Horn going to Southampton
George de Sancta Maria, A, 1 fardel with 3 cloths 16 yds. w.g.

376. 7 Mar. In a cart of John Bolt going to Southampton

Gabriel Urse, A, 2 bales with 142 pcs. Welsh straits, £33

377. 7 Mar. In a cart of John Bolt going to Southampton
Gabriel Urse, A, 2 bales with 126 pieces Northern [cloth], £42

378. 7 Mar. In a cart of William Kent going to Southampton
Gabriel Urse, A, 2 bales with 135 pcs. Northern straits, £45

379. 7 Mar. In a cart of William Rede going to Southampton
Gabriel Urse, A, 2 bales with 136 pcs. Northern straits, £45 6s.8d.

380. 7 Mar. In a cart of William Sellam going to Southampton
Gabriel Urse, A, 2 bales with 138 pcs. Welsh straits, £36 13s.4d.

381. 7 Mar. In the ship of Peter Johnson [of Flushing]
Said master, A, ½ cloth w.g.

382. 8 Mar. In a certain barge going to Gravesend
Peter Jesse, D, 1 bale with 16 cloths w.g.
Richard Henle, D, 1 bale with 20 cloths w.g.

383. 8 Mar. In a cart of John Rede going to Southampton
Jeronimo Typolo, A, 2 bales with 1 cloth 8 yds. w.g.; 72 pcs. Welsh
  straits, 20 rolls frieze, £37 6s.8d.

384. 9 Mar. In a cart of Henry Colyare going to Southampton
Laurence Mean, A, 1 bale 1 fardel with 3 cloths 8 yds. w.g.; 87 pcs.
  Welsh straits, £29

385. 9 Mar. In the ship of Peter Jacobisson [of Arnemuiden]
William Grenewolt, H, 1 bale with 12 cloths w.g.
Herman Plough, H, 1 bale with 25 cloths w.g.; 20 goads Welsh straits,
  13s.4d.
John Greverard, H, 1 bale with 18 cloths w.g.; 25 goads Welsh straits,
  16s.8d.
Albert Falland, H, 1 bale with 24½ cloths w.g., 4 yds. cloth of half grain;
  84 goads Welsh straits, 2 maunds with 9 M. 7 C. seasoned and 3 C.
  summer rabbit-skins, £22 16s.8d.
John Russenthorp, H, 1 bale with 15½ cloths w.g.; 25 goads cotton
  russet, 16s.8d.
Hans Stut, H, 1 bale with 18 cloths w.g.; 40 goads Welsh straits, 1
  maund with 6 M. 5 C. seasoned and 3 M. summer rabbit-skins, £16
John Sewyk, H, 1 bale with 21 cloths w.g.; 1 roll frieze, 13s.4d.
James Williamson, A, 3 C. summer rabbit-skins, 6 brls. honey, £3
  13s.4d.
James Florisson, A, 6 cloths 16 yds. w.g.
Laurence Tyman, A, 8 M. seasoned and 6 M. summer rabbit-skins, £22
Luke Neckar, A, 1 fardel with 23 pcs. cotton russet, £8 13s.4d.
James Falk, A, 3 M. seasoned and 3½ M. summer rabbit-skins, £9 10s.

Christiano Mowe, A, 5 pipes 1 hhd. beer, 43s.4d.

Simon Johnson, A, 2 brls. with 12 C. lbs. pewter vessels, £17 6s.8d.

John Petyrson, A, 2 brls. with 13 C. lbs. pewter vessels, £17 6s.8d.

Marcello Maurys, A, 42 weys rendered tallow, 5 brls. honey, 2 brls. with 24 doz. candles, £27 13s.4d.

James Florisson, A, 2 cloths w.g.

Henry Lathuson, A, 2 bales with 38 cloths 8 yds. w.g.; 70 goads Welsh straits, 4 cades sprats,[1] 50s.

John Salmer, H, 1 bale with 13 cloths 8 yds. w.g.; 20 goads Welsh straits, 13s.4d.

George Tak, H, 1 bale with 20 cloths w.g.; 60 goads Welsh straits, 40s.

Gerard Lesbern, H, 1 bale with 18 cloths w.g.; 34 goads Welsh straits, 23s.4d.

Arnold van Stalle, H, 1 bale with 16 cloths w.g.; 20 goads Welsh straits, 13s.4d.

Herman Overcamp, H, 1 bale with 22 cloths w.g.; 50 goads Welsh straits, 33s.4d.

William Scapehuson, H, 3 bales with 66 cloths w.g.; 67 goads Welsh straits, 46s.8d.

John van Strawlyn, H, 1 bale with 18 cloths w.g.; 48 goads Welsh straits, 33s.4d.

Hans Culle, H, 1 bale with 40 cloths w.g.; 21 goads Welsh straits, 13s.4d.

Matthew Blyterswyke, H, 1 bale with 14 cloths w.g.; 20 goads Welsh straits, 13s.4d.

Tylman Barkys, H, 1 bale with 18 cloths w.g.; 41 goads Welsh straits, 26s.8d.

Matthew Hynkylman, H, 1 bale with 19 cloths w.g.; 40 goads Welsh straits, 26s.8d.

Peter Hownfler, A, 8 pipes beer, 53s.4d. (26s.8d. *del.*)

Gerard van Grove, H, 1 bale with 15 cloths w.g.; 15 goads Welsh straits, 10s.

[1] '4 cades sprats' entered in another hand in this account and in *S*.

386. 9 Mar. In the ship of John de Albistro [of San Sebastian]
John[1] Chaverr' of Guipúzcoa, Sp, 11 [*S* 11½] yds. cloth w.g.

[1] 'A' in marg.

[m.16]
387. 9 Mar. In the ship of Martin de Geldo
John[1] Bilbishose of Guipúzcoa, Sp, 10 yds. cloth w.g.

[1] 'A' in marg.

388.[1] 12 Mar. In a cart of John Long going to Bristol
Alexander Portinarius, A, 3 bales with 50 cloths 8 yds. w.g.

[1] *S* entries **388–428** missing. ?Whole membrane

389. 12 Mar. In a wagon of Nicholas Packer going to Bristol

Michael Sepryell', A, 2 bales with 31 cloths w.g.

390. 12 Mar. In a wagon of Nicholas Packer going to Bristol
Michael Sepryell', A, 3 bales with 44 cloths w.g.

391. 12 Mar. In a wagon of Nicholas Packer going to the port of Bristol
Cosma Spenyll', A, 3 bales with 39 cloths w.g., 2 cloths 16 yds in grain.

392. 12 Mar. In the ship of William Mogot [of Harfleur]
Thomas Deodemey, A, 24 brls. pitch, £4
Laurence Varrell', A, 1 vat 1 bag with 52 doz. horns, £5
John de la Pomerye, A, 3 lasts 9 brls. pitch, 3 brls. tar, £8
John Molon', A, 20 brls. pitch, £4; 10 yds. cloth w.g.

393. 12 Mar. In a cart of John Belt going to Southampton
Gabriel Urse, A, 3 bales with 41 cloths w.g.

394. 12 Mar. In a cart of William Spigot going to Southampton
Gabriel Urse, A, 3 bales with 43 cloths 16 yds. w.g.

395. 14 Mar. In the ship of John de Albisto [of San Sebastian]
Said master of Guipúzcoa, Sp, 1 cloth 6 yds. w.g.
John de Serrago of Guipúzcoa, Sp, 10 yds. cloth w.g.
John Chevers of Guipúzcoa, Sp, 18 yds. cloth w.g.
Peter Sanches of Guipúzcoa, Sp, 1 fardel with 5 cloths 8 yds. w.g.
Domyngo de Golongas of Guipúzcoa, Sp, 1 fardel with 8 cloths 10 yds.
  w.g.
Martin de Leso of Guipúzcoa, Sp, 1 fardel with 16 yds. cloth w.g.
Peter Valedelede of Guipúzcoa, Sp, 2 bales with 36 cloths 16 yds. w.g.
John Delsak of Guipúzcoa, Sp, 1 fardel with 2½ cloths w.g.
John Urtice of Guipúzcoa, Sp, 20 yds. cloth w.g.
Sancheo de Turrey of Guipúzcoa, Sp, ½ cloth w.g.

396. 14 Mar. In a cart of Thomas Arnold going to Southampton
Jeronimo Typolo, A, 3 bales with 50 cloths 20 yds. w.g.

397. 14 Mar. In a cart of William Johnson going to Southampton
Jeronimo Typolo, A, 2 bales with 52 cloths w.g.

398. 14 Mar. In the ship of Lubert van Boke
Matthew Hynkylman, H, 1 bale with 44½ cloths w.g., 2 pcs. double
  worsted; 14 goads Welsh straits, 10s.
Lambert Rotard, H, 1 fardel with 6 cloths w.g.; 300 goads Welsh straits,
  £10
Gerard Lesbern, H, 1 bale with 28½ cloths w.g.; 25 goads Welsh straits,
  16s.8d.
Herman Ovyrcamp, H, 1 bale with 23 cloths w.g., 3 yds. cloth of half
  grain; 50 goads Welsh straits, 33s.4d.
William Scapehuson, H, 1 bale with 18 cloths w.g.; 20 goads Welsh
  straits, 1 basket with 4 cades sprats, 18s.4d.

John van Strawlyn, H, 1 bale with 17 cloths w.g. (16 yds. *del.*); 40 goads Welsh straits, 26s.8d.

Henry Lathuson, H, 1 bale with 27 cloths 16 yds. w.g.; 70 goads Welsh straits, 46s.8d.

Hans Stut, H, 1 bale with 26 cloths w.g.; 23 goads Welsh straits, 16s.8d.

John Sewik, H, 1 bale with 20 cloths w.g.; 1 roll frieze, 13s.4d.

Herman Plough, H, 1 bale with 24 cloths w.g.; 21 goads Welsh straits, 13s.4d.

Albert Falland, H, 1 bale with 25 cloths w.g.; 76 goads Welsh straits, 50s.

Edward Johnson, A, 2 M. seasoned and M. 5 C. summer rabbit-skins, 5 doz. fox-skins, £6

John Kaynys, A, 18 yds. cloth w.g.; 7 pcs. Welsh straits, 46s.8d.

Thomas Screven, D, 1 fardel with 5 cloths w.g.

399. 14 Mar. In the ship of Lamb[ert] Wilbertson [of Flushing]
Peter Johnson, A, 10 qrs. peas, 26s.8d.

400. 15 Mar. In a cart of William Sellam going to Southampton
Jeronimo Friscobaldo, A, 1 fardel with 6 cloths 20 yds. w.g., 4 yds. cloth of half grain, 2 pcs. single worsted and for the aforesaid 2 pcs. single worsted, 20s.

401. 16 Mar. In a cart of Peter Jamys going to Southampton
Luke Valarise, A, 1 bale with 17 cloths w.g.; 22 pcs. Welsh straits, £10

402. 16 Mar. In a cart of Peter Jamys going to Southampton
Luke Valarise, A, 2 fardels with 38 pcs. Welsh straits, £12 13s.4d.

403. 16 Mar. In a cart of Peter Jamys going to Southampton
Luke Valarise, A, 2 bales 2 fardels with 25½ cloths w.g.; 30 pcs. Welsh straits, £10

404. 16 Mar. In the ship of John Brasse [of Bergen-op-Zoom]
Margaret Claysson, A, 2 brls. with 24 doz. candles, 26s.8d.

405. 17 Mar. In a cart of Robert Sparowe going to Southampton
Bastean Michaell', A, 2 bales with 5 cloths w.g.; 36 pcs. Welsh straits, £12

406. 17 Mar. In a cart of John Bedyll going to Southampton
Bastean Michaell', 2 bales with 98 pcs. Welsh straits, £32 13s.4d.

407. 17 Mar. In a cart of John Rede going to Southampton
Gabriel Urse, A, 3 bales with 55 cloths w.g.

408. 17 Mar. In the ship of James Rachburgh [of London]
John Fysshare, D, 2 bales with 48 cloths, 16 yds. w.g.
Godfrey Speeyng, D, 1 fardel with 7 cloths w.g.

Andrew Petirson, A, 5 brls. honey, 53s.4d.
John Crace, D, 2 bales with 34 cloths 16 yds. w.g.
Nicholas Buk, A, 60 flitches bacon, £3
Peter Joye, D, 1 bale with 14 cloths w.g.
John Warner, D, 1 fardel with 7½ cloths w.g.
John Chambyr, D, 1 fardel with 10 cloths w.g.
John Fysshare, D, 1 fardel with 3½ cloths w.g., 31 pcs. double worsted
William Weston, D, 2 fardels with 17 cloths w.g., 9 pcs. double worsted
William Redye, D, 1 fardel with 12 pcs. double worsted
Richard Mason, D, 18 yds. cloth w.g., 7 pcs. double worsted

409. 19 Mar. In the ship of Corbrand Johnson
Said master, A, 11 qrs. peas, 3 qrs. oats, £3

410. 20 Mar. In the ship of Martin de Geldo
Peter de Carryan of Guipúzcoa, Sp, 2 fardels with 19 cloths 8 yds. w.g.,
    1½ yds. cloth in grain, 2½ yds. cloth of half grain
John de Rane of Guipúzcoa, Sp, 1 fardel with 6 cloths w.g.
Said master of Guipúzcoa, Sp, 13 yds. cloth w.g.
Peter Misteryk of Guipúzcoa, Sp, ½ cloth w.g.
Martin Lopyan of Guipúzcoa, Sp, 4 bales 1 fardel with 65 cloths w.g.
Peter Valedelede of Guipúzcoa, Sp, 4 bales 1 fardel with 89 cloths w.g.,
    22 yds. cloth in grain, 4 yds. of half grain
Frank de Matholo of Guipúzcoa, Sp, 2 bales 1 fardel with 28 cloths 18
    yds. w.g.
Peter Embeto of Guipúzcoa, Sp, 2 bales with 21½ cloths w.g.
Allowiso de Lyon of Guipúzcoa, Sp, 3 bales 1 fardel with 41 cloths 16
    yds. w.g.
John Semelso of Guipúzcoa, Sp, 8 bales with 89 cloths w.g.
Peter de Castro of Guipúzcoa, Sp, 6 bales 3 fardels with 112 cloths w.g.,
    5 rolls with 5½ cloths in grain, 1 cloth 8 yds. of half grain
Peter Gusmes of Guipúzcoa, Sp, 2 bales 1 fardel with 27 cloths 16 yds.
    w.g., 1 roll with 1 cloth 16 yds. in grain, 1 cloth 20 yds. of half grain
Peter de Garevare of Guipúzcoa, Sp, 1 fardel with 4 cloths 16 yds. w.g.
Peter de Gayndes of Guipúzcoa, Sp, 1 fardel with 1 cloth 22 yds. w.g.
Peter Villalouse of Guipúzcoa, Sp, 5 yds. cloth in grain

411. 20 Mar. In the ship of John Gole [of Caen]
James Gelebrand, D, 2 bales with 31 cloths 8 yds. w.g.

412. 21 Mar. In the ship of Michael Meyr [of Antwerp]
Simon Coppis, A, 160 qrs. rye, £24

413. 21 Mar. In a cart of Edmund Colyfox
Lewis Bonyvise, A, 3 bales 1 fardel with 46 cloths 16 yds. w.g.

414. 21 Mar. In a cart of Thomas Arnold going to Southampton
Ralph Nigro, A, 1 bale with 11 cloths 8 yds. w.g.; 10 pcs. Welsh straits
    cont. 150 goads, 3 pcs. Kendals, £4 6s.8d.

415. 22 Mar. In a cart of Peter Jamys going to Southampton
Andrew Gylys, A, 1 fardel with 6 cloths 16 yds. w.g.

[m.16d.]
416. 22 Mar. In a cart of Thomas Arnold going to Southampton
Luke Valarise, A, 2 bales with 36 cloths 18 yds. w.g.

417. 22 Mar. In a cart of John Rede going to Southampton
Lewis Bonyvise, A, 2 bales 1 fardel with 30 cloths 8 yds. w.g.

418. 22 Mar. In a cart of John Rede going to Southampton
Bernard Barbarigo, A, 3 bales with 48 cloths w.g., 6 yds. cloth of half
  grain; 63 pcs. Welsh straits, £21

419. 22 Mar. In the ship of Peter Mengill [of Antwerp]
Peter Wolf, A, 2 M. seasoned and 2 M. summer rabbit-skins, 2 doz. fox-
  skins, £6 6s.8d.

420. 22 Mar. In a cart of Peter Jamys going to Southampton
Lewis Bonyvise, A, 2 bales with 10 cloths w.g.; 34 pcs. Welsh straits,
  £11 6s.8d.

421. 26 Mar. In the ship of Walter Johnson [of Gouda]
Martin Johnson, A, 1 maund with 2 M. seasoned and 2 M. summer
  rabbit-skins, £6
James Falk, A, 1 basket with 3 C. lbs. pewter vessels, M. C. seasoned
  and 2 M. C. summer rabbit-skins, £8
John Evingar, A, 12 hhds. beer, 40s.
Clays Loo, A, 180 qrs. rye, £27

422. 27 Mar. In the ship of John Hervey
Thomas Randyll, D, 1 cloth w.g.

423. 27 Mar. In the ship of Richard Avise
Richard Fabyan, A, 20 brls. pitch, 8 brls. tar, 1 brl. with 31 doz. candles,
  2 C. lbs. copperas, 4 horns, £8 6s.8d.

424. 28 Mar. In the ship of Robert Bygg [of London]
George Lews, A, 1 maund with 9 M. seasoned and 10 M. summer
  rabbit-skins, £28
John Vandermasson, A, 1 maund with 2 M. 6 C. seasoned rabbit-skins,
  1 basket with 9 C. seasoned and 13 C. summer rabbit-skins, £9 6s.8d.
Peter Capper, A, 1 maund with 2 M. seasoned and 2 M. summer rabbit-
  skins, £6
Peter Matheuson, A, 1 basket with M. seasoned and M. summer rabbit-
  skins, £3
Lewis Ansan, A, 1 fardel with 5 pcs. Welsh straits, M. 5 C. seasoned
  and 2 M. summer rabbit-skins, £6 13s.4d.
Oliver Danyell, D, 1 bale with 20 cloths w.g.

John Durham, D, 2 bales with 28 cloths w.g.

John Kyrkebye, D, 1 fardel with 7 cloths w.g.

Thomas Wynnam, D, 1 bale with 24 cloths w.g.

John Chambir, D, 1 bale 1 fardel with 28 cloths w.g., 5 pcs. double worsted

John Chambyr, D, 1 bale with 51 pcs. double worsted, 4 pcs. single worsted

Peter Joye, D, 1 bale with 14 cloths w.g.

William Millet, D, 1 bale with 24 cloths w.g.

William Scalder, D, 1 bale with 12 cloths w.g.

Nicholas Nyandeser, D, 1 fardel with 9 cloths 8 yds. w.g.

Richard White, D, 1 bale with 30 cloths w.g.

John Benet, D, 1 bale with 10 cloths w.g.

William Weston, D, 1 bale with 10 cloths w.g.

John Gose, D, 1 bale with 21 cloths w.g.

Nicholas Loo, A, 2 cloths w.g.; 50 fox-skins, 26s.8d.

John Hall, D, 1 bale with 24 cloths w.g.

John Romayn, A, 4 brls. with 40 doz. candles, 9 flitches bacon, 3 C. seasoned rabbit-skins, 8 flitches bacon, £3 10s.

425. 28 Mar. In the ship of Matthew Brom'

Said master, H, 1 brl. with 1 cloth 10 yds. w.g.

Herman Overcamp, H, 1 bale with 25 cloths w.g.; 20 goads Welsh straits, 13s.4d.

Gerard Lesbern, H, 2 bales with 33 cloths w.g.; 320 goads Welsh straits, £10 13s.4d.

Hans Stut, H, 2 bales with 55 cloths w.g.; 105 goads Welsh straits, £3 13s.4d.

Albert Falland, H, 1 bale with 50 cloths w.g.; 125 goads Welsh straits, £4 13s.4d.

William Scapehuson, H, 2 bales with 37½ cloths w.g.; 45 goads Welsh straits, 30s. (16s.8d. *del.*)

Hillibrand van Vuno, H, 1 bale with 25 cloths w.g.; 20 goads Welsh straits, 13s.4d.

Tylman van Howell, H, 1 bale with 30 cloths w.g.; 186 goads Welsh straits, £6 6s.8d.

Hans Stut, H, 1 maund with 4 M. 5 C. seasoned and M. summer rabbit-skins, £12

Hans Culle, H, 2 bales with 51 cloths w.g., 7 yds. cloth of half grain; 61 goads Welsh straits, 40s.

Matthew Hinkylman, H, 1 bale with 21 cloths w.g.; 21 goads Welsh straits, 13s.4d.

Hans Culle, H, 1 maund with 5 M. seasoned and 9 C. summer rabbit-skins, £13

Henry Floskyn, H, 1 bale with 27 cloths w.g.; 18 goads Welsh straits, 13s.4d.

426. 28 Mar. In a cart of John Bedyll going to Southampton

Gabriel Urse, A, 1 bale with 13 cloths w.g.

Jeronimo Typolo, A, 2 bales with 36 cloths 16 yds. w.g.

427. 28 Mar. In a cart of Robert Sparowe going to Southampton
Jeronimo Typolo, A, 3 bales with 44 cloths 16 yds. w.g.

428. 30 Mar. In a certain barge going to Poole
John Quevers of Guipúzcoa, Sp, 8 yds. cloth w.g.

429. 30 Mar. In a cart of Richard Pynhorn going to Southampton
Maryn' [*S* Mawrume] Monsenigo, A, 3 bales with 47 cloths 8 yds. w.g.

430. 30 Mar. In a cart of Richard Pynhorn going to Southampton
Maryn' Monsenygo, A, 3 bales 1 fardel with 48½ cloths w.g.; 2 pcs.
Welsh straits [*S* cotton russet], 13s.4d.

431. 2 Apr. In a cart of John Jamys going to Southampton
Maryn' Monsenygo, A, 2 bales with 23 cloths 20 yds w.g.; 30 pcs. Welsh
straits [*S* cotton russet], £10

432. 2 Apr. In a cart of William Sellam going to Southampton
Maryn' Monsenygo, A, 2 bales with 63 pcs. Welsh straits [*S* cotton
russet], £21

433. 2 Apr. In a cart of William Sellam going to Southampton
Maryn' Monsenygo, A, 2 bales with 128 pcs. Welsh straits [*S* cotton
russet], £42 13s.4d.

434. 3 Apr. In a cart of William Johnson going to Southampton
Lewis Bonevise, A, 3 bales with 36 cloths w.g.; 7 pcs. Welsh straits [*S*
cotton russet], 46s.8d.

435. 3 Apr. In a cart of William Ekley going to Southampton
Bernard Barbarigo, A, 2 bales with 40 pcs. broadcloth w.g. with broad
selvages ('brode lysts') cont. 20 cloths; 24 pcs. Welsh straits [*S* cotton
russet], £8

436. 3 Apr. In a cart of Thomas Arnold going to Southampton
Luke Valeryse, A, 2 bales with 38 pcs. broadcloth w.g. with broad
selvages cont. 19 cloths

437. 3 Apr. In a cart of Thomas Arnold going to Southampton
Luke Valerise, A, 2 bales with 38 pcs. broadcloth w.g. with broad
selvages cont. 19 cloths

438. 4 Apr. In a cart of William Esylton [*S* Eslinton] going to
Southampton
Maryn' Monsenigo, A, 2 fardels with 4 cloths 8 yds. w.g.; 37 pcs. Welsh
straits [*S* cotton russet], £12 6s.8d.

Bartholomew Fusan, A, 9 pcs. Welsh straits [*S* cotton russet], £3

439. 5 Apr. In a cart of Richard Marchall going to Southampton
Lewis Bonevise, A, 2 bales 2 fardels with 29 cloths 16 yds. w.g.; 3 pcs.
Welsh straits, 20s.

440. 6 Apr. In the ship of Clays Byll [of Danzig]
Hans Stut, H, 2 bales with 54 cloths 4 yds. w.g.; 58 goads Welsh straits
[*S* cotton russet], 3 maunds with 23 M. 9 C. seasoned and 8 M.
summer rabbit-skins, £69
Tylman Barkys, H, 1 maund with 6 M. seasoned and 2 M. summer
rabbit-skins, £18
Herman Overcamp, H, 1 bale with 26 cloths w.g.; 40 goads Welsh straits
[*S* cotton russet], 1 maund with 5 M. 5 C. seasoned and M. 5 C.
summer rabbit-skins, £15 6s.8d.
Gerard Lesbern, H, 2 bales with 45 cloths w.g.; 300 [*S* 305] goads Welsh
straits, £10
Albert Falland, H, 4 maunds with 28 M. 6 C. seasoned and 3 M.
summer rabbit-skins, £71
Roger van Feld, H, 1 bale with 26 cloths w.g.; 200 goads Welsh straits [*S*
cotton russet], £6 13s.4d.
James van Werd, H, 2 bales with 50 cloths w.g.; 180 goads Welsh straits,
£6
Herman Plough, H, 2 bales with 50 cloths w.g.; 110 goads Welsh straits,
£3 13s.4d.
Hillibrand van Vuno, H, 1 bale with 25 cloths w.g.; 26 goads Welsh
straits [*S* cotton russet], 16s.8d.
Matthew Hynckylman, H, 1 bale with 22 cloths 9 yds. w.g.; 19 goads
Welsh straits [*S* cotton russet], 13s.4d.
Tylman Barkys, H, 1 bale with 22 cloths w.g.; 140 goads Welsh straits,
£4 13s.4d.
Hans Culle, H, 1 bale with 20 cloths w.g.; 225 goads Welsh straits [*S*
cotton russet £7 5s.], 1 maund with 5 M. seasoned and M. 6 C.
summer rabbit-skins, £17 5s. [*S* £10]
Henry Floskyn [*S* Folskyn], H, 1 bale with 26 cloths w.g.; 20 goads
Welsh straits [*S* cotton russett], 13s.4d.
Albert Falland, H, 2 bales with 50 cloths w.g., ½ pc. double worsted; 122
goads Welsh straits [*S* cotton russet], £4
[m.17]
Herman Plough, H, 1 bale with 14½ cloths w.g.; 20 goads Welsh straits [*S*
cotton russet], 13s.4d.
William Prune, D, 1 fardel with 8½ cloths w.g.
John Sparowe, D, 1 fardel with 7 cloths w.g.
Lambert Rotard, H, 1 bale with 15 cloths w.g.; 20 goads Welsh straits,
13s.4d.
Hans Stut,[1] H, 1 maund with 4 M. seasoned rabbit-skins, 1 brl. with 3
doz. lampreys, 1 basket with 1,000 oranges, £9
Henry Floskyn [*S* Fulskyn], H, 1 fardel with 6 cloths 9 yds. w.g., 3 yds.
cloth of half grain; 7 goads Welsh straits, 5s.

Roger van Feld, H, 1 bale with 17 cloths w.g.; 190 goads Welsh straits [*S* cotton russet], £6 6s.8d.

Lambert Rotard, H, 1 bale with 10 cloths w.g.; 20 goads Welsh straits [*S* cotton russet], 13s.4d.

[1] Entries from Hans Stut to Lambert Rotard repeated and deleted.

441. 7 Apr. In a cart of John Perys

Michael Sepriell', A, 1 fardel with 6 cloths 16 yds. w.g., 4 pcs. single worsted; for the aforesaid 4 pcs. worsted and 4 pcs. Welsh straits [*S* cotton russet], £3 6s.8d.

442. 9 Apr. In the ship of Simon Pecheford

John Gibbis, D, 2 bales with 36 cloths 20 yds. w.g., 1 cloth 16 yds. in grain [*S* cont. 40 yds.]

Hugh Jenkyn, D, 8 yds. cloth w.g.

John Fysshe, D, 2 bales with 30 cloths w.g.

Robert Godwyn, D, 2 bales with 34 cloths 8 yds. w.g., 7 pcs. double worsted

John Jakes, D, 1 bale with 14 cloths 16 yds. w.g.

Richard Langton, D, 1 bale with 30 cloths 16 yds. w.g.

John Baylie, D, 1 fardel with 8½ cloths w.g.

William Colyns, D, 3 bales with 49 cloths w.g.

John Halle, D, 1 fardel with 3 cloths w.g.

Robert Tate, D, 1 bale with 10½ cloths w.g.

Richard Ormyzed, D, 1 cloth w.g.

443. 9 Apr. In the ship of Patrick Michaelson

John Bett, D, 1 fardel with 2 cloths w.g.

William Norton, D, 1 fardel with 4 cloths 8 yds. w.g.

444. 9 Apr. In a cart of Peter Jamys going to Southampton

Victor Compayn', A, 1 bale with 11 cloths 16 yds. w.g.

Paul Larka, A, 3 bales with 36 cloths w.g.

445. 9 Apr. In a cart of William Sellam going to Southampton

Thomas Kyppyng, D, 2 bales with 22 cloths 16 yds. w.g.

446. 10 Apr. In the barge of Peter Fornandus [of Viana]

Said master, A, 1 fardel with 4½ cloths w.g.; 20 yds. Welsh straits [*S* cotton russet], 10s.

Vasco Perus, A, 1 fardel with 3 cloths 8 yds. w.g.; 42 yds. Welsh straits [*S* cotton russet], 20s.

Alfonso Yanus, A, 1 fardel with 4 cloths w.g.; 18 yds. Welsh straits, 20 yds. frieze, 20s.

Alfonso de Roche, A, 9 brass kettles, 9 [*S* pewter] pots, 5 platters, 5 pewter dishes, 25s.

447. 10 Apr. In the ship of Thomas Gurley going to Sandwich
Paul Larka, A, 2 C. flax, 20s.

448. 10 Apr. In a cart of Thomas Arnold going to Southampton
William Freman, D, 46 cloths. 20 yds. w.g., 6 yds. cloth of half grain

449. 10 Apr. In a cart of William Long going to Southampton
Peter Friscobaldo, A, 1 fardel with 2 cloths 16 yds. of half grain

450. 10 Apr. In the ship of William Tabbard [of Boston]
Laurence Swarfeld, D, 1 bale with 24 cloths 8 yds. w.g.
John Colyns, D, 1 bale with 34 cloths w.g.
Robert Drayton, D, 1 bale with 18 cloths w.g.
William Scalder, D, 1 bale with 24 cloths w.g.
Henry Wynger, D, 1 bale with 30 cloths w.g.
Nicholas Wylde, D, 2 bales with 59 cloths w.g.
Roger Arnold, D, 1 bale with 16 cloths w.g.
William Brown, D, 1 bale with 30 cloths w.g.
John Nancathan, D, 1 bale with 30 cloths w.g.
William Geffrey, D, 1 bale with 24 cloths w.g.
Richard Laken, D, 1 bale with 18 cloths w.g.
John Haynes, D, 1 bale with 21 cloths w.g.
Robert Bangyll, D, 1 bale with 24 cloths w.g.
William Alburgh, D, 1 bale [with] 36 cloths w.g.
John Paret, D, 1 bale with 22½ cloths w.g.
Oliver Danyell, D, 1 bale with 23 cloths w.g.
Ralph Bere, D, 1 bale with 25 cloths 6 yds. w.g.
George Hawkyn, D, 1 bale with 18 cloths w.g.
William Bentley, D, 1 fardel with 8 cloths w.g.
Tylman van Howell, H, 1 bale with 21 cloths w.g.
William Scapehuson, H, 1 bale with 40 cloths w.g.
Albert Falland, H, 1 bale with 25 cloths w.g.; 63 goads Welsh straits [S
    cotton russet], 43s.4d.
John Fisshare, D, 1 bale with 27 cloths w.g.
Robert Boys, D, 1 bale with 34 cloths w.g.
Robert Squyer, D, 1 bale with 10 cloths w.g.
John Pasmer, D, 1 bale with 29 cloths w.g.
William Wilcok', D, 1 bale with 22 cloths w.g.
Robert Ryngbelle, D, 1 bale with 18 cloths w.g.
Robert Billesdon, D, 2 bales with 60 cloths w.g.
William Jenk', D, 1 bale with 10 cloths w.g.
Stephen Jannys, D, 1 bale with 20 cloths w.g.
John Mathew, D, 1 bale with 30 cloths w.g.
John Warner, D, 1 bale with 28 cloths w.g.
John Pykton, D, 1 bale with 33 cloths w.g.
Richard White, D, 1 bale with 16 cloths w.g.
Everard Southerman, H, 1 bale with 19 cloths w.g.; 68 goads Welsh
    straits [S cotton russet], 46s.8d.

Thomas Lok, D, 1 bale with 35 cloths 8 yds. w.g.
John Raynold, D, 1 bale with 36 cloths w.g.
Richard Eyryk, D, 1 bale with 24 cloths w.g.
Henry Frost, D, 1 bale with 14 cloths 16 yds. w.g.
Roger Hevyn, D, 1 bale with 33 cloths w.g.
Nicholas Bodyn, D, 1 bale with 32½ cloths w.g.
Thomas Lee, D, 1 bale with 30 cloths w.g.
Thomas Lok, D, 1 bale with 18 cloths w.g.
John Gose, D, 1 bale with 24 cloths w.g.
Richard Langton, D, 1 bale with 28 cloths w.g.
John Russinthorp, H, 1 bale with 17 cloths w.g.; 63 goads Welsh straits [*S* cotton russet], 43s.4d.
John Russinthorp, H, 1 bale with 18 cloths w.g.; 60 goads Welsh straits [*S* cotton russet], 40s.
Peter Syber, H, 1 bale with 36 cloths w.g.; 120 goads Welsh straits [*S* cotton russet], £4
John van Armysbery, H, 1 bale with 17 cloths w.g.; 60 goads Welsh straits [*S* cotton russet], 40s.
Matthew Bliterswyk, H, 1 bale with 14 cloths w.g.; 40 goads Welsh straits [*S* cotton russet], 26s.8d.
John van Armysbery, H, 2 bales with 34 cloths w.g.; 120 goads Welsh straits [*S* cotton russet], £4
Henry Cantlowe, D, 1 bale with 30 cloths w.g.
Thomas Hore, D, 1 bale with 30 cloths w.g.
John Chambre, D, 1 bale with 35 cloths w.g.
[*S* John van Armysbery, H, 1 bale with 17 cloths w.g.; 36 goads cotton russet, 45s.]

451. 10 Apr. In the ship of John Yoman [of London]
Laurence Swarfeld, D, 1 bale with 22 cloths w.g.
Cornelius Johnson, A, 1 bale with 34 pcs. Welsh straits [*S* cotton russet], £11 6s.8d.
James Bolle, A, 1 bale with 26 pcs. Welsh straits, [*S* ½ roll] frieze, £9
Peter Nelson, D, 1 bale with 16 cloths w.g.
John Rose, D, 1 bale with 30 cloths w.g.
Robert Eyrik, D, 1 fardel with 4 cloths w.g.
John Colyns, D, 1 bale with 33 cloths w.g.
Henry Wynger, D, 1 bale with 30 cloths w.g.
Thomas Wynnam, D, 1 bale with 26 cloths w.g.
Robert Drayton, D, 1 bale with 14½ cloths w.g.
William Clerk, D, 1 bale with 30 cloths w.g.
Thomas Bowes, D, 1 bale with 21 cloths w.g.
Matthew Falk, A, 4 brls. starch, 30s.
Roger Arnold, D, 1 fardel with 7 cloths w.g., 6 pcs. double worsted
Nicholas Wilde, D, 2 bales with [*S* 41] cloths w.g.
John Nawcathan, D, 1 bale with 30 cloths w.g.
William Scalder, D, 1 bale with 42 cloths 16 yds. w.g.
Richard Laken, D, 1 bale with 11 cloths 6 yds. w.g., 7 pcs. double worsted

Robert Bangyll, D, 1 bale with 14 cloths w.g.

William Alburgh, D, 1 bale with 30 cloths w.g.

William Bent[ley], D, 1 bale with 14 cloths w.g.

William Rice, D, 1 bale with 21 cloths w.g.

Robert Billesdon, D, 1 bale with 21 cloths w.g.

[m.17d.]

Albert Falland, H, 1 bale with 26 cloths w.g.; 61 goads Welsh straits [*S* cotton russet], 40s.

William Scapehuson, H, 1 bale with 17 cloths w.g.; 92 goads Welsh straits [*S* cotton russet], £3

Tylman van Howell, H, 1 bale with 36 [*S* 26] cloths w.g.

Hans Stut,[1] H, 2 bales with 56 cloths w.g.; 40 goads Welsh straits, 26s.8d.

Everard Southerman, H, 1 bale with 19 cloths w.g.; 60 goads Welsh straits, 40s.

Richard Close, D, 1 bale with 24 cloths 8 yds. w.g.

John Pasmer, D, 1 bale with 24 cloths w.g.

William Wilcok', D, 1 bale with 20 cloths w.g.

Richard White, D, 1 bale with 30 cloths w.g.

Robert Ryngbell, D, 1 bale with 17 cloths 8 yds. w.g.

Robert Squyer, D, 1 bale with 27 cloths w.g.

Thomas Lok, D, 1 bale with 34 cloths w.g.

William Redye, D, 1 bale with 16 cloths w.g.

John Raynold, D, 1 bale with 35 cloths w.g.

John Crace, D, 1 bale with 26 cloths w.g.

William Banknot, D, 1 bale with 25 cloths w.g.

William Rollisley, D, 1 bale with 27 cloths w.g.

John Kyrkbye, D, 1 bale with 16 cloths 6 yds. w.g.

Stephen Jannys, D, 1 bale with 20 cloths w.g.

Thomas Lok, D, 1 bale with 22 cloths w.g.

Thomas Hore, D, 1 bale with 10 cloths w.g.

John Chambre, D, 1 bale with 30 cloths w.g.

Roger Hewyn, D, 1 bale with 21 cloths w.g.

Thomas Lee, D, 2 bales with 40 cloths w.g.

John Gose, D, 1 bale with 23 cloths w.g.

John Pykton, D, 1 bale with 30 cloths w.g.

Hillibrand van Vuno, H, 1 bale with 22 cloths w.g.; 62 goads Welsh straits, 43s.4d.

Peter Syber, H, 1 bale with 24 cloths w.g.; 100 goads Welsh straits [*S* cotton russet], £3 6s.8d.

John Russynthorp, H, 1 bale with 19 cloths w.g.; 48 goads Welsh straits, 33s.4d.

John Questynburgh, H, 1 bale with 18 cloths w.g.; 100 goads Welsh straits, £3 6s.8d.

John van Armysbery, H, 1 bale with 17 cloths w.g.; 30 goads Welsh straits, 20s.

John van Armysbery, H, 1 bale with 17 cloths w.g.; 60 goads Welsh straits, 40s.

John Malet, D, 1 bale with 18 cloths w.g.

¹ *S* entries from here to **467** missing. ?Whole membrane.

452. 10 Apr. In the ship of Thomas Coys [of London]
Nicholas Alwyn, D, 1 bale with 14 cloths w.g.
James Bolle, A, 1 bale with 30 pcs. Welsh straits, 1 hhd. with 32 doz. lbs. starch, £11
George Hawkyn, D, 1 bale with 21 cloths w.g.
Thomas Wynnam, D, 1 bale with 24 cloths w.g.
William Scalder, D, 1 bale with 10 cloths w.g.

453. 10 Apr. In the ship of William Petyte [of Weymouth]
Robert Billesdon, D, 1 bale with 19 cloths w.g.
William Wilcok', D, 1 bale with 20 cloths w.g.
Nicholas Wylde, D, 1 bale with 30 cloths w.g.
John Haynes, D, 1 bale with 21 cloths w.g.
John Nancathan, D, 2 bales with 26 cloths 20 yds. w.g.
Robert Drayton, D, 1 bale with 21 cloths w.g.
Thomas Lok, D, 1 bale with 22 cloths w.g., 18 pcs. double worsted
John Crase, D, 1 bale with 30 cloths w.g., 11 pcs. double worsted
John Raynold, D, 1 bale with 28 cloths 16 yds. w.g.
John Pykton, D, 1 bale with 30 cloths w.g.
Thomas Lee, D, 1 bale with 30 cloths w.g.
Peter Syber, H, 1 bale with 18 cloths w.g.; 60 goads Welsh straits, 40s.
John Russinthorp, H, 1 bale with 17 cloths w.g.; 48 goads Welsh straits, 34s.4d.
John van Armysbery, H, 1 bale with 17 cloths w.g.; 60 goads Welsh straits, 40s.

454. 10 Apr. In the ship of John Smolt
Cornelius Johnson, A, 1 basket with M. seasoned and 5 C. summer rabbit-skins, 1 hhd. with 39 doz. lbs. starch, 2 brls. honey, 5 hhds. 2 pipes beer, 1 pipe flour, 2 brls. with salt meat, £7
Peter Wolf, A, 2 M. 5 C. seasoned and 2 M. summer rabbit-skins, 14 fox-skins, 12 cat-skins, £7 13s.4d.
James Falk, A, 1 maund with 15 C. seasoned and 2 M. 8 C. summer rabbit-skins, 2 doz. fox-skins, £6
Armews de Sonwell, A, 4 brls. butter, 1 brl. with 12 doz. candles, 9 flitches bacon, £3 6s.8d.
Martin Johnson, A, 15 C. seasoned and 15 C. summer rabbit-skins, £4 10s.
James Laurence, A, 8 C. seasoned and summer rabbit-skins, 1 brl. with salt meat, 30s.
Clement Goget, A, 3 brls. with salt meat, 1 brl. with 50 lbs. rendered tallow, 20s.

455. 10 Apr. In the ship of Robert Alcok [of London]
George Hawkyn, D, 1 bale with 24 cloths w.g.
Thomas Wynnam, D, 1 bale with 24 cloths w.g.
Cornelius Johnson, A, 1 bale with 32 pcs. Welsh straits, £10 13s.4d.

Armews de Sonwell, A, 6 brls. butter, 53s.4d.

Laurence Tyman, A, 1 maund with 3 M. seasoned and 3 M. summer rabbit-skins, 12 fox-skins, 5 nets, £9 6s.8d.

Peter Segir, A, 1 basket with 12 pcs. Welsh straits, 4½ rolls frieze, £6 13s.4d.

Peter de Castro of Guipúzcoa, Sp, 1 bale with 17 cloths 22 yds. w.g., 4 yds. cloth in grain

456. 10 Apr. In the ship of John Wodeles [of London]

John Rose, D, 1 bale with 25 cloths w.g.

William Clerk, D, 1 bale with 21 cloths w.g.

Robert Drayton, D, 1 bale with 16 cloths w.g.

Henry Cantlowe, D, 1 bale with 16 cloths w.g.

Thomas Wynnam, D, 1 bale with 24 cloths w.g.

Nicholas Wylde, D, 1 bale with 30 cloths w.g.

William Brown, D, 1 bale with 30 cloths w.g.

John Nancathan, D, 1 bale with 30 cloths w.g.

William Welbek, D, 1 chest with 6 cloths 18 yds w.g.

William Jenk', D, 1 bale with 24 cloths w.g.

John Haynes, D, 1 bale with 11 cloths w.g.

Laurence Swarfeld, D, 1 fardel with 6 cloths w.g.

Ralph Bere, D, 1 bale with 25 cloths 8 yds. w.g.

William Alburgh, D, 1 bale with 27 cloths w.g.

William Rice, D, 1 bale with 14 cloths w.g.

William Wilcok', D, 1 bale with 22 cloths w.g.

Robert Boys, D, 1 bale with 30 cloths w.g.

John Pasmer, D, 1 bale with 24 cloths w.g.

Thomas Goldsmyth, D, 1 bale with 21 cloths w.g.

Robert Squyer, D, 1 bale with 27 cloths w.g.

Robert Ryngbell, D, 1 bale with 17 cloths 8 yds. w.g.

Richard Close, D, 1 bale with 26 cloths 16 yds. w.g.

Robert Billesdon, D, 2 bales with 48 cloths w.g.

Walter Violet, D, 1 bale with 12 cloths w.g.

John Kyrkebye, D, 1 bale with 14½ cloths w.g.

John Warner, D, 1 bale with 17 cloths w.g.

Thomas Lok, D, 1 bale with 31½ cloths w.g.

Thomas Quadryng, D, 1 bale with 15 cloths w.g.

John Raynold, D, 1 bale with 32 cloths w.g.

John Pykton, D, 1 bale with 30 cloths w.g.

Thomas Hore, D, 1 bale with 30 cloths w.g.

William Peryn, D, 1 fardel with 6 cloths w.g.

Stephen Jannys, D, 1 bale with 15 cloths 8 yds. w.g., 3 cloths in grain

Thomas Lok, D, 1 bale with 18 cloths w.g.

John Chambre, D, 1 bale with 30 cloths w.g.

Thomas Lee, D, 2 bales with 42 cloths w.g.

John Paynter, D, 3 cloths w.g.

William Boteler, D, 1 bale with 14 cloths w.g.

Peter Syber, H, 1 bale with 18 cloths w.g.; 62 goads Welsh straits, 43s.4d.

John Russinthorp, H, 1 bale with 18 cloths w.g.; 68 goads Welsh straits, 46s.8d.

John Questinburgh, H, 1 bale with 16 cloths w.g.; 200 goads Welsh straits, £6 13s.4d.

John van Armysbery, H, 2 bales with 33 cloths w.g.; 122 goads Welsh straits, £4

457. 14 Apr. In a cart of Peter Jamys going to Southampton
John Spinell', A, 1 bale 2 rolls with 19 cloths w.g.

458. 14 Apr. In the ship of William Prowde
William Norton, D, 1 cloth w.g.

459. 14 Apr. In a cart of William Johnson going to Southampton
Lewis Bonyvise, A, 2 bales 2 fardels with 3 cloths 13 yds. w.g.; 59 pcs. Welsh straits, £19 13s.4d.

460. 16 Apr. In a cart of William Long going to Southampton
Peter Friscobaldo, A, 1 fardel with 2 cloths w.g., 6 pcs. single worsted; and for the aforesaid 6 pcs. single worsted, £3

461. 16 Apr. In a cart of Peter Jamys going to Southampton
Bastean Michaell', A, 1 fardel with 19 yds. cloth w.g.; 12 pcs. Welsh straits, £4

462. 18 Apr. In a cart of William Sellam
Frederyk Prioll', A, 2 bales with 53 pcs. Welsh straits, £17 13s.4d.

[m.18]
463. 19 Apr. In a cart of William Sellam
Thomas Kyppyng, D, 2 bales with 24 cloths w.g.

464. 19 Apr. in the ship of Diego Vincent [of Viana]
Gunsalvo Fernandus, A, 2 fardels with 13 cloths w.g.; 2 pcs. Welsh straits, 46 pewter pots and pieces, 40s

464A. 19 Apr. In the ship of Ferot de la Crosse [of Réville]
William Amound, A, 1 fardel with 5 cloths 18 yds. w.g.

465. 26 Apr. In the ship of William Tabbard [of Boston]
Peter Rovere of Guipúzcoa, Sp, 1 bale with 10 cloths 16 yds. w.g.
William Whetewey, D, 1 bale with 28 cloths 16 yds. w.g.
Roger Bonyfaunt, D, 2 bales with 66 cloths w.g.
John Colet, D, 1 bale with 20 cloths w.g., 4 pcs. double worsted
Nicholas Morton, D, 1 bale with 26 cloths w.g.
Alan Hobard, D, 1 bale with 41 cloths w.g.
William Herryot, D, 1 bale with 20 cloths w.g.
Peter Joye, D, 1 bale with 18 cloths w.g.
Robert Sowthwode, D, 2 bales with 63 cloths w.g.
John Benham, D, 1 bale with 32 cloths w.g.
William Elysson, D, 1 bale with 14 cloths 16 yds. w.g.

William Purches, D, 1 bale with 33 cloths w.g.
John Pellam, D, 1 bale with 30 cloths w.g.
John Benham, D, 1 bale with 10 cloths w.g., 8 pcs. double worsted
Thomas Mayn, D, 1 bale with 20 cloths w.g.
John Hosyare, D, 2 bales with 49 cloths w.g.
John Bayly, D, 1 fardel with 5 cloths w.g.
Oliver Danyell, D, 1 fardel with 4½ cloths w.g.
Nicholas Alwyn, D, 1 bale with 21 cloths w.g.
Thomas Gylbert, D, 1 bale with 13 cloths 8 yds. w.g.
William Hamlyn, D, 1 fardel with 5 cloths w.g.
Edmund Talwyn, D, 1 bale with 20 cloths w.g.
Nicholas Morton, D, 2 bales with 39 cloths 16 yds. w.g.
Robert Brown, D, 1 fardel with 8 cloths 16 yds. w.g.
Henry Cantlowe, D, 1 bale with 16 cloths w.g.
John Millet, D, 1 bale with 18 cloths w.g.
Thomas Fabyan, D, 1 bale with 33 cloths w.g.
John Fysshare, D, 1 bale with 33 cloths 18 yds. w.g.
John Brampton, D, 1 bale with 12 cloths w.g.
John Darbe, D, 1 bale with 19 cloths 8 yds. w.g.
Roger Bonyfaunt, D, 1 fardel with 4 cloths 8 yds. w.g.
William Sholdwell, D, 1 fardel with 5 cloths 3 yds. w.g.
William Brett, D, 1 fardel with 7 cloths w.g.
John Rose, D, 1 bale with 14 cloths w.g.
John Salvo, A, 1 bale with 27 pcs. Welsh straits, £19
John Fysshe, D, 1 bale with 14 cloths w.g.
William Heton, D, 1 bale with 10 cloths w.g.
William Venables, D, 1 fardel with 3 cloths 8 yds. w.g.
Thomas Robynson, D, 1 bale with 23 cloths w.g.
William Bryt, D, 1 bale with 18 cloths w.g.
John Colet, D, 1 fardel with 4½ cloths w.g., 11½ pcs. double worsted
Stephen Chirche, D, 1 fardel with 5 cloths 18 yds. w.g.
Thomas Smyth, D, 1 fardel with 6 cloths 16 yds. w.g.
Roger van Feld, H, 1 bale with 24 cloths w.g.; 50 goads cotton russet, 33s.4d.
Hans Stut, H, 1 bale with 25 cloths w.g.; 32 goads cotton russet, 23s.4d.
John van Strawlyn, H, 1 bale with 22 cloths w.g.; 40 goads Welsh straits, 26s.8d.
Roger Manfeld, D, 1 bale with 13 cloths 18 yds. w.g., 7 pcs. double [worsted]

466. 26 Apr. In the ship of John Wodeles [of London]
William Kyng, D, 1 fardel with 2 cloths 8 yds. w.g.
John Colet, D, 1 bale with 24 cloths w.g.
William Herriot, D, 1 bale with 14 cloths w.g.
Thomas Petyte, D, 1 bale with 12 cloths w.g., 3 pcs. double worsted
Nicholas Morton, D, 1 bale with 27 cloths w.g.
Roger Bonyfaunt, D, 1 bale with 33 cloths w.g.
Thomas Screven, D, 1 bale with 27 cloths w.g.
Robert Sowthwode, D, 2 bales with 63 cloths w.g.

Peter Joye, D, 1 bale with 16 cloths w.g.
Richard Twyg, D, 1 bale with 12 cloths w.g.
Thomas Bowes, D, 1 bale 1 fardel with 4 cloths w.g.
Robert Basset, D, 4 fardels with 10 cloths w.g.
John Fysshare, D, 1 fardel with 5 cloths w.g.
Stephen Chirche, D, 1 fardel with 7 cloths w.g.
Roger van Feld, H, 1 bale with 20½ cloths w.g.; 36 goads Welsh straits, 23s.4d.
Albert Falland, H, 1 bale with 25 cloths w.g.; 60 goads Welsh straits, 40s.

467. 26 Apr. In the ship of John Yoman [of London]
William Dolfynbye, D, 1 bale with 18 cloths 16 yds. w.g.
Roger Bonyfaunt, D, 1 bale with 30 cloths w.g.
Richard Rawson, D, 1 fardel with 3 cloths w.g., 21 pcs. double worsted
William Scalder, D, 1 bale with 27 cloths w.g.
Robert Sowthwode, D, 1 bale with 30 cloths w.g.
John Gloyse, D, 1 bale with 19 cloths w.g.
John Fysshare, D, 1 bale with 33 cloths w.g., 15 pcs. double worsted
John Broke, D, 1 bale with 10 cloths w.g.
John Benyngton, D, 1 bale with 18 cloths w.g.
Robert Pecche, D, 1 fardel with 3 cloths w.g.
Robert Hardben, D, 1 fardel with 5 cloths w.g.
William Mannyng, D, 1 bale with 16 cloths w.g.
Tylman Barkys, H, 1 bale with 42 cloths w.g.
Anthony Jamys, A, 2 hhds. with 32 [*S* 22] doz. lbs. starch, 1 hhd. with 12 pcs. pewter, 3 pewter pots, 1 [*S* 3] old brass pot, 2 candlesticks, 20s

468. 26 Apr. In the ship of William Petyte [of Weymouth]
Roger Bonyfaunt, D, 1 bale with 33 cloths w.g.
William Geffrey, D, 1 bale with 18 cloths w.g.
John Benet, D, 1 fardel with 9 cloths w.g.
Peter Joye, D, 1 bale with 18 cloths w.g.
John Benham, D, 1 bale with 34 cloths 4 yds. w.g., 14 pcs. double worsted
John Pellam, D, 2 bales with 56 cloths w.g.
John Hall, D, 1 bale with 20 cloths w.g.
Richard Capell [*S* Chapell], D, 1 bale with 10 cloths w.g.
Robert Sowthwode, D, 1 bale with 22 cloths w.g., 32 pcs. double worsted
Thomas Bradburye, D, 1 bale with 31 cloths w.g.
John Brampton, D, 1 fardel with 8 cloths w.g.
Simon Smythe, D, 2 bales with 32 cloths w.g.
William Bryt [*S* Brut], D, 1 bale with 26 cloths w.g.
Thomas Mayn, D, 1 bale with 15 cloths w.g.
John Fyssh', D, 1 bale with 10 cloths w.g.
John Warner, D, 1 fardel with 6 cloths w.g.
William Geffrey, D, 1 fardel with 7 cloths w.g.
William Bryt, D, 1 bale with 10 cloths w.g.

John Haynes, D, 1 fardel with 8 cloths w.g.

William Mannyng, D, 1 bale with 14 cloths w.g.

William Colyns, D, 2 bales with 34 cloths 8 yds. w.g.

Roger van Feld, H, 1 bale with 22 cloths w.g.; 50 goads Welsh straits [*S* cotton russet], 33s.4d.

Hans Stut, H, 1 bale with 25 cloths w.g.; 23 goads Welsh straits [*S* cotton russet], 15s.

John van Strawlyn, H, 1 bale with 24 cloths w.g.; 40 goads Welsh straits [*S* cotton russet], 26s.8d.

Hans Stut, H, 1 bale with 25 cloths w.g.; 24 goads Welsh straits [*S* cotton russet], 16s.8d.

469. 26 Apr. In the ship of Anthony Brabander [of Middelburg]

Henry Lathuson, H, 1 bale with 25 cloths w.g.

Anthony Odindale, H, 1 bale with 18 cloths w.g.; 20 goads Welsh straits [*S* cotton russet], 13s.4d.

[m.18d.]

Matthew Hynkylman, H, 1 bale with 31½ cloths. w.g.

Tylman Barkys, H, 1 bale with 41 cloths w.g.; 20 goads Welsh straits, 13s.4d.

Gerard Lesbern, H, 1 bale with 26 cloths w.g.; 200 goads cotton russet, £6 13s.4d.

Matthew Hynkylman, H, 1 bale with 25 cloths w.g.; 20 goads Welsh straits [*S* cotton russet], 13s.4d.

William Scapehuson, H, 1 bale with 40 cloths w.g.

Hans Cull, H, 1 bale with 25 cloths w.g.; 19 goads cotton russet, 13s.4d.

George Tak, H, 1 bale with 16 cloths w.g.; 62 goads cotton russet, 40s.

Tylman van Howell, H, 1 bale with 25 cloths w.g.; 223 goads cotton russet, £7 8s.4d.

Hans Stut, H, 2 bales with 53 cloths w.g.; 32 goads cotton russet, 23s.4d.

Herman Overcamp, H, 1 bale with 24 cloths w.g.; 60 goads cotton russet, 40s.

William Grenewolt, H, 1 bale with 16 cloths w.g.; 65 goads cotton russet, 43s.4d.

Herman Plowgh, H, 1 bale with 25 cloths w.g.; 20 goads cotton russet, 13s.4d.

Albert Falland, H, 1 bale with 26 cloths w.g.; 61 [*S* 60] goads cotton russet, 40s.

Arnold van Stalle, H, 1 bale with 25 [*S* 15] cloths w.g.; 124 goads cotton russet, £4 3s.4d.

Hillebrand van Vuno, H, 1 bale with 25 cloths w.g.

Henry Bevyr, H, 1 bale with 14 cloths w.g.; 18 goads Welsh straits [*S* cotton russet], 13s.4d.

William Grenewod [*S* Grenewolt], H, 1 bale with 14 cloths w.g.; 20 goads cotton russet, 13s.4d.

Henry Lathuson, H, 1 bale with 31½ cloths w.g.

John Kele, A, 5 pcs. tin, £12 10s.

Nicholas Johnson, A, 1 maund with 4 M. seasoned and 2 M. summer rabbit-skins, £10

470. 26 Apr. In the ship of Peter Jacobisson [of Arnemuiden]

Herman Plough, H, 1 bale with 25 cloths w.g.; 19 goads cotton russet, 13s.4d.

Anthony Odyndale, H, 1 bale with 18 cloths w.g.; 20 goads cotton russet, 13s.4d.

Matthew Blytterswyke, H, 1 bale with 14 cloths w.g.; 40 goads cotton russet, 26s.8d.

Tylman Barkys, H, 1 bale with 18 cloths w.g.; 20 goads cotton russet, 13s.4d.

Henry Lathuson, H, 2 bales with 65 cloths w.g.

Matthew Hynkylman, H, 1 bale with 25 cloths w.g.; 22 goads cotton russet, 13s.4d.

Herman Overcamp, H, 1 bale with 26 cloths w.g.; 45 goads cotton russet, 30s.

Gerard Lesbern, H, 1 bale with 33 cloths w.g.; 160 goads cotton russet, £5 6s.8d.

William Scapehuson, H, 1 bale with 40 cloths w.g.

Hans Culle, H, 1 bale with 28½ cloths w.g.; 21 goads cotton russet, 13s.4d.

Tylman van Howell, H, 1 bale with 29 cloths 16 yds. w.g.; 40 goads cotton russet, 26s.8d.

John Stakylhuson, H, 1 bale with 17 cloths w.g.; 40 goads cotton russet, 26s.8d.

George Tak, H, 1 bale with 19 cloths w.g.; 60 goads cotton russet, 26s.8d. [*S* 40s.]

William Scapehuson, H, 1 bale with 25 cloths w.g.

Gerard van Grove, H, 1 bale with 18 cloths w.g.; 100 goads cotton russet, £3 6s.8d.

Hans Stut, H, 2 bales with 52 cloths w.g.; 40 goads cotton russet, 26s.8d.

William Grenewold, H, 1 bale with 16 cloths w.g.; 61 goads cotton russet, 26s.8d. [*S* 40s.]

Everard Southerman, H, 1 bale with 19 cloths w.g.; 60 goads cotton russet, 26s.8d. [*S* 40s.]

James van Werd, H, 1 bale with 25 cloths w.g.; 20 goads cotton russet, 13s.4d.

John Salmer, H, 1 bale with 14 cloths w.g.; 2 mattresses, 20 goads cotton russet, 20s.

Arnold van Stalle, H, 1 bale with 15 cloths w.g.; 68 goads cotton russet, 45s.

Albert Falland, H, 1 bale with 26 cloths w.g.; 61 goads cotton russet, 40s.

Lambert Rotard, H, 1 bale with 19 cloths w.g., 5 yds. cloth in grain, 3 pcs. double worsted; 160 goads cotton russet, £5 6s.8d.

Roger van Feld, H, 1 bale with 20 cloths w.g.; 45 goads cotton russet, 30s.

Henry Bevir, H, 1 bale with 15 cloths w.g.; 18 goads cotton russet, 13s.4d.

Tylman Barkys, H, 1 bale with 20 cloths 8 yds. w.g., 4 yds. cloth in grain; 140 goads cotton russet, £4 13s.4d.

Anthony Odindale, H, 1 bale with 19 cloths w.g.; 20 goads cotton russet, 13s.4d.

John Claisson, A, 2 maunds with 3 M. seasoned and 14 M. summer rabbit-skins, £20

Marcello Maurys, A, 7 baskets with 7 weys rendered tallow, £4 6s.8d.

George Perus, A, 1 fardel with 5 cloths w.g.

Edward Johnson, A, 2 M. seasoned and summer rabbit-skins, 6 fox-skins, 1 brl. with 3 C. lbs. [S old] pewter vessels, £7

Nicholas Johnson, A, 2 maunds with 4 M. seasoned and 8 M. summer rabbit-skins, £16

471. 26 Apr. In the ship of Lubert van Boke [of the Steelyard]

Herman Plough, H, 1 bale with 26 cloths w.g.; 28 goads cotton russet, 20s.

Anthony Odindale, H, 1 bale with 18 cloths w.g.; 21 goads cotton russet [S Welsh straits], 13s.4d.

Henry Lathuson, H, 1 bale with 24 cloths w.g.

Matthew Hynkylman, H, 1 bale with 31 cloths w.g.; 51 goads cotton russet, 33s.4d.

Herman Overcamp, H, 1 bale with 25 cloths w.g.; 20 goads cotton russet, 13s.4d.

Gerard Lesbern, H, 1 bale with 25 cloths w.g.; 90 goads cotton russet, £3

William Scapehuson, H, 1 bale with 21 cloths w.g.; 20 goads cotton russet, 13s.4d.

George Tak, H, 1 bale with 18 cloths w.g.; 56 goads cotton russet, 36s.8d.

Tylman Barkys, H, 1 bale with 18 cloths w.g.; 44 goads cotton russet, 30s.

Hans Culle, H, 1 bale with 16 cloths w.g.; 20 goads cotton russet, 13s.4d.

William Grenewolt, H, 1 bale with 16 cloths w.g.; 64 goads cotton russet, 43s.4d.

Hans Stut, H, 2 bales with 50 cloths w.g.; 45 goads cotton russet, 30s.

Lambert Rotard, H, 1 bale with 18 cloths w.g.; 140 goads cotton russet, £4 13s.4d.

Albert Falland, H, 1 bale with 26 cloths w.g.; 60 goads cotton russet, 40s.

Hillibrand van Vuno, H, 1 bale with 30 cloths w.g.; 205 goads cotton russet, £6 16s.8d.

Hans Hasturberch, H, 1 bale with 34 cloths w.g.

Henry Bevir, H, 1 bale with 15 cloths w.g.; 20 goads cotton russet, 13s.4d.

John Kele, A, 5 pcs. tin, £12 10s.

[m.19]
472. 26 Apr. In the ship of Robert Alcok [of London]

Gerard Lesbern, H, 1 bale with 25 cloths w.g.; 90 goads cotton russet, £3

George Tak, H, 1 bale with 18 cloths w.g.; 41 goads cotton russet, 26s.8d.

Hans Stut, H, 1 bale with 27 cloths w.g.; 20 goads cotton russet, 13s.4d.

Tylman Barkys, H, 1 bale with 23 cloths w.g.; 24 goads cotton russet, 16s.8d.

Arnold Howell, H, 2 M. seasoned and summer rabbit-skins, 10 flitches bacon, 1 hhd. with 34 doz. lbs. starch, 20 lbs. [*S* old] pewter vessels, £4 13s.4d.

Michael Sepriell', A, 1 fardel with 7 cloths 16 yds. w.g., 5 yds. cloth of half grain

Thomas Screven, D, 1 fardel with 9 cloths 4 yds. w.g.

Peter Joye, D, 1 fardel with 9 cloths w.g.

John Ebrall, D, 1 fardel with 7 cloths w.g.

Thomas Smyth, D, 1 bale with 20 cloths w.g.

Thomas Braybroke, D, 1 fardel with 6 cloths w.g.

Edmund Talwyn, D, 1 fardel with 6 cloths w.g.

John Ebrall, D, 1 bale with 13 cloths w.g., 2 pcs. double worsted

Nicholas Morton, D, 1 fardel with 9 cloths w.g.

Thomas Smyth, D, 1 fardel with 7 cloths 16 yds. w.g.

John Hurflench [*S* Hurlflinche], D, 1 cloth w.g.

John Baskervile, D, 1 fardel with 1 cloth 20 yds. w.g., 3 pcs. double worsted

473. 26 Apr. In the ship of John Ochea

Said master, of Guipúzcoa, Sp, 1 bale 1 fardel with 21 cloths w.g.

Peter Savale of Guipúzcoa, Sp, 1 fardel with 1 cloth 10 yds. w.g.

Martin Darbeto of Guipúzcoa, Sp, 1 bale 1 fardel with 18 cloths 10 yds. w.g.

Peter de Lagando of Guipúzcoa, Sp, 1 bale 3 fardels with 29 cloths 5 yds. w.g., 1½ yds. cloth in grain [*S* 1 yd. cloth of half grain]

John de Garria [*S* Carrya] of Guipúzcoa, Sp, 1 fardel with 7 cloths w.g.

Francis Fernandus of Guipúzcoa, Sp, 1 fardel with 5 cloths 6 yds. w.g.

Alfonso de Cevilia [*S* Ceviola] of Guipúzcoa, Sp, 92 cloths 8 yds. w.g.

Bernard Baldore of Guipúzcoa, Sp, 2 rolls with 18 yds. cloth w.g., 3 yds. cloth of half grain

Alfonso de Lyon of Guipúzcoa, Sp, 1 fardel with 9 cloths w.g., 3 cloths in grain

Martin Lopian [*S* Lupyana] of Guipúzcoa, Sp, 5 bales with 64 cloths w.g., 1½ cloths in grain

Peter de Castro of Guipúzcoa, Sp, 5 bales with 70 cloths w.g., 2 rolls with 3 cloths in grain

474. 26 Apr. In the ship of Thomas Coys [of London]

George Tak, H, 1 bale with 18 cloths w.g.; 58 goads cotton russet, 40s.

William Bentley, D, 1 cloth w.g.

John Cobbe, D, 1 fardel with 7 cloths w.g.

John Baldrye, D, 1 bale with 16 cloths 22 yds. w.g.

Robert Upnore, D, 1 bale with 12 cloths w.g.

Andrew Rogger, D, 1 bale with 12 cloths w.g.

Thomas Kellet, D, 1 bale with 14 cloths 8 yds. w.g.

Thomas Screven, D, 1 fardel with 2 cloths w.g., ½ pc. double worsted

John Warner, D, 1 fardel with 5 cloths w.g.

John Paynter, D, 1 fardel with 7 cloths w.g.

John Haynes, D, 2 bales with 22 cloths w.g.

William Brytt, D, 1 fardel with 4½ cloths w.g.

John Pellam, D, 1 fardel with 9 cloths w.g.

John Pikton, D, 1 fardel with 8 cloths w.g.

Stephen Chirche, D, 1 fardel with 5 cloths 18 yds. w.g.

Walter Ayleworth, D, 1 fardel with 3 [*S* white] cloths w.g.

John Chambre, D, 1 fardel with 13 pcs. double worsted

Roger Grove, D, 1 bale with 20 cloths w.g.

Bernard Senterion [*S* Barnabas Senturyon], A, 1 brl. with 6 [*S* C.] bundles ostrich feathers, £4

John Gylis, A, 42 pcs. cotton russet, 30 flitches bacon, £15

475. 26 [*S* 21] Apr. In the ship of John Yanus

Gonsalvo Rodrigus of Guipúzcoa, Sp, 1 fardel with 6 cloths 20 yds. w.g.

Andrew Alvis, A, 1 fardel with 6 cloths 16 yds. w.g.; 47 yds. [*S* goads] cotton russet, 51 pewter pcs. and pots, 2 brass kettles, 40s.

Gomves Bryan of Guipúzcoa, Sp, 1 fardel with 8 cloths w.g.

Francis Fornandus, A, 1 fardel with 5 cloths w.g.; 14 yds. [*S* goads] cotton russet, 5s.

Gonsalvo Rodr[i]gus, A, 1 brass bell weight 3 C. 28 [*S* 3 C. 1] lbs., £3 13s.4d.

Rodrigo Yanus, A, 2 fardels with 8 cloths w.g.; 100 yds. [goads *del.*] cotton russet, 40s.

476. 26 Apr. In the ship of Nicholas Thorn [of Arnemuiden]

Tylman Barkys, H, 2 bales with 42 cloths w.g.; 40 goads cotton russet, 26s.8d.

John van Strawlyn, H, 3 bales with 55 cloths 3 yds. w.g.; 85 goads cotton russet, 56s.8d.

Gerard Lesbern, H, 1 bale with 25 cloths w.g.; 20 goads cotton russet, 13s.4d.

Herman Overcamp, H, 1 bale with 11 cloths w.g.; 20 goads cotton russet, 13s.4d.

Albert Falland, H, 1 bale with 25 cloths w.g.; 60 goads cotton russet, 40s.

Roger van Feld, H, 1 bale with 21 cloths 20 yds. w.g.; 70 goads cotton russet, 46s.8d.

John Russenthorp, H, 1 bale with 13 cloths 6 yds. w.g.; 20 goads cotton russet, 13s.4d.

Anthony Odyndale, H, 1 bale with 18 cloths 7 yds. w.g.; 21 goads cotton russet, 13s.4d.

Arnold van Stalle, H, 1 bale with 15 cloths w.g.; 204 goads cotton russet, £6 16s.8d.

Arnold van Stalle, H, 1 chest with 2 cloths 2 yds. w.g., 5 yds. of half grain, 2 pcs. double worsted

William Scapehuson, H, 1 bale with 16 cloths w.g.; 105 goads cotton russet, £3 10s.

Hans Culle, H, 1 bale with 24 cloths w.g.; 20 goads cotton russet, 13s.4d.

John Questynburgh, H, 1 bale with 15 cloths w.g.; 38 goads cotton russet, 26s.8d.

Hillybrand van Vuno, H, 1 bale with 16 cloths w.g.; 11 goads cotton russet, 6s.8d.

Goswyn Redekyrke, H, 1 bale with 14 cloths w.g.; 20 goads cotton russet, 13s.4d.

Hans Stut, H, 2 bales with 54 cloths w.g.; 50 [*S* 49] goads cotton russet, 33s.4d.

John van Armysbery, H, 1 bale with 15 cloths w.g.; 60 goads cotton russet, 40s.

John Claysson, A, 2 maunds with 7 M. seasoned and 8 M. summer rabbit-skins, £22

Florence Skynner, A, 5 C. seasoned and 5 C. summer rabbit-skins, 3 doz. fox [*S* skins], 45s.

477. 26 Apr. In a cart of Peter Jamys going to Southampton
Lewis Bonyvise, A, 2 fardels with 11 cloths 8 yds. w.g.

[m.19d.]
478. 26 Apr. In the ship of Peter Mengell [of Antwerp]
John Kele, A, 2 blocks tin, 6 hhds. beer, £6 [*S* 2 blocks tin, 3 hhds. beer, £5 10s., 3 hhds. beer, 10s.]
Peter Syber, H, 1 brl. with 12 doz. [*S* lbs.] candles, 13s.4d.

479. 30 Apr. In a cart of John Bedyll going to the port of Bristol
Simon Harries, D, 3 fardels with 29 cloths 8 yds. w.g.

480. 30 Apr. [*S* 2 May] In a cart of William Johnson going to Bristol
John Stok[are], D, 1 bale 4 fardels with 54 cloths 20 yds. w.g.

481. 30 Apr. In a cart of Peter Jamys going to Southampton
Michael Sepriell', A, 1 bale with 11 cloths 8 yds. w.g.
Edward Brampton, D, 1 fardel with 4 cloths w.g.

[**481A.** *S* 8 May. In a cart of John Perus going to Southampton
Michael Sepriell', A, 1 bale with 11 cloths 8 yds. w.g.

481B. 8 May. In a cart of Peter Jamys going to Southampton
Edward Brampton, D, 1 fardel with 4 cloths w.g.]

482. 30 Apr. On 5 horses of John Ryse going to Southampton
Edward Brampton, D, 5 fardels with 20 cloths w.g.

483. 30 Apr. In the ship of Nicholas Morcok
Said master, D, 1 cloth 10 yds. w.g.

484. 9 May. In the ship of Oliver Carmewe
Said master, Breton,[1] 1 fardel with 9 cloths 8 yds. w.g.
Elyott Abey, Breton, 1 fardel with 8 cloths 8 yds. w.g.
Nicholas Abbey,[2] Breton, 1 fardel with 7 cloths 16 yds. w.g.

[1] By the thirty year commercial treaty of 1468 between England and Brittany merchants were only to pay the customs, tolls etc. previously accustomed, in effect, at denizen rates (T. Rymer, *Foedera* (1704–35), XI, p. 619).
[2] marg. 'B. In the ship of J. Gode.'

485. 14 May. In the ship of Elyot Labye of [Guérande]
Said master, Breton, 1 fardel with 2 cloths 20 yds. w.g.

486. 15 May. In a cart of William Sellam going to Winchelsea
Alexander Portynale, A, 3 bales with 41 cloths 16 yds. w.g.

487. 18 May. In the ship of John Furnandus
Said master, A, 1 fardel with 4 cloths w.g.; 5 yds. Welsh straits [*S* 10 yds. cotton russet], 5s.
Peter Alfownce [*S* Alfonso], A, 2 fardels with 9 cloths 8 yds. w.g.
Fernando Yanus, A, 1 fardel with 4 cloths 4 yds. w.g.; 1 pc. cotton russet, 6s.8d.
Martin Yanus, A, 1 fardel with 1 cloth 4 yds. w.g.; 20 yds. [*S* goads] cotton russet, 2 coverlets, 20 pewter pots and pieces [*S* 8 pots 18 pieces], 12 calfskins, 1 brass kettle, 1 coffer 'ongr' [*S* covering], 46s.8d.
Nicholas Gromet, A, 1 cloth 6 yds. w.g.
Edward Brampton, D, 1 fardel with 3 cloths 8 yds. w.g.
John Tordecelis of Guipúzcoa, Sp, 1 fardel with 9 cloths w.g.

488. 10 May. In the ship of John Goode
William Tregull', John Dexter and William Colyns, Ds, 3 bales 4 fardels with 72 cloths 16 yds. w.g.
[*S* William Tregyll', 3 cloths 8 yds. w.g.; John Dexter, 2 fardels with 9 cloths 8 yds. w.g.; William Collyns, 3 bales 1 fardel with 60 cloths w.g.]

489. 10 May [*S* 18 May]. In the ship of John de Santandera [of San Sebastian]
William Herryot, D, 5 bales with 54 cloths w.g.
Richard Odiham, D, 6 bales 1 fardel 1 chest with 75 cloths w.g., 1 cloth 8 yds. in grain, ½ cloth of half grain
Alexander Portinarius, A, 1 bale with 20 cloths 16 yds. [*S* 16 cloths 20 yds.] w.g.
John Marchall, D, 1 fardel with 6 cloths w.g., 4 yds. cloth in grain
Richard Isaac, D, 1½ cloths w.g.
Lewis Bonevise, A, 2 fardels with 18 cloths 8 yds. w.g.
Rowland Brocton, D, 1 fardel with 2 cloths 8 yds. w.g.
Anthony Grace, A, 3 bales with 105 doz. tanned calfskins, £17 10s.
Stephen de Villa Sole of Guipúzcoa, Sp, ½ cloth 2 yds. w.g.
Martin Lopyan of Guipúzcoa, Sp, 2½ cloths w.g.

490. 20 May. In a cart of Peter Jamys going to Southampton
Ciprian Furnarius, D, 1 fardel with 3 cloths 6 yds. w.g., 4 yds. cloth in grain

491. 24 May. In the ship of Martin de Laborda
John Ochea of Guipúzcoa, Sp, 3 bales 1 fardel with 40 cloths w.g.
Peter Valedelede of Guipúzcoa, Sp, 1 bale with 13 cloths 16 yds. w.g.
John Hoyo of Guipúzcoa, Sp, 1 bale 1 fardel with 21 cloths w.g.
Alowenso Degomell [*S* Domyngo] of Guipúzcoa, Sp, 4 bales 1 fardel
    with 41 cloths 8 yds. w.g., 18 yds. cloth in grain, 1 cloth 1 yd. of half
    grain
John de Galeguns of Guipúzcoa, Sp, 1 cloth w.g.
John Perus of Guipúzcoa, Sp, 1 cloth w.g.
Peter de Castro of Guipúzcoa, Sp, 7 bales with 128 cloths 16 yds. w.g.

492. 28 May. In the ship of John Tutor[1]
Said master, Breton, 1 fardel with 2 cloths 10 yds. w.g.

> [1] On 21 May 1481 John Tutor, master and owner of a ship called the *Magdalene* of
> Crozon ('Crowdon') in Brittany, received a warrant for payment for freightage of
> wines for the king and their carriage to Windsor (P.R.O. Warrants for the Privy Seal,
> P.S.O. 1/49, no. 2541B).

493. 29 May. Upon 2 horses of Thomas Bisshopp going to Plymouth
Ralph Astry, D, 2 fardels with 8 cloths 3 yds. w.g., 2 yds. cloth in grain

494. 2 June. In a wagon of William Nassh going to Bristol
Thomas Spens, D, 1 bale 3 fardels with 42 cloths w.g.

495. 2 June. In the ship of Cornelius Frank [of Sluis]
Anthony Jacob, A, 1 bale with 20 doz. tanned calfskins, £3 6s.8d.

496. 2 June. Upon 4 horses of Thomas Baker going to Bristol
Barnabas Senturion, A, 4 fardels with 5 cloths 8 yds. in grain, 11 cloths 8
    yds. w.g.

497. 4 June. In the ship of John Cordon
Said master, Breton, 1½ yds. cloth of half grain [*S* in grain], 14 yds. cloth
    w.g.

498. 4 June. In the ship of Walter Culvercok [of Dartmouth]
Richard Rysyng, D, 2 fardels with 10 cloths w.g.
William Brytt, D, 1 bale with 22 cloths 16 yds. w.g., 10 pcs. double
    worsted
Richard Batte, D, 1 bale with 16 cloths w.g.
Richard Snawe, D, 1 bale with 13 cloths w.g.
Henry Wynger, D, 1 bale with 23 cloths w.g.
Peter Joye, D, 1 bale with 13 cloths w.g.
Ralph Bere, D, 1 bale with 25 cloths w.g.

John Goos, D, 1 bale with 30 cloths w.g.

John Fysshare, D, 1 bale with 19 cloths 16 yds. w.g., 6 pcs. double worsted

John Haynes, D, 1 bale with 11 cloths w.g.

Roger Hungate, D, 1 bale with 28 cloths 8 yds. w.g.

Richard Rawson, D, 1 fardel with 2 cloths w.g.

Thomas Kellet, D, 1 bale with 16 cloths w.g.

John Kyrkbye, D, 1 bale with 42 cloths w.g.

John Hosyare, D, 1 bale with 32 cloths w.g.

Thomas Bradbury, D, 1 bale with 16 cloths w.g.

John Fysshare, A, 1 bale with 40 cloths w.g.

Henry Bryan, D, 1 bale with 15 cloths w.g.

Thomas Pikynham, D, 1 bale with 19 cloths w.g.

Thomas Gerrard, D, 1 bale with 22 cloths w.g.

John Stanley, D, 1 bale with 13 cloths w.g.

William Alburgh', D, 1 bale with 28 cloths w.g.

Thomas Fabian, D, 1 bale with 28 cloths 16 yds. w.g., 34 pcs. double worsted

John Raynold, D, 1 bale with 34 cloths w.g.

Robert Southwode, D, 2 bales with 60 cloths w.g.

William Eton [S Heton], D, 1 fardel with 8 cloths 8 yds. w.g., 1 pc. double worsted

John Crace, D, 1 bale with 30 cloths w.g.

Thomas Hore, D, 1 bale with 30 cloths w.g.

[m.20]

William Capell, D, 1 bale with 16 cloths w.g.

Richard Wether, D, 1 fardel with 6 cloths w.g.

Richard Wight [S White], D, 1 bale with 15 cloths w.g.

John Millet, D, 1 bale with 27 cloths w.g.

John Colet, D, 1 bale with 22 cloths w.g.

William Banknot, D, 1 bale with 31 cloths w.g.

William Lambard, D, 1 bale with 12 cloths w.g.

William Purches, D, 1 bale with $20\frac{1}{2}$ cloths w.g., 1 [S $2\frac{1}{2}$] pc. double worsted

John Chambre, D, 2 bales with 56 cloths w.g.

William Fyncham, D, 1 bale with 30 cloths 16 yds. w.g.

John Cobbe, D, 1 fardel with 7 cloths w.g.

Walter Povy, D, 1 bale with 34 cloths w.g.

John Hosiare, D, 1 bale with 12 cloths w.g.

Henry Halle, D, 1 bale with 30 cloths w.g.

John Brampton, D, 1 bale with 26 cloths w.g.

Philip Ball, D, 1 bale with 24 cloths w.g.

Peter Jay, D, 1 bale with 17 cloths w.g.

Thomas Brykill [S Brikles], D, 1 fardel with $3\frac{1}{2}$ cloths w.g., 3 pcs. double worsted

John Skyrwythe, D, 1 bale with 27 cloths w.g.

Cipriano Furnarius, D, 1 roll with 6 yds. cloth in grain, 8 yds. cloth of half grain, 1 cloth w.g.

Nicholas Alwyn, D, 1 bale with 19 cloths w.g.

Henry Cantlowe, D, 1 bale with 16 cloths w.g.
John Pykton, D, 1 bale with 30 cloths w.g.
William Weston, D, 1 bale with 10 cloths w.g., 5 pcs. double worsted
William Bufford [*S* Burford], D, 1 bale with 14 cloths w.g.
John Pellam, D, 2 bales with 45 cloths w.g.
Thomas Bradbury, D, 1 bale with 16 cloths w.g.
Thomas Mayn, D, 1 fardel with 6 cloths w.g.
John Spylman, D, 2 bales with 30 cloths w.g.
Thomas Abraham, D, 1 bale with 21 cloths 18 yds. w.g.
John Raynold, D, 1 vat with 3 cloths 8 yds. w.g.
William Hayle, D, 1 bale with 15 cloths w.g.
John Benham, D, 1 bale with 20 cloths w.g.
Roger Grove, D, 1 bale with 24 cloths w.g., 22 pcs. double worsted
Thomas Calowe, D, 1 fardel with 8 cloths w.g.
Richard Carter, D, 1 bale with 18 cloths w.g.
John Pellam, D, 1 fardel with 9 cloths w.g.
Robert Jakson, D, 1 bale with 11 cloths 18 yds. w.g.
John Pykton, D, 1 bale with 30 cloths w.g.
William Scapehuson, H, 1 bale with 19 cloths 11 yds. w.g., 4½ yds. cloth
  in grain, 8 yds. cloths of half grain; 27 goads cotton russet, 18s.8d. [*S*
  18s.4d.]
John Russenthorp, H, 2 bales with 36 cloths w.g.; 192 [*S* 189] goads
  cotton russet, £6 8s.4d.
Peter Syber, H, 1 bale with 18 cloths w.g.; 80 goads cotton russet,
  53s.4d.
Godard Slotkyn, H, 1 bale with 18 cloths w.g.; 60 goads cotton russet,
  40s.
John van Armysbery, H, 1 bale with 18 cloths w.g.; 1 grs. points, 60
  goads cotton russet, 43s.4d.
John Stakylhuson, H, 1 bale with 18 cloths w.g.; 50 goads cotton russet,
  33s.4d.
John Questynburgh, H, 1 bale with 17½ cloths w.g.; 90 [*S* 80] goads
  cotton russet, £3
Matthew Blytterswyke, H, 1 bale with 18 cloths w.g.; 60 goads cotton
  russet, 40s.
Everard Southerman, H, 1 bale with 17 cloths w.g.; 3 bonnets, 2 grs.
  points, 75 goads cotton russet, £3
Hans Culle, H, 1 bale with 22 cloths w.g.; 21 goads cotton russet,
  13s.4d.
John de Salvo, A, 2 bales 1 roll with 21 cloths 2 yds. w.g. [*S* 1 bale with 1
  cloth w.g., 2 bales with 40 pcs. cloth with broad selvage cont. 20
  cloths. w.g.], 4 yds. cloth in grain, 3 yds. cloth of half grain
Walter Violet, D, 1 fardel with 9 cloths w.g.

499. 4 June. In the ship of Thomas Payn [of London]
William Bryt, D, 1 bale with 18 cloths w.g.
Richard Batt, D, 1 bale with 21 cloths w.g.
John Thomas, D, 1 bale with 19½ cloths w.g.
William Wilcok', D, 1 bale with 20 cloths w.g.

Nicholas Wilde, D, 1 bale with 13 cloths w.g.
Robert Bangyll, D, 1 bale with 22 cloths w.g.
John Chambre, D, 1 bale with 33 cloths w.g.
Roger Hungate, D, 1 bale with 18 cloths 16 yds. w.g.
Henry Bulstrod, D, 1 fardel with 9 cloths 4 yds. w.g., 10 pcs. double worsted
John Hosiar, D, 1 bale with 32 cloths w.g.
Robert Kervile, D, 1 bale with 21 cloths w.g.
John Kyrkbye, D, 1 bale with 15 cloths w.g.
Roger Grove, D, 1 bale with 22 cloths w.g.
John Salford, D, 1 bale with 23 cloths w.g.
William Branfeld [*S* Bornflette], D, 1 bale with 20 cloths w.g.
William Whetewey, D, 1 bale with 15 cloths 8 yds. w.g., 25 pcs. double worsted
Richard Wether, D, 1 bale with 18 cloths w.g.
Thomas Lok, D, 1 bale with 12 cloths w.g.
William Twig, D, 1 bale with 16 cloths w.g.
John Pasmer, D, 1 bale with 35 cloths w.g.
William Alburgh, D, 1 bale with 27 cloths w.g.
John Raynold, D, 1 bale with 33 cloths w.g.
John Fysshare, D, 1 bale with 22 cloths w.g.
William Beynton, D, 1 bale with 20 cloths w.g.
William Peryn, D, 1 bale with 24 cloths 8 yds. w.g.
John Crace, D, 1 bale with 30 cloths w.g.
Thomas Lee, D, 1 bale with 15 cloths w.g.
William Capell, D, 1 bale with 22 cloths w.g.
John Pikton, D, 1 bale with 30 cloths w.g.
Robert Southwode, D, 1 bale with 30 cloths w.g.
Thomas Gerrard, D, 1 bale with 24 cloths w.g.
John Goos, D, 1 bale with 30 cloths w.g.
Richard White, D, 1 bale with 15 cloths w.g.
Roger Hungate, D, 1 fardel with 3 cloths w.g.
Richard Mason [*S* Manson], D, 1 bale with 16 cloths w.g.
William Bard, D, 1 bale with 23 cloths w.g.
William Herryot, D, 1 bale with 12 cloths w.g.
Robert Kervile, D, 1 bale with 24 cloths w.g.
John Hawkyn, D, 1 bale with 20 cloths w.g.
John Shelwyng, D, 1 bale with 20 cloths 16 yds. w.g.
Thomas Poplet, D, 1 fardel with 4 cloths w.g.
Robert Southwode, D, 1 bale with 14 cloths w.g.
Richard Eyryk, D, 1 bale with 12 cloths w.g.
Thomas Somer, D, 1 bale with 18 cloths w.g.
John Fysshe, D, 1 bale with 30 cloths w.g.
John Paynter, D, 1 bale with 32 cloths w.g.
Henry Hall, D, 1 bale with 27 cloths w.g.
John Pellam, D, 1 bale with 33 cloths w.g.
John Fysshare, D, 1 bale with 36 cloths w.g.
John Kyrkbye, D, 8 cloths 16 yds. w.g.
John Pykton, D, 1 bale with 33 cloths w.g.

William Jenk', D, 1 bale with 20 cloths w.g.
Robert Pech, D, 1 bale with 15 cloths 16 yds. w.g.
John Fysshare, D, 1 bale with 31 cloths w.g., 6 pcs. double worsted
James Fromlod, D, 1 bale with 14 cloths w.g.
William Bentley, D, 1 bale with 10 cloths w.g.
John Paynt', D, 1 fardel with 6 cloths w.g.
[m.20d.]
John Brampton, D, 1 bale with 18 cloths w.g.
John Goos, D, 1 fardel with 6 cloths w.g.
Walter Povye, D, 1 fardel with 6 cloths w.g.
Richard Langton, D, 1 bale with 10 cloths w.g.
John Shelwyng, D, 1 bale with 16 cloths 8 yds. w.g.
Thomas Poplot, D, 1 fardel with 2 cloths w.g.
John van Armysberye, H, 1 bale with 18 cloths w.g.; 60 goads cotton
   russet, 40s.
Peter Syber, H, 1 bale with 18 cloths w.g.; 80 goads cotton russet,
   53s.4d.
John Questynburgh, H, 1 fardel with 7 cloths w.g., 1 cloth of half grain;
   110 goads cotton russet, £3 13s.4d.
Hans Culle, H, 1 bale with 25 cloths w.g.; 30 goads cotton russet, 20s.
Augustine de Loretto, A, 1 roll with 1 cloth 7 yds. w.g.

500. 4 June. In the ship of John Roke [of London]
William Bryt, D, 1 bale with 10 cloths w.g.
Robert Bangyll, D, 1 bale with 24 cloths w.g.
Henry Winger, D, 1 bale with 20 cloths w.g.
Thomas Somer, D, 1 bale with 14 cloths w.g.
Robert Southwode, D, 2 bales with 66 cloths w.g.
William Geffrey, D, 1 bale with 20 cloths w.g.
John Goos, D, 1 bale with 30 cloths w.g.
Roger Hungate, D, 1 fardel with 5 cloths 8 yds. w.g.
Thomas Kellet, D, 1 bale with 12 cloths w.g.
John Kirkebye, D, 1 bale with 13 cloths 18 yds. w.g.
Roger Grove, D, 1 bale with 17 cloths w.g., 23 pcs. double worsted
John Hasyar, D, 1 bale with 28 cloths w.g.
Richard Wether, D, 1 bale with 27 cloths w.g.
Henry Holgyll, D, 1 bale with 25 cloths 18 yds. w.g.
John Robynson, D, 1 fardel with $8\frac{1}{2}$ cloths w.g.
Peter Lucas, D, 1 bale with 21 cloths w.g.
William Twig, D, 1 bale with 30 cloths w.g.
John Cotton, D, 1 bale with 20 cloths w.g.
William Scalder, D, 1 bale with 22 cloths w.g.
John Ebrall, D, 1 bale with 10 cloths 8 yds. w.g.
John Raynold, D, 1 bale with 33 cloths w.g.
William Beynton, D, 1 bale with 20 cloths w.g.
John Hungirford, D, 1 fardel with 10 pcs. double worsted
Robert Aldernes, D, 1 bale with 11 cloths 8 yds. w.g.
Thomas Hore, D, 1 bale with 22 cloths w.g.
Thomas Lee, D, 1 bale with 20 cloths w.g.

John Pikton, D, 1 bale with 31 cloths w.g.
Robert Ryngbell, D, 1 bale with 16 cloths w.g.
Richard Laykyn, D, 1 fardel with 5 cloths 8 yds. w.g.
John Broke, D, 1 bale with 30 cloths w.g.
John Chambre, D, 1 bale with 31 cloths w.g., 2 pcs. double worsted
Richard Bryn, D, 1 fardel with 3 cloths w.g.
William Alburgh [*S* Albrough], D, 1 bale with 12 cloths w.g.
Roger Bonyfaunt, D, 1 bale with 21 cloths w.g.
Thomas Roche, D, 1 fardel with 6 cloths 4 yds. w.g.
Thomas Bowes, D, 1 bale with 24 cloths w.g., 5 pcs. double worsted
John Crace, D, 1 fardel with 4 cloths w.g., 12 pcs. double worsted
John Jaye, D, 1 bale with 12 cloths w.g.
John Shelwyng', D, 1 bale with 28 cloths w.g.
John Pellam, D, 1 bale with 30 cloths w.g.
William Colyns, D, 1 fardel with 2½ cloths w.g.
John Warner, D, 1 bale with 28 cloths w.g.
John Skyrwithe, D, 1 bale with 18 cloths w.g.
Thomas Bowrn, D, 1 bale with 16 cloths 20 yds. w.g.
William Bentley, D, 2 fardels with 5 cloths w.g.
Thomas Quadryng', D, 1 bale with 30 cloths w.g.
William Norton, D, 1 bale with 10 cloths w.g.

501. 4 June. Upon 2 horses of John Osban [*S* Osborn] going to the port of Bristol
Enygo de Matroano of Guipúzcoa, Sp, 2 fardels with 6 cloths 8 yds. w.g., 1½ cloths in grain

502. 4 June. In the ship of Jasper [*S* Casper] Boke [of Hamburg]
Henry Lathuson, H, 6 bales with 169 cloths w.g.; 593 [*S* 615] goads cotton russet, £20
George Tak, H, 1 bale with 15 cloths w.g.; 282 goads cotton russet, £9 3s.4d.
Gerard Lesbern, H, 1 bale with 25 cloths w.g.; 18 goads cotton russet, 13s.4d.
Gasper Boke, H, 1 bale with 35 cloths w.g.; 22 goads cotton russet, 13s.4d.
Gerard Lesbern, H, 1 bale with 30 cloths w.g.
William Scapehuson, H, 1 bale with 31 cloths w.g.
Tylman van Howell, H, 1 bale with 40 cloths w.g.
Eggard Meire, H, 2 bales with 68 cloths 6 yds. w.g.; 280 goads cotton russet, £9 6s.8d.
Hans Hosterberche, H, 2 bales with 43 cloths 8 yds. w.g.
Hans Culle, H, 2 bales with 62 cloths w.g.; 222 goads cotton russet, £7 8s.4d.
Matthew Hynkylman, H, 1 bale with 29 cloths 5 yds. w.g.; 50 goads cotton russet, 33s.4d.
Hans Stut, H, 1 bale with 25 cloths w.g.; 58 goads cotton russet, 40s.
William Scapehuson, H, 1 bale with 31½ cloths w.g.; 41 goads cotton russet, 26s.8d.

Hans Swalyngburgh, H, 1 bale with 27 cloths w.g.; 328 goads cotton russet, £11

Albert Falland, H, 1 bale with 25 cloths w.g.; 65 goads cotton russet, 43s.4d.

Herman Plough, H, 1 bale with 22½ cloths w.g.; 21 goads cotton russet, 13s.4d.

Hans Culle, H, 1 bale with 11 cloths w.g.; 15 goads cotton russet, 10s.

Hans Stut, H, 2 bales with 45 cloths w.g.; 195 goads cotton russet, £6 11s.8d.

503. 4 June. In the ship of Lubert van Boke [of the Steelyard]

Tylman Barkys, H, 1 bale with 24 cloths w.g.; 18 goads cotton russet, 13s.4d.

Hans Culle, H, 1 bale with 40 cloths w.g.; 160 goads cotton russet, £5 6s.8d.

Gerard Lesbern, H, 1 bale with 29 cloths w.g.

Godard Slotkyn, H, 1 bale with 17 cloths w.g.; 93 goads cotton russet, £3 3s.4d.

Ingilbright Sevenek, H, 1 bale with 20 cloths w.g.; 70 goads cotton russet, 46s.8d.

Stephen Brawnche, H, 1 bale with 13 cloths w.g.; 90 goads cotton russet, £3

[m.21]

Lambert Rotard, H, 1 bale with 6½ yds. cloth of half grain, 3½ yds. cloth w.g., 1½ pcs. [S 1 pc. 2 ells] double worsted; 518 goads cotton russet, £17 6s.8d.

John van Derbeson, H, 1 bale with 16 cloths w.g., 3 yds. cloth of half grain; 35 goads cotton russet, 23s.4d.

George Tak, H, 1 fardel with 9 cloths w.g.; 40 goads cotton russet, 26s.8d.

John Stakylhuson, H, 1 bale with 18 cloths w.g.; 65 goads cotton russet, 43s.4d.

Henry [S van der] Bevir, H, 1 fardel with 9 cloths w.g.; 280 goads cotton russet, £9 6s.8d.

Albert Falland, H, 1 bale with 25 cloths w.g.; 67 goads cotton russet, 43s.4d.

Arnold van Stalle, H, 1 bale with 18 cloths w.g.; 67 goads cotton russet, 43s.4d.

John Salmer, H, 1 bale with 12 cloths w.g.; 2 rolls frieze, 26s.8d.

Anthony Odyndale, H, 1 bale with 24 cloths 8 yds. w.g.; 30 goads cotton russet, 20s.

George Foot, H, 1 bale with 17 cloths w.g.; 68 goads cotton russet, 46s.8d.

John Russynthorp, H, 1 fardel with 9 cloths w.g.; 20 goads cotton russet, 13s.4d.

William Scapehuson, H, 1 bale with 31 cloths w.g.; 41 goads cotton russet, 26s.8d.

Lady Margaret, Duchess of Burgundy, A, 1 bale with 10 cloths 8 yds. w.g.; C. 80 lbs. pewter vessels, 53s.4d.

504. 4 June. In the ship of Clais [*S* Nicholas] Jacobisson [of Middelburg]
Peter Wolf, A, 9 brls. with 108 doz. candles, 1 corf with C. 50 lbs.
pewter vessels, 12 weys rendered tallow, M. seasoned and 2 M. summer rabbit-skins, 18 fox-skins, 4 cat-skins, £17 13s.4d.

Arnold Howell, A, 5 weys rendered tallow, 1 brl. with 12 doz. candles, £3
Henry Hanyskyn, A, 1 basket with 5 C. seasoned and M. summer
rabbit-skins, 5 [*S* 3] doz. fox-skins, 46s.8d.

James Falk, A, M. seasoned and M. summer rabbit-skins, £3

505. 4 June. In the ship of Robert Foster [of London]
Stephen Chirch, D, 1 fardel with 3 cloths w.g.
William Haile, D, 1 bale with 15 cloths w.g.
Nicholas Niandeser, D, 1 bale with 16 cloths w.g.
John Pekeryng, D, 1 bale with 10 cloths 16 yds. w.g., 32 pcs. double
worsted.
John Skyrwith, D, 1 fardel with 7½ cloths w.g.
Laurence Swarfeld, D, 1 fardel with 9 cloths 16 yds. w.g.
Robert Ryngbell, D, 1 bale with 14 cloths 16 yds. w.g.
Philip Buntyng, D, 1 fardel with 5 cloths w.g.
John Trewinard, D, 1 bale with 12½ cloths w.g.
Richard Langton, D, 1 bale with 16 cloths w.g.
John Durham, D, 1 fardel with 9 cloths w.g.
William Redye, D, 1 fardel with 2 cloths w.g., 8 pcs. double worsted
Thomas Petyte D, 1 bale with 10½ cloths w.g.
John Bolt, D, 1 fardel with 5 cloths w.g.
Thomas Abraham, D, 1 bale with 18 cloths w.g.
John Bolt, D, 1 fardel with 3 cloths w.g.
Ingilbright Sevenek, H, 1 bale with 18 cloths w.g.; 50 goads cotton
russet, 33s.4d.
Matthew Bliterswyk, H, 1 bale with 18 cloths w.g.; 60 goads cotton
russet, 40s.
Edward Johnson, A, 6 C. seasoned and 6 C. summer rabbit-skins, 3
doz. fox-skins, 2 doz. cat-skins, 46s.8d.
Nicholas Jamys, A, M. seasoned and M. summer rabbit-skins, 5 doz.
fox-skins, £3 13s.4d.

506. 4 June. In the ship of William Petyte [of Weymouth]
Ingilbright Sevenek, H, 1 bale with 18 cloths w.g.; 90 goads cotton
russet, £3
John Russenthorp, H, 1 bale with 20 cloths w.g.; 66 goads cotton russet,
43s.4d.
John van Armysbery, H, 1 bale with 17 cloths w.g.; 80 goads cotton
russet, 53s.4d.
Ingilbright Sevenek, H, 1 bale with 17 cloths w.g.; 150 goads cotton
russet, £5
Matthew Bliterswyke, H, 1 bale with 16 cloths 2 yds. w.g.; 103 goads
cotton russet, £3 13s.4d.
Peter Syber, H, 1 bale with 18 cloths w.g.; 88 goads cotton russet, £3
John Stakylhuson, H, 2 bales with 36 cloths w.g., 8 yds. cloth of half

grain; 105 [*S* 110] goads cotton russet, £3 13s.4d.

John van Armysbery, H, 1 bale with 22 cloths w.g.; 2 bonnets, 374 goads cotton russet, £12 10s.

Matthew Bliterswyke, H, 1 bale with 15 cloths 9 yds. w.g.; 120 goads cotton russet, £4

Gerard van Grove, H, 1 bale with 18 cloths w.g.; 60 goads cotton russet, 40s.

John van Derbeson, H, 1 bale with 18½ cloths w.g.; 19 goads cotton russet, 13s.4d.

Goswyn Redekyrk, H, 1 bale with 18 cloths w.g.; 40 goads cotton russet, 26s.8d.

Hans Culle, H, 1 bale with 28 cloths w.g.; 20 goads cotton russet, 13s.4d.

John van Strawlyn, H, 1 bale with 25 cloths w.g.; 40 goads cotton russet, 26s.8d.

Roger van Fell [*S* Feld], H, 1 bale with 18 cloths w.g.; 20 goads cotton russet, 13s.4d.

Godfrey Spyring, D, 1 fardel with 4 cloths 16 yds. w.g.

Nicholas Sudbery, D, 1 bale with 14 cloths 8 yds. w.g.

John Sewalle, D, 1 bale with 12 cloths w.g.

John Nanthatan [*S* Nancatham], D, 1 bale with 10 cloths w.g.

Thomas Burgoyn, D, 1 fardel with 3 cloths w.g.

Roger Bonyfaunt, D, 1 fardel with 6 cloths w.g.

Richard Snawe, D, 1 fardel with 4 cloths w.g.

John Rose, D, 1 bale with 27 cloths w.g.

Thomas Bate, D, 1 fardel with 7 cloths w.g.

John Raynold, D, 1 bale with 16 cloths w.g.

Robert Brikylsworth, D, 1 fardel with 4 cloths w.g.

John Pykton, D, 1 bale with 21 cloths w.g.

William Jeffrey, D, 1 fardel with 4 cloths w.g.

Richard Langton, D, 1 fardel with 4 cloths w.g.

Edmund Talwyn, D, 1 cloth w.g.

Charles Harryson, A, 1 maund with M. seasoned and 3 [*S* 4] M. summer rabbit-skins, £5

[m.21d.]

507. 4 June. In the ship of John Wodeles [of London]

John Brampton, D, 1 fardel with 6 cloths w.g.

William Jenk' D, 1 fardel with 7 cloths w.g.

Thomas Lok, D, 1 bale with 12 cloths w.g.

Thomas Abraham, D, 1 bale with 19½ cloths w.g.

William Clerk, D, 1 bale with 14 cloths w.g.

Roger Bonyfaunt, D, 1 bale with 21 cloths w.g.

John Goos, D, 1 bale with 14 cloths 20 yds. w.g.

Robert Brikylsworth, D, 1 fardel with 5 cloths w.g.

John Rose, D, 1 bale with 11 cloths w.g.

John Robynson, D, 1 chest and fardel with 19 cloths 16 yds. w.g.

William Velbek, D, 2 chests with 7 cloths 6 yds. w.g.

Thomas Abraham, D, 1 fardel with 6 cloths w.g.

Thomas Screven, D, 1 bale with 24 cloths w.g.

Richard Twigg, D, 1 bale with 11 cloths w.g.

Gilbert Keys, D, 1 cloth w.g.

Thomas Skirwith, D, 1 bale with 11 cloths 8 yds. w.g.

John Rose, D, 1 fardel with 24 pcs. double worsted

William Jenk', D, 1 cloth w.g.

William Jeffrey, D, 1 fardel with 7 cloths w.g.

Stephen Braunche, H, 1 fardel with 4 cloths w.g.

Robert Boys, D, 1 fardel with 6 cloths 8 yds. w.g.

Thomas Screven, D, 1 fardel with 9 cloths w.g.

Simon Harryes, D, 1 bale with 15 cloths w.g.

Ingilbright Sevenek, H, 1 bale with 18 cloths w.g.; 100 goads cotton russet, £3 6s.8d.

John Questynburgh, H, 1 bale with 12 cloths 5 yds. w.g.; 432 goads cotton russet, £14 6s.8d.

Matthew Bliterswyke, H, 1 bale with 18 cloths w.g.; 66 goads cotton russet, 45s.

Peter Syber, H, 2 bales with 36 cloths w.g.; 180 goads cotton russet, £6

John Stakylhuson, H, 1 bale with 18 cloths w.g.; 60 goads cotton russet, 40s.

Ingilbright Sevenek, H, 1 bale with 11 cloths w.g.; 400 goads cotton russet, £13 6s.8d.

John Russynthorp, H, 1 bale with 11 cloths w.g.; 130 goads cotton russet, £4 6s.8d.

Gerard van Grove, H, 1 bale with 17½ cloths w.g.; 60 goads cotton russet, 40s.

Goswyn Rodinkerk, H, 1 bale with 19 cloths w.g.; 80 goads cotton russet, 53s.4d.

John van Armysbery, H, 1 bale with 13 cloths w.g.; 80 goads cotton russet, 53s.4d.

John Stakylhuson, H, 1 bale with 15 cloths w.g.; 60 goads cotton russet, 40s.

508. 4 June. In the ship of Peter Jacobisson [of Arnemuiden]

Gerard Lesbern, H, 1 bale with 38 cloths w.g.

Hillibrand van Vuno, H, 1 bale with 26½ cloths w.g.; 25 goads cotton russet, 16s.8d.

Ingilbright Sevenek, H, 1 bale with 18 cloths w.g.; 80 goads cotton russet, 53s.4d.

John Questinburgh, H, 1 bale with 18 cloths w.g.; 70 goads cotton russet, 46s.8d.

Stephen Braunche, H, 1 bale with 15 cloths w.g.; 102 goads cotton russet, £3 8s.4d.

Ingilbright Sevenek, H, 1 bale with 18 cloths w.g.; 80 goads cotton russet, 53s.4d.

Matthew Bliterswyke, H, 1 bale with 18 cloths w.g.; 61 goads cotton russet, 40s.

John van Derbeson, H, 1 bale with 18 cloths w.g.; 38 goads cotton russet, 26s.8d.

Matthew Hynkylman, H, 1 bale with 15 cloths w.g.; 18 goads cotton russet, 13s.4d.

John van Armysbery, H, 1 bale with 18 cloths w.g.; 60 goads cotton russet, 40s.

George Tak, H, 1 bale with 16 cloths w.g.; 66 goads cotton russet, 45s.

Peter Syber, H, 2 bales with 32 cloths w.g.; 240 goads cotton russet, £8

Goswyn Rodynkerk, H, 1 bale with 18 cloths w.g.; 45 [*S* 40] goads cotton russet, 30s.

Matthew Bliterswyke, H, 1 bale with 15 cloths w.g.; 170 goads cotton russet, £5 13s.4d.

Hans Culle, H, 1 bale with 21 cloths w.g.; 17 goads cotton russet, 11s.8d.

John Stakilhuson, H, 2 bales with 28 cloths w.g.; 80 goads cotton russet, 6 bonnets, 1 brl. with 3½ C. pewter vessels, 3 doz. ox-tongues, 2 brls. with 26 doz. candles, £9

Arnold van Stalle, H, 1 bale with 18 cloths w.g.; 57 goads cotton russet, 40s.

Anthony Odindale, H, 1 bale with 15 cloths w.g.; 31 goads cotton russet, 20s.

John Salmer, H, 1 bale with 17 cloths 16 yds. w.g.; 3 rolls [*S* Welsh] frieze, 40s.

John Russenthorp, H, 1 bale with 15 cloths w.g., 1 cloth 9 yds. in grain; 88 goads cotton russet, £3

Albert Falland, H, 1 bale with 25 cloths w.g.; 76 goads cotton russet, 50s.

Frank Savage, H, 1 bale with 10 cloths 8 yds. w.g.; 3 rolls Welsh frieze, 46s.8d.

William Grenewold, H, 100 qrs. wheat, £33 6s.8d.

John van Armysbery, H, 1 bale with 18 cloths w.g.; 80 goads cotton russet, 53s.4d.

Hans Culle, H, 1 bale with 28 cloths w.g.; 26 goads cotton russet, 16s.8d.

Roger van Feld, H, 1 bale with 22 cloths w.g.; 21 goads cotton russet, 13s.4d.

George Foot, H, 1 bale with 13 cloths w.g.; 109 goads cotton russet, £3 13s.4d.

Marcello Maurys, A, 60 qrs. wheat, £20

James Falke, A, 1 maund 2 baskets with 4 M. seasoned and 4 M. summer rabbit-skins, 2 doz. cat-skins, 6 nets, £12

John Docher, A, 1 maund 5 baskets with 13 weys rendered tallow, 1 hhd. ½ brl. with 40 doz. lbs. starch, £8 6s.8d.

Laurence Gil, D, 1 fardel with 2½ cloths w.g.

John Semewaye, A, 1 cloth w.g.; 30 lbs. pewter vessels, 1 brass basin, 2 salt-cellars, 9 pcs. pewter vessels, 1 flitch bacon, [*S* 1 cheese, 1 brl. salt meat], 13s.4d.

Leonard Swallyn, [A,] 1 brl. 2 firkins with 30 doz. lbs. starch, 15s.

Face Sumbre, A, 16 yds. [cloth] w.g.

509. 19 June. In a cart of Thomas Arnold going to Southampton

Michael Sepriell', A, 1 fardel with 9 cloths 20 yds. w.g.

510. 19 June. In the ship of Philpot Betowe [*S* Betstowe]
Said master, A, 1 fardel with 2 cloths 16 yds. w.g.; 3 pcs. cotton russet,
17 brls. pitch and tar, £6 13s.4d.

[m.22]
511. 19 June. In the ship of Hayn' Wilberdson
William Grenewold, H, 65 qrs. wheat, £21 13s.4d.

512. 22 June. In the ship of John Bargeman [of Reimerswaal]
John Evyngar, A, 4 pipes 1 hhd. beer, 30s.

513. 23 June. In the ships of Cornelius Quatell, Cornelius Stenburgh
and George Bras [of Bergen-op-Zoom]
Lady Margaret, Duchess of Burgundy,[1] A, 60 live oxen, A, £30

> [1] At the end of her visit to Edward IV in 1480, the Duchess of Burgundy was granted
> the right to buy 1,000 oxen and 2,000 rams yearly and to ship them to Flanders,
> Holland or Zeeland free of custom or subsidy (*C.P.R. 1476–85*, p. 236).

514. 25 June. In the ship of Thomas Grey
John Fynkyll, D, 14 bales with 218 cloths w.g.
Robert Godwyn, D, 2 bales with 23 cloths 20 yds. w.g.
Simon Harryes, D, 5 fardels with 47 cloths 18 yds. w.g.
Thomas Spens, D, 8 bales with 100 cloths w.g.
John Thwayt', D, 4 bales with 65 cloths w.g.
Edward Fynkell, D, 1 fardel with 4 cloths w.g.
Edward Gower, D, 1 fardel with 7 cloths w.g.

515. 26 June. In the ship of Robert Johnson [of Middelburg]
William Grenewold, H, 70 qrs. wheat, £23 6s.8d.

516. 28 June. In the ship of Giles van Gent [of Reimerswaal]
Andrew Petirson, A, 3½ brls. 2 [*S* 3½] firkins honey, 2½ brls. candles, 2
pipes beer, 1 hhd. with rye-meal [*S* 'ryeflor'], £3 6s.8d.

517. 28 June. In a cart of Henry Cole going to Southampton
Jordon Deputes, A, 4 bales with 52 cloths w.g.

518. 28 June. In the ship of Marise Styvare
Said master, A, 1 vat with 4 cloths 4 yds. w.g.; 1 roll frieze, 13s.4d.

519. 30 June. In the ship of Henry Bret [of Ostend]
Said master, A, 16 yds. cloth w.g.

520. 30 June. In the ship of Nicholas Langbene
Thomas Kays, D, 16 yds. cloth w.g.
Lady Margaret, Duchess of Burgundy,[1] A, 80 qrs. wheat, £26 13s.4d.

> [1] 14 June 1481, grant of licence to the Duchess of Burgundy to export 1,000 qrs. wheat
> and 1,000 qrs. barley, paying custom (P.R.O. Treaty Roll, C.76/165, m.8).

521. 6 July. In the ship of Masse Sture [*S* Story] [of Ostend]

Lady Margaret, Duchess of Burgundy, A, 100 qrs. wheat, £33 6s.8d.

522. 2 July. In the ship of John Smolt
William Grenewold, H, 50 qrs. wheat, £16 13s.4d.

523. 6 July. In the ship of Robert Alcok [of London]
John Cobbe, D, 1 bale with 14 cloths w.g.
Thomas Smyth, D, 1 fardel with 7 cloths w.g.
John Cobbe, D, 1½ cloths w.g.
Richard Awbrie, D, 1 bale with 18 cloths w.g.
Henry Savage, D, 1 bale with 13 cloths 20 yds. w.g.
Henry Lathuson, H, 1 bale with 25 cloths w.g.; (203 goads cotton russet, £6 16s.8d. *del.*)
Hans Stut, H, 1 bale with 25 cloths w.g.; 17 goads cotton russet, 11s.8d.
Hans Culle, H, 1 bale with 10 cloths w.g.; 486 goads cotton russet, £16 5s.
Tylman Barkys, H, 1 bale with 19 cloths w.g.; 20 goads cotton russet, 13s.4d.
Peter Laurenson, A, 17 sacks [S with 8½ qrs.] mustard seed, £8 6s.8d.
William Scapehuson, H, 1 bale with 20 cloths w.g.; 203 goads cotton russet, £6 16s.8d.

524. 10 July. In the ship of John Lopus
Martin de Debia of Guipúzcoa, Sp, 16 yds. [cloth] w.g.
Martin de Sistona of Guipúzcoa, Sp, 1 cloth 16 yds. w.g.
Peter de Savale of Guipúzcoa, Sp, 2 bales with 26 cloths w.g.
Pascualle Diakos of Guipúzcoa, Sp, 1 bale with 13½ cloths w.g.
Michael Vergare of Guipúzcoa, Sp, 1 fardel with 5 cloths 2 yds. w.g.
Martin de Soarto of Guipúzcoa, Sp, 8 yds. cloth w.g.

525. 12 July. In the ship of Richard Johnson
Peter de Castro of Guipúzcoa, Sp, 2 bales with 39 cloths 10 yds. w.g.

526. 12 July. In the ship [S cart] of Thomas Long
Peter Wolf, A, 9 brls. with 4 weys rendered tallow, 40s.

527. 14 July. In the ship of Anthony Brabander [of Middelburg]
Walter Richardson, A, 2 firkins with 14 doz. [S lbs.] candles, 13s.4d.
Matthew Grenestrete, A, 3 brls. 1 kilderkin with 44 doz. candles, 53s.4d.
Donas Bernard, A, 9 yds. cloth w.g.; 44 lbs. pewter vessels, 8 pcs. pewter vessels [S 1 basin, 1 laver, 1 pot, 6 brass candlesticks, 1 pewter salt-cellar], 13s.4d.
Simon van Broke, A, 1 fardel with 2 cloths w.g.
Hans Culle, H, 1 bale with 752 goads cotton russet, £25
Hans Stut, H, 1 bale with 23 cloths w.g.; 66 goads cotton russet, 46s.8d.
Albert Falland, H, 1 bale with 21 cloths w.g.; 96 goads cotton russet, £3 5s.
Roger van Feld, H, 1 bale with 25 cloths w.g.; 20 goads cotton russet, 13s.4d.

Henry Lathuson, H, 1 bale with 27 cloths w.g.
John Stakylhuson, H, 1 bale with 18 cloths w.g.; 9 bonnets, 40 goads cotton russet, 40s.
Tylman Barkys, H, 1 bale with 15 cloths 3 yds. w.g.; 20 goads cotton russet, 13s.4d.
John Salmer, H, 1 fardel with 8 cloths w.g.; 17 goads cotton russet, 11s.8d.

528. 16 July. In the ship of John de Bedea
Said master of Guipúzcoa, Sp, 1 bale with 10½ cloths w.g.
Sawncheus de Leveano of Guipúzcoa, Sp, 2 fardels with 14 cloths 16 yds. w.g.
Martin Howgard of Guipúzcoa, Sp, 1 fardel with 4 cloths w.g.
Florence Stean of Guipúzcoa, Sp, 1 fardel with 2 cloths w.g.
Peter Valedelede of Guipúzcoa, Sp, 1 bale with 12 cloths w.g.
Peter de Senyowre of Guipúzcoa, Sp, 1 fardel with 2 cloths 20 yds. w.g.
John de Erosta of Guipúzcoa, Sp, 1 fardel with 7 cloths w.g.
John Sawnches of Guipúzcoa, Sp, 6 cloths 20 yds. w.g.
Martin de Gargara of Guipúzcoa, Sp, 1 fardel with 8 cloths w.g.
Ochea de Arreata of Guipúzcoa, Sp, 2 fardels with 14 cloths w.g.
Domyngo de Rola of Guipúzcoa, Sp, 3 fardels with 15 cloths 16 yds. w.g.
Peter de Savogale of Guipúzcoa, Sp, 1 fardel with 7 cloths 8 yds. w.g.
Sawnchio Minys Jake of Guipúzcoa, Sp, 4 fardels with 26 cloths w.g.
Lopus Deteres of Guipúzcoa, Sp, 5 cloths 17 yds. w.g.
Sawnchio Mynisyake [*S* Menseake] of Guipúzcoa, Sp, 11 yds. cloth w.g.
Martin de Strokesa of Guipúzcoa, Sp, 8 yds. [cloth] w.g.

529. 16 July. In the ship of Peter de Savegale
Peter Valedelede of Guipúzcoa, Sp, 2 bales with 22 cloths 16 yds. w.g., 3 cloths 20 yds. in grain, 2 cloths 8 yds. of half grain
John de Sent John of Guipúzcoa, Sp, 1 bale 1 fardel with 11 cloths 6 yds. w.g., 4 yds. cloth in grain, 3 yds. cloth of half grain
John Revore of Guipúzcoa, Sp, 1 bale with 12 cloths 16 yds. w.g.
Martin de Ryaga of Guipúzcoa, Sp, 2 fardels with 7 cloths 15 yds. w.g.
Fortunio de Novia of Guipúzcoa, Sp, 2 bales with 19 cloths 6 yds. w.g., 1 cloth 8 yds. of half grain
John Revore of Guipúzcoa, Sp, 1 fardel with 5 cloths w.g.
John Sancheodores of Guipúzcoa, Sp, 1 fardel with 9 cloths 10 yds. w.g., 3 cloths in grain
Alfonso de Lyon of Guipúzcoa, Sp, 3 bales with 36 cloths 8 yds. w.g.
Giles Martino of Guipúzcoa, Sp, 1 fardel with 2 cloths 8 yds. w.g.
John de Sowte of Guipúzcoa, Sp, ½ cloth w.g., ½ pc. double worsted [m.22d.]
Peter de Castro of Guipúzcoa, Sp, 2 bales with 30 cloths 8 yds. w.g., 3 cloths in grain

530. 16 July. In the ship of Peter de Traco
Peter Valedelede of Guipúzcoa, Sp, 1 bale with 12 cloths 16 yds. w.g.

531. 18 July. In the ship of John de Roka
John Markena of Guipúzcoa, Sp, 4 fardels with 19 cloths 6 yds. w.g., 7 yds. cloth in grain, 6 yds. cloth of half grain
Gumsalvo Garcea of Guipúzcoa, Sp, 1 fardel with 5 cloths w.g.
John Loriaga of Guipúzcoa, Sp, 1 fardel with 7 cloths w.g.
John de Sent John of Guipúzcoa, Sp, 4 fardels with 23 cloths 18 yds. w.g.
Fortunio de Novia of Guipúzcoa, Sp, 3 bales with 32 cloths 16 yds. w.g.
Peter Valedelede of Guipúzcoa, Sp, 2 fardels with 9 cloths 16 yds. w.g.
John de Sanchio [*S* John Sancheo de Doras] of Guipúzcoa, Sp, 1 bale 1 fardel with 15 cloths 10 yds. w.g., 6 cloths 6 yds. in grain, 1 cloth 8 yds. of half grain
Ocheo Darbolanch of Guipúzcoa, Sp, 1 fardel with 5 cloths w.g.
Alowiso [*S* Alfonso] de Lyon of Guipúzcoa, Sp, 3 bales with 39 cloths w.g.
Peter de Castro of Guipúzcoa, Sp, 1 bale with 16 cloths w.g., 3 rolls with 4½ cloths in grain
Peter Arranda [*S* Arranat] of Guipúzcoa, Sp, 1 bale with 13 cloths 8 yds. w.g.

532. 18 July. In the ship of Martin de Gaunce
Said master of Guipúzcoa, Sp, 20 yds. cloth w.g.

533. 18 July. In a cart of Peter Jamys going to Southampton
Cipriano Furnarius, D, 3 bales with 38 cloths w.g.

534. 23 July. In the ship of John Turnour [of London]
Peter Hardyng, D, 1 fardel with 1 cloth w.g.

535. 23 July. In the ship of John Benet
John Semer, D, 2 bales with 28½ cloths w.g.
William Nicoll, D, 1 fardel with 2 cloths w.g.
William Fyncham, D, 4 bales with 67 cloths w.g.
Thomas Spens, D, 1 fardel with 3 cloths w.g.
Richard Odyham, D, 2 fardels with 15 cloths 8 yds. w.g.
Ralph Astrye, D, 1 bale with 13 cloths w.g.

536. 24 July. In the ship of Edmund Jacobson
Lambert Jacobson, A, 21 yds. cloth w.g.; 6 [*S* 16] lbs. starch, 20d.
Peter Hownfler, A, 10 pipes beer, £3 6s.8d.

537.[1] 24 July. In the ship of John Lopus
Enego de Areola of Guipúzcoa, Sp, 1 fardel with 5 cloths 4 yds. w.g.
Martin de Areola of Guipúzcoa, Sp, 1 bale with 10 cloths 6 yds. w.g.
Peter de Ochea of Guipúzcoa, Sp, 1 fardel with 4 cloths 19 yds. w.g.

[1] Follows **529** in *S*.

538. 24 July. In the ship of Bartholomew Johnson
James van Alice, A, 4½ weys cheese, 20 Suffolk cheeses, £3

James Bose, A, 2 brls. with 24 doz. [*S* lbs.] candles, 30s.

539. 27 July. In the ship of John Stephens [of Fowey]
William Isaac, D, 3 bales with 40 cloths w.g., 1 pipe with 1 cloth 11 yds.
w.g. [*S* in grain]
Richard Isaac, D, 3 bales with 38 cloths w.g.
John Towneshend, D, 5 bales with 50 cloths 10 yds. w.g.
Thomas Terre, D, 2 bales with 35 cloths 20 yds. w.g.
Robert Basset, D, 3 bales with 65 cloths w.g.

540. 27 July. In a cart of Peter Jamys going to Southampton
John Thwayt', D, 3 bales 1 fardel with 36 cloths 8 yds. w.g.

541. 27 July. In the ship of Cornelis Nese [of Middelburg]
Said master, A, 1 cloth 16 yds. w.g.; 4 baskets with 4 weys rendered
tallow, 8 pipes beer, £5
John Clerk, D, 1 fardel with 3 cloths w.g.
Joyes Vanderhage, A, 1 brl. butter, 6 weys cheese, £4

542. 1 Aug. In the ship of Peter Jacobisson [of Arnemuiden]
Marcello Mawris, A, 110 qrs. wheat, £36 13s.4d.
Dorito Jamys, A, 1 brl. with 24 doz. [*S* lbs.] candles, 1 firkin verjuice,
26s.8d.
Matthew Falk, A, 1 brl. with 26 doz. lbs. starch, 13s.4d.
Frederick Hegyll, A, 1 fardel with 11 pcs. double worsted; for the
aforesaid 11 pcs. double worsted, £11
John Greverard, H, 1 bale with 16 cloths w.g.; 17 goads cotton russet,
13s.4d.
Peter Eksted, H, 1 bale with 20 cloths w.g.; 20 goads cotton russet,
13s.4d.
John van Armysbery, H, 2 bales with 34 cloths w.g.; 66 goads cotton
russet, 43s.4d.
Frank Savage, H, 1 brl. with 6 C. lbs. pewter vessels, £8
John Salmer, H, 1 bale with 12½ cloths w.g.; 1½ rolls frieze, 20s.
Henry Bevir, H, 1 bale with 18 cloths w.g.; 34 goads cotton russet,
23s.4d.
Gerard van Grove, H, 1 bale with 16 cloths w.g.; 20 goads cotton russet,
13s.4d.
John van Strawlyn, H, 1 bale with 21½ cloths w.g.; 20 goads cotton
russet, 13s.4d.
John Russenthorp, H, 1 bale with 13 cloths w.g.; 21 goads cotton russet,
13s.4d.
Anthony Odindale, H, 1 bale with 12 cloths w.g.
John van Derbeson, H, 1 fardel with 1 cloth w.g.; 304 goads cotton
russet, £10 3s.4d.
Hans Stut, H, 1 bale with 26 cloths w.g.; 18 goads cotton russet, 13s.4d.
William Scapehuson, H, 1 bale with 25 cloths 15 yds. w.g., 3 yds. cloth
of half grain
Matthew Blitterswyk, H, 1 bale with 23 cloths 19 yds. w.g.; 1 mantle 100
goads cotton russet, £3 13s.4d. (6s.8d. *del.*)

Peter Wesell, H, 1 bale with 10 cloths 10 yds. w.g.; 4 bonnets, 15 goads cotton russet, 13s.4d.

John van Armysbery, H, 1 bale with 12 cloths w.g.; 20 goads cotton russet, 13s.4d.

Herman Plough, H, 1 bale with 25 cloths w.g.; 25 goads cotton russet, 16s.8d.

543. 1 Aug. In the ship of John Wilbordson
Marcello Maurys, A, 80 qrs. wheat, £26 13s.4d.

544. 4 Aug. In the ship of Robert Dearte [of Dieppe]
Nicholas Symors [*S* Somers], A, 6 butts rumney, 1 pc. lead cont. 7 C. lbs. 3 qrs., 12 cheeses, 3 brls. pitch, 1 pc. double worsted, £22
For the aforesaid pc. of double [*S* worsted], A[1]
John Elyot, A, 20 pcs. copper plate cont. 7½ C. 24 [*S* 18] lbs., 12½ C. 46 [*S* 16] lbs. copper, 12 galley pots, 1 brl. orpiment [*S* cont. 52 lbs.], £17

[1] Indicates worsted exported by an alien merchant which was liable both for cloth and petty custom.

545. 4 Aug. In the ship of John Wolcok
John Townesend, D, 1 bale 1 fardel with 22 cloths 16 yds. w.g.
John Bayly, D, 1 bale with 11 cloths 16 yds. w.g.
Richard Odyham, D, 1 bale with 10 cloths 16 yds. w.g.
Ralph Astry, D, 2 bales with 28 cloths w.g., 1 cloth 7 yds. in grain, 1 cloth of half grain

[m.23]
546. 4 Aug. In the ship of Cornelius Johnson
John Evingar, A, 10 pipes beer, £3 6s.8d.

547. 4 Aug. In the ship of John Bargeman [of Reimerswaal]
William Bentley, D, 1 cloth w.g.
John Rogger, D, 16 yds. cloth w.g.

548. 7 Aug. In the ship of Peter Mengyll [of Antwerp]
John Stakylhuson, H, 4 brls. with 40 doz. [*S* lbs.] candles, 40s.

549. 7 Aug. In the ship of Martin Perus
John Perus of Guipúzcoa, Sp, 1 fardel with 3 cloths 10 yds. w.g.
Martin Lopean [*S* Lopiana] of Guipúzcoa, Sp, 6 bales with 77 cloths w.g.
Said master of Guipúzcoa, Sp, 4 cloths w.g.
Martin de Legete of Guipúzcoa, Sp, 18 yds. [cloth] w.g.
Lopus de Solola of Guipúzcoa, Sp, 1 chest with 1 cloth 20 yds. w.g.
John Sawenches of Guipúzcoa, Sp, 1 bale with 10 cloths 8 yds. w.g., 3 cloths in grain

550. 9 Aug. In the ship of Nicholas Fere [*S* Clais Feryng]
John Gylys, A, 1 chest with 50 cheeses, 25s.
John Evingar, A, 11 pipes beer, £3 13s.4d.

551. 9 Aug. In the ship of Clays [*S* Nicholas] Jacobisson [of Middelburg]
Said master, A, 1 vat 1 pipe 1 brl. with 165 doz. [*S* lbs.] candles, £8 5s.
Cowred [*S* Conratt] Bone, A, 3 pipes beer, 20s.

552. 9 Aug. In the ship of Robert Foster [of London]
William Brit [*S* Brett], D, 1 fardel with 2 cloths w.g.

553. 9 Aug. In the ship of Nicholas [*S* Clais] Thorn [of Arnemuiden]
Peter van Worskyn, A, 1 basket with 12 pcs. cotton russet, 1 hhd. with salt meat, £4 13s.4d.
Paul Godfrey, A, 10 pipes beer, £3 6s.8d.
James Cornelius, A, 4 brls. with 6 C. 34 lbs. rendered tallow, ½ brl. with 5 doz. [*S* 50 doz. lbs.] candles, 40s.
Henry Henrikson [*S* Harryson], A, 2 baskets with 2 weys rendered tallow, 26s.8d.
John Greverard, H, 2 bales with 34 cloths w.g.; 47 goads cotton russet, 31s.8d.
John van Armysbery, H, 3 bales with 43 cloths w.g.; 85 goads cotton russet, 55s.8d. [*S* 56s.8d.]
Peter Eksted, H, 1 bale with 25 cloths w.g.; 42 goads cotton russet, 26s.8d.
Gerard van Grove, H, 1 bale with 16 cloths w.g.; 20 goads cotton russet, 13s.4d.
Ingylbright Sevenek, H, 1 bale with 15 cloths w.g.; 160 goads cotton russet, £5 6s.8d.
Henry Bevir, H, 1 bale with 18 cloths w.g.; 21 goads cotton russet, 13s.4d.
John van Strawlyn, H, 2 bales with 38 cloths w.g.; 60 goads cotton russet, 40s.
John Russynthorpp, H, 1 fardel with 8 cloths w.g.; 19 goads cotton russet, 13s.4d.

554. 13 Aug. In the ship of John Goldisburgh [of London]
William Remyngton, D, 1 cloth 5 yds. w.g.

555. 25 Aug. In the ship of Thomas Calwey
William Mill, D, 1 fardel with 2 cloths w.g.

556. 25 Aug. In the ship of Martin de Mesketa
Gabriel Furnarius, A, 3 bales with 36 cloths 8 yds. w.g.
Barnabas Senturion, A, 6 bales with 69 cloths 18 yds. w.g.
Nicholas Lomlyn', A, 1 bale with 10 cloths 8 yds. w.g.
Laurence Gryll', A, 1 bale with 15 cloths 16 yds. w.g.; 4 M. lbs. tin in bars, £48

John Baptista Gentill', A, 5 cloths 16 yds. w.g.
Ocheo Pylote of Guipúzcoa, Sp, 1 fardel with 2 cloths 4 yds. w.g.
Said master of Guipúzcoa, Sp, 1 fardel with 9 cloths w.g.
Domyngo de Mesketa of Guipúzcoa, Sp, 1 fardel with 3 cloths 18 yds. w.g.

557. 25 Aug. In the ship of Cornelius Stenburgh [of Bergen-op-Zoom]
Adrian Mawson, A, 120 goads cotton russet, 20 yds. frieze, 1 brl. with 18 [*S* 13] doz. lbs. candles, £3 6s.8d.
Corryn Gysbright, A, 9 baskets with 10 weys rendered tallow, £8
Cornelius Williamson, A, 2 baskets with 4 C. lbs. rendered tallow, 36s.8d.
John Evingar, A, 10 pipes beer, £3 6s.8d.
Gerard van Stonburgh, A, 30 pipes beer, £10

558. 25 [*S* 27] Aug. Upon 2 horses of John Colston going to Bristol
Peter Joye, D, 3 fardels with 12 cloths w.g.

559. 25 Aug. In the ship of Richard Lull
John Luff, D, 1 fardel with 2 cloths 8 yds. w.g.
Adrian Mews [*S* Muse], D, 1 bale with 12 cloths w.g.
Oliver Bredesley, D, 6 fardels with 31½ cloths w.g.
Peter Jesse, D, 3 bales with 35 cloths 6 yds. w.g.
Richard Henle, D, 1 bale with 14 cloths w.g.

560. 25 Aug. In the ship of Peryn Vare
Said master, A, 1 fardel with 4 cloths 16 yds. w.g., ½ pc. [*S* 4 ells] double worsted; for the aforesaid pc. double worsted, 10s.; 1 brass bell weight 4 C. 50 lbs., £5

561. 25 Aug. In the ship of Copyn Welle [of Antwerp]
Simon Harryson, A, 2 brls. with 4 C. lbs. rendered tallow, 2 pcs. cotton russet, £3
Anthony Jacobisson, A, 1 fardel with 6 cloths 16 yds. w.g.
Cornelius Smyth, A, 1 brl. with 18 doz. [*S* lbs.] candles, 4 brls. with 48 doz. lbs. starch, 46s.8d.
Philip Bussh, A, 4 yds. cloth w.g.; 8 pcs. cotton russet, 13½ brls. 5 baskets with 21 weys rendered tallow, 1 hhd. 1 brl. [*S* and 1 firkin] salt meat, £18
Gerard de Loye, A, 1 fardel with 13 pcs. cotton russet, 2 brls. with salt meat, £5
Laurence Tyman, A, 1 fardel with 12 pcs. cotton russet, £4
John Welbek, A, 6½ weys cheese, 2 brls. with salt meat, 1 brl. with 12 doz. lbs. candles, 1 firkin butter, £5 6s.8d.
James Falke, A, 4 pipes beer, 2 brls. with salt meat, 1 brl. with 22 doz. lbs. starch, 6 nets, 4 cheeses, £3; 5 yds. cloth w.g.
Conrat Bone, A, 5 weys cheese, £4

562. 25 Aug. In a wagon of William Nassh going to Bristol

Peter de Gassmore of Guipúzcoa, Sp, 3 bales with 32 cloths 8 yds. w.g.

563. 28 Aug. In the ship of Robert Monk [of London]
William Newton, D, 2 cloths 16 yds. w.g.
Nicholas Wyndebak, D, 1 fardel with 2½ cloths w.g.
John Mandefeld, D, 1 fardel with 7 cloths w.g.

564. 29 Aug. In the ship of Otys Code
Robert Godwyn, D, 1 bale with 11 cloths 8 yds. w.g.
William Isaac, D, 4 bales 1 fardel with 75 cloths w.g.
William Fox, D, 2 fardels with 15½ cloths w.g.
John Kyrkebye, D, 1 bale 2 fardels with 29½ cloths w.g.
Thomas Spens, D, 5 bales with 78½ cloths w.g.
John Fynkyll, D, 4 bales with 46 cloths w.g.

565. 3 Sept. In the ship of Thomas Joosson (Johnson *del.*) [of Bergen-op-Zoom]
James Bolle, A, 1 bale with 31 pcs. cotton russet, 1 hhd. with 30 doz. lbs. starch, 80 lbs. old pewter vessels, 1 chest with 24 [*S* 80] cheeses, £12 6s.8d.
John Hase, A, 31½ brls. with 36 weys rendered tallow, £24
Nicholas Andrew, A, 12 brls. with 24 [*S* 28] C. lbs. rendered tallow, £10
James Laurence, A, 6 brls. with salt meat, 3 brls. with 44 doz. lbs. starch, 2 brls. with 23 doz. lbs. candles, £6
[m.23d.]
John Powles [*S* Paulus], A, 1½ weys cheese, 20s.
John Gilys, [A,] 1 hhd. verjuice, 1 brl. with salt meat, 26s.8d.
John Claysson, A, 1 basket with M. seasoned and 2 M. summer rabbit-skins, £4
Matthew Lodowikson, A, 1 brl. with honey, 10 weys cheese, 1 brl. with 16 doz. lbs. starch, 1 kilderkin with white potters' earth, 1 brl. with 12 doz. [*S* lbs.] candles, £7

566. 3 Sept. In the ship of Hans Rutyng [of Danzig]
Lambert Rotard, H, 1 bale with 20 cloths w.g.; 20 goads cotton russet, 13s.4d.
Luke Wynke, H, 1 fardel with 6 cloths 7 yds. w.g.
George Mulver [*S* Mullier], H, 1 bale with 24 cloths w.g.
Herman Overcamp, H, 1 bale with 26 cloths w.g.; 60 goads cotton russet, 40s.
Said master, H, 2 bales with 41½ (11 yds. *del.*) cloths w.g.; 40 (39 *del.*) goads cotton russet, 1 coverlet, 30s.
Lambert Rotard, H, 1 vat with 15 yds. cloth w.g.; 2 C. lbs. pewter vessels, 53 pewter pots, £5
Roger van Feld, H, 1 bale with 25 cloths 4 yds. w.g.; 60 goads cotton russet, 40s.
Matthew Hynkylman, H, 1 bale with 20 cloths w.g.; 17 goads cotton russet, 11s.8d.
George Mulver, H, 1 bale with 25 cloths w.g.; 1 basket with 2 C. 16 lbs. pewter vessels, 56s.8d.

Hans Stut, H, 1 bale with 25 cloths w.g.; 20 goads Welsh straits [*S* cotton russet], 13s.4d.

James van Werd, H, 2 bales with 48 cloths w.g.; 167 [*S* 127] goads cotton russet, £5 13s.4d.

Herman Plough, H, 1 bale with 25 cloths w.g.; 25 goads cotton russet, 16s.8d.

Peter Eksted, H, 2 bales with 60 cloths 16 yds. w.g.; 123 goads cotton russet, £4 13s.4d. (16s.8d. *del.*)

Herman Overcamp, H, 2 bales with 46 cloths w.g., $\frac{1}{2}$ pc. double worsted; 42 goads cotton russet, 1 chest with 27 pewter pots [*S* 3 pottle-pots, 2 doz. quart pots], £3 (33s.4d. *del.*)

Gerard Lesbern, H, 1 bale with 15 cloths w.g.; 20 goads cotton russet, 13s.4d.

Hans Stut, H, 2 bales with 50 cloths w.g.; 40 goads cotton russet, 26s.8d.

Hillibrand van Vuno, H, 2 bales with 62 cloths 4 yds. w.g.; 83 goads cotton russet, 56s.8d.

Tylman Barkys, H, 1 bale with 21 cloths w.g.; 41 goads cotton russet, 26s.8d.

Matthew Hynkylman, H, 1 bale 1 brl. with 23 cloths 18 yds. w.g.; 29 goads cotton russet, 12 coverlets, 20s.

Peter Eksted, H, 1 bale with 24 cloths 7 yds. w.g., $10\frac{1}{2}$ yds. cloth in grain, 1 pc. double worsted; 20 goads Welsh straits, 13s.4d.

Hans Mulver, H, 1 bale with $23\frac{1}{2}$ cloths w.g.; 18 goads cotton russet, 13s.4d.

Hans Stut, H, 1 bale with 26 cloths w.g.; 16 goads cotton russet, 11s.8d.

Hans Mulver, H, 1 bale with 17 cloths 17 yds. w.g.; 13 goads cotton russet, 10s. (8s.4d. *del.*)

567. 3 Sept. In the ship of Clays Bartyles [of Danzig]

Said master, H, 1 bale 1 fardel with 20 cloths w.g.; 20 goads cotton russet, 13s.4d.

Clays Stene, H, 1 fardel with 9 cloths 4 yds. w.g.; 11 coverlets, 1 bench-cover, 4 brls. 2 bags with MD lbs. pewter vessels, 1 brl. 1 pipe (7 ropes *del.*) with 151 pewter pots, £15

Said master, H, 1 fardel with 4 cloths 18 yds. w.g., 6 yds. cloth in grain; 8 pcs. [*S* tapestry] coverlets, 8 yds. cotton russet, 20s.

Gerard Lesbern, H, 1 bale with 17 cloths w.g., 6 pcs. double worsted; 20 goads cotton russet, 13s.4d.

Herman Overcamp, H, 2 bales with 47 cloths w.g.; 70 goads cotton russet, 4 brls. with M lbs. pewter vessels, 2 doz. [*S* pewter] pottle-pots, 2 doz. quart pots, 2 doz. pint-pots, £18 13s.4d.

Hillibrand van Vuno, H, 1 bale with 27 cloths w.g.; 20 goads cotton russet, 13s.4d.

Matthew Hynkylman, H, 1 bale with 20 cloths w.g.; 20 goads cotton russet, 13s.4d.

Lambert Rotard, H, 1 bale with 15 cloths 10 yds. w.g., 9 yds. cloth in grain, $5\frac{1}{2}$ pcs. double worsted; 31 coverlets, 1 brl. with $5\frac{1}{2}$ C. lbs. pewter vessels, £18 (£12 13s.4d. *del.*)

145

Hans Stut, H, 1 bale with 35 cloths 16 yds. w.g.; 20 goads cotton russet, 13s.4d.

Herman Plough, H, 1 bale with 25½ cloths w.g.; 60 goads cotton russet, 40s.

Tylman Barkys, H, 1 bale with 26 cloths w.g.; 40 goads cotton russet, 26s.8d.

Hans Culle, H, 2 bales with 51 cloths w.g.; 21 goads cotton russet, 13s.4d.

Peter Eksted, H, 2 bales with 50 cloths w.g.; 147 goads cotton russet, £4 16s.8d.

Roger van Feld, H, 1 bale with 25 cloths 5 (3 *del.*) yds. w.g., 4 yds. cloth in grain; 80 goads cotton russet, 53s.4d.

Roger van Feld, H, 1 bale with 15 cloths 7 [yds.] w.g., 7 yds. cloth in grain

Matthew Hynkylman, H, 1 bale with 24½ cloths w.g.; 24 goads cotton russet, 16s.8d.

James van Werd, H, 1 bale with 24 cloths w.g.; 65 goads cotton russet, 46s.8d.

Said master, H, 1 bale with 14 cloths 18 yds. w.g.; 9 goads cotton russet, 6s.8d.

Hans Stut, H, 2 bales 1 chest with 52 cloths w.g., 7 yds. cloth in grain, 1 cloth 4 yds. of half grain; 40 goads cotton russet, 26s.8d.

Henry Lathuson, H, 3 brls. with 11½ [*S* 21] yds. [cloth] w.g.; 2½ C. lbs. pewter, 1 ell double worsted, 6 hats, 3 gallon pots, 3 doz. pottle-pots, 3 doz. quart pots, 3 doz. pewter pint-pots, £9

Hans Stut, H, 1 bale with 29 cloths w.g.; 56 goads cotton russet, 6 coverlets, 53s.4d.

Herman Plough, H, 1 bale with 16 cloths w.g.; 28 goads cotton russet, 20s.

Peter Eksted, H, 1 bale 1 chest with 26 cloths w.g.; 67 goads cotton russet, 43s.4d.

Hans Mulver, H, 1 bale with 27 cloths w.g.; 1 chest with 3 C. lbs. pewter vessels, 14 [*S* 4 pewter] pots, 15 goads cotton russet, £5 6s.8d.

568. 3 Sept. In the ship of John Yoman [of London]

James Bolle, A, 2 bales with 51 pcs. cotton russet, 3½ [*S* 2] rolls frieze, £19 6s.8d.

John Crace, D, 1 bale with 30 cloths w.g.

Robert Howgate, D, 1 fardel with 4 cloths 8 yds. w.g.

Thomas Lee, D, 1 bale with 23 cloths w.g.

Henry Wynger, D, 1 bale with 27 cloths w.g.

Robert Drayton, D, 1 bale with 16 cloths w.g.

John Kyrkbye, D, 1 bale with 13 cloths 18 yds. w.g.

Nicholas Bodyn, D, 1 bale with 13 cloths w.g.

John Nanchaton, D, 1 bale with 30 cloths w.g.

Roger Bonyfaunt, D, 1 bale with 19 cloths 8 yds. w.g.

Thomas Quadryng, D, 1 bale with 12 cloths w.g.

John Millet, D, 1 bale with 27 cloths w.g.

Robert Squyer, D, 1 bale with 27 cloths w.g.

Laurence Sqwarfeld, D, 1 bale with 31 cloths 16 yds. w.g.

William Dolfynby, D, 1 fardel with 3 cloths 16 yds. w.g.

[m.24]

Nicholas Morton, D, 1 bale with 30 cloths w.g.

Henry Frank, D, 1 bale with 13 cloths w.g.

John Chambre, D, 1 bale with 44 cloths w.g.

Peter de Castro of Guipúzcoa, Sp, 1 bale with 14 cloths 16 yds. w.g., 10 yds. cloth in grain

John Benet, D, 1 bale with 30 cloths w.g.

John Benyngton, D, 1 bale with 18 cloths w.g.

Roger Graunt, D, 1 bale with 18 cloths w.g.

John van Armysbery, H, 1 bale with 18 cloths w.g.; 50 goads cotton russet, 33s.4d.

John Russenthorp, H, 1 bale with 18 cloths w.g.; 67 goads cotton russet, 45s. 1 bale with 18 cloths w.g.; 80 goads cotton russet, 53s.4d. [*S* 147 goads cotton russet, £5]

Simon Harries, D, 1 bale 2 fardels with 31 cloths w.g.

Thomas Bancroft, D, 2 bales with 26 cloths 18 yds. w.g.

John Kyrkebye, D, 1 bale with 6½ cloths w.g.

William Burwell, D, 1 fardel with 6 cloths w.g.

Anthony Odyndale, H, 1 bale with 18 cloths w.g.; 20 goads cotton russet, 13s.4d.

William Scalder, D, 1 bale with 13 cloths 8 yds. w.g.

Robert Peche, D, 1 bale with 25 cloths 8 yds. w.g.

Robert Boys, D, 1 bale with 31 cloths w.g.

William Ryse, D, 1 bale with 16 cloths w.g.

Henry Halle, D, 1 bale with 21 cloths w.g.

John Pykton, D, 1 bale with 21 cloths w.g.

Thomas Lee, D, 1 fardel with 9 cloths w.g.

John Ebrall, D, 1 fardel with 7 cloths 16 yds. w.g.

Hans Culle, H, 1 bale with 18 cloths w.g.; 102 goads cotton russet, £3 6s.8d.

Stephen Branche, H, 1 bale with 12 cloths 3 yds. w.g.; 177 goads cotton russet, £6

Godard Slotkyn, H, 1 bale with 17 cloths 7 yds. w.g.; 5 rolls frieze, 368 goads cotton russet, £15; 3 yds. cloth of half grain

Robert Ryngbell, D, 1 bale with 14 cloths w.g.

John Ferr, D, 1 bale with 2 cloths w.g.

Peter Joye, D, 1 bale with 14 cloths w.g.

John Hosiar, D, 1 bale with 30 cloths w.g.

John Ebrall, D, 1 fardel with 16 pcs. double worsted

William Scapehuson, H, 2 bales with 43 cloths w.g.; 82 goads cotton russet, 53s.4d.

John Questynburgh, H, 1 bale with 18 cloths w.g.; 83 goads cotton russet, 56s.8d.

Tylman Barkys, H, 1 bale with 18 cloths w.g.; 41 goads cotton russet, 26s.8d.

Peter Syber, H, 1 bale with 10 cloths w.g.; 160 goads cotton russet, £5 6s.8d.

Roger van Feld, H, 1 bale with 23 cloths 16 yds. w.g., 1½ cloths in grain; 40 goads cotton russet, 26s.8d.

Richard Hartwell, D, 1 fardel with 6 cloths w.g.

Laurence Gylis, D, 1 cloth w.g.

Thomas Lok, D, 1 fardel with 6 cloths w.g.

Thomas Gerrard, D, 1 fardel with 20 cloths w.g.

Matthew Bliterswyke, H, 1 bale with 18 cloths w.g.; 100 goads cotton russet, £3 6s.8d.

John van Strawlyn,[1] H, 1 bale with 30 cloths w.g.; 40 goads cotton russet, 26s.8d.

John van Strawlyn,[1] H, 1 bale with 30 cloths w.g.; 40 goads cotton russet, 26s.8d.

Hans Stut, H, 1 bale with 26 cloths w.g.; 21 goads cotton russet, 13s.4d.

John Greverod, H, 1 bale with 20 cloths w.g.; 54 goads cotton russet, 36s.8d.

William Geffrey, D, 1 bale with 10 cloths w.g.

John Barker, D, 1 fardel with 3 cloths 18 yds. w.g.

[1] These two identical entries also occur in *S*.

569. 3 Sept. In the ship of John Wodelez [of London]

Cornelius Johnson, A, 1 bale with 34 pcs. cotton russet, £11 6s.8d.

Roger Hungate, D, 1 bale with 21 cloths w.g.

John Gose, D, 1 bale with 27 cloths w.g.

Thomas Lee, D, 1 bale with 20 cloths w.g.

Robert Drayton, D, 1 bale with 19 cloths 8 yds. w.g.

Henry Cantlow, D, 1 bale with 21 cloths w.g.

John Nanchaton, D, 1 bale with 20 cloths w.g.

Oliver Danyell, D, 1 bale with 25 cloths w.g.

Robert Southwod, D, 1 bale with 30 cloths w.g.

John Salmer, H, 1 bale with 23 cloths w.g.; 69 goads cotton russet, 46s.8d.

John Hosyer, D, 1 bale with 14 cloths w.g.

William Bryt, D, 1 bale with 19 cloths w.g.

Richard Twig, D, 1 bale with 17 cloths w.g.

Robert Boys, D, 1 bale with 30 cloths 18 yds. w.g.

John Rose, D, 2 bales with 50 cloths w.g.

Nicholas Morton, D, 1 bale with 32 cloths w.g.

William Heeryot, D, 1 bale with 14 cloths w.g.

John Chambre, D, 1 bale with 65 cloths w.g.

John Haynes, D, 1 bale with 20 cloths w.g.

William Jeffrey, D, 1 bale with 27 cloths w.g.

Edward Johnson, D, 1 bale with 16 cloths w.g.

Roger Arnold, D, 1 bale with 31 cloths 6 yds. w.g., 10 pcs. double worsted

William Shugburgh, D, 1 bale with 12 cloths 4 yds. w.g.

George Hawkyn, D, 1 bale with 18 cloths w.g.

John Benet, D, 1 bale with 23 cloths w.g.

William Jenk', D, 1 bale with 14 cloths w.g.

Thomas Lok, D, 1 bale with 18 cloths 7 yds. w.g., 14 pcs. double worsted

Roger Bonyfaunt, D, 1 bale with 16 cloths w.g.

Roger Graunt, D, 1 bale with 18 cloths w.g.

Peter Syber, H, 1 bale with 14 cloths w.g.; 5 rolls frieze, 45 goads cotton russet, £5

John Pikton, D, 1 bale with 30 cloths w.g.

Peter Joye, D, 1 bale with 20 cloths w.g.

William Whetewey, D, 1 bale with 26 cloths 16 yds. w.g.

Richard Wethir, D, 1 bale with 21 cloths w.g.

Richard Close, D, 1 bale with 27 cloths 16 yds. w.g.

Thomas Goldsmyth, D, 1 bale with 20 cloths w.g.

John Jakes, D, 1 bale with 16 cloths w.g.

John Dockyng, D, 1 bale with 15 cloths 8 yds. w.g.

John Benyngton, D, 1 fardel with 6 cloths 6 yds. w.g.

Robert Brykylsworth, D, 1 fardel with 6 cloths w.g.

Edward Johnson, D, 1 bale with 12 cloths w.g.

John Questynburgh, H, 1 bale with 18 cloths w.g.; 83 goads cotton russet, 56s.8d.

John Pellam, D, 1 bale with 28 cloths w.g.

Thomas Abraham, D, 1 bale with 12 cloths w.g.

Roger van Feld, H, 1 bale with 21½ cloths w.g., 1½ cloths in grain; 50 [*S* 56] goads cotton russet, 33s.4d.

John Russynthorp, H, 1 bale with 25 cloths w.g.; 80 goads cotton russet, 53s.4d.

570. 3 Sept. In the ship of John Roke [of London]

John Gose, D, 1 bale with 30 cloths w.g.

Richard Wethir, D, 1 bale with 28 cloths w.g.

John Salmer, H, 1 bale with 3 cloths 8 yds. w.g.; 720 goads cotton russet, £24

John Hosyer, D, 1 bale with 30 cloths w.g.

Robert Bangill, D, 1 bale with 21 cloths w.g.

William Bret, D, 1 bale with 15 cloths w.g., 10 pcs. double worsted

John Raynold, D, 1 bale with 31 cloths 8 yds. w.g.

John Fysshar, D, 1 bale with 14 cloths w.g.

John Pasmer, D, 1 bale with 20 cloths w.g.

Hillibrand van Vuno, H, 1 bale with 33½ cloths w.g.

Edward Redeknapp, D, 1 fardel with 7 cloths 16 yds. w.g.

John Broke, D, 1 bale with 24 cloths w.g.

Nicholas Taylour, D, 1 fardel with 6 cloths 16 yds. w.g.

[m.24d.]

John Cras [*S* Crace], D, 1 bale with 31 cloths 16 yds. w.g., 12 pcs. [*S* double] worsted

John Kyrkbye, D, 1 bale with 13½ cloths w.g.

Simon Smyth, D, 1 bale with 20 cloths w.g.

John Warner, D, 1 bale with 26 cloths w.g.

Thomas Kellet, D, 1 bale with 23 cloths w.g.

Matthew Hynkylman, H, 1 bale with 16 cloths w.g., 6 pcs. double worsted; 3 rolls frieze, 53s.4d.

John Russinthorp, H, 1 bale with 18 cloths w.g.; 93 goads cotton russet, £3 3s.4d.

Robert Southwode, D, 1 bale with 30 cloths w.g.

Thomas Hore, D, 1 bale with 31 cloths 8 yds. w.g.

Richard Eyryk, D, 1 fardel with 9 cloths w.g.

Thomas Bate, D, 1 bale with 20 cloths w.g.

John Pellam, D, 1 bale with 30 cloths w.g.

William Bentley, D, 1 fardel with 8 cloths w.g.

John Colyns, D, 1 bale with 25 cloths w.g., 2 pcs. double worsted

William Beyngton, D, 1 bale with 27 cloths w.g.

Thomas Pekenam, D, 1 bale with 24 cloths w.g.

Frank Savage, H, 1 bale with 10 cloths w.g.; 20 goads cotton russet, 13s.4d.

Robert Harben [*S* Hardbem], D, 1 bale with 22 cloths w.g.

Thomas Goldsmyth, D, 1 bale with 10 cloths w.g.

Edmund Talwyn, D, 1 bale with 10 cloths 16 yds. w.g.

William Colyns, D, 1 bale with 16 cloths w.g.

Robert Ryngbell, D, 1 bale with 10 cloths w.g.

William Ryng, D, 1 fardel with $2\frac{1}{2}$ cloths w.g.

Richard Feldyng, D, 1 fardel with 6 cloths w.g.

John Gybbes, D, 1 bale with $21\frac{1}{2}$ cloths w.g.

William Scapehuson, H, 1 bale with 42 cloths w.g.

John Fysshe, D, 1 bale with 13 cloths w.g.

Roger Grove, D, 1 bale with 16 cloths 6 yds. w.g., 16 pcs. double worsted

William Grenewolt, H, 1 bale with 15 cloths 6 yds. w.g., 4 pcs. double worsted; 20 goads cotton russet, 13s.4d.

Roger van Feld, H, 1 bale with $20\frac{1}{2}$ cloths w.g.; 50 goads cotton russet, 33s.4d.

John Brampton, D, 1 fardel with 3 cloths w.g.

John Pykton, D, 1 bale with 18 cloths w.g.

Henry Halle, D, 1 fardel with 6 cloths w.g.

Thomas Halis, D, 4 fardels with 8 cloths 8 yds. w.g.

Anthony Odindale, H, 1 bale with 18 cloths w.g.; 20 goads cotton russet, 13s.4d.

William Twigg', D, 1 bale with 26 cloths w.g.

571. 3 Sept. In the ship of John Bawdewyn [of Calais]

John Fysshare, D, 1 bale with $27\frac{1}{2}$ cloths w.g.

Thomas Lee, D, 1 bale with 20 cloths w.g.

Richard Wethir, D, 1 bale with 21 cloths w.g.

Thomas Burgoyn, D, 1 bale with 24 cloths w.g.

Robert Drayton, D, 1 bale with 18 cloths w.g.

Nicholas Alwyn, D, 1 bale with 27 cloths w.g.

John Nanchaton, D, 1 bale with 27 cloths w.g.

Richard Eyryk, D, 1 bale with 21 cloths w.g.

William Martyn, A, 12 pipes Toulouse woad, £24

Roger Bonyfaunt, D, 1 bale with 29 cloths w.g.

Oliver Danyell, D, 1 bale with 27 cloths w.g.

Thomas Somer, D, 1 bale with 18 cloths w.g.

William Bentley, D, 1 bale with 16 cloths w.g.

John Rose, D, 1 bale with 32 cloths w.g.

Roger Arnold, D, 1 bale with 29½ cloths w.g.

Richard Laken, D, 1 bale with 29 cloths w.g.

William Bryt, D, 1 bale with 20 cloths w.g.

John Bayly, D, 1 bale with 20 cloths 6 yds. w.g.

Nicholas Morton, D, 1 bale with 24 cloths w.g.

Ralph Vivoldus [*S* Wynoldis], D, 1 fardel with 3 cloths w.g.

Richard Mason, D, 1 bale with 18 cloths w.g.

Robert Bangyll, D, 1 bale with 21 cloths w.g.

Henry Bulstrode, D, 1 bale with 30 cloths w.g.

Hillibrand van Vuno, H, 1 bale with 20 cloths w.g.; 160 goads cotton russet, £5 6s.8d.

William Norton, D, 1 bale with 23 cloths w.g.

Richard Laken, D, 1 fardel with 4 cloths w.g., 1 pc. double worsted

Gerard Lesbern, H, 1 bale with 30 cloths w.g.; 80 goads cotton russet, 53s.4d.

John Mathew, D, 1 bale with 30 cloths 16 yds. w.g.

Thomas Borne, D, 1 bale with 17 cloths 16 yds. w.g.

William Alburgh [*S* Albrugh], D, 1 bale with 15 cloths w.g., 2 pcs. double worsted

Stephen Muschamp, D, 1 bale with 24 cloths w.g.

Henry Wynger, D, 1 bale with 10 cloths w.g.

William Purches, D, 1 bale with 36 cloths w.g.

William Heton, D, 1 bale with 20 cloths w.g.

John Benham, D, 1 bale with 30 cloths w.g.

John Warner, D, 1 bale with 30 cloths w.g.

John Russynthorp, H, 1 bale with 37 cloths w.g.; 162 [*S* 160] goads cotton russet, £5 6s.8d.

Peter Siber, H, 1 bale with 18 cloths w.g.; 124 goads cotton russet, £4 3s.4d.

Roger Graunt, D, 1 bale with 18 cloths w.g.

Thomas Fabyan, D, 1 bale with 32 cloths w.g.

Edward Johnson, D, 1 bale with 16 cloths w.g.

Robert Southwod, D, 1 bale with 20 cloths w.g., 5 pcs. double worsted

John Shelwyng, D, 1 bale with 16 cloths w.g.

John Pellam, D, 1 bale with 30 cloths w.g.

John Nanchaton, D, 1 fardel with 3 cloths w.g.

John Colyns, D, 1 bale with 22 cloths w.g.

John Chambre, D, 1 bale with 38 cloths w.g.

Roger Mandevile [*S* Mandfeld], D, 1 bale with 10 cloths 8 yds. w.g.

John Williams, A, 6 yds. cloth w.g.; 2 pcs. cotton russet, 5 flitches bacon, 4 weys rendered tallow, £4

John Broke, D, 1 bale with 20 cloths w.g.

John Trewynard, D, 1 bale with 13 cloths w.g.

Walter Povy, D, 1 bale with 34 cloths w.g.

William Banknot, D, 1 bale with 19 cloths w.g.

John Raynold, D, 1 bale with 14 cloths w.g.

Thomas Screven, D, 1 bale with 16 cloths 16 yds. w.g.

Robert Dod, D, 1 fardel with 3½ cloths w.g.

John Benet, D, 1 bale with 14 cloths w.g.

William Scapehuson, H, 2 bales with 48½ cloths w.g.; 543 goads Welsh straits [*S* cotton russet], £17 6s.8d.

Roger Grove, D, 1 bale with 22 cloths w.g.

Richard Odiham, D, 1 bale with 14 cloths w.g.

Robert Squyer, D, 1 bale with 12 cloths w.g.

Robert Squyer, D, 1 fardel with 8 cloths w.g.

Roger van Feld, H, 1 bale with 24 cloths w.g.; 50 goads Welsh straits [*S* cotton russet], 33s.4d.

Robert Billesdon, D, 1 bale with 24 cloths w.g.

Richard Wymond, D, 1 bale with 32 cloths w.g.

John van Armysbery, H, 1 bale with 15 cloths w.g.; 103 goads Welsh straits [*S* cotton russet], £3 10s. [*S* £3 6s.8d.]

John Questynburgh, H, 1 bale with 14 cloths 19 yds. w.g.; 292 goads Welsh straits [*S* cotton russet], £9 13s.4d.

John Prince, D, 1 bale with 10 cloths w.g.

John Pasmer, D, 1 bale with 30 cloths w.g.

572. 3 Sept. In the ship of Thomas Cokcok [*S* Cockot]
John de Mayn, D, 2 cloths w.g.

[m.25]
573. 3 Sept. In the ship of John Capp [of London]
John Crace, D, 1 bale with 30 cloths w.g.

Roger Hungate, D, 1 bale with 23 cloths 16 yds. w.g.

John Gose, D, 1 bale with 27 cloths w.g.

Thomas Lee, D, 1 bale with 27 cloths w.g.

Richard Wethir, D, 1 bale with 24 cloths w.g.

Henry Wynger, D, 1 bale with 27 cloths w.g.

John Mille, D, 1 fardel with 5 cloths w.g.

Robert Drayton, D, 1 bale with 18 cloths w.g.

John Kyrkebye, D, 1 bale with 13 cloths 18 yds. w.g.

Nicholas Bodyn, D, 1 bale with 18 cloths w.g.

William Redye, D, 1 bale with 21 cloths 6 yds. w.g.

William Martyn, A, 12 pipes Toulouse woad, £24

Roger Bonyfaunt, D, 1 bale with 33 [*S* 23] cloths w.g.

Richard Estgate, D, 1 bale with 14 cloths w.g., 27 pcs. double worsted

Thomas Somer, D, 1 bale with 18 cloths w.g.

William Bentley, D, 1 bale with 10 cloths w.g.

Robert Ryngbelle, D, 1 bale with 18 cloths w.g.

Robert Southwod, D, 1 bale with 33 cloths w.g.

John Rose, D, 1 bale with 32 cloths w.g.

Richard Lakyn, D, 1 bale with 29½ cloths w.g., 14 pcs. double worsted

Thomas Gerrard, D, 1 bale with 30 cloths w.g.

John Pykton, D, 1 bale with 30 cloths w.g.

John Baylye, D, 1 bale with 20 cloths 6 yds. w.g.

John Millet, D, 1 bale with 27 cloths w.g.

William Banknot, D, 1 bale with 23 cloths w.g.

Nicholas Morton, D, 1 bale with 27 cloths w.g.

John Rose, D, 1 bale with 62 pcs. double worsted, 4 pcs. single worsted [*S* stamin]

Peter Joye, D, 1 bale with 20 cloths w.g.

Thomas Bradburye, D, 1 fardel with 7 cloths w.g., 20 pcs. double worsted

William Jenk', D, 1 bale with 12 cloths w.g.

Ralph Bere, D, 1 bale with 27 cloths w.g.

John Fysshare, D, 1 bale with 38 cloths w.g., 13 pcs. double worsted

William Andrew, D, 1 fardel with 5 cloths w.g.

Gerard Lesbern, H, 1 bale with 38 cloths w.g.; 60 goads cotton russet, 40s.

John Pasmer, D, 1 bale with 20 cloths w.g.

George Hawkyn, D, 1 bale with 27 cloths w.g.

Laurence Swarfeld, D, 1 bale with 30 cloths w.g.

Andrew Rogger, D, 1 bale with 12 cloths w.g.

Alexander Portynale [*S* Portinarius], A, 1 bale 1 fardel with 26 cloths w.g., 2 pcs. double worsted; [*S* for the aforesaid] 2 pcs. double worsted, 2 pcs. cotton russet [*S* Welsh straits, 1 mantle], 53s.4d.

John Mathew, D, 1 bale with 25 cloths 8 yds. w.g.

Edward Johnson, D, 1 bale with 16 cloths w.g.

John Thomas, D, 1 bale with 28 cloths w.g.

Henry Cantlow, D, 1 bale with 21 cloths w.g.

Edward Redknapp, D, 1 fardel with 6 cloths 10 yds. w.g., $27\frac{1}{2}$ pcs. (3 ells *del.*) double worsted

John Benet, D, 1 bale with 24 cloths w.g.

Thomas Lok, D, 1 bale with 21 cloths w.g., 16 pcs. double worsted

Roger Graunt, D, 1 bale with 18 cloths w.g.

Robert Flecer [*S* Flecher], D, 1 bale with 20 cloths w.g.

John van Armysbery, D [*sic* for H], 1 bale with 18 cloths w.g.; 60 goads cotton russet, 40s.

Godard Slotkyn, H, 1 bale with 17 cloths w.g.; 100 goads cotton russet, £3 6s.8d.

John Russenthorp, H, 1 bale with $37\frac{1}{2}$ cloths w.g.; 162 [*S* 180] goads Welsh straits, £6 (6s.8d. *del.*)

Peter Syber, H, 1 bale with 18 cloths w.g.; 100 goads cotton russet, £3 6s.8d.

William Bret, D, 1 bale with 14 cloths w.g.

Ingilbright Sevenek, H, 1 bale with 24 cloths w.g., 4 yds. cloth of half grain; 105 goads Welsh straits [*S* 108 goads cotton russet], £3 10s.

Richard Mason, D, 11 cloths 8 yds. w.g.

William Norton, D, 1 fardel with 6 cloths w.g.

John Chambre, D, 1 bale with 40 cloths w.g.

Thomas Berewyk, D, 1 bale with 12 cloths w.g.

Robert Bangill, D, 1 bale with 21 cloths w.g.

John Pellam, D, 1 bale with 30 cloths w.g.

John Pykeryng, D, 1 bale with $18\frac{1}{2}$ cloths w.g.

John Colyns, D, 1 bale with 23 cloths w.g., 3 pcs. double worsted
William Beyngton, D, 1 bale with 33 cloths 8 yds. w.g.
William Lamberd, D, 1 fardel with 1 cloth w.g.
Gilbert Kays, D, 1 fardel with 3½ cloths w.g.
William Purches, D, 1 bale with 31 cloths 18 yds. w.g.
Henry Halle, D, 1 bale with 30 cloths w.g.
John Broke, D, 1 bale with 21 cloths w.g.
John Haynes, D, 1 bale with 24 cloths 8 yds. w.g.
John Fyssh, D, 1 bale with 21 cloths w.g.
Edmund Talwyn, D, 1 bale with 20½ cloths w.g.
John Colet, D, 1 bale with 19 cloths w.g., 34 pcs. double worsted
John Hosyer, D, 1 bale with 32 cloths w.g.
William Scapehuson, H, 1 bale with 18 cloths w.g.; 72 goads cotton
  russet, 46s.8d. (13s.4d. *del.*)
William Scapehuson, H, 1 bale with 25 cloths w.g.; 20 goads Welsh
  straits [*S* cotton russet], 13s.4d.
Arnold van Stalle, H, 1 bale with 15 cloths w.g.; 13 goads cotton russet,
  10s.
John Salmer, H, 1 brl. with 7 C. lbs. pewter vessels, £9 6s.8d.
John Questynburgh, H, 1 bale with 10 cloths w.g.; 60 goads cotton
  russet, 40s.
Roger van Feld, H, 1 bale with 23 cloths 16 yds. w.g., 1½ cloths of half
  grain (in grain *del.*); 50 goads Welsh straits [*S* cotton russet], 33s.4d.
John Warner, D, 1 bale with 10 cloths w.g.
Thomas Stoge, D, 1 bale with 1 cloth 20 yds. w.g.
William Grenewolt, H, 1 bale with 17 cloths w.g.; 20 goads cotton
  russet, 13s.4d.
Simon Bartot, D, 1 bale with 30 cloths 16 yds. w.g.
Peter Joye, D, 1 fardel with 8 cloths w.g.

574. 3 Sept. In the ship of Hans Haugyn [*S* Hawgen] [of Hamburg]
Hans Swalyngburgh, H, 1 bale with 11 cloths w.g.; 48 goads cotton
  russet, 33s.4d.
Matthew Hynkylman, H, 1 fardel with 5 cloths 16 yds. w.g.; 216 goads
  cotton russet, £7 3s.4d.
Hans Stut, H, 1 bale with 16 cloths 18 yds. w.g.; 2 coverlets, 20 goads
  cotton russet, 20s.
Gerard Lesbern, H, 1 bale with 25 cloths w.g.; 170 goads cotton russet,
  £5 13s.4d.
Hillibrand van Vuno, H, 1 bale with 27 cloths w.g.; 20 goads cotton
  russet, 13s.4d.
Lambert Rotard, H, 1 bale with 31 cloths 3 yds. w.g.
Henry Lathuson, H, 2 bales with 46 cloths w.g.; 202 [*S* 206] goads cotton
  russet, £7
Herman Plough, H, 1 bale with 25 cloths 4 yds. w.g.; 28 goads cotton
  russet, 20s.
Henry Lathuson, H, 2 bales with 34½ cloths w.g., 9 yds. cloth in grain, ½
  cloth of half grain; 348 goads cotton russet, 5 rolls frieze, £15
Peter Eksted, H, 2 bales with 50 cloths w.g.; 126 goads cotton russet, £4

6s.8d. [*S* £4]

Hans Hosterberch, H, 1 bale with 18 cloths 20 yds. w.g.

William Scapehuson, H, 1 bale with 38 cloths w.g., 2 pcs. double worsted

Henry Lathuson, H, 3 bales with 68 cloths 18 yds. w.g.; 360 goads cotton russet, 6 rolls frieze, 13 cheeses, £16

Hans Stut, H, 2 bales with 55 cloths w.g.; 40 goads cotton russet, 26s.8d.

Henry Lathuson, H, 1 bale with 11 cloths w.g.; 80 tawed lambskins, 53s.4d.

[m.25d.]

575. 3 Sept. In the ship of Robert Foster [of London]

Henry Wynger, D, 1 bale with 10 cloths w.g.

Robert Eyrik, D, 1 fardel with 6 cloths w.g.

John Bughall, D, 1 fardel with 3 cloths 8 yds. w.g.

Henry Cantlowe, D, 1 bale with 18 cloths w.g.

William Gunny [*S* Gunnyth], D, 1 fardel with 5 cloths w.g.

William Redy, D, 1 chest with 3 cloths 8 yds. w.g., 26 pcs. double worsted

Edward Johnson, A, 1 fardel with 26 rolls frieze, 16 rolls cotton russet, £22 13s.4d.

William Brit, D, 1 bale with 16 cloths 8 yds. w.g.

John Gose, D, 1 bale with 9 cloths w.g.

Nicholas Morton, D, 1 bale with 10 cloths w.g.

John Gylis, A, 1 fardel with 18 yds. cloth w.g.; 9 pcs. cotton russet, 1 chest with 1½ weys cheese, 26 lbs. pewter vessels, 1 flitch bacon, £4 6s.8d.

Thomas Petite, D, 1 bale with 21 cloths 16 yds. w.g.

Walter Povy, D, 1 bale with 18 cloths w.g.

John Durham, D, 1 bale with 13 cloths w.g.

John Rose, D, 1 fardel with 2 cloths w.g.

William Bentley, D, 1 fardel with 6 cloths 8 yds. w.g.

John Benet, D, 1 fardel with 6 cloths 18 yds. w.g.

Frank Justynyan, A, 1 bale with 20 pcs. cloth with broad selvages cont. 10 cloths w.g.

Lewis Gremold', A, 1 fardel 1 roll with 2 cloths 18 yds. w.g., 7 yds. cloth of half grain

John Hosyar, D, 1 fardel with 7 cloths w.g.

John Durham, D, 1 fardel with 3 cloths 16 yds. w.g.

John Chambire, D, 1 fardel with 6 cloths w.g.

John Hosyer, D, 1 bale with 27 cloths w.g.

576. 3 Sept. In the ship of James Spisholt [of Danzig]

Paul Kortume, H, 1 fardel with 1 cloth (22½ yds. *del.*) w.g.; 2 goads cotton russet, 60 lbs. pewter, 7 pottle-pots, 12 quart pots, 6 pint-pots, 33s.4d.

Roger van Feld, H, 1 bale with 25 cloths w.g.; 20 goads cotton russet, 13s.4d.

Peter Eksted, H, 2 bales with 50 cloths w.g.; 123 goads cotton russet, £4

3s.4d.

Herman Overcamp, H, 1 bale with 26 cloths w.g.; 60 goads cotton russet, 40s.

Gerard Lesbern, H, 1 fardel with 5 cloths w.g.; 5 goads cotton russet, 3s.4d.

Said master, H, 1 cloth 5 yds. w.g.; 12 coverlets, 36 lbs. pewter vessels, 53s.4d.

Roger van Feld, H, 1 bale with 16 cloths w.g., 4 yds. in grain, 1 pc. double worsted; 20 goads cotton russet, 13s.4d.

Herman Plough, H, 1 bale with 24 cloths 3 yds. w.g.; 28 goads cotton russet, 20s.

Hans Stut, H, 3 bales with 77 cloths w.g., 3½ yds. cloth in grain; 57 goads cotton russet, 40s.

Hillibrond van Vuno, H, 1 bale with 25 cloths w.g.; 20 goads cotton russet, 13s.4d.

577. 3 Sept. In the ship of Simon Pecheford

Matthew Hynkylman, H, 1 bale with 19 cloths w.g.; 28 goads cotton russet, 20s. [*S* 40s.]

Stephen Branche, H, 1 bale with 8 cloths w.g.; 213 goads cotton russet, £7 3s.4d.

Christian Paynter, D, 2 bales with 31 cloths w.g.

Robert Dode, D, 1 fardel with 5 cloths w.g.

William Scapehuson, H, 1 bale with 40 cloths w.g.

Tylman van Howell, H, 1 bale with 25 cloths w.g.

Hillibrand van Vuno, H, 1 bale with 16 cloths w.g.; 163 goads cotton russet, £5 5s. [*S* £5 10s.]

Arnold van Stalle, H, 1 bale with 14 cloths w.g.; 20 goads cotton russet, 13s.4d.

John van Armysbery, H, 1 bale with 12 cloths w.g.; 490 goads cotton russet, £16 6s.8d.

John Hawes, A, 10 pcs. double worsted; for the aforesaid pcs. of double worsted and 4 brls. with salt meat, £11 6s.8d.

Hans Culle, H, 1 bale with 19 cloths w.g.; 100 goads cotton russet, £3 6s.8d.

Thomas Raven [*S* Rawyn], D, 1 bale with 15 cloths w.g.

William Grenewolt, H, 1 bale with 17½ cloths w.g.; 21 goads cotton russet, 13s.4d.

Thomas Abraham, D, 1 fardel with 20 pcs. double worsted

John Russenthorp, H, 1 bale with 14 cloths w.g.; 150 goads cotton russet, £5

Frank Savage, H, 1 brl. with 6 C. lbs. pewter vessels, £8

Roger van Feld, H, 1 bale with 24 cloths w.g.; 60 goads cotton russet, 40s.

Christian Paynter, D, 1 fardel with 5 cloths w.g.

Hans Stut, H, 1 bale with 26 cloths w.g.; 26 goads cotton russet, 16s.8d.

Marcello Maurys, A, 2½ weys cheese, 26s.8d.

Robert Billesdon, D, 2 bales with 39 cloths w.g.

William Peryn, D, 1 fardel with 7 cloths w.g.

John Salvo, D,[1] 1 bale with 20 pcs. cloth with broad selvages cont. 10 cloths w.g.

Peter Syber, H, 1 fardel with 6 cloths w.g.; 140 goads cotton russet, £4 13s.4d.

John Salmer, H, 1 bale with 13 cloths 8 yds. w.g.; 17 goads cotton russet, 11s.8d.

Laurence Swarfeld, D, 1 bale with 17 cloths w.g.

William Bentley, D, 1 fardel with 5½ cloths w.g.

Gerard van Grove, H, 1 bale with 18 cloths w.g.; 20 goads cotton russet, 13s.4d.

Thomas Rawyn, D, 1 fardel with 4 cloths 2 yds. w.g.

Godard van Boston, H, 1 bale with 18 cloths w.g.; 20 goads cotton russet, 13s.4d.

John van Armysbery, H, 1 bale with 15 cloths w.g.; 140 goads cotton russet, £4 13s.4d.

John Collard, D, 1 fardel with 8 cloths w.g.

William Twigg, D, 1 bale with 32 cloths w.g.

Lambert Rotard, H, 1 bale with 9 cloths w.g., 3 pcs. double worsted; 200 goads cotton russet, £6 13s.4d.

[1] John de Salvo, born in Genoa, previously described as an alien (see above, **465, 498**) was granted letters of denization on 22 June 1481 (*C.P.R. 1476–85*, 282).

578. 10 Sept. In the ship of Anthony Brabander [of Middelburg]

Gerard Lesbern, H, 1 bale with 18 [*S* 28] cloths w.g.; 20 goads cotton russet, 13s.4d.

Tylman van Howell, H, 1 bale with 35 cloths w.g.

Hillibrand van Vuno, H, 1 bale with 17 cloths w.g.; 106 goads cotton russet, £3 13s.4d.

William Scapehuson, H, 1 fardel with 5 cloths 15 yds. w.g.; 606 [*S* 128] goads cotton russet, £20 6s.8d.

Arnold van Stalle, H, 1 bale with 14 cloths w.g.; 16 goads cotton russet, 10s.

John van Creke, A, 30 cheeses, 20s.

John Willyams, A, 2 pipes beer, 13s.4d.

Matthew Bliterswyke, H, 1 bale with 10 cloths w.g.; 100 goads cotton russet, £3 6s.8d.

Hans Stut, H, 1 bale with 27 cloths w.g.; 20 goads cotton russet, 13s.4d.

Said master, A, 4 pipes 1 hhd. beer, 30s.

William Scapehuson, H, 1 chest with 19½ yds. [*S* cloth] w.g.; 35 lbs. pewter vessels, 13s.4d.

Lambert Rotard, H, 1 bale with 16 cloths w.g.; 140 goads cotton russet, 90 tawed lambskins, £5

Peter Eksted, H, 1 bale with 25 cloths w.g.; 48 goads cotton russet, 33s.4d.

John van Strawlyn, H, 1 bale with 31 cloths w.g., 1½ cloths in grain; 130 goads cotton russet, £4 6s.8d.

Courte Bone, A, 3 brls. with salt meat, 15s.

Tylman Barkys, H, 1 bale with 24 cloths 3 yds. w.g.; 63 goads cotton russet, 43s.4d.

Godard van Beston, H, 1 bale with 19 cloths w.g.; 20 goads cotton russet, 13s.4d.

579. 10 Sept. In a cart of John Bisshop going to Bristol
Michael Sepriell', A, 3 bales 1 fardel with 45 cloths w.g., 2 cloths 8 yds. in grain

[m.26]
580. 10 Sept. In a cart of Thomas Willas
John Stephenis, A, 2 bales with 32 cloths 9 yds. w.g., 2½ (8 yds. *del.*) cloths in grain

581. 10 Sept. In the ship of John Stephenis [of Oporto]
Said master, A, 9 baskets with 2 M. D. lbs. pewter, 91 pcs. lead weight 5 M. [S and 50] lbs., 51 pcs. copper weight 2 M. lbs., 12 brls. pitch, £90
Thomas Hay, D, 2 fardels with 16 cloths w.g.
Edward Brampton, D, 1 bale 1 fardel with 25 cloths 18 yds. w.g.
Peter Gunsavo [S Gumsalvo], A, 6 yds. w.g.
Thomas Pope, D, 1 bale with 13½ cloths w.g.

582. 10 Sept. In the ship of Peter Everyday [of Middelburg]
Ingylbright Hugson, A, 24 pipes beer, 1 brl. with salt meat, £8 6s.8d.
Peter Ewyn, A, 4 pipes beer, 26s.8d.

583. 10 Sept. In the ship of Thomas Andrew [of London]
William Fyncham, D, 1 fardel with 8 cloths w.g.
James Vergeant, D, 1 bale with 10 cloths w.g.
William Horton, D, 3 bales with 42 cloths w.g.
Ralph Astry, D, 1 bale 1 fardel with 16½ cloths w.g., 6 yds. cloth in grain
Nicholas Mattok, D, 1 bale with 10 cloths w.g., 1 cloth 21 yds of half grain, 1 bale with 11½ cloths w.g.
Robert Leycroft, D, 1 fardel with 9 cloths w.g.
William Fyncham, D, 1 fardel with 9 cloths w.g.
Thomas Bower, D, 1 fardel with 7 cloths w.g.
John Stokar, D, 2 bales with 18 cloths w.g.

584. 10 Sept. In the ship of Robert Bown
Michael Malbrayn, A, 82 cheeses cont. 7 weys, £4 6s.8d.
Robert Brown, D, 1 fardel with 2 cloths w.g.
William Colyns, D, 1 cloth 6 yds. w.g.

585. 10 Sept. In the ship of Richard Grene
William Remyngton, D, 1 fardel with 1 cloth 8 yds. w.g.
Thomas Bower, D, 1 fardel with 6 cloths w.g.
Richard Philpot, D, 1 bale with 14 cloths w.g.
William Remyngton, D, 1 cloth w.g.

James Fromlod, D, 1 fardel with 9 cloths 8 yds. w.g.

586. 10 Sept. In the ship of Clays Henrikson [of Middelburg]
John Ewingar, A, 13 pipes beer, £4 6s.8d.

587. 15 [*S* 13] Sept. In the ship of William Smyth
Robert Godwyn, D, 1 bale 1 fardel with 18 cloths w.g.
Richard Odyham, D, 1 cloth of half grain
John Kyrkeby, D, 1 fardel with 7 cloths 14 yds. w.g.
Peter de Vynaw, D, 1 fardel with 9 cloths w.g.
John Marchall, D, 1 fardel with 9 cloths w.g.
Anthony Bawdet, D, 36 doz. blowing horns, £3 13s.4d.

588. 18 Sept. In the galley of Bernard Bondymere [of Venice]
William Herryot, D, 2 fardels with 18 cloths w.g.
Allowiso George, A, 3 bales with 75 pcs. cotton russet, 3 bales with 200 doz. tanned calfskins, C. 40 lbs. pewter vessels, £60 6s.8d.
Francis Pascalego, A, 2 bales with 100 doz. tanned calfskins, £16 13s.4d.
Francis de Meso, A, 2 bales with 49 cloths 4 yds. w.g.; 40 pcs. cotton russet, 123 doz. tanned calfskins, £34 3s.4d.
Sancta Maria Pero, A, 1 bale with 19 cloths 8 yds. w.g.
Nicholas Dydo, A, 3 bales with 179 doz. tanned calfskins, £29 16s.8d.
Nicholas Caruso, A, 3 cloths 8 yds. w.g.; 2 pcs. cotton russet [*S* Welsh straits], 13s.4d.
Ralph Caruso, A, 1 cloth 8 yds. w.g.
John de Squetery, A, 16 yds. cloth w.g.; 2 pcs. cotton russet, 4 doz. tanned calfskins, 26s.8d.
Maryn de Sent George, A, 9½ cloths w.g.
Pero [*S* Petro] de Bodna, A, 8 cloths 6 yds. w.g.; 1 pc. cotton russet, 6s.8d.
John de Monte Beango [*S* Beanco], 7 cloths 20 yds. w.g.
George de Catero, A, 9 cloths w.g.; 8 pcs. cotton russet, 53s.4d.
George de Sancta Maria, A, 12½ cloths w.g.
Luke Camsa, A, 35 cloths w.g.; 8 pcs. cotton russet, 48 doz. tanned calfskins, £10 13s.4d.
John Camsa, A, 8 cloths 22 yds. w.g.; 8 pcs. cotton russet, 53s.4d.
Lazaro de Zeta, A, 3 cloths w.g.
Stephen Caruso, A, 4 cloths 16 yds. w.g.; 5 pcs. cotton russet 33s.4d.
Nicholas Summa, A, 2 cloths w.g.; 5 rolls frieze, 211 doz. tanned calfskins, £38 10s.
Nicholas Daldamo, A, ½ cloth w.g.; 2 pcs. cotton russet, 20 lbs. pewter vessels, 20s.
Michael [*S* Nicholas] de Sancta Maria, A, 10 cloths 20 yds. w.g.; C. lbs. pewter vessels, 26s.8d.
Domyngo de Bodna, A, ½ cloth w.g.
Nicholas de Catero, A, 8 yds. cloth w.g.; 5 pcs. cotton russet, 1 roll frieze, 22 doz. tanned calfskins, £6
Beasio de Sent John, A, 8 yds. cloth w.g.; 1 pc. cotton russet, 6s.8d.

Andrew de Squetery, A, 16 yds. cloth w.g.; 10 lbs. pewter vessels, 3s.4d.

Nicholas de Squterye, A, 7 cloths 16 yds. w.g.; 4 pcs. cotton russet, 24 doz. tanned calfskins, 14 lbs. pewter vessels, £5 10s.

George de Lago, A, 8 cloths 4 yds. w.g.; 4 pcs. cotton russet, 1 qr. pewter vessels, 33s.4d.

Nicholas Sozina, A, 3 cloths 10 yds. w.g.

Dimitrio de Sent George, A, 20 cloths 16 yds. w.g.; 1 pc. cotton russet, 6s.8d.

Novello Dantyvore, A, 6½ cloths w.g.; 7 pcs. cotton russet, 28 [*S* 38] doz. tanned calfskins, £7

Novello de Sancta Maria, A, 8 cloths 16 yds. w.g.; 1 pc. cotton russet, 6s.8d.

John de Camsa, A, 24 cloths w.g.; 2 pcs. cotton russet, 10 doz. tanned calfskins, 46s.8d.

John Dantyvore, A, 4½ cloths w.g.; 3 pcs. cotton russet, 20s.

Pero de Sancto Leo, A, 3 cloths 16 yds. w.g.; 10 doz. tanned calfskins, 33s.4d.

Pero de Squetery, A, 8 yds. cloth w.g.; 1 pc. cotton russet, 6s.8d. [*S* 2 pcs. 13s.4d.]

Michael Dantyvore, A, 2 cloths 16 yds. w.g.

Allesio de Bedia, A, 7½ cloths w.g.

George de Squtery, A, 6 yds. cloth w.g.

George de Sancta Maria, A, 2 cloths 15 yds. w.g.

Allewiso de Cattero, A, 1½ cloths w.g.

Luke de Squetery, A, 1 cloth w.g.

John de Ludryn', A, 16 yds. cloth w.g.

Paul de Lago, A, 5 cloths w.g.

Ralph de Monte Pesulo, A, 2 cloths 18 yds. w.g.; 2 pcs. cotton russet, 13s.4d.

Beasio de Dulsenio, A, 1 cloth w.g.

Nadallo Sozina, A, 2 cloths w.g.

Nicholas Angelo, A, 5 cloths w.g.; 14 pcs. cotton russet, 70 lbs. pewter vessels, £5 6s.8d.

Allowiso George, A, 12 pcs. cotton russet, C. 10 [*S* 140] lbs. pewter vessels, 3 bales with 200 doz. tanned calfskins, £39

Novello de Lago, A, 4 cloths 8 yds. w.g.; 1 pc. cotton russet, 10 lbs. pewter vessels, 10s.

George[1] de Squetery, A, 3 yds. cloth w.g.; 12 lbs. pewter vessels, 9 doz. tanned calfskins, 33s.4d.

[m.26d.]

Pero Pastrovico, A, 4 cloths 20 yds. w.g.; 1 pc. cotton russet, 6s.8d.

Ralph de Sent George, A, 2 cloths 16 yds. w.g.; 1 pc. cotton russet, 6s.8d.

Beasio de Lago, A, 2 cloths 23 yds. w.g.

Pero Buldon, A, 15 cloths 16 yds. w.g.; 1 pc. cotton russet, 6s.8d.

Ralph de Sent Nicholo, A, 2 cloths w.g.; 16 pcs. cotton russet, £5 6s.8d.

Nicholas Sent George, A, 17 cloths 18 yds. w.g.; 8 pcs. cotton russet, 20 lbs. pewter vessels, 50 doz. tanned calfskins, £8 6s.8d.

Stephen Catero, A, 3 fardels with 6 cloths w.g.

Pero [*S* Petro] de Sent Michaell', A, 15 cloths 8 yds. w.g.; 18 pcs. cotton russet, £6

Pero [*S* Petro] de Sancta Maria, A, 8 cloths w.g.; 4 doz. tanned calfskins, 13s.4d.

Francis Navo, A, 1 cloth w.g.; 24 pcs. cotton russet, £8

Nicholas Mazerachio, A, 15 cloths w.g.; 4 pcs. cotton russet, 26s.8d.

George de Sent George, A, 6½ cloths w.g.

Stephen de Lago, A, 20 cloths w.g.; 11 pcs. cotton russet, £3 13s.4d.

Allegreto de Catero, A, 4 cloths 16 yds. w.g.

Dayemo Caliger, A, 7 doz. tanned calfskins, 23s.4d.

Nicholas Sozina, A, 8 cloths w.g.; 1 pc. cotton russet, 6s.8d.

George de Sancta Maria, A, 19 cloths 18 yds. w.g.; 10 pcs. cotton russet, £3 6s.8d.

Ralph Compayn', A, 16 yds. cloth w.g.   .

Nicholas Dantyvore, A, 1 cloth 20 yds. w.g.

Manonia de Candia, A, 16 yds. cloth w.g.

George Carpenter, A, 8 doz. Welsh cloths, £5 6s.8d.

Ralph de Castello Novo, A, 2 cloths 20 yds. w.g.; C. 50 lbs. pewter vessels, 40s.

Damyan Pastrovico, A, 2 cloths 6 yds. w.g.

Thomas Canever, A, 1 cloth w.g.

'Comito'[2] of the galley, A, 10 cloths w.g.

Angelo de Nicholo, A, 46 cloths w.g.; 3 fothers 3 [*S* 1] qrs. lead, 109 doz. tanned calfskins, £33 3s.4d.

Stephen Kateryn, A, 1 cloth w.g.; 20 pcs. cotton russet, 88 doz. tanned calfskins, £20 13s.4d.

Lewis Conteryn', A, 16 blocks tin, £40

Jeronimo Barrel', A, 2 C. 3 qrs. pewter vessels, £3 13s.4d.

George de Sancta Maria, A, 42 doz. tanned calfskins, £7

Damyan de Catero, A, 7 cloths 21 yds. w.g.; 2 pcs. cotton russet, 13s.4d.

Nicholas Daspolet, A, 8 yds. cloth w.g.

Damyan de Sancta Maria, A, 13 cloths w.g.

Nicholas de George, A, 1 cloth w.g.; 9 doz. bellows, 1 pipe with 400 [*S* 440] wooden dishes, 26s.8d.

Nicholas Sozina, A, 16 yds. cloth w.g.; 1 [*S* 3] doz. tanned calfskins, 3s.4d.

Nicholas de Sent Georgo, A, 2 cloths 16 yds. w.g.; 2 pcs. cotton russet, 13s.4d.

Luke Nigro, A, 3 cloths w.g.

Peter Pilote of Guipúzcoa, Sp, 3 cloths w.g.

Anthony Remore, A, 1 brl. with 172 lbs. pewter vessels, 1 small sack with 100 tawed lambskins, £3

Bernard Bondymer, A, 16 cloths w.g.; 4 small brls. 1 runlet with 6 C. lbs. pewter vessels, 114 doz. tanned calfskins, 63 pcs. cotton russet, £48

Stephen Fesaunt, A, 1 bale with 83 [*S* 80] pcs. cotton russet, £28

Luke de Catero and Ralph de Sent George, As, 12 cloths 3 yds. w.g.

Ralph de Sent George, A, 9 yds. cloth w.g.; 27 pcs. cotton russet, 28 doz. tanned calfskins, C. lbs. pewter vessels, £15
Luke de Catero, A, 4 cloths 20 yds. w.g.; 40 lbs. pewter vessels, 10s.

[1] 'A' in margin.
[2] The mate, see above, **156**.

589. 18 Sept. In the ship of Robert Laverok [of Fowey]
Thomas Terre, D, 1 bale with 20 cloths w.g.
Thomas Watt', D, 2 bales with 42 cloths w.g.
John Trewinard, D, 1 bale with 12 cloths 10 yds. w.g.
John Banestir, D, 1 bale with 13 cloths 6 yds. w.g.
Thomas Skelton, D, 1 bale with 14 cloths w.g.
John Fysshe, D, 1 bale with 12 cloths w.g.
Richard Langton, D, 1 bale with 16 cloths w.g.

590. 18 Sept. In the ship of Thomas Jorde
Thomas Watt', D, 2 bales with 38 cloths w.g.
John Gybbis, D, 2 bales with 29 cloths 16 yds. w.g.
John Gybbis, D, 1 fardel with 2 cloths 16 yds. w.g.
James Fromlod, D, 1 bale with 13 cloths 16 yds. w.g., 3 cloths in grain
John Bekeryng', D, 1 fardel with 2 cloths 16 yds. w.g.
John Banester, D, 1 bale with 16 cloths 16 yds. w.g.
Robert Godwyn, D, 1 bale with 19 cloths 4 yds. w.g.
Richard Chapell, D, 2 bales with 29 cloths w.g.
Richard Langton, D, 1 bale with 14 cloths w.g.
Richard Langton, D, 1 bale with 16 cloths w.g.
John Gibbes, D, 1 bale with 15½ cloths w.g.
John Fysshe, D, 1 bale with 21 cloths w.g.
Nicholas Mattok, D, 1 bale with 11½ cloths w.g., 2 cloths of half grain
Richard Clynche, D, 1 fardel with 5 cloths w.g.

591. 18 Sept. In the ship of Thomas Payn [of London]
Robert Leycroft, D, 1 fardel with 9 cloths w.g.
John Gibbes, D, 1 bale with 12 cloths 16 yds. w.g.
James Fromlod, D, 1 bale with 13 cloths 16 yds. w.g., 1½ cloths in grain
William Wynk, D, 1 fardel with 6 cloths w.g.
Thomas Lowed, D, 1 fardel with 7 cloths 8 yds. w.g.
Thomas Watt', D, 2 bales with 36 cloths w.g.
John Trewinard, A, 1 bale with 11 cloths 16 yds. w.g.
John Bekeryng', D, 1 fardel with 2 cloths 16 yds. w.g.
John Banester, D, 2 bales with 27 cloths 8 yds. w.g.
Robert Goodwyn, D, 1 bale with 20 cloths w.g.
Edward Wode, D, 1 fardel with 3 cloths w.g.
Richard Chapell, D, 2 bales with 33 cloths w.g.
John Fysshe, D, 1 bale with 12 cloths w.g.
William Fyncham, D, 1 fardel with 9 cloths w.g.
Richard Langton, D, 2 bales with 28 cloths w.g.
Thomas Skelton, D, 1 bale with 14 cloths w.g.
Robert Tate, D, 1 bale with 13 cloths w.g.

Richard Chapell, D, 1 bale with 13 cloths w.g.
Richard Clynche, D, 1 fardel with 6 cloths w.g.
Thomas Gerrard, D, 1 bale 1 fardel with 22 cloths w.g.
John Alstone, D, 2 bales with 20 cloths w.g.
Thomas Bukyngham, D, 1 fardel with 7 cloths w.g.
William Perysson, D, 1 cloth 20 yds. w.g.

[m.27]
592. 22 Sept. In the ship of Nicholas Barbour [of Fowey]
John Peynter, Robert Buk and William Nycoll by Richard Odyham
   their factor,[1] Ds, 10 bales 2 fardels with 200 cloths 8 yds. w.g.
Robert Goodwyn, D, 2 bales 1 fardel with 37½ cloths w.g.
William Fyncham, D, 1 fardel with 9 cloths w.g.
John Tutsam', D, 1 bale with 14 cloths w.g.
Richard Isaac, D, 2 bales with 20 cloths w.g.
William Breware, D, 2 cloths w.g.
George Bulstrode, D, 1 bale with 10 cloths w.g.

[1] On 12 December 1480 Peynter, Buk and Nicholl, merchants of Plymouth, and their
factors had been granted a licence to export and import goods in a ship or ships of not
more than 200 tuns for one voyage without payment of duties (P.R.O. Treaty Roll C
76/164, m.7).

593. 22 Sept. In the ship of Martin Sanchis,
Michael de Rautari of Guipúzcoa, Sp, 14 yds. cloth w.g.
Peter Valedelede of Guipúzcoa, Sp, 5 bales with 72 cloths 8 yds. w.g.
Peter de Castro of Guipúzcoa, Sp, 7 bales 1 fardel with 111 cloths 8 yds.
   w.g., 4 rolls with 4 cloths in grain
Martin Lopean [S Lopiana] of Guipúzcoa, Sp, 3 bales with 51 cloths 16
   yds. w.g., 1 cloth of half grain
Allowiso de Lyon of Guipúzcoa, Sp, 2 bales 1 fardel with 34 cloths 16
   yds. w.g.
Domyngo de Colyns, [S Colongas] of Guipúzcoa, Sp, 1 cloth w.g.
Thomason de Spice of Guipúzcoa, Sp, 2 cloths 4 yds. w.g.
John Retorto of Guipúzcoa, Sp, 20 [S 22] yds. w.g.
Peter de Salvo of Guipúzcoa, Sp, 1 fardel with 5½ cloths w.g.

594. 22 [S 24] Sept. In the ship of Robert Alcok [of London]
Richard Snawe, D, 1 fardel with 4 cloths w.g.
John Evington, D, 2 fardels with 3 cloths 6 yds. w.g., 12 yds. cloth of
   half grain, 17 pcs. double worsted
James Falk, A, 3 brls. with D. lbs. rendered tallow, 1 brl. with 14 doz. [S
   lbs.] candles, 53s.4d.
William Redye, D, 1 chest with 5 pcs. double worsted
John Gose, D, 1 fardel with 4 cloths w.g.
William Bentley, D, 1 cloth w.g.
Thomas Lok, D, 1 fardel with 2 cloths w.g., 2 pcs. double worsted
John Fysshare, D, 1 fardel with 4 cloths w.g., 22 pcs. double worsted
Henry Holgyll, D, 1 fardel with 9½ cloths w.g.
John Benet, D, 1 fardel with 4 cloths w.g.
John Cotton, D, 1 fardel with 6 cloths 20 yds. w.g.

Thomas Smythe, D, 1 fardel with 6 cloths w.g.

Thomas Johnson, A, 6 pipes beer, 40s.

John van Strawlyn, H, 1 bale with 14 cloths w.g., 1½ cloths of half grain, 2 pcs. double worsted; 20 goads cotton russet, 13s.4d.

[m.27d.]

595. 22 Sept. In the ship of Ditcloffe Soltman [*S* Slotman]

The Lord Edward King of England by Marcellus Mawrys, A, his factor,[1] 2 maunds with 1,186 'passlades' lambskins and 174 'mesandes' lambskins, £13 10s.

John Evinger, A, 5 weys cheese, 10 pipes beer, £6 6s.8d.

Hans Culle, H, 1 bale with 23 cloths w.g.; 20 goads cotton russet, 13s.4d.

Anthony Odindale, H, 1 bale with 10 cloths w.g.; 20 goads cotton russet, 13s.4d.

Matthew Hynkylman, H, 1 bale with 17 cloths w.g., 1 pc. double worsted; 170 goads cotton russet, £5 13s.4d.

Said master, H, 1 fardel with 9 cloths 4 yds. w.g.

Arnold Moldyk, H, 1 bale with 15 cloths w.g.; 20 goads cotton russet, 13s.4d.

Godard van Beston, H, 1 bale with 16 cloths w.g.; 40 goads cotton russet, 26s.8d.

Peter Eksted, H, 1 bale with 25 cloths w.g.; 67 goads cotton russet, 46s.8d.

Herman Plough, H, 1 bale with 24 cloths w.g.; 20 goads cotton russet 13s.4d.

Said master, H, 1 brl. with 18 [*S* 10] stocks of trenchers, 36 cheeses, 20s.

Deryk Isbright [*S* Gysbryght], A, 3 pipes beer, 20s.

[1] This shipment was almost certainly made by the factor on his own behalf since Mawrys, the King's goldsmith, had on 8 April 1481 been granted a licence to export 50,000 'passelades and mesandes' (diseased or damaged lambskins) over the next three years without payment of custom (P.R.O. Treaty Roll C 76/164, m.14).

596. 22 [*S* 27] Sept. In the ship of William Parker

Roger Arnold, D, 1 bale with 11 [*S* 10] cloths 6 yds. w.g., 9 pcs. double worsted

William Twig, D, 1 fardel with 2 cloths w.g.

John Gay, D, 1 fardel with 7 cloths w.g.

John Wheteley, D, 1 fardel with 5 cloths w.g.

Hugh Clopton, D, 1 fardel with 3 cloths w.g.

Thomas Kyppyng', D, 1 fardel with 6 cloths 16 yds. w.g.

597. 27 Sept. In a cart of William Johnson [*S* going to Southampton]

Peter de Castro of Guipúzcoa, Sp, 2 bales with 34 cloths 8 yds. w.g.[1]

[1] *S.* follows 'these 29 membranes the said William Weston, surveyor, delivered here by his own hands on 9 November 21 Edward IV and took oath' (see above p. xxvii).

ADDITIONAL DOCUMENTS

i. Accounts of the Staplers' Company of wool customed at London for shipment to Calais, Michaelmas 1480 – Michaelmas 1481 (extracted from accounts for all wool ports, P.R.O., L.T.R. Foreign Accounts, E 364/115 m.3, 116 m.2).

598. 7 Dec. 1480. 991 sacks 12 cloves of wool and 26,370 woolfells making 109¾ sacks 30 fells of Richard Pontesbury, Owin Rideley, Richard Gardeyn, John Henne, Thomas Fabian, Hugh Clopton, William Stokker, John Stokker, William Browne, Thomas Otley, Robert Flemmyng, John Benyngton, John Broke, Thomas Pontesbury, William Waryn, Thomas Croke, Roger Grauntoft, John Nyng, Thomas Graunger, Richard Drake, Richard Brente, Peter Shelton, Christopher Broune, John Wryght, Richard Nonneley, Robert Adlyn, John Tame, John Wryght and John Wetherard, Robert Biffeld, William Gasgill, Richard Haddon, William Norton, Roger Wigston, William Adam, William Higons, William Lynde, Thomas Ilom, Robert Michell, William Milys, Roger Wigston and John Wygston, William Horne, Robert Broke, John Nessefeld, Gerard Canizian, William Howson, Thomas Bretayne, William Pondman, Roger Kynton, John Odyn, Roger Grauntoft and Richard Cely, merchants of the Staple.

599. 12 Dec. 42 sacks 19 cloves of wool and 1,417 woolfells making 5¾ sacks 37 fells of Roger Kynton, Thomas Grafton, Richard Garden, John Benyngton, Robert Flemmyng and William Miles, merchants of the Staple.

600. 13 Dec. 2,099½ sacks 17 cloves of wool and 103,793 woolfells making 432¼ sacks 53 fells of Robert Onley, John Nyng, Roger Grauntoft, Thomas Otley, Barnard Symond, Nicholas Alwyn, Thomas Grafton, Richard Gardyn, Thomas Gilbert, John Nesseffeld, Thomas Ilom, William Lord Hastyngs, James Alie, Thomas Pontesbury, Adam Knyght, William Horne, Nicholas Alwyn, Henry Cantlowe, William Bondman, John Whichecote, Richard Pontesbury, Thomas Betson, Robert Michel, Thomas Croke, William Gasgill, Robert Biffeld, Roger Kynton, John Oneley, Richard Oneley, Hugh Clopton, Richard Chester, Robert Houghton, Henry Kebill, Walter Ayleworth, Richard Braytoft, John Tame, William Lynde, Richard Hadon, John Thirkell, Richard Nonneley, Christopher Broune, Thomas Bretayne, John Broke, William Waren, William Miles, Alexander Mottrom, Robert Billesdon, John Elys, Robert Basset, Robert Croke, Thomas Croke, Gerard Canizian, Stephen Gibson, Thomas Feldyng, Robert Stokker, John Wetherard, Ralph Lymyngton,

Richard Mariot, Peter Selton, William Norton, John Exnyng, John Brasebrygge, John Tate, William Higons, Robert Tate, John Tate, William Stokker, John Stokker, William Hill, John Pelet, Richard Cely, Henry Wayte, William Walford, William Tailour, Richard Penreth, William Trayford, William Wyse, Thomas Wynham, William Perys and Richard Brente, merchants of the Staple.

601. 21 July 1481. 778 sacks of wool and 194,363 woolfells making 809¾ sacks 23 fells of Gerard Canyzian, William Dalton, Richard Pontesbury, John Oneley, Henry Kebyll, Hugh Went, Robert Flemyng, Richard Chester, Richard Nonneley, John Broke, Roger Wygston, Thomas Bretayn, John Tame, Roger Wygston, John Wygston, Thomas Wynham, John Tate senior, John Bradshawe, William Lynde, William Bentham, Thomas Betson, John Pelet, John Benyngton, Hugh Clopton, Richard Feldyng, William Waren, William Higons, Thomas Fabyan, Richard Gardener, Robert Hardbene, John Nessefeld, Henry Cantlowe, Nicholas Allewyn, Thomas Grafton, William Taillour, John Goldsmyth, Thomas Pontysbury, Thomas Burton, William Stokker, John Stokker, Walter Ayleworth, Richard Brent, Richard Chawry, Roger Kynton, John Saundyrs, Stephen Gybson, Richard Haddon, William Miles and Alexander Mottrom, merchants of the Staple.

602. 26 Sept. 839½ sacks 18 cloves of wool and 235,142 woolfells making 979¾ sacks 2 fells of Thomas Otley, Thomas Wymbyssh, John Elys, John Wryght, John Wetherard, Richard Cely senior, Thomas Burton, Hugh Went, Thomas Bretayn, William Dalton, Roger Wygston, William Heryot, Henry Kebyll, William Horne, William Brown, John Benyngton, William Trayford, Richard Pontysbury, Richard Chestyr, Thomas Wynham, John Croke, Thomas Croke, William Miles, Alexander Mottrom, Adam Knyght, John Broke, Hugh Clopton, William Norton, William Lord Hastyngs, William Maryon, Richard Cely junior, Robert Flemyng, Nicholas Alwyn, Henry Cantlowe, John Wetherard, Richard Brent, Stephen Gybson, John Saundyrs, Thomas Betson, John Stokker, Walter Ayleworth, Roger Grauntoft, Thomas Hayward, Henry Colet, John Tame, Robert Byllysdon, John Ways, Robert Tate, John Tate, William Goldwyn, Richard Braytoft junior, Thomas Pontysbury, John Neffeld, Thomas Fabyan, Thomas Graunger, Richard Drake, John Mede, William Pers, William Lynde, Owin Rydley, Richard Haddon, Robert Oneley, Robert Adlyn, Charles Vellers, John Odyn, Thomas Gylbert, William Salford, Nicholas Broun, Richard Nonneley, Peter Shelton, William Hygons, Thomas Grafton, Robert Stokker, Wiliam Bentham, Harold Staunton, Richard Chawry, Christopher Brown and William Adam, merchants of the Staple.

[**603.** 4 Apr. 1481. 62½ sacks 9 cloves of wool of the King by William Slyfeld, D, his factor, shipped to Calais

604. 25 May 1481. 63½ sacks 7 cloves of wool of William Heryot, shipped in a ship of John Santander of San Sebastian called *Sancta Clara*, towards the straits of Marrok][1]

[1] P.R.O. Enrolled Wool Customs Accounts, E 356/22, m.33. Total London wool exports 1480–1481, 7,216 sacks (*England's Export Trade*, p. 68). There were also 1,028 ox-hides exported by alien merchants (Enrolled Customs Account, loc. cit.).

ii. Account of Anthony Earl Ryvers, Chief Butler of England, of the custom of 2s. for each tun of wine imported by alien merchants into London, Michaelmas 1480 – Michaelmas 1481 (extracted from an account for all the ports, P.R.O., K.R., Various Accounts, E 101 Bnd. 82/22 m.1.).

605. 11 Nov. 1480. In the ship of John Mathewson called *Christofer* of Dordrecht
Matthew Blittiswyk, A, 5 roods wine

606. 18 Nov. In the ship of John de Albistur called *le Sancta Maria* of San Sebastian
John de Albistur, A, 6 tuns wine

607. 9 Dec. In the ship of Richard Sayer called *le Bartilmewe* of London
Lewis Bonvise, A, 4 tuns 1 pipe wine

608. 22 Dec. In the ship of Henry Costians called *le Hert* of Dordrecht
John Bees, A, 6 roods wine

609. 23 Dec. In the ship of Thomas Horn called *le Thomas* of London
Lewis Bonvise, A, 5 tuns 1 pipe wine

610. 2 Jan. 1481. In the ship of Thomas Keten called *le Mary Dawbeney*
Lewis Bonvise, A, 8 tuns 1 pipe wine

611. 13 Jan. In the ship of John Demode called *le Margaret* of Dieppe
John Demode, A, 10 tuns wine

612. 19 Feb. In the ship of Evan Potesten called *le Genet* of Le Conquet
Evan Potesten, A, 2 tuns wine

613. 7 Mar. In the ship of Ellis Arnold called *le Kateryn* of London
Lewis Bonvise, A, 4 tuns 1 pipe wine

614. 10 Mar. In the ship of Thomas Coyse called *le Petir Stokker* [of London]
Lewis Bonvise, A, 4 tuns 1 pipe wine

615. 2 Apr. In the ship of Thomas Bette called *le Kateryn Charlez* [of London]
Peter Dalgey and others, As, 8 tuns wine

616. 3 Apr. In the ship of Thomas Grey called *le Peter Fynkell*

Jenycote de Carrys, A, 2 tuns wine

617. 16 Apr. In the ship of Elyot Laby called *le Margaret* of Guérande
Peter Friscabawde and other As., 17 tuns 1 pipe wine

618. 24 May. In the ship of Roger Higgys [of Plymouth]
Jordan de Putez, A, 1 pipe wine

619. [14 June] In the galley of Bernard Bondymer [of Venice]
Bernard Bondymer and other As, 46 tuns 1 pipe wine
Constantine Companyon, A, 1 butt wine

620. 4 Sept. In the ship of Richard Sayer called *le Christofer* of
'Middleton'[1]
Lewis Bonvise, A, 5 tuns wine

   [1] ? Middleton, Sussex, Chichester division, on coast 3m. E. of Bognor.

621. 5 Sept. In the ship of John Lokyngton called *le Jesus* of London
Lewis Bonvise, A, 5 tuns 1 hhd. wine

622. 23 Sept. In the ship of Thomas Gourley
Lewis Bonvise, A, 4 tuns 1 pipe wine

Total of wine 159 tuns,[1] custom £15 18s.

   [1] Total denizen and alien wine imports into London 1480–1481, 3820 tuns, including 50 tuns of sweet wine (P.R.O. Enrolled Tunnage and Poundage Accounts, E 356/22, m.45). The account also records the export by denizen and alien merchants, all said to be factors of the Italian merchant Alan de Monteferrato who acted on behalf of the king, of the following metals: 147 thousandweight of tin valued at £10 per thousandweight, 13 thousandweight of pewter valued at £13 6s.8d. per thousandweight and 116 fothers 15 C. of lead valued at £4 per fother. In 1471, following an earlier grant of 1466, Monteferrato had been licensed to export 10,000 blocks of tin, 2,000 barrels of pewter vessels and 1,000 fothers of lead without paying custom or subsidy and Monteferrato probably re-sold the licences. (Enrolled Tunnage and Poundage Account, loc. cit.; J. Hatcher, *English Tin Production and Trade Before 1550* (Oxford, 1973), 123–4, 166, 176).

APPENDIX

List of London Particular Customs Accounts, 1461–1509[1]
(a) Wool Custom and Subsidy

Ref. no.	Date[2]	Description	No. of Membranes or Folios
E.122/73/32	3 March– 1 Aug. 1461	Particulars of account of John Poutrell and Nicholas Sharp, collectors	24 fos.
73/35	Michaelmas 1462– 16 July 1463	Particulars of account of John Smyth and Thomas Thorndon, collectors	12 fos. (printed in Gras, 601–5)
73/36	10 March– 7 July 1464	Controlment of Thomas Stratton, controller	1 m.
73/37	23 July– 10 Dec. 1464	Particulars of account of Robert Rufford and John Brampton, collectors	8 fos.
79/2	Michaelmas 1467– 31 May 1468	Controlment of Robert Iseham, controller	5 ms.
162/1	31 May– 25 Dec. 1468	Particulars of account of William Chattok and Roger Appleton, collectors	7 fos. (slightly damaged at head and foot)
203/5	21 Aug.– 10 Nov. 1469	Particulars of account of William Chattok and John Otir, collectors	4 fos.
194/21	Michaelmas 1476– Michaelmas 1477	Controlment of Henry Danvers, controller	1 m.
73/40	5 July 1478– Michaelmas 1479	Particulars of account of John Fitzherbert and Robert Plomer, collectors	56 fos.
78/2	19 June– 27 Sept. 1483[3]	Controlment of Nicholas Sothworth, controller	3 ms. (damaged and faded in places)

[1] Omits small, undated fragments.
[2] The period of account is that stated at the head of the account unless otherwise noted.
[3] Dates of first and last entries.

Appendix

Ref. no.	Date	Description	No. of Membranes or Folios
78/5	Michaelmas 1487–Michaelmas 1488	Particulars of account of William Tysted and Henry Assheborn, collectors	28 fos.
78/6	Michaelmas 1487–Michaelmas 1488	Controlment of above by Nicholas Suthworth, controller	6 ms.
78/8	Michaelmas 1489–Michaelmas 1490	Controlment of John Shurley, controller	6 ms. (right-hand margin damaged)
78/10	Michaelmas 1490–Michaelmas 1491	Particulars of account of William Tysted and Henry Assheborn, collectors	12 fos.
78/11	Michaelmas 1490–Michaelmas 1491	Controlment of above by John Shurley, controller	2 ms. (badly damaged and faded)
79/3	Michaelmas 1491–Michaelmas 1492	Particulars of account of William Tysted and Henry Assheborn, collectors	16 fos.
73/4	Michaelmas 1493–Michaelmas 1494	Particulars of account of William Tysted and Henry Assheborn, collectors	37 fos.
80/1	Michaelmas 1493–Michaelmas 1494	Controlment of above by John Shurley, controller	8 ms.
203/6	Michaelmas 1495–Michaelmas 1496	Particulars of account of William Tysted and Henry Assheborn to 8 July when Assheborn died and of Tysted alone 9 July onwards	47 fos. (some slightly damaged)
79/9	Michaelmas 1501–Michaelmas 1502	Particulars of account of William Tystede and William Bulstrode gent., collectors	32 fos.
79/14	Michaelmas 1505–25 April 1506	Controlment of John Shirley gent., controller	1 m. (faded in places)
79/17	Michaelmas 1507–Michaelmas 1508	Particulars of account of Richard Cholmeley kn. and William Bulstrode gent., collectors	30 fos.

(b) Petty Custom

Ref. no.	Date	Description	No. of Membranes or Folios
E.122/194/11	Michaelmas 1461–20 May 1462	Controlment of Master William Hatclyff, controller	11 ms. (slightly faded in places)
194/12	15 October 1462–2 July 1463	Controlment of Ralph Hastyngs, gent., controller	8 ms. (ms. 5–8, export section, damaged)
194/15	Michaelmas 1463–27 Jan. 1464	Particulars of account of William Haydok and Thomas Gay, collectors	9 ms. (slightly faded in places)
73/33	9 Feb.–19 Feb. 1470[4]	Controlment of Ralph Hastynges, controller	1 m. (damaged)
194/19	Michaelmas 1471–4 Aug. 1472	Particulars of account of John Roger and Thomas Belletour, collectors	18 ms. (some slightly damaged)
73/34	4 Aug. 1472–Michaelmas 1473	Particulars of account of Thomas Billetour and John Brokford	16 ms. (badly damaged)
194/20	Michaelmas 1472–Michaelmas 1473	Controlment of above by Thomas Fowler, controller	18 ms.
194/22	20 November 1477–9 July 1478	Particulars of account of Peter Draper and Henry Davers, collectors	19 ms. (badly damaged)
194/23	20 November 1477–13 July 1478	Controlment of above by Thomas Fowler, controller	17 ms.
194/24	Michaelmas 1480–Michaelmas 1481	Rolls of William Weston, surveyor	27 ms. (later ms. damaged)
194/25	Michaelmas 1480–Michaelmas 1481	Controlment of Thomas Fowler, controller	27 ms. (printed in this edition)
194/26	9 April–26 June 1483	Particulars of account of Robert Fitzherbert and William Martyn, collectors	9 ms. and fragments (badly damaged)
73/41	9 April–24 July 1483	Controlment of Thomas Fowler, controller	3 ms. (imports only, damaged)
162/5	22 May–23 July 1483[5]	Controlment of Thomas Fowler, controller	4 ms. (exports only)

[4] First and last entries in account.   [5] First and last entries in account.

Appendix

Ref. no.	Date	Description	No. of Membranes or Folios
78/3	22 Aug.– 17 Oct. 1485	Particulars of account of William Birte (or Brette) and Thomas Litley, collectors of petty custom and tunnage and poundage	8 ms. (stained and damaged in places)
78/9	Michaelmas 1490–Michaelmas 1491	Controlment of Simon Digby, controller	18 ms.
80/2	Michaelmas 1502–Michaelmas 1503	Particulars of account of William Trefry and William Holybrond, collectors	30 ms.
80/3	Michaelmas 1502–Michaelmas 1503	Controlment of the above by Simon Digby, controller	29 ms. (damaged in places)
79/12	18 Jan.–Michaelmas 1506	Particulars of account of William Grene and John Warnet, collectors	23 ms.
80/4	Michaelmas 1506–Michaelmas 1507	Controlment of Simon Digby, controller	34 ms. (some damaged and faded)
80/5	Michaelmas 1507–Michaelmas 1508	Particulars of account of John Millys, surveyor	34 ms. (faded in places)

(c) Tunnage and Poundage

E.122/194/14	2 Feb.– 6 Aug. 1463	Particulars of account of Ralph Wolseley and John Colrede, collectors	2 ms. (exports only)
194/13	11 Feb.– 6 Aug. [1463]	No heading but almost certainly belongs with above account	5 ms. (imports only)
194/16	6 Aug.–Michaelmas 1463	Controlment of Thomas Mauncell, controller	7 ms.
194/18	19 Nov. 1465– 6 Apr. 1466	Particulars of account of Robert Cousyn and John Roggers	10 ms.
194/17	6 Apr.– 1 May 1466	Particulars of account of William Hyde and John Thomas, collectors	2 ms.
194/17	6 Apr.– 1 May 1466	Controlment of above by John Forster, controller	2 ms.

Appendix

Ref. no.	Date	Description	No. of Membranes or Folios
78/3	22 Aug.– 17 Oct. 1485	see Petty Custom Account of same date	
78/7	Michaelmas 1487– Michaelmas 1488	Controlment of John Myllys, controller	11 ms.
79/5	Michaelmas 1494– Michaelmas 1495	Controlment of John Myllys, controller	31 ms. (some damaged and faded)

GLOSSARY AND INDEX OF
COMMODITIES

References in Roman numerals are to pages in the introduction; all other references are to serial numbers in the text. All the commodities in the text are listed below and the English (unless identical with the modern form), Latin or French spelling of the MS is given in round brackets. A reference is provided to each entry for a commodity, with the exception of a few very common commodities, e.g. woollen cloth, for which the first six references only are given. Descriptions are provided of the less familiar commodities and weights and measures. The following books have been especially useful in supplementing the *Oxford English Dictionary*:

S. W. Beck, *The Draper's Dictionary* (1886)

Claude Blair, *European Armour circa 1066 to circa 1700* (1953)

E. M. Carus-Wilson (ed.), *The Overseas Trade of Bristol in the later Middle Ages* (1937)

H. Hall and F. J. Nicholas (eds.), 'The Noumbre of Weyghtes' in *Select Tracts and Table Books Relating to English Weights and Measures, 1100–1742* (Camden Society, 3rd series, xli, 1929)

E. M. Veale, *The English Fur Trade in the later Middle Ages* (Oxford, 1966)

T. S. Willan (ed.), *A Tudor Book of Rates* (1962)

R. E. Zupko, *A Dictionary of Weights and Measures for the British Isles: the Middle Ages to the Twentieth Century* (American Philosophical Society, 1985)

ashes (cineres), wood-ashes for making lye, the alkalised water used in cloth manufacture, 1, 13, 32, 40, 88, 106, 114–15, 117, 120–2, 125, 127, 137, 141, 143, 169–71, 182, 197, 202, 204, 206, 212–13; *see also* pot ashes

awl blades (alblad', alleblad', alle bladys), 24, 30, 37, 60, 139, 147, 181, 184

awl hafts (allehaft', alhaft'), handles of awls, 91, 181

axes, coopers' (couper axes), 205

Backs, ? metal backs for hearths, 183

bacon (bakon, baconus), 220, 266, 305, 354, 374, 408, 424, 454, 472, 474, 508, 571, 575

bags (bagg', bag'), 1, 26, 30, 38, 94, 96, 100, 102, 139, 174, 181, 183–4, 186; for children (pro pueris), 1

bag rings (bag reng', ryng'), 1, 26, 102, 174, 183–4

balances (balanc'), 24–5, 30, 70, 94, 181–2, 184, 186; latten (latonis), 79

balls (pile), probably tennis balls, 5, 9, 11, 23, 25, 60, 68, 82, 84–6, 92, 95–7, 100, 138, 140, 143, 147, 159, 172, 178–9, 187; *see also* chasing balls

band, a weight for iron, 24 stone in 1600 (Zupko)

barbers' stones (barbour stonys), 46

barley (ordeum), 61

barrel, a cask and a measure of capacity, varying with the commodity, e.g. 8 barrels of wine and oil to the tun, 12 barrels of herring to the last

basan leather (basen ledd'), lower quality leather made from sheepskin, 103, 147, 182

'bascheron' (basskeron), a measure (amount unknown) of battery (q.v.)

basins (basyns, bason), 90, 94, 121, 368, 527; barbers' (barbours), 90; 'bottom of a basyn', 82; brass (enea), 508; latten (latonis), 23

bast ropes (bast ropis), made from the inner bark of the lime tree, 169–70

battery (battry), articles of metal wrought by hammering, basins, kettles, etc., 1, 10, 33–5, 37, 59, 77–8, 90, 94–5, 97, 100, 117, 134, 139, 147, 150–1, 154, 159, 181, 183, 189, 204, 206–8, 211, 237

baudekin (bawdkyn', bawdekyns), a rich embroidered silk cloth, 33, 184, 190

bays, bay berries, fruit of the laurel or bay-tree, 107, 111, 116

beads (bed', bedys'), 114, 139, 152, 156, 181, 190; black (blak), 180; bone, 94, 139; boxwood (box), 27, 30, 33, 183–4; coral (corall'), 156; glass (glas, glas-

sez), 17, 23, 25, 27, 33, 94, 147, 153, 156, 162, 178, 181–2; jet (cole, kole), 23, 27, 33, 82, 91–2, 181, 207; red, 94; wooden (treen, lignea), 17, 20, 23–4, 37, 90, 93, 139, 153, 165, 178; *see also* mistletoe beads

bead-stones (bedeston'), ?beads for rosaries, 147

bead strings (bede stryng'), 1

beaver skins (bevirs), 190

beaver wombs (bevir wombys), beaver skins from the belly, 170

beer, (beir', beyr), 169–70, 222, 225, 243, 291, 298, 301, 305, 312, 342, 349, 354–5, 385, 421, 454, 478, 512, 516, 536, 541, 546, 550–1, 553, 557, 561, 577, 582, 586, 594–5

bellows (belowes), 588

bells (bell'), 17, 24, 46, 56, 139, 153, 174, 180–1, 184–5; brass (campana enea), 475, 560; latten (latonis), 24, 114; sheep's (ovium, shepis), 178, 184; *see also* Anthony's bells, sacring-bells

bench-covers (banker'), 139, 290, 567

bevors, plate (bavers plate), plate defence for the chin and neck, 114, 139

bills (billes), long-handled weapons, 117

bits (bytt', bittes, bittez), 2, 30, 56, 82, 117, 197; horse bits, 207

'blowers', bellows, 170

blowing horns (blowyng horns), 587

boards (bord'), between which shanks (q.v.) were packed, four skins at a time

boards for shoemakers (ligna pro sutoribus), 10, 169–70, 206

bocals (bocal'), glass bottles or jugs with short wide necks, 156

bocasin (bocarsyn'), a cotton fabric of the fustian type, 134

bodkins (botkyns, botkins), 25, 56, 94, 184

bolsters (bolstr'), 183

'bolt wombs', fur of, 204

bonnets (caleptra, bonnet'), 93–4, 121, 498, 506, 508, 527, 542; double (dupl', dowble), 121, 205; half grain (dimidium granum), dyed partly with grain (q.v.), 227; scarlet, 166; single, 121, 205, 290; without grain (sine grano), 227; *see also* steel bonnets

books (libri), xxxvi, 1, 139, 156; painted (depicti), 178; *see also* histories, printed books

boots of calaber fur (boot' de calabre fur-res), 30

borax (borace), 156

bord Alexander (bord' Alisaundr', Alasaundr', Alizandr'), a rich striped silk originally from Alexandria, 2, 93, 141 bottles (bottell'), glass (glasse), 96, 114, 178; pint (pynt'), 23; tin (tyn'), 147; *see also* wicker bottles

bowls, round maple (ciphi maple rotundi), 212

bowstaves (bowstav', boustaves, bowstawes), 15, 16, 32, 59, 77, 156, 169–70, 197, 200

boxes, 94, 139

Brabant linen cloth (telum lineum Braband'), 1, 9, 17, 21, 23–4, 26, 30, 33–5, 82, 91, 120–1, 134, 139, 144, 165, 173, 177–9, 181, 184, 186, 189, 196, 205; raw (rawe), 121

Brabant stones (brabanstone), ? floor tiles, 179

brace (brac'), a measure of length, about 64 inches

brace, mail (brace' mayle), complete armour for the arm, 114

brass (eneus), 311

brazil (brasill'), a red wood of the Sappan tree from which dye was obtained, 156

breastplates (brest plate), 58, 114, 187

breeches of mail (brechis mayle), 196

bricks (breke), 148

brigandines (brigandynes, brigandeyns), body armour composed of iron rings or small iron plates, sewed upon canvas, linen or leather, 15, 93, 114, 129–30, 139, 196; *see also* nails, brigandine

bristles (bristell'), 17, 25–6, 33, 117, 178–81, 183

brooches (broches, brochis), 23, 165; brooch pins (spang' tong'), 174

brooms (bromes), 23

Bruges thread (filum Brug'), 184

Brunswick linen cloth (telum lineum Browneswyche, Browneswyk', Browneswiche), 10, 184, 190

brushes (broosh', brusches, brusshes, brusshis'), 4, 23, 26, 34, 46, 60, 85, 87, 93, 96, 103, 130, 144, 153, 172, 178–82, 184, 187, 205, 208; flax (flex), 94, 139, 174, 181; hair (here), 176, 190; stable (casch', craissh, crasche, cressh'), 26, 35, 56, 94, 147, 180; weavers' (wevir'), 93

Brussels leather (Brusell' leddir), 106

Brussels linen cloth (telum lineum Brussell'), 35, 37, 174, 181, 183

buck skins (buk pelles), 169–70

buckets (bokett'), 113

buckles (bokles), 2, 37, 40, 45, 94, 114, 174, 180, 184; hose (calege bokles), 189; latten (latonis), 1, 26, 28, 34, 96, 100, 114, 183

buckram (bokeram, bokram, bukram), could either be a coarse stiff linen or a fine one, 34, 45, 95, 103, 121, 134, 141,

156, 159, 183–4; of Constance (custans), 159; *see also* treillis

budge skins (pelles bogy), lambskins imported from north Africa and southern Europe, 30, 35, 134, 139, 174, 181, 189; Spanish (Spaynyssh'), 174; *see also* shanks

bullions (bullyons), knobs or bosses of metal, 58

Burgundy cloth (burgeis, borgoyn), 177

busk (buske), a coarse linen used for lining and stiffening, 24, 26, 28, 33, 35, 37, 56, 77–8, 94–5, 97, 114, 138, 159, 177, 181, 183, 187; white (album), 35

butter (butirum), 298, 305, 349, 454–5, 541, 561

buttons (botons), 20, 103

C (centum, centena, centenarium)
  (a) a measure of weight, either decimal or the hundred-weight of 112 lbs. For 'great wares', i.e. woad, madder, alum, wax, dates, soap, copper, pewter, etc., C. was equal to 112 lbs. For 'subtle wares', i.e. pepper and other spices, Spanish grain, etc., C. was equal to 100 lbs.
  (b) a measure of number varying with the commodity. The 'long hundred' of 120 was used for stockfish, eels, and most other fish, and certain other commodities such as bowstaves and rabbit-skins. For certain linen cloths, e.g. Herford and Osnabruck, C. appears to equal 200 ells (q.v.) in this account. The 'short hundred' (100) was used for Holland and some other varieties of linen and many small manufactures. The 'great C' of clapholt contained 24 'short hundreds'

cable, ship's (cabill' navis), 99

caddis (cadas, cades), a worsted yarn, 56, 94; coarse (cors'), 174, 184

caddis webs (cadas webbes), worsted tape, 139

Caen-stone (canestone), building stone from Caen in Normandy, 70, 80

calaber furs (calabr'), squirrel skins, originally from Calabria, S. Italy, but later from other parts of southern and central Europe, 37, 184, 186–7, 189, 192; wombs (wombes), belly fur, 189; *see also* boots

calamine (calmyn'), zinc ore for use in making brass alloy, xxxv, 30, 82

cade, a cask of herring holding five long hundreds (600), twenty to the last (q.v.)

calfskins (pelles vitulorum), 487; tanned

176

(tanette), 250, 256, 262, 310, 332, 489, 495, 588

camlet (chamelott', chamelet), a long-haired cloth made of such materials as camel and goat hair, 33, 121, 156; long, 156; short coarse, 156

candles (candele), 220, 225, 237, 243, 266, 277, 279, 293, 295, 298, 302, 305, 312–13, 317, 332, 342, 344, 354–6, 360, 385, 404, 423–4, 454, 478, 504, 508, 516, 527, 538, 542, 548, 551, 553, 557, 561, 594

candles, pipes for (pipes pro candels, candell' pipes), 139, 178, 184; *see also* candlesticks

candle-snuffers (candell' snoffers), 122, 139, 176, 184; *see also* snuffers

candlesticks (candelstykk', candylstick', candelstikk', candelabrum), 25, 93, 121, 135, 139, 159, 183, 368, 467; brass, 527; 'iron stickyng', 33; tin (tyn), 35; wire (wyron), 174

candle-wick (candellweke, candelewek, candelwyk), 35, 159, 168–70, 181, 197, 204; candle yarn (candell' yern') 184

cans (cannys), 170

canvas (canvas, kanvas), 4, 32, 45, 70, 89, 93–4, 159, 166, 179, 182, 184, 206; barras (barowe), coarse linen cloth imported from Holland, 95, 183; Brabant (braban'), 94; Burgundy (burgon'), 186; spruce (sprewes), of Prussia, 32, 169–70

canvas linen cloth (telum lineum canvas), 4, 29

caps (cappis, capelle), 34, 157; double, with double turn-ups or facings, 34, 93, 103; single, 34, 93, 103; worsted, 205

capers (capres), 156

card-boards (carde bord'), boards for wool-cards (q.v.), 23

card heads (card hed), 157

cards *see* wool-cards

carpets, (carpett'), 156

caskets (caskett', kaskett', kark'), 26, 30, 33, 40, 93–4, 106, 117, 120, 147, 152, 174

cassia fistula (casa fistola), a laxative derived from senna leaves and cassia pods, 156

cats fur (catte furr'), 28; wild (furres wild catt'), 139

cat-skins (pelles mureligorum), 454, 504–5, 508

chafing-dishes (chafyng disshes), 139, 183; earthen (erthe), 113; latten (latonis), 121

chalcedony (calcedons), a precious (or semi-precious) stone, with a lustre like

wax, 30, 35, 184–5; imitation (counterfet), 27–8, 45, 82, 92, 94, 183, 186

chamfron (chamfre), armour for a horse's head, 93

chasing balls (chasyng ball'), 27

cheeses (chesis, casei), 205, 225, 237, 243, 266, 290, 298, 305, 308, 312, 349, 508, 541, 544, 550, 561, 565, 574–5; Suffolk (Suff'), 538

chess boards (ches bord'), 27

chess-men (chesmen), 174

chests (cista), 165, 197

cinnamon (cynamonum, canella), 83, 156

citronade (sitrenade, citrenade), candied citron or orange peel, 156

clapholt (clappholt), small split timber, usually oak, for barrel-staves or panelling, 32, 168–70, 197

clarions, shrill trumpets, 20

clasps (clapsis, clapsez), 1, 56, 82, 84, 92, 94, 184

clavichord wire (clavicord weir), 174, 185

cloth, woollen (pannus), broadcloth, standard 1½–2 yds. wide and 24 yds. long: with broad selvages (largus cum brode lysts), 435–7, 498, 575, 577; half grain (de dimidio grano), dyed partly with the scarlet dye grain, 309, 319, 333–4, 368–594 *passim*; in grain (in grano), dyed with grain, 228, 262–3, 309, 315, 319–593 *passim*; without grain (sine grano), 69, 216–597 *passim*; *see also* cotton russet, 'forlaken', frieze, Kendals, Northern, Welsh straits, worsted

cloths, miscellaneous (panni), 34, 179, 182; *see also* painted cloths, stained cloths

cloth of gold, 156

clout (clowt'), a measure of weight, of silk: 4 lbs.; also a piece of cloth containing a number of pins, needles, etc.

clove, a measure of weight, used for wool: 7 lbs.

cloves (clowes), 156

coal-fish (coll'), allied to cod, 163

cocks, 181

codfish (pisces cod'), 197

codsheads (cod' hed'), 71–2, 74

coffers (cofers, coffers), 20, 25, 30, 32–3, 36, 82, 84, 103, 106, 121, 147, 152, 156, 169–70, 181, 184, 197, 205, 207; covering of, 487; of cypress (cipres), 156, 184

Cologne thread (filum Col'), a linen yarn normally dyed blue, 1, 2, 27–8, 30, 33–7, 54, 56, 58, 77, 94–5, 97, 147, 151, 154, 174, 177, 181, 183, 185, 187, 189; white and blue (album et blodium), 78

coloquintida (coloquintica), the bitter-apple used as a purgative, 156 combs (pectina, combys, kombes, kombis), 2, 4, 23, 26, 40, 46, 70, 79, 84, 109–10, 140, 176, 181–2, 184, 191; ivory (yvery, every), 40, 45, 185; wooden (treen, ligni), 93, 114, 165; *see also* kempsters' combs

compasses, 1, 24, 28, 56, 84, 139, 174, 176, 183–4, 205

confections, mixed drugs or comfits, 156

coopers' irons (couper irons), 103

copper (cuprum, coper), 32, 125–6, 147, 168–70, 185, 311, 324, 356, 544, 581; beaten (bet), 94; broad (brod), 169; split (spliter), 169–70, 181, 185, 190

copper gold (coper gold), ?red gold, gold with a small alloy of copper to enhance its colour, 26, 92, 94, 100

copper plate (plate coper, cupri), 32, 94, 169–70, 177, 183, 544

copper rolls (roll' coper), 28, 30

copperas (coprose), sulphate of copper used in dyeing, tanning and making ink, 10, 13, 125–6, 168, 423

'coppyn' (copin) hats, probably high-crowned hats of the form of a sugar-loaf (*O.E.D. sub* copintank), 17, 23, 27, 30, 84, 89, 91, 94, 96, 144, 179, 181, 184

coral (corall'), 156; white (album), 35; *see also* beads

cords (cord'), 120

cordwain (cordewyn'), Spanish leather, 1

cork (corke), 14, 16, 77, 101, 107, 111, 116, 138, 140–1, 165; for slippers, 116

corses (corsys), ribbons or bands used as girdles; of Oudenarde thread (filum Outenard'), 58; worsted, 37

corslets (corsett'), light half-armour covering the upper body, 94, 96, 114

cottons, woollen cloth, 1, 34, 159

cotton russet, cheap woollen cloth, 308, 385, 465, 469–595, *passim*; *see also* Welsh straits

couch-bed (couche bed'), 141

counters (countours), pieces of metal or other material used in counting or keeping accounts, 27, 92, 94, 174, 178; of horn, 178

counters (countours, counters tables), tables or desks for counting money, 32, 169–70, 172, 177, 185, 197

coverings for pots (couveryng' pro pott'), 33

coverlets (coverlet', coopertoria), 34, 77, 94, 103, 124, 183, 204, 290, 324, 349, 487, 566–7, 574, 576; tapestry (tapstry, tapserye), 56, 83, 139, 175, 567

cow and calf *see* arrow-root

crane, an upright revolving axle with a horizontal arm, fixed by a fireplace,

for suspending a pot or kettle over the fire, 56

crocks, earthen (erthen crock'), 163

cropling *see* stockfish

crossbows (cros bowes), 25, 184; *see also* thread, trusses, windlass

crosses, 139; copper (coper), 147; latten (latonis), 94; mother of pearl (modir perle), 174; tin (tynne), 131

crucifixes, 178

cruets (cruett'), small vessels for sacramental wine, holy water or chrism, 27, 94, 100, 183–4; tin (tyn'), 33

cruses (crusys, cruc'), earthenware pots or jars, 5, 20–1, 23, 31, 55, 87, 96, 138, 140–1

cuirasses (curas), 93

cupboards (copbord), 93, 135, 147, 172

curtain rings (cortein ryng', curteyn'), 94, 181, 185

curtains (corteyns), 155

cushion-cloths (quisshon clothis, quosshyn clothis, quoisshon leves), 77, 135, 139, 181, 183

cushions (quysshons, quysshyns, quesshons, cusshyns), 139, 141, 324; leather (leddir), 30, 56, 181, 184; round, 204; skins for (pelles pro), 181

cypress cloth (cipres), 93

Cyprus kerchiefs (cipers kerchieff'), 156

D, a measure equal to 5 C. (q.v.)

daggers (armicudia), 20, 23, 25, 30, 33, 37, 45–6, 90, 93–4, 103, 106, 117, 121, 139, 152, 171, 174, 176, 183–6; sheaths for, 165

damask (damaske), costly figured silk, 184

dials, sundials, clocks or compasses, 184

dates (dactuli), 12, 156, 198, 203

diaper, a linen cloth, woven with small, often geometric, patterns, 26, 106, 175, 177, 204; *see also* napkins, tablecloths, towels

dicker, a measure of ten, used here for razors

dishes (dic', dischis, dys), 79; pewter (electri), 446; wooden (ligni), 588

distaffs (distaves), 23, 178–9; cases for (cases pro rokk'), 103; coverings for (coveryng pro distaves), 165

dog-hooks (dogk hok'), 100

dog-stones (dog' stonn', dogstonys), stones used for millstones, 1, 30–1, 147, 150, 183

dolls *see* puppets

Dornick linen cloth (telum lineum dornyk), a fine linen cloth taking its name from Doornik in Flanders, 23

dossals (dusshels), ornamental cloths to cover the backs of chairs, 205

Ghentish Holland cloth (Gent' Hod'), a linen cloth, 36, 77, 184, 186

Ghentish linen cloth (telum lineum Gentish), 6, 81, 181, 183; coarse, 174

gilt cases, 60

gimlets (gemelott', gemelett'), 46, 174, 181

ginger (gynger, zinziber), 35, 147, 156; green (viride), 56, 60, 114, 143, 156

gipsers, purses, pouches or wallets suspended from a belt or girdle, 93: with rings (cum ryng'), 93

girdles (zone), xxxvii, 27, 94, 114, 117, 165, 181, 187; gilt (deaurate), 156; latten (latonis), 2, 26–7, 35, 56, 94, 120, 147, 165; leather (leddir'), 23, 26, 33, 37, 46, 56, 100, 102, 147; silk (serice), 178; thread (fili'), 82, 92, 94; wire (weir'), 23–4, 26–8, 37, 82, 94, 140, 174, 183–4, 186; with aglets (cum aglett', auglett'), 100, 174, 184; *see also* corses

girdle hooks (zone hok'), 140

girth-webs (gerthe webbes), woven material of which girths are made, 90

glass (vitrum, glasse), 10, 87, 109, 125–6, 131, 141, 159, 166, 178–9

glasses (glassez, vitra), 34–5, 46, 56, 83, 117, 156, 172, 178, 180–3; 'cole', 20; crystal drinking (drynkyng cristall'), 162; drinking (drynkyng), 21, 23, 35, 94, 156, 173, 176, 178–9; foot (fote), 87, 179; great (magna), 23, 93; table, 215; ivory (yvery), 33; ? pouring (pere), 91; standing (stondynglassez), 174; *see also* looking glasses, pots, 'trumpe' glasses

gloves (cirotece), 1, 25–6, 30, 40, 45, 56, 82, 91, 93–4, 114, 117, 120, 147, 166, 174, 183–4, 207, 215

goad, a measure of cloth, 4½ ft.

goatskins (gote pelles), 139, 204

gold, rolls of, 2

gold pipes (gold pippes), tubes or rolls on which gold thread was wound, 35

gold skins (gold' pelles), 5, 96, 156, 184

gold thread (gold' filum), 184

gold weights (gold weyght'), for weighing gold, 46, 79; latten (latonis), 46; wooden (treen), 4

gorgets (gorgett'), collar of armour enclosing the neck and extending down over the top of the chest and back, 24, 60, 85, 93–4, 106, 114, 117, 121, 139, 159, 196; Dutch (douche), 196; mail (mayle), 93, 139

grain (granum), scarlet dye for cloth made from the dried body of the grain-like insect *kermes*: of Portugal (Portingale), 16, 201; of Seville (Civile), 12,

37, 198; of Spain (Hispanie), 16, 130, 152, 198, 203

graters, 26, 139, 178, 182

graving hafts (gravynghaft'), handles of engraving tools, 91

grey skins (pelles grey, greywork), the grey backs of winter squirrel skins, 1, 34, 146–7, 170, 190, 192, 204; coarse (cours), 126, 139, 168

griffin's egg (grypes hegg'), 156

gull-fish (gull'), small fish allied to the cod, 128

gum (gumma), 12

gunpowder (gunne poudir), 181

guns (gonnys), 150

gunstones (gonnestones), cannon-balls, 173, 176

gussets (gussett', gossett'), pieces of mail or plate filling up spaces at the joints in a suit of armour, 93, 114

Habergeons (habergons, habergens), sleeveless coats or jackets of mail or scale armour, 24, 58, 93, 103, 114, 121, 183, 196, 205

haddock, dry (hadd' drie), 160

hafts, 139

Hainault linen cloth (telum lineum Henegoys, Henoud', Hennoud', Henogos), 1, 10, 13, 95, 97, 184

hair (here), 2, 37

Hamburg linen cloth (telum lineum Hamburgh'), 126

hammers (hamers, mallys), 1, 27, 136

hangers, type of short sword originally hung from the belt, 46, 176, 187: blades, 94

Hannovers (hennovers), linen cloth, 13, 34, 125–6, 140, 168, 181, 186–7

hare skins (har' pelles), 146

harness, coarse (cors harneys), ? cheap armour, 106

harness, complete (complet harneys, harnes), probably a light half-armour. (cf. Blair, 118–9), 82, 89, 121, 129, 139

harness barrel (harnes bar'), for storing armour, 23

harp-strings (harp stryng', harpstring'), 33, 92, 186

hart skin (hert' pellis), 26

hastrey linen cloth (telum lineum haustr'), 28, 33, 35, 37, 77, 94, 97, 178, 181, 183, 187

hatbands (hatbond'), 26, 82, 100, 185

hats (hatt'), 34, 124, 567; boys' (pro pueris), 124; children's (childr'), 117; double (dowble), 117, 124; felt, 23, 26, 63; rolls for, 175; single, 117, 124; split, 213; *see also* coppyn, St. Omer, straw hats

mirrors (specula, merrours, mirrours), 23, 25–6, 35, 45, 56, 79, 82–3, 89, 93, 102–3, 121, 139, 152, 165, 174, 176, 184–5, 205, 215; barbers' (barbours), 184; of Nuremburg (Norburgh, Norborough), 23, 37, 60, 84, 94, 178–9

mistletoe (mystelyn), 35

mistletoe beads (mistell' bed', mystell'), 26–7, 82, 94, 103, 147, 181, 186; imitation (conterfet), 147, 153, 207

mittens (mitt'), 25

mortars (mort'), 185

mount (monys), a measure of plaster, 30 cwt.

musk-balls (muske ball'), receptacles for musk, 17, 35, 82, 207

mustard (cenapium), 368

mustard-querns (mustarde quernes), small hand-mills for grinding mustard seed, 147

mustard seed (mustardsede, semen cenapii), 237, 523

mustard stones, stones on which to pound mustard seed, 193

Nails (clavi, nayll', naile), 11, 23, 90, 93–4, 96, 100, 102–3, 114, 134, 147, 154, 159, 176, 180–2, 187, 189–90; brigandine (brigandyn'), 56, 94, 117, 156, 183; card (carde), for wool-cards, 147; latten (latonis), 147, 174; patten (pattyn'), 27, 159; red (rede), 147; *see also* lath-nails

napkins (napkens), 1, 85, 93; diaper, 26, 85

needle-cases (nedil cas'), 183, 185

needles (nedles, nedyll', nedels), 24, 33, 139, 153, 156, 174, 180, 184–5, 190; tack (tak), 187; *see also* pack-needles, sail-needles

nest, a measure (three) of counters, coffers, chests, bits etc.

nets (rethis), 305, 455, 508, 561

'Niperfeld' linen cloth (telum lineum Niperfeld'), ? of Nivelles, 13, 125–6, 168

Northern cloth (North'), a cheap woollen cloth produced in the West Riding of Yorkshire, 377; straits (stricti), single width (1 yd.), 378–9

nutcrackers (notcrakkers, notte crakkers), 174, 205

nutmegs (notmyg', notmug'), 156, 185, 187

nuts (nuces, nott'), 156; filberts (avelana), 61, 67, 70, 85, 92

Oars (orys), 68, 125, 171, 330

oats (avena), 409

oil (oleum), 12, 16, 59, 82, 97, 100, 112, 137, 150, 156, 201; *see also* linseed oil, rush oil, train oil

oil of spikenard (oleum spike, oleum de spyke), 79, 117

olives, 68

onion seed (semen caparum), 35

onions (cepe), 14, 55

oranges (oreng', oryng'), 42, 101, 107, 111–12, 116, 440

orchil (orgyll'), a purplish red dye obtained from lichens, 121

orpiment (orpyment, orpyn'), yellow arsenic, used as a pigment, 156, 544

osier rods (virge de osyer), 164

osmund (osmond'), high quality iron, 10, 13, 32, 58, 77, 94, 125–6, 150, 168–70, 197

Osnabrück linen cloth (telum lineum Osynbrug'), 1–3, 24, 28, 33, 35, 37, 58, 77, 95, 139, 141, 147, 168, 183, 204, 207

ostrich feathers (estrich fethers), 474

Oudenarde thread (filum Outenard'), a linen thread, 1, 23

oxen, live (boves vivi), 513

ox-hides, 604n.

ox-tongues (lingue bovium), 508; salt (salce), 368

Pack-needles (pak nedels, nedles), 92, 103, 147, 181, 185

packthread (pak filum, packyng thread), 11, 23, 45, 60, 89, 100, 159, 165, 176, 178, 181, 184, 204

padlocks, 184, 190

'pailes', ? spangles, 20

painted cloths (panni depicti), hangings for a room, painted or worked with figures, mottoes or texts, 25, 30–1, 34, 77, 83, 93–4, 97, 103, 121, 130, 144, 147, 174, 176–8, 180–2, 184, 205, 215

pane, a number of skins sewn together to form a fur lining

pans (pannys), 33; copper, 35, 184

paper, 26, 30, 43, 46, 60, 79, 84, 178, 184, 204, 215; black (nigrum), 118, 182; brown, 5, 23, 86, 208; painted (depictum), 23, 26, 30, 33, 45, 144, 174, 180, 184; silver (silv'), 34, 114; white (album), 23, 78; wrapping (spendable), 24, 179; writing (scribable, skrybable), 12, 178; *see also* printed papers

papers, paper packets of pins, points etc.

papers of the Passion of Christ (papers de passione Christi), 184

Paris cloth, imitation (conterfet), 159

Paris thread (parys thred'), 28

pavingstones (pavingston', pavyngstones), 9, 23, 68, 85–6, 96, 119, 172, 176, 179; white (alba), 118, 178

(b) of fruit: 12 quarterns to the sort (q.v.)

querns (quernys): hand, 183; *see also* mustard-querns, pepper-querns

quilts (quilt', quylte), 26, 56, 60, 155, 159, 178, 181

quintal (quintall'), a weight of 100 lbs. or a hundred-weight (112 lbs.); probably 112 lbs. for wax

Rabbit-skins (pelles cuniculorum), seasoned (sesinate), from animals taken in winter, 349, 354, 385, 398, 419, 421, 424–5, 440, 454–5, 469–70, 472, 476, 504–6, 508, 565; summer (stages), out of season, 233, 243, 273, 295, 298, 349, 354, 385, 398, 419, 421, 424–5, 440, 454–5, 469–70, 472, 476, 504–6, 508, 565

raisins (racemi, raysons), 12, 42, 61, 112; of Corinth (Cor'), currants, 48, 156

rattles (ratell'), 178

razors (rasours, rasers), 4, 24, 30, 33, 46, 56, 70, 94, 114, 139, 153, 174, 178, 180, 184–5

red hides (hid' rubra), 5, 23, 56, 58, 60, 82, 139

red lasch (lassh, lois rubra), a fine kind of red leather, perhaps morocco, 94, 102, 139

red skins (pelles rubra), summer squirrel skins or red leather, 1, 27, 45, 120, 138–9, 147, 169–70, 174, 177–8, 183–4; ? for bowyers (russe pelles pro bowers), 16

resin (rosyn'), 127, 163

rests (rist'), lance-rests, 114, 197

ribbons (rybans), 156, 181, 184

rings (ryng'), 147, 183, 207; black (nigra), 82, 94, 139, 184; copper with stones (coper ryng' cum lapidibus), 156; iron, 120, 147; latten (latonis), 24, 26, 30, 117, 147, 184, 196; tin (tynne), 46; white and black (alba et nigra), 35; *see also* bag rings, curtain rings, pouch rings

roasting pans (rosting pann'), 21

rods (rodd'), 127; *see also* osier rods

ropes *see* bast ropes

Rumney (romney), a sweet wine of Greek origin, 360, 544

running glasses (rynnyng glasses), hour-glasses, 26, 184

rush oil (russhe oile), 169

rye (sigalum, selignus), 61, 412, 421; rye-meal (rye mele), 516

Sack, a measure of weight used for wool: 364 lbs. For customs purposes 240 woolfells were equated with one sack

sacring-bells, small bells rung at the elevation of the host, 94, 180–1, 185

saffron (crocus), 61, 77, 178, 180

sail-needles (sayle nedyll'), 92

sail thread (sayle filum), 32

St. Omer hats (Sertomerhattes, Sentomers hattes'), felt hats, 1, 24, 26, 30, 93, 106, 134

sallets (salett'), a light head-piece of armour without visor, 93–4, 96–7, 102–3, 106, 114, 129, 139, 196; leather coverings for (koveryng' led' pro salett'), 129; *see also* archers' sallets

salmon (samon), 57, 64, 120, 123, 134, 166

salt (sal): Bay (de Baye), cheap salt from Bourgneuf Bay, Brittany, 29; Berflete (barflet), 214; white (album), 148, 163

salt-cellars (salt', saltsalers), 27, 100, 508; pewter, 527

saltpetre (saltpetir), 59, 121, 168, 177, 200

sanders (saundrz), an ointment made from powdered sandalwood, 156

sarcenet (sarcynet), a very fine and soft silk material, 184

sarcocolla (circacola), a gum resin from Persia or Arabia, used in medicine, 156

satin (satan', saten'), 184; black (noir), 156; green (vert), 156; red and black (rubrum et nigrum), 33; tawny (tawney), 33

saws (saues), 205

says (sayes), a light-weight cloth usually made from worsted and woollen yarn, 179; fine (fyn'), 156; *see also* thread, yarn

schönwerk (skonewark), the finest and most highly priced squirrel skins, presumably from the far north, taken at the height of the winter, 170

scissors (cisours, sesers, sisoures, sisers, sesours), 79, 84, 181, 184–5

'scone Jesus', ? scones stamped with the figure of Christ, 23

scouring tiles (scowryng tyle), 215; *see also* Flanders scouring stones

seam of herring (heryng' sayme), fish oil or grease, 135

sendal (syndale), a fine silk cloth, 156

setwall (sedevall'), the root of the valerian plant, used in medicine, 156

shafts, 184

shanks (shank'), furs made of skins from legs of budge (lambskins), 37, 45, 134, 139; budge (bogy), 146; tavelon, often used to indicate a bundle of four skins of black budge but sometimes meaning the individual skins, 33, 189

sheaf, a weight or measure
(a) of iron: 5–6 lbs.
(b) of glass: quantity uncertain

stockfish (fungia), cod and other gadoid fish cured by drying hard in the air, 1, 10, 13, 34, 40, 56, 58, 77, 88, 114, 117, 120, 122, 125–6, 168, 178, 199, 204; cropling (croplyng'), an inferior kind of stockfish, 19; titling (tytlyng'), a small size of stockfish, 22, 59

stones (ston'): jet (geet), 185; white (albe), 23; *see also* dog-stones, millstones

stools (stolys), 197

straw, a measure of weight, used for wax, usually between 8 and 11 quintals (q.v.)

straw hats (hatt' straminis, strawen hatt'), 86–7, 90, 93–7, 134, 139–40, 143, 175, 178

string thread (stryng filum, streng'), 26, 56, 94, 184

stringing yarn (stringyng yern', streng' yern'), 26, 176

sturgeon, 10, 13, 32, 68, 117, 168, 206

succade, fruit preserved in sugar, either candied or in syrup, 156

sugar (sugour), 12, 15, 16, 47–8, 107, 116, 201, 215; broken (broke), 215; loaves (loves, pannes), 35, 156; of Messina (Missene), 156; powdered (pouder), 15, 156

sum (somme), a measure of number (ten thousand) used for nails: (Willan, *Rates*, 41)

swords (gladii), 24, 37, 83, 93–4, 117, 120, 134, 139, 183; sheaths for (shethis), 197

Table-cloths (table clothe, mappa, pannus), 152, 176, 183, 215; diaper, 28, 93, 155

table-mats (warnappis), 175

tablemen (tabilmen), pieces used in board games, especially backgammon, 46

tables, 174, 181; painted (depicta), 93

tables with images (cum ymag'), pictures painted on boards or other flat surfaces, 103

tabor pipes (taber pipes), pipe played alongside a drum, 114, 181

taffeta (tapheta), 33, 177

tallow, rendered (cepum molton'), 225, 237, 243, 266, 277, 288, 298, 302, 305, 332, 342, 349, 356, 385, 454, 470, 504, 508, 526, 541, 553, 557, 561, 565, 571, 594

tapestry (tapstr'), 30, 159; *see also* coverlets

tar (tarr', terr'), 10, 13, 32, 88, 125–6, 136, 138, 140, 169–70, 197, 204, 212, 332, 360, 368, 392, 423, 510

teazles (tasyll', tasell'), prickly flower-heads of the fuller's teazle used to raise a nap on the surface of cloth, 1, 20, 34, 45, 63, 83, 93, 103, 106, 130, 137, 140, 146–7, 152, 176, 178, 205, 215

terrets (terrett'), ring to which a string, ribbon or chain is attached, e.g. on a dog's collar or to attach a leash to the jesses of a hawk, 26

thimble-cases (themels casez), 84

thimbles (thymels, themels), 20, 26, 28, 56, 94, 156, 174, 176, 180–1, 184–5; latten (latonis), 156

thread (filum), 94, 139, 176, 180, 184; blue (blodium), 23, 25, 30, 45, 58, 77, 82, 93–4, 96, 103, 134, 140, 165, 179, 181–2, 184, 186, 189; brown, 168; for crossbows (pro crossebowes), 120; for hats (pro hatt'), 117, 124; raw (rawe), 103, 169; say, 181; sewing (sewyng), 169; white (album), 77, 176, 179, 181, 184, 189; *see also* Bruges, Cologne, gold thread, Oudenarde, packthread, Paris, sail thread, string thread

ticks (tykes), linen bed coverings, 1, 21, 26, 70, 80, 91, 103, 178, 183, 185, 189, 204

timber, a bundle of forty skins

tin (stannum), xxxv, 295, 305, 349, 469, 471, 478, 556, 588, 622n.

tinfoil (tynne foyle), 182

tin-glass (tyn' glasse, ten glas), bismuth, added to fine pewter to produce a harder and more durable alloy, xxxv, 178, 183

titling *see* stockfish

tongs, 181–2

tongues, salt (lingue salce), 305; *see also* ox-tongues

towels, towelling (towell'), 85, 155; diaper, 26, 28, 166, 183

toys (japes), 33

train oil (trane), fish or whale oil, 10, 32, 107, 125–6, 165, 169–70, 179, 184, 197, 199

trays (treys), 126

treacle (triacle), a medicinal compound of spices and drugs (Flemish) or a syrup (Genoese), 114, 156

treillis (trilles, terlyson), a stout or coarse kind of cloth similar to buckram, 157, 177

trenchers (trenchours), 169–70, 197, 595

trivets (trevett'), tripods, 181

troughs (trowes), 169–70

trowels (trowell'), 182

'trumpe' glasses, ? flared or trumpet-shaped glasses, 156

trumpets (trumpes), 26, 181; latten (latonis), 156

trusses for crossbows (trosses pro crossebowes), 120

187

GENERAL INDEX

References in Roman numerals are to pages in the introduction; all other references are to serial numbers in the text. The places of origin and other identifications of merchants, shipmasters and officials, unless taken from the Petty Customs Account, are given in square brackets. Variant spellings in the MSS of personal and place names are given in round brackets. The following books have been especially useful in identifying persons and places:

Acts of Court of the Mercers' Company 1453–1527

Calendar of Plea and Memoranda Rolls of the City of London, 1458–82, ed. P. E. Jones (1961)

Calendar of Letter-Books of the City of London: Letter-Book L, ed. R. R. Sharpe (1912)

Hansisches Urkundenbuch 1471–85, ed. W. Stein (Leipzig, 1907)

Hanserecesse 1477–1530, vols. 1 & 2, ed. D. Schafer (Leipzig, 1881–3)

A. Hanham, *The Celys and Their World* (Cambridge, 1985).

Abbey, Nicholas, Breton merchant, 484

Abey, Elyott, Breton merchant, 484

Abraham, Thomas, denizen merchant [London stapler and grocer], 498, 505, 507, 569, 577

Acon, John van, alien merchant [of Aachen], 181

Actoris *see* Auctoris

Adam, William, stapler, 598, 602

Adlyn, Robert, stapler [of Calais], 598, 602

Adrianson (Adryandson)
  Cornelius, shipmaster of Middelburg, 194
  Walter, shipmaster of Antwerp, 96

Albright, Isbrand, shipmaster, 66

Alburgh (Albrough, Albrugh), William, denizen merchant [London mercer], 450–1, 456, 498–500, 571

Albustro (Albisto, Albistro, Albistur), John de, shipmaster of San Sebastian and Spanish merchant of Guipúzcoa, 328, 386, 395, 606

Alcok, Robert, shipmaster of London, 91, 153, 455, 472, 523, 594

Alder, Richard, denizen merchant, 228

Aldernes, Robert, denizen merchant [London haberdasher], 500

Alfonso (Alfownce), Peter, shipmaster and alien merchant of Portugal, 116, 487

Alice, James van, alien merchant, 538

Alie, James, stapler, 600

Alstone, John, denizen merchant, 591

Alverus, Lopo, alien merchant, 324

Alvis, Andrew, alien merchant, 475

Alvolus, Andrew, alien merchant, 111

Alwyn (Allewyn), Nicholas, denizen merchant [London stapler and mercer], 309, 452, 465, 498, 571, 600–2

Amberos (Ambros), John, alien merchant, 275, 292, 333

Amersham (Hakmersham), Bucks., steward of, xlv

Amound *see* Hamond

Ancona, Italy, merchant of: Gracia, Augustine, 28

Andrew(e)
  Nicholas, alien merchant, 565
  Peter, alien merchant, 15
  Thomas, shipmaster of London, 110, 300, 583
  William, denizen merchant [London mercer], 573

Andrewson (Andreson, Andrianson)
  Copyn, shipmaster of Flushing and alien merchant, 74, 160
  Peter, alien merchant, 160

Andwarp, John van, alien merchant, 139

298, 305, 308–9, 349, 440, 465–6, 468, 470, 476, 506, 508, 527, 566–71, 573, 576–7

Feldyng
Richard, denizen merchant and stapler [and London mercer], 570, 601
Thomas, stapler [and London mercer], 600

Fere (Feryng), Nicholas, shipmaster, 550

Fernandus (Fernando, Fornandus)
Francis, alien merchant, 111, 475
Francis, Spanish merchant of Guipúzcoa, 473
Gonsalvo, alien merchant, 107, 464
Peter, shipmaster and alien merchant of Viana, 101, 446
Vasco, alien merchant, 42

Ferr, John, denizen merchant, 568

Fesaunt, Stephen, alien merchant, 156, 588

Fitzherbert
John [King's Remembrancer and London customs collector], xvii n.
Robert [London draper and customs collector] xv n., xxix, p. 1
Robert (? same) [London customs surveyor], xix n.

Flanders
revolt in, xlii
ships of, xxxviii–xxxix; *see also* Ostend, Sluis

Fleccher (Flecer, Flecher), Robert, denizen merchant, 312, 573

Fleet, James, alien merchant, 204

Flemmyng (Flemyng), Robert, stapler [conductor of wool fleets], 598–9, 601–2

Florence, Italy, merchants of, xlii; *see also* Barde, John de; Course, Anthony; Friscobaldo, Jeronimo and Peter; Portinarius, Alexander; Stroce, Mark

Florenson (Florens), Hugh, alien merchant, 181, 204

Floresson (Florenson, Florisson), James, alien merchant and shipmaster of Purmerend, 53, 58, 385

Floskyn (Folskyn, Fulskyn) Henry, Hanse merchant, 425, 440

Floure, William [Gravesend customs searcher], xx n.

Flushing (Flisshyng, Flusshyng), Zeeland, ships and masters of, 55, 71–5, 142, 160, 162–3, 214, 381, 399

Fondemars *see* Demers

Fons
John, alien merchant, 15
Luke, alien merchant, 349

Foot, George, Hanse merchant, 503, 508

Forest, Rowlond, alien merchant, 184

Foster, Robert, shipmaster of London, 174, 505, 552, 575

Founs (Fownse), Digo, shipmaster and alien merchant of Viana, 14, 303

Fowey, Cornwall
goods going to, 372
ships of, xlii, 42, 198, 201, 323, 539, 589, 592

Fowler (Fuller), Thomas, London customs controller and collector, xv n., xix n., xxv n., xliii–xlv, p. 1

Fox
John, alien merchant, 35, 94, 97
Lewis, alien merchant, 98
William, denizen merchant, 564

Frank
Cornelius, shipmaster and alien merchant of Sluis, 127, 495
Henry, denizen merchant, 568

Frankenberch, Henry, alien merchant, 1, 23, 30, 34, 103, 178

Frankfurt, Germany, merchant of *see* Rewe, Andrew

Freman, William, denizen merchant, 448

Friscobaldo (Friscabawde)
Jeronimo, alien merchant [of Florence], 400
Peter, alien merchant [of Florence], 449, 460, 617

Frise (Fryse)
Henry, shipmaster, 34, 302
James, alien merchant, 23, 37, 114–15, 118, 120, 178–9, 183, 298
John, alien merchant, 298

Froddesham, Edward [London goldsmith and searcher's clerk], xx n.

Fromlod, James, denizen merchant, 499, 585, 590–1

Frost, Henry, denizen merchant, 308, 450

Fryk, Henry, Hanse merchant, 10, 40, 58

Furnandus, John, shipmaster and alien merchant, 487; *see also* Fernandus

Furnarius
Ciprian, denizen merchant [esquire of the king's household], 236, 490, 498, 533
Gabriel, alien merchant [of Genoa], 12, 16, 56, 130, 200, 216–18, 239–40, 244–5, 250, 255–6, 270–2, 294, 556

Furner'
Catayne, alien merchant, 203
Dennis, shipmaster of Harfleur, 70, 368

Fusan, Bartholomew, alien merchant, 438

Fustaryno, Paul, alien merchant, 156

Fyncham, William, denizen merchant [London mercer], 498, 535, 583, 591–2

Fynkyll
Edward, denizen merchant, 228, 514
John, denizen merchant [London draper], 228, 514, 564

John, carrier with horses, 482; *see also* Aryse

William, denizen merchant, 568

Rysyng, Richard, denizen merchant, 498

Ryvers, Anthony Wydeville, earl, Chief Butler, xxxi, p. 167

St. Osyth (St. Osys, St. Osiis), Essex, ships and masters of, 108, 188

Salford

John, denizen merchant [London mercer], 499

William, stapler [London mercer], 602

Salman, Datleff, shipmaster of Hamburg, 199

Salmer, John, Hanse merchant [of Dinant], xli, 1, 33, 35, 37, 59, 77–8, 90, 94–5, 97, 134, 147, 150–1, 154, 159, 183, 185, 189, 204, 206–8, 243, 279, 290, 298, 302, 305, 309, 313, 317, 349, 354, 385, 470, 503, 508, 527, 542, 569–70, 573, 577

Saltash, Cornwall, ship of, 203, 331

Salvage, Anthony, alien merchant [of Genoa], 200, 203

Salvo

John (de), alien, later denizen, merchant [of Genoa], 465, 498, 577

Peter de, Spanish merchant of Guipúzcoa, 593

Sambre (Sumbre), Bonyfas (Face), alien merchant, 146, 508

San Sebastian, prov. Guipúzcoa, Spain, ships and masters of, 328, 386, 395, 489, 604, 606

Sancheodores (de Sanchio, Sancheo de Doras), John, Spanish merchant of Guipúzcoa, 529, 531

Sanches, Peter, Spanish merchant of Guipúzcoa, 395

Sanchis, Martin, shipmaster, 593

Sancta Maria

Damyan de, alien merchant, 588

George de, alien merchant, 156, 242, 375, 588

Michael de, alien merchant and galley seaman, 156, 588

Nicholas de, alien merchant, 156

Novello de, alien merchant, 156, 588

Pero de, alien merchant, 588

Sancto George (Sancto Georgio, Sent George)

Dymytrio, alien merchant, 156, 588

George de, alien merchant, 156, 588

Maryn' de, alien merchant, 156, 588

Nadale de, alien merchant, 156

Nicholas de, alien merchant, 588

Ralph, alien merchant, 298

Ralph de, alien merchant, 156, 588

Sancto Leo Grobissa (Sancto Leo), Pero de, alien merchant, 156, 588

Sancto Mores, Nicholas de, alien merchant, 166

Sancto Nicholo (Sent Nicholo)

Damyan, alien merchant, 181

Ralph de, alien merchant and galley crossbowman, 156, 588

Stephen de, alien merchant, 156

Sandwich, Kent

customs officials of, xv

goods going to, 250, 256, 447

Santandera (Santander), John de, shipmaster of San Sebastian, 489, 604

Sarrasto, Saba de, shipmaster and Spanish merchant of Guipúzcoa, 265

Sarro (Serro)

Anthony de, alien merchant [of Genoa], 43, 200

John, alien merchant, 250

Saundyrs, John, stapler, 601–2

Savage

Frank, Hanse merchant [of Dinant], 34, 37, 90, 94–5, 100, 134, 139, 150, 181, 211, 290, 302, 305, 508, 542, 570, 577

Henry, denizen merchant, 523

Savale (Desavala), Peter (de), Spanish merchant of Guipúzcoa, 262, 473, 524

Savogale (Savegale), Peter de, shipmaster and Spanish merchant of Guipúzcoa, 528–9

Sawnches (Sawenches), John, Spanish merchant of Guipúzcoa, 528, 549

Sayer

Richard, shipmaster of London, 607

Richard, shipmaster of Middleton, 620

Scalder, William, denizen merchant, 424, 450–2, 467, 500, 568

Scalstreate (Scalstret)

Gerard, alien merchant, 312

John van, alien merchant, 31

Scapehuson (Scaphuson), William, Hanse merchant [of Soest], 3, 5, 8, 10, 13, 28, 32, 35–7, 58, 77, 125–6, 147, 150, 159, 168, 177, 181, 183, 185, 187, 189–90, 204, 293, 301, 308–9, 313, 349, 354, 385, 398, 425, 450–1, 469–71, 476, 498, 502–3, 523, 542, 568, 570–1, 573–4, 577–8

Scheldt, river, xxxix, xlii

Sconborowe, Gerard, alien merchant, 21

Scot, John [London tronager], xx n.

Screven, Thomas, denizen merchant, 228, 398, 466, 472, 474, 507, 576

Scutery (Squetery, Squterye)

Andrew de, alien merchant, 588

George de, alien merchant, 156, 588

John de, alien merchant and galley crossbowman, 156, 588

Luke de, alien merchant, 156, 588

Nicholas de, alien merchant, 156, 588

LONDON RECORD SOCIETY

The London Record Society was founded in December 1964 to publish transcripts, abstracts and lists of the primary sources for the history of London, and generally to stimulate interest in archives relating to London. Membership is open to any individual or institution; the annual subscription is £12 ($22) for individuals and £18 ($35) for institutions. Prospective members should apply to the Hon. Secretary, Miss Heather Creaton, c/o Institute of Historical Research, Senate House, London, WC1E 7HU.

The following volumes have already been published:

17. *London Politics, 1713–1717: Minutes of a Whig Club, 1714–17*, edited by H. Horwitz; *London Pollbooks, 1713*, edited by W. A. Speck and W. A. Gray (1981)
18. *Parish Fraternity Register: fraternity of the Holy Trinity and SS. Fabian and Sebastian in the parish of St Botolph without Aldersgate*, edited by Patricia Basing (1982)
19. *Trinity House of Deptford: Transactions, 1609–35*, edited by G. G. Harris (1983)
20. *Chamber Accounts of the sixteenth century*, edited by Betty R. Masters (1984)
21. *The Letters of John Paige, London merchant, 1648–58*, edited by George F. Steckley (1984)
22. *A Survey of Documentary Sources for Property Holding in London before the Great Fire*, by Derek Keene and Vanessa Harding (1985)
23. *The Commissions for Building Fifty New Churches*, edited by M. H. Port (1986)
24. *Richard Hutton's Complaints Book*, edited by Timothy V. Hitchcock (1987)
25. *Westminster Abbey Charters, 1966–c.1214*, edited by Emma Mason (1988)
26. *London Viewers and their Certificates, 1508–1558*, edited by Janet S. Loengard (1989)
27. *The Overseas Trade of London: Exchequer Customs Accounts, 1480–1*, edited by H. S. Cobb (1990)

Most volumes are still in print; apply to Hon. Secretary. Price to individual members £12 ($22) each, to non-members £20 ($38) each.